The

SEMINOLES

of Florida

The
SEMINOLES
of Florida

James W. Covington

University Press of Florida
Gainesville / Tallahassee / Tampa / Boca Raton
Pensacola / Orlando / Miami / Jacksonville

This book is dedicated to two fine teachers: E. E. Dale of the University of Oklahoma and Father John Bannon, S. J., St. Louis University.

Second printing 1993

Printed in the United States of America on acid-free paper ♾

Library of Congress Cataloging-in-Publication Data

Covington, James W.
 The Seminoles of Florida / James W. Covington.
  p. cm.
 Includes bibliographical references and index.
 ISBN 0-8130-1196-5
  1. Seminole Indians—History. 2. Seminole Indians—Government
relations. 3. Seminole Indians—Social conditions. I. Title.
E99.S28C73 1992
975.9'004973—dc20   92-40978
                                                        CIP

The University Press of Florida is the scholarly publishing agency for the
State University System of Florida, comprised of Florida A & M
University, Florida Atlantic University, Florida International University,
Florida State University, University of Central Florida, University of
Florida, University of North Florida, University of South Florida, and
University of West Florida.

University Press of Florida, 15 Northwest 15th Street, Gainesville, FL 32611

CONTENTS

MAPS

PREFACE

This book was a long time in the making. I developed a fondness for the American Indian as a child in St. Louis, Missouri, reading again and again the accounts of Tecumseh, Pontiac, and Geronimo in *Famous American Indians* and later relating those stories to young campers in the YMCA summer camps where I was employed. After World War II, I worked at Muskogee High School, Muskogee, Oklahoma, where the agency for the five civilized tribes was located and which was near Fort Gibson, where the Seminoles disembarked from river steamers after their trip from Florida. It was my first opportunity to see a number of Indians living an ordinary life. I also visited Bacone College at Muskogee, a two-year Baptist college for American Indians.

The University of Oklahoma with its good library, fine teaching staff, and excellent press offered an opportunity to work for a doctorate in U.S. history. Dr. E. E. Dale suggested that, as little had been published on the Ute Indians, I should select them as the subject for a dissertation. Accordingly, my topic was "Federal Relations with the Utes, 1848–1890." Dr. Dale, one of the country's foremost authorities on the American Indian, gave helpful advice concerning federal relations, and his course on the American Indian was useful from the historical side. I undertook most of the basic research for the dissertation in that major depository of American Indian records, the National Archives in Washington, D.C.

After graduation, my first college teaching position, in January 1950, was in the Department of History at the University of Tampa. With Florida so far from the Ute Indians of Colorado, New Mexico, and Utah, I looked forward to developing a knowledge of the Native Americans who had lived in the Tampa area and who were still in the state. I did so slowly, visiting reservations, talking to Seminoles, writing articles, and reading papers at state and national scholarly meetings.

Several Seminoles and white friends of the Seminoles have been helpful in the preparation of the text, Joe Dan Osceola, Bobby Henry, and

Buffalo Tiger among the former, John Goggin, Albert DeVane, Charles Knight, Ethel Cutter Freeman, and Robert Coulter among the latter.

Present-day writers of Seminole history owe a debt to those who earlier recorded their views of the tribe and how the whites treated them. The first historian to make use of the store of materials at the National Archives was Grant Foreman. Although he included early relations and removal of all five civilized tribes in two of his books, *The Five Civilized Tribes* and *Indian Removal,* the chapters devoted to the Seminoles contributed to my basic understanding of the subject. Others who made important contributions to my understanding of the pre–Civil War period include historians John Mahon, Kenneth Porter, Frank Laumer, J. Leitch Wright, and Mark Boyd and anthropologists John Goggin, William Sturtevant, Brent Weisman, and Charles Fairbanks.

Concerning the postbellum period there have been worthy contributions from anthropologists Louis Capron, Alexander Spoehr, Merwyn Garbarino, Patsy West, William Sturtevant, and Ethel Freeman Cutter and from historians Robert T. King, Harry A. Kersey, Jr., and Charles Coe.

It is regrettable that no Florida Seminoles have written articles or books on the history of the Seminole Tribe of Florida, although the Miccosukees have been gathering information and some literature; perhaps this effort will spark some written material from the Seminole perspective. Evidence from the Seminole position can be found in taped interviews at the University of Florida's Oral History Archives and in the pamphlet "20th Anniversary of Tribal Organization, 1957–1977," Seminole Tribe of Florida, August 20, 1977. The Seminole view is needed, as Alice Marriott showed in her well-researched book *Ten Grandmothers,* in which a white minister proud of his Kiowa dialect was called by Kiowas "preacher who cannot be understood."

The
SEMINOLES
of Florida

1

The Seminoles Come to Florida

lthough the Seminoles and Florida have been linked for many years, the tribe was part of the Creek Confederacy in Alabama and Georgia for a far longer time and was a relatively late arrival on the peninsula: the Apalachees, Calusas, Timucuans, and other smaller tribes arrived much earlier.

The original tribes of Florida, which may have numbered as many as 100,000 persons, were virtually extinct when the Lower Creeks began making permanent settlements on the peninsula in the latter half of the eighteenth century. The peaceful and semicivilized Apalachees were the first Florida tribe to suffer almost complete annihilation. Governor James Moore of South Carolina, with 50 colonial soldiers and 1,000 Lower Creeks, invaded the Apalachee area in 1704, destroying most of the Spanish missions and carrying off some 300 Apalachee men and 1,000 women and children to be settled on the present-day borders of South Carolina and Georgia and a considerable number of Apalachee slaves to be sold in the West Indies.[1] Some Apalachees eluded the English and escaped to Pensacola, Mobile, and St. Augustine. Eventually a handful returned from Georgia, where Moore had settled some of the migrants along the Okmulgee River, but for all practical purposes the Apalachee missions had ceased operations.[2]

Carolina slave raiders, migrations, disease, and war with the Spanish all contributed to the extermination of the Timucuans living in northeastern and central Florida during the sixteenth century when the Spanish explorers arrived. Learning of Moore's success in capturing Florida's Native Americans, various parties of whites, Yamassees, and Lower Creeks moved southward to raid the practically defenseless villages, and by 1705 thirty-two towns had been destroyed by raiders from the north.[3]

Streams and rivers like the St. Johns provided excellent avenues into Florida; in 1702 one party of thirty-three Yamassees led by Captain Thomas Nairne paddled for six days along the river before going ashore and seizing Timucuans as they hunted, fished, and gathered firewood. In a report in 1709 Nairne informed the Earl of Sunderland that "the garrison of Saint Augustine is by this war [Queen Anne's War] reduced to the bare walls, their castle and Indian towns all consumed either by us in our invasion of that place or by the Indian subjects since who in quest of booty are now obliged to go down as far as the point of Florida as the firm land will permit, they have drove the Floridians to the islands of the Cape, have brought in and sold many hundreds of them and daily now continue that trade."[4] Finally, the smallpox, measles, bubonic plague, influenza, and yellow fever introduced by the Europeans may have reduced the population by half or more.[5]

Over the years historians and anthropologists have searched for significant facts concerning the final years of the savage Calusa Indians, who lived along the lower Gulf Coast south of Tampa Bay. When Pedro Menéndez de Avilés landed near Calusa headquarters in 1566, the tribe (numbering perhaps as many as 15,000) gave the Spaniards a rough time, finally forcing them to abandon San Antonio, a station the Spanish had established. But diseases took their toll on the tribe, and after 1600 little was heard of the Calusas.[6] In 1743 the Jesuits established a mission, Santa Maria, near the mouth of the Miami River to serve nearly 200 persons representing what remained of the Calusa, Key, and Boca Raton tribes. At and near the mission tribe members fished and gathered wild fruits, but in September of each year they were taken by Cuban fishermen to the Keys and to the area near the mouth of the Caloosahatchee River, where they worked for the Cubans.[7] An early name for Key West was Cayo Hueso (Bone Key): according to a local legend, early in the eighteenth century American Indians from the mainland killed many of the natives, and the piles of bones left scattered about gave the island its name.[8] If these early Key West inhabitants were Calusas and not Key Indians, only a portion of them were killed, for as late as 1754 they were causing the Spanish authorities trouble.[9] In 1775 an English observer reported that Key Vacas and Key West were refuges for Calusas hiding from the Creeks and that eighty Calusa families had migrated to Cuba in 1763.[10] There is no further record of them, and it is not known whether they stayed in Cuba or returned to Florida after 1783, when Britain returned the territory to Spain.

Gradually, Spanish control of Florida receded to a few surviving Timucuan, Apalachee, and Yamassee villages clustered for the most part around St. Augustine and St. Marks. Florida's Native American population rapidly declined, and by 1759 only three villages remained under Spanish protection. These settlements included seventy-nine Yamassees at Tolomato and Nuestra Senora de la Leche and twenty-five in a village near San Marcos de Apalache.[11] In 1764, after relinquishing St. Augustine to the English, the Spanish carried with them to Havana eighty-nine Yamassees: twenty men, thirty-two women, and thirty-seven children. There is no mention of Apalachees or Timucuans living in or near St. Augustine at this time, but there likely was some intermarriage with the Spanish and Yamassee inhabitants.[12]

At the same time that Florida tribes were being decimated, the Creek Confederation, which included some sixty towns and a population of nearly 20,000 scattered throughout Georgia, Alabama, and fringe areas, was thriving. This confederation represented a clash of cultures, languages, and environments, with only rarely a common goal or front.[13] English traders classified the confederation into two principal divisions, the Upper Creeks, who lived along the Coosa and Tallapoosa branches of the Alabama River and primarily spoke the Muskogee dialect, and the Lower Creeks, who resided in the valleys of the Chattahoochee and Flint rivers along the lower Alabama and Georgia borders and primarily spoke the Mikasuki dialect.[14] Small matrilineal communities or *huti* were found usually along the banks of a river or stream or near a spring. Crops raised included corn, melons, beans, and pumpkins, and when the soil became unproductive, the villagers moved to another site. Agriculture and hunting were carried on solely for subsistence purposes, and little or no effort was made to dispose of surplus commodities during this period.

Seminole migration into Florida came in three phases. Between 1702 and 1740 the Seminoles made raids against the Spaniards and their Apalachee allies; although they acquired much knowledge of the Florida terrain, they made no significant settlements during this period. Between 1740 and 1812, at least six Seminole villages were established in the northern part of Florida; small parties explored the entire peninsula in search of deer, bear, and other game and made contact with Cuban fishermen. The third phase came between 1812 and 1820, when pressures in Alabama and Georgia forced many Upper and Lower Creeks to move into Florida.

The first Seminoles were really Creeks who had migrated to Florida, and so they operated under the Creek form of government. Each of the hutis was part of a larger division known as the square ground town or *talwa,* where the leader of the town, the *micco,* lived. The talwa village, averaging several hundred persons, had as its highest official a leader or micco chosen by a general council of elders representing several clans. Selection of the leader was restricted to one clan, however, so the position might be deemed hereditary, although the chief could be impeached and removed by the council.[15]

Duties of the town chief included issuing invitations to feasts and dances, receiving envoys, and presiding at the meeting of the town council. Other town council officials included the vice-chief, *micco apokta;* assistant leaders, *micalgi;* ceremonial leaders, *heniha;* the war speaker, *holibonaya;* and the top two classes of warriors. Although the council selected officials from a certain clan, those chosen had to possess the ability and skill to retain their positions; if misfortune happened during their tenure, they could be replaced by a person from another clan.[16] During councils or busks, the men sat in cabinlike structures, the micco and his advisers, the henihas on the west side of the square ground, the war speaker and warriors on the south side, and visitors and other men of the town on the east and north sides.

Representatives from all of the towns considered matters of importance at a general assembly held in May, usually in the most important town, Coweta or Tukabahchee. Before beginning discussions the men enjoyed a pipe, and because a clear head was needed to deliberate important matters, they drank the black drink (cassina), which the older men passed around the circle. The meeting was held in the center of the town, where three cabins were erected on each side of a square. The significance of the rising sun in their religion dictated that the cabin of the most important chief face the east. Nine of the cabins were painted red, but those facing the setting sun and occupied by older men were painted white to denote old age and virtue. Only the important leaders entered the assembly cabin, and they could not leave or sleep until all matters had been discussed. Women prepared food and drink—roast meat, bread, and fermented meal—served by lesser leaders.[17]

Selection of warriors and their leaders took place differently. Fighting men were placed in four classes: *imala,* low; *labotskalgi,* higher; *imala lakalgi,* still higher; and *tustenuggee,* highest. Judging from his record of deeds performed on the battlefield the micco and town council selected the tustenuggee. When a fighting force was needed, the tustenuggee placed a red two-foot-long war club in his village square and sent a similar club to the leader of each band, who placed it in his square, began a count of the sticks sent along with the club to mark the days before the raid, and had a drummer keep a steady beat to summon all people in the town to the council house, where the number of warriors needed was announced.[18] The needed number stayed in an enclosure, drinking war medicine and packing the weapons and parched corn flour that their wives brought. At the end of three days the town leader, carrying a sacred bundle, went to the general meeting, where leaders from other towns had assembled, and the tustenuggee reported what had been planned.

Once a town's warriors had assembled in their enclosure, the war leader was in complete control, distributing war medicine made from the brew of herbs and roots, which the men drank for three days. According to one European witness, the war medicine served a good purpose by preventing the men from drinking hard liquor, which would make them drunk and useless as fighters; it also served as a slight purgative, which reduced infection from possible wounds.[19] Possibly to avoid infection from clothing that would be carried into the body by buckshot, the warriors fought virtually naked. As soon as they left the town, the men, with the leader at their head, moved in single file, each walking in the footsteps of the leader and the last man concealing the prints with grass. When a stop was ordered, the men formed a circle, a gun at the side of each and the leader sitting opposite the only opening in the circle. By hand signal the leader informed the warriors when to sleep and when to arise and move from the circle.[20]

Most important in the social organization of the Creeks was the clan. Among the Upper Creeks, clans such as Raccoon, Bear, Wind, Bird, Alligator, Deer, and Panther were found in the white, or peace, towns.[21] (The Creeks fell into two ill-defined divisions or moieties known as red, or war, towns and white, or peace, towns. Such divisions were not important, for one town shifted divisions when it lost a ball game, and little is known of the system concerning identity of towns as peace or war towns.) A Creek could not marry within a clan, and clan kinship was acknowledged from the female side.[22] That is, a male Deer married a female Raccoon, and all children born of the union were Raccoons. A Raccoon could not marry another Raccoon but had to choose from the ranks of the other clans. Among the Creeks, the micco came from the ranks of one clan, usually the most important one in the town, but a general council of males was selected from several clans.[23] These headmen were chosen from the white moiety or group of clans including the Wind, Snake, and Bird clans.[24]

At the annual Green Corn Dance those who had committed crimes faced charges. Some who tried to escape punishment were sometimes captured and brought back. No one was confined, but some who committed adultery were disfigured or beaten, and others were excluded from ceremonies and rituals until they demonstrated that they had been rehabilitated by the shaman. When there was little chance of reform or when a serious crime such as murder had taken place, leaders of the clan met and decided upon a sentence—money payment, exile, or execution.[25]

Division of labor between the sexes was similar to that of other American Indians of the southeast. Women made clothing, pottery, and mats, collected firewood and game when it was killed near the town, dressed skins, and prepared food.[26] Men made implements of war, built houses and canoes, hunted, traded, and took part in the wars.

Rather severe restrictions were imposed on the Creek women. During her monthly periods, a woman lived in a small hut erected some distance from her home; afterward she cleansed herself in a stream, dressed in fresh clothing, and returned home.[27] When the time of childbirth approached, a woman went again to a remote hut and, usually with no help, gave birth.[28] When a child was born, its father fasted for four days and its mother returned to her normal schedule of meals, but for one month she did not prepare food for her husband or sleep with him.

Creek women had complete child-rearing responsibility until the children were able to provide for themselves, partly because the father belonged to one clan, the mother and children to another. In each clan there was usually a man who watched over the children, lectured those who needed advice at the Green Corn Dance, and took care of necessary punishment.[29] Children were never struck or whipped, but when slight correction was needed their mother scratched them on the legs and thighs with a needle.

With the exception of some instruction by their mothers, girls received little formal education, but boys performed many services: lighting fires, finding and carrying firewood, cooking the black drink, and doing all of the required work in the public square. Release from their lowly status came when they performed a brave act during a war or a hunt.

When the time of marriage approached, the prospective husband sent a female relative to the female relations of his would-be wife. After these representatives had met and approval had been given, the bridegroom gathered gifts, usually clothing, which were taken to the bride by his female relatives. If accepted, he went to the home of the bride and remained there. After the bridegroom had erected his own home and given the products of a hunt to the bride, the marriage was considered valid.[30] Should the male desire to acquire other wives he could do so, but the first wife was considered the most important one. Either party could request a divorce, but the wife kept the children.

Children received names shortly after birth; a girl usually retained hers throughout life, but a boy, given an early name such as "little rabbit" or "smells of urine," received a second name when he reached the age of a warrior and had performed some courageous feat, and sometimes a third name after he had performed another, more outstanding exploit. A young warrior retained the name of his mother and could not have a wife until he brought back a scalp from a raid. It is believed that the most famous Seminole, Osceola, was named Billy Powell in adolescent years and after maturity was given the name Asi-yaholo from *asi* (Black Drink) and *yaholo* (singer)—a reference to the sons of the attendant who offered the black drink to the participants at the Green Corn ceremony.[31] The name was corrupted, probably by whites, to Osceola, and today many Seminoles bear the name Osceola in honor of the nineteenth-century hero. The possibility of one man having three names—an Indian one, a translated version, and one given by whites—led to considerable confusion among the frontier people and later among writers trying to identify Creeks.[32]

A listing of Apalachee villages in 1704 indicates early migrations of Creek bands into the Florida Panhandle. The villages of San Carlos de Chatos and San Pedro de los Chines are believed to have included many Chatot Indians belonging to a Lower Creek band, and another village, San Francisco de Oconoi, was probably composed of Oconees, a second Lower Creek band.[33] These villages soon lost their Lower Creek identity and became part of the Apalachee mission chain.

Lieutenant Antonio Matheos moved into present-day Georgia in 1685 to enforce Spain's will on the Lower Creeks living along the Chattahoochee and Flint rivers. For a time he was partially successful, but under the influence of English traders the Lower Creek villagers moved northeastward to the upper Okmulgee River, where they lived for twenty-five years.[34] In the Okmulgee River location, Creeks from the towns of Coweta, Kasinta, Tuskegee, Kolomi, and others became friendly with English traders, and tribal raiders from these towns seized people from Florida and sold them as slaves in Carolina. Consequently, many Lower Creek warriors became knowledgeable about the geography of Florida.

Yamassees, Apalachees, Savannahs, and their Lower Creek allies started a conflict, the Yamassee War, in 1715 against the colonists in South Carolina. By mistreating and overcharging the American Indians, frontier traders brought on this brief but bloody war, which ended with the defeat of the Yamassees, their retreat to the gates of St. Augustine, and the migration of their allies to southwestern Georgia, where they settled in an area extending from the falls of the Chattahoochee to a point some fifty miles downriver.[35] The new locations did not satisfy all the Lower Creeks, and they indicated to the Spanish that they wanted to settle on the fertile lands abandoned by the Apalachees. In 1716, 1717, and 1718, Lieutenant Diego Peña traveled into Lower Creek territory to secure allegiance to Spain and to ascertain how many Lower Creeks wanted to settle in Florida. He recommended that they select village sites along the banks of rivers and creeks.[36]

When the Spanish established Fort San Marcos de Apalache on the Gulf of Mexico (present-day St. Marks), the migration of Lower Creek bands into Florida proper was more actively encouraged. Although Peña could not convince Brims, leader of Coweta, that a Spanish alliance was necessary, he learned from the pro-Spanish nephew of Brims that six villages of Yamassee, Yuchi, or Apalachee would shortly move to Apalachee.[37] Unfortunately, the Spanish lacked money to purchase gifts for the bands and thus were unable to secure their migration. Chiscalachisle, a Creek Yuchi leader, visited San Marcos de Apalache, but when he was not offered gifts and was served meager food, he decided that his people ought to stay in southern Georgia.[38] Only a Yamassee group and some Apalachees from Pensacola and the hill country of Georgia moved into the Apalachee area.[39]

The Spanish established a trading post at Apalachee in 1744, but the storehouse was quickly emptied and never refilled. The Lower Creeks, comparing gifts given by the Spanish with those of their English and French rivals, complained, "King of Spain no good. English goods, give much, much. Captain . . . does not give what el Mico sends."[40] From time to time, wandering bands came into Apalachee to check if Spanish gifts had become available. Usually only warriors visited the post, but when a tribal conflict threatened in 1747, men, women, and children swarmed the place.[41] At Pensacola, the Upper Creek Tallapoosa band settled near the fort, but when gifts were not distributed at frequent intervals, it moved away.

During this initial phase of expansion into Florida, the Lower Creek bands, with the exception of several small villages in the Apalachee area, made little or no attempt to form permanent establishments. They came to Florida on slave raids and as English allies in the wars against the Spanish, but they did not remain. The Spanish did their best to enlist the aid of these possible allies, but because they failed to deliver sufficient gifts the Indians remained in Georgia and Alabama.

The second phase of Creek expansion, which saw some permanent Lower Creek settlements established in Florida and extensive hunting in the area, occurred because of power politics and because of the great success of trade between whites and American Indians. The Creeks' dependence upon whites' goods forced them to cast aside their practice of killing game only for their immediate needs; they began to kill as much game as possible to trade skins for guns, flints, powder, blankets, dyes, beads, iron utensils, and assorted odds and ends. The Europeans became dependent upon their trade for deerskins used in the manufacture of saddles, aprons, book covers, breeches, shoes, gloves, and other items. In order to find the rapidly vanishing herds of deer, Creek hunters made longer and longer trips and often remained away from their families for several months.[42] After securing sufficient pelts on their hunt they brought the furs to a white or American Indian factor in the village who did the actual bargaining. After the transaction the factor sent the goods by mule or horse train to the trading house headquarters in Charleston, Savannah, or Pensacola. To the hunters the relatively untapped Florida wilderness was a virtual promised land, filled with vast numbers of deer, bear, and other game.

With the settlement of Georgia by the English in 1732, the excursions by the English and their American Indian allies into Florida became more frequent. A band of Tallapoosas and Yuchis raided Picolata in 1735, destroying it and forcing the Yamassees and Timucuans living there to flee to St. Augustine. In 1738 a Creek attack took place at Fort Pupo, less than thirty miles from St. Augustine, and a short time later Spanish cattlemen observed Lower Creeks camped near roads on tracts throughout central Florida. James Oglethorpe invaded Florida from Georgia in 1739 during the War of Jenkins' Ear with a force of 2,000 whites and a large number of Lower Creeks. Besides laying siege to the Castillo de San Marcos at St. Augustine, bands of Lower Creeks taking part in this foray explored the area west of the St. Johns River and became familiar with the lakes, hammocks, swamps, and rivers.

It is difficult to ascertain definite reasons for the migration of the first Lower Creek bands into Florida and the making of permanent settlements. William Bartram relates in detail the travels of one of these Lower Creek bands, the Oconee, led by Cowkeeper. According to the story told to Bartram, Cowkeeper's band had settled along the Oconee River in Georgia but, because of the proximity of frontier settlements, had migrated to the lands held by the Upper Creeks. Unhappy with this location, they decided to move southeast toward the Atlantic Ocean. En route they saw the plains and the lake at Alachua Prairie and there built the town known as Alachua or Latchaway. Because of the smell of decaying fish and swarms of mosquitoes, Cowkeeper and his people later abandoned Latchaway and moved to Cuscowilla, located several miles away near present-day Micanopy.

Bartram talked to a trader who knew the Lower Creeks well and learned another possible reason for the Oconee migration into Florida. Because the cultivation of maize and beans exhausted the soil, southern bands constantly needed to change their old sites for more fertile ones. Surrounded by hostile tribes—Cherokees, Chickasaws, and Choctaws—the Lower Creeks sought to migrate to Florida, where there was no need to expect a battle whenever they changed village sites.[43] At first, tribes allied with the Spanish gave the newcomers a difficult time, but the arrival of other Creek bands forced the Spaniards and their allies to retreat into a defensive area around St. Augustine.[44]

The bands moving into Florida comprised two groups speaking "the related, but not mutually intelligible, Muskogee (Creek) and Mikasuki (Hitchiti) languages."[45] It was difficult to identify a person or even a band as being pure Muskogee or Mikasuki. The vast majority of personal names listed in books and papers pertaining to the period were given in Muskogee, but some of the persons listed were known definitely to have been Mikasuki. Probably many persons spoke both languages, and the interpreters used Muskogee as the official language in transacting business with the whites and the Mikasukis because more people knew Muskogee than Mikasuki and non-Muskogee speakers adopted the Muskogee tongue. These bands scattered across northern Florida—along the Apalachicola and the lower Suwannee rivers, throughout Tallahassee and the Alachua Prairie, and along stretches of the St. Johns River—and established "towns . . . each a political unit with little sense of commonness."[46] During these early years the Seminoles were considered part of the Creek Confederacy, and they maintained political ties with their counterparts in Alabama and Georgia. Because of poor communication, however, these ties were broken.

Although the name *Seminole* has been applied by whites to virtually all of Florida's American Indians since 1763, the translation *runaway* has not been accepted by the Native Americans. As early as 1771 Englishman John Stuart, the American Indian agent, called the Florida natives *Seminoles* because he had learned that it meant *wild people*. Although William Bartram used the same term during his travels in Florida, only Cowkeeper's band, which had settled near Alachua Prairie (also called Paynes Prairie), showed that they were determined to cast off the influence of the Creek Confederation. The word *Seminole* as used by Muskogee speakers is taken from the Spanish term *cimarron* or runaway, but this designation was disliked by the American Indians. Perhaps the translation *pioneer* or *adventurer* would be more suitable.[47] For the purposes of this book, any Alabama or Georgia Creek who made a permanent move to Florida will be termed a Seminole; the Muskogee-speaking Seminoles will be referred to as Muskogees and the Mikasuki-speaking Seminoles as Mikasukis. The reader should not confuse these Lower Creek Mikasuki-speaking Seminoles with the later group that called itself the Miccosukee Tribe of Indians of Florida. This group broke away from the Seminoles for political, not ethno-linguistic, reasons and is composed of both Mikasuki- and Muskogee-speaking Indians.

The largest Seminole camps in Florida during the 1760s were in present-day Alachua, Leon, and Levy counties. Cuscowilla included some thirty dwellings, a population of several hundred persons, cornfields, herds of cattle and horses, and a considerable number of Yamassee slaves.[48] Because the Spanish had limited trade facilities, pottery making continued but on a reduced basis, and the flintlock obtained in trade was supplemented by the bow and arrow. According to Bartram, Cuscowilla consisted of a number of wood-frame buildings erected about an open square with a council house at the center and several smaller outlying settlements. Each home had its own vegetable garden in which corn, beans and squash were cultivated, but coontie (Zamia integrifolia) and wild potatoes gathered from the woods supplemented the diet.[49] Large fields held in common extended two miles from the settlement of Cuscowilla to the edge of Paynes Prairie.[50] Meat products were supplied by the large herds of cattle, a lesser number of pigs, and wild game. So attractive was the Alachua area with its rich soil that by 1764 migrants from the Creek towns of Oconee, Apalachicola, Sawokli, and Chiaha had moved into the region.

White King was the leader of a second settlement, Talahasochte, located on the west bank of the Suwannee River in present-day Levy County; it contained approximately the same number of houses as Cuscowilla.[51] Its inhabitants built cypress canoes that could hold as many as twenty or thirty men, and they made frequent trips to the Florida Keys, the Bahamas, and Cuba. On the excursions to Cuba they traded deerskins, furs, dried fish, honey, and bear oil for cigars, coffee, rum, and sugar.[52] Archaeological work at this village has revealed that Spanish olive jars, English ceramics, razors, knives, gun parts, and articles of personal adornment had been obtained by White King and his people. Many of the European items came from a trader who lived at the village for some time. In addition to Talahasochte and Cuscowilla a third town lay on the west bank of the St. Johns River near present-day Palatka.

During the first Spanish period (1513–1763) Seminole pressure against white settlements in Florida increased to such a degree that the inhabitants of San Marcos de Apalache and St. Augustine were forced to stay near their town limits, and sea contacts replaced land communication between the two settlements.[53] Cowkeeper (Ahaya), the leader at Cuscowilla, claimed to have killed eighty-six Spaniards, and he made his successor as leader promise to kill fourteen more.[54]

Before the Seminoles could assert full control of northern Florida, they had to conquer the Yamassees, who had migrated to Florida in 1715 and become Spanish allies. The Seminoles made several raids against Yamassee villages located near Spanish settlements. According to accounts told by the Creeks to the English, the last band of Yamassees was trapped in a bend of the St. Johns River and, except for about forty or fifty men, was exterminated. William Bartram saw the place where the slain Yamassees were allegedly buried.[55] According to a Seminole tradition, Seminoles had killed the Yamassee men and married their women.[56] Bartram noted in 1773 that many Yamassee slaves captured by Cowkeeper were fairly well treated and that children born to the Yamassee women and Seminole men were not considered slaves.[57]

The Treaty of Paris signed on February 10, 1763, transferred Florida from the Spanish to the British. It was an area about which the British knew little, one that was not self-supporting but that was inhabited by bands of American Indians who had almost pushed the Spanish into the sea. The majority of non-Seminoles in Florida able to escape a life of slavery or absorption by the Lower Creeks went to Cuba in 1764 with the Spanish when they left Florida.[58]

Life under the militarily weak Spanish in Florida had meant an almost

Seminole Settlements in Florida Containing More than Five Families (before 1770)
Source: Based largely on Mark Boyd, "A Map of the Road from Pensacola to St. Augustine," *Florida Historical Quarterly* 17 July 1938): 15-23.

independent existence for the Seminoles, but English rule meant treaties to be signed, observance of set prices for furs, and regulation of the traders by British authority. Under the British, John Stuart, American Indian agent for the Southern District, set American Indian policy for Florida. First he appointed agents to represent the government in American Indian affairs at Mobile, Pensacola, and St. Augustine, and in July 1764 he held a meeting with Cowkeeper and other leaders at St. Augustine. According to Stuart, Cowkeeper's band at Cuscowilla had been detached from the main body of Creeks for some time and was kept friendly to the English by gifts of silver ornaments and guns. Stuart held a conference at St. Marks on September 13, 1764, with leaders from five nearby towns, including Tallahassee or Tonaby's Town, Mikasuki (also called Newtown), Chiskatalofa, Tamathli, and Ochlockonee (the last three from the area where the Flint and Chattahoochee rivers joined).[59]

When the British took control of Florida in 1763, they noted two settlements in Apalachee that had been established some time after 1755—Tonaby's Town at present-day Tallahassee (parent town of the Muskogee speakers) and Newtown at Lake Miccosukee (parent town of the Mikasuki speakers). Tonaby's Town reportedly contained thirty-six houses and thirty warriors, and Newtown sixty houses and seventy warriors. Tonaby, a famous Coweta band member, had lived near San Marcos de Apalache, and his band supplied food and provided protection to the small garrison there. With the decline of the fort Tonaby probably moved his village north to present-day Tallahassee. Newtown or Miccosukee was founded by people from Coweta. At first they followed Tonaby's lead, but by 1775 Kinache from Mikasuki had become the most important leader in the area.

In November 1765, at a conference at Picolata on the St. Johns River, Stuart, James Grant, governor of East Florida, and thirty-one Lower Creek leaders signed an agreement. (Picolata rather than St. Augustine had been selected because the Creeks were afraid to cross the St. Johns with their horses.) The meeting was held in a pavilion constructed of pine branches for the roof and walls. Grant and Stuart sat at a table facing the open end, and fifty or more Creeks sat on blanket-covered benches. The Lower Creek leaders had advanced into the area bearing a peace pipe, which was passed about the audience. Governor Grant, doing most of the talking through three interpreters, stated his case:

> The Great King after driving the French and Spanish from this land was most graciously pleased to appoint me to govern the white people in this part of his new conquered dominions.
>
> I know and love the red people. I have lived long with them and as I am acquainted with their customs and manners, the Great King knew that I will do everything in my power to keep up peace and harmony between his white subjects and red children who the Great King wishes to live together as brethren should do.
>
> You are apprehensive and have been told that the white people are desirous of getting possession of your hunting grounds. Your fears are ill founded for I am ordered by the Great King not to take any lands which are of use to you even if you should agree to give them up. You may judge from that how careful your Father the Great King is of your interests and welfare. . . .
>
> Your profession is hunting, you therefore must have a large tract of country, but it is in your interest to have your brothers the English near you. They only can supply you in exchange for your skins with cloths to

cover you, your wives and children, with guns, powder, and balls for
your hunting and with a number of other things which you cannot make
for yourselves though you cannot exist without them.[60]

Captain Alec from a red Yuchi town, a good friend of the English, and
Tallechea of the Okmulgees made conciliatory replies to Grant. Tallechea
spoke the following words:

I hope the Governor and Beloved Man will agree to the limits which
were prepared by us at Augusta, and that a line from St. Sevilla to
Picolata and along the road to St. Augustine will hence forward will [*sic*]
be the boundary, and that you will not allow the white people [to] settle
beyond the road leading from this place to our nation.

We have people who will take notice and observe what lands are
settled which we hope will not be beyond the now mentioned.

There is no occasion for a fort on the other side of the river. Let the
path remain open, that our people may go and see [the] Governor when
they choose.

You will consider that the presents which are now to be given us may
last for a year but will afterwards not [last] and [will] become of no
value, but the land which we now give will last forever.

I now have the happiness of speaking to the Governor and desire
should any people or cattle stray beyond the line and die or be lost, that
the red people may not be blamed for it.[61]

As Tallechea noted in his talk, the Lower Creeks consented to give up 2
million acres of land in northeastern Florida, a much larger tract than the
English had anticipated.

The Treaty of Picolata negotiated in 1765 was signed mostly by
Lower Creeks from Georgia, for the English believed that the Georgia
towns controlled the land and people in Florida. Cowkeeper was con-
spicuous by his absence, but Weoffke signed for him. The Creek and
Seminole leaders received silver medals in varying sizes, depending on
the importance of the leaders, that bore the portrait of the English ruler;
three of them, including Cowkeeper, were made great medal chiefs, and
four others received small medals. In addition, hoes, guns, linen, blankets,
and kettles were distributed among them.[62] Shrewd Cowkeeper, who
had fought the Spanish and their Yamassee allies to a standstill by laying
siege to St. Augustine for many years, gained the same type of control
over the British without the use of arms by staying aloof and meeting
with the governor in private. As a result, the British sent him a great

medal, provided his people with traders, and did not bother his villages.

When two traders detected Seminoles stealing cattle along the St. Marys River and were killed when they interfered, a second congress was held at Picolata in 1767. Sixty-nine Creeks and Seminoles attended. Grant, not wanting to disturb the delicate balance of trade, did not threaten them but tried to prevent another such occurrence. Although Stuart, Grant's superior, wanted some punishment meted out, Philoke from Cuscowilla, whose two sons were involved in the killing, was given a great medal by the British, and all left the meeting with friendly feelings. From details of this council it seems evident that Cowkeeper's band had separated completely from the main body of Creeks.[63]

The American Indians had all along preferred to trade with the English, from whom they received better quality at lower prices than the Spanish had offered. It was therefore easy for English firms to operate in Florida under their own flag and administration. One of the first such firms, headed by James Spalding, expanded from a base at Frederica on St. Simons Island to establish posts stretching from Sunburg, Georgia, to present-day Volusia County, Florida. Two of Spalding's well-known posts were on the St. Johns River, his lower store at present-day Stoke's Landing six miles south of Palatka and his upper store five miles south of Lake George.[64]

Panton, Leslie and Company, which later acquired the Spalding stores, began operating in Florida in 1782–83. The most important item at the first store established by William Panton at Cowford on the St. Johns River was gunpowder, needed for warfare and for killing white-tailed deer. Other trade articles included blue and red stroud (a cheap cloth), blankets, woolen goods, cotton and linen cloth, handkerchiefs, shoes, cheap rifles, muskets, kettles, iron pots, lead, flints, nails, fishhooks, ribbons, hats, paints, rum, and brandy.[65] Overseer John Hambly cured and tanned the deerskins he received from the Seminoles before shipping the skins to England. Writing in September 1776 Panton claimed he had 32,000 deerskins stored and could have had many more if gunpowder in large quantities could be supplied to him.

Relations between the Seminoles and whites during the British occupation of Florida were excellent. From 1763 to 1783 the whites never numbered more than several thousand; Loyalist refugees flooding St. Augustine and nearby towns increased the population to 10,000. The British kept the terms of their pacts, and the traders were fair in their dealings. In William Bartram's travels through the heart of Seminole country he met with the most friendly of receptions. The influx of Creek bands became greater during the British period. By 1767 they had established a village at Chukochatty (near present-day Brooksville) some distance south of Cowkeeper's town, and seven more towns appeared by 1774.

Unfortunately for the Seminoles, the British lost both Florida and the thirteen North American colonies as a result of the American Revolution and were forced to leave Florida and central North America. When the British retreated from Georgia and South Carolina in 1782 and prepared to surrender Florida to Spanish authorities in 1783, Seminole leaders, fearing the advance of the white Americans, attempted to secure some assurances that British support would continue. To allay their fears Governor Patrick Tonyn and Lieutenant Colonel Thomas Brown, superintendent of American Indian affairs, granted a license to Panton, Leslie and Company on January 15, 1783, to continue their American Indian trade. As a consequence, a post under the management of Charles McLatchy opened in the fall of 1783 on the west bank of the Wakulla River.[66]

Thomas Forbes, representing Panton, Leslie and Company, visited London and tried to convince the Spanish ambassador that the only way for Spanish Florida to hold its own against Georgia traders was to allow a steady flow of British products into Florida. Because the Spanish had no firm that could supply goods to the Seminoles, authorities in May 1784 granted a temporary stay to Panton, Leslie to remain in Florida; however, the firm could handle only commodities that were heavily taxed.[67] At a final conference at or near St. Augustine attended by the British governor and by Kinache of Mikasuki, Five Bones of Coweta, and Long Warrior of Cuscowilla, the Seminoles showed their distress that the English were leaving and surrendering the land to the Spanish. Cowkeeper told the English that his band would kill all Spaniards that entered his territory.

Vicente Manuel de Zéspedes, the incoming Spanish governor of East Florida, realized that American Indian trade was one of his difficult problems and turned to Panton, Leslie to supply the natives' needs. When the white Americans who controlled Georgia and Alabama proved tough competitors for the Lower Creek trade, Governor Zéspedes and his counterpart, West Florida governor Arturo O'Neill at Pensacola, decided to grant a monopoly of the fur trade to Panton, Leslie; the firm had the necessary know-how, funds, and equipment to handle the job. The selection of the Panton firm came as a result of the visits of Seminole and

Creek leaders to St. Augustine where Zéspedes, having few presents to give to the delegations, was saved embarrassment by a steady flow of presents advanced on credit by John Leslie.[68]

Alexander McGillivray, an Upper Creek and the son of a Scottish trader and Creek mother, had organized the 45,000 Creeks, Choctaws, Chickasaws, and Cherokees into a loose confederation with which he tried to play the American whites against the Spanish to the profit of the Creeks. He succeeded. In the treaty between the Creeks and Spaniards signed at Pensacola May 31 and June 1, 1784, by Governor Arturo O'Neill, Governor Esteban Miro, Martin Navarro, superintendent of Louisiana, and McGillivray, McGillivray was referred to as the representative of many towns, including those of the Seminoles or wanderers. Although no land was relinquished in the pact, Spain proclaimed her control over the Creek lands, and prices were established for the exchange of dressed skins and various articles including guns, linen, shirts, and handkerchiefs.[69] As a result of the treaty Panton's store, situated on a hill behind the town of Pensacola, became a trade center for the Creeks and Seminoles, and Spain became protector of the American Indians against land-hungry Georgia whites.[70]

Both Spanish and white American authorities at this time were taking note of the Seminoles as separate bands who were still part of the Creek Confederation. Governor Zéspedes in December 1784 gave a talk at St. Augustine on the subject of peace and trade to the "chiefs and warriors of the Creek and Seminole Indians."[71] In response the Native Americans stated that they regarded the governor as a friend and brother and that they desired peace and stores maintained at the St. Johns River, Apalachee, and Pensacola.[72] In a 1788 meeting held at Rock Landing on the Oconee River in Georgia, white representatives followed orders to list separately Upper Creeks, Lower Creeks, and Seminoles.[73]

Relations between the Seminoles, the Lower Creeks, and the Spaniards were good. Under Governor Manuel de Zéspedes and his successor, Juan Nepomuceno de Quesada, presents purchased from private firms with drafts on the Royal Treasury usually included trade items that the Seminoles and Creeks wanted and that went to their leaders or designated agent at Apalachee, Pensacola, or St. Augustine. The leaders in turn distributed the presents to the others. To a chief, for example, might go a woolen blanket and shirt, tobacco, a looking glass, a large knife, a razor, two casks of rum, and a supply of powder, lead, and flint. A warrior might receive a woolen blanket, a shirt, a razor, a large knife, one cask of rum, and less ammunition. A woman could expect linen, woolen stripping, velveteen, beads, needles, and a looking glass, while a girl might receive only woolen cloth and some inferior cloth.

When American Indians visited St. Augustine and camped in the plaza they received a pound of bread, honey, a pound of rice, and tobacco and clay pipes, and they left after four to five days with enough food to supply them on the trip home. In addition, the governor gave some leaders and warriors guns, saddles, kettles, coats of fine cloth, and hats.[74]

When Enriqué White became governor of East Florida in 1796 he was forced to reduce the money spent for such presents, for the sum was proving too great a proportion of the provincial budget. Because White had previously been governor of West Florida, he recognized the leaders from western Florida who were receiving presents both at Pensacola and St. Augustine. Although some councilmen advised ending the presentation of presents, White favored only a reduction, for he feared an uprising. With previous records incomplete and bands moving from one spot to another, it was difficult to designate one post for any band to receive its presents, and White continued to reward those who also received gifts at Pensacola.

The first test of power between the Seminoles and the United States came as a result of a boundary-marking party's foray into Seminole land. With the signing of the Treaty of San Lorenzo in 1795, a boundary commission of Spanish and U.S. representatives traveled from the Mississippi River eastward marking the thirty-first parallel as the boundary line. By 1799 the commission had reached the neighborhood of towns along the lower Flint River that were controlled by the Tame King and his Creeks but that fell within the jurisdiction of Kinache and his warriors from Lake Miccosukee. Although American Indian agent Benjamin Hawkins and the Creek tribal council had provided eighty warriors as protection for the surveyors, and although these guards had been supplied with flour and meat by Andrew Ellicott, who was in charge of the U.S. surveying team, they proved of little help.[75] When the Seminoles and Lower Creeks came on a visit purportedly to scout the camp of the surveying party, they stole without hindrance by the guards as many articles, including horses, as they could safely carry away from the tents.[76]

Following this incident Kinache, who was cut from the same cloth as Seminole leaders Osceola, Wildcat, and Sam Jones, returned with a large group of warriors and, in an act of defiance, told Ellicott that he would not surrender the fourteen horses stolen earlier by his people. Finally, after the

Seminoles had stolen more horses from a corral at night and had robbed a schooner's crew of all its possessions, Ellicott decided to protect his party by quickly moving from the mouth of the Flint down the Apalachicola to St. George Sound and into the Gulf of Mexico. After resuming his work again on the St. Marks River, Ellicott blamed the Spanish governor for not making the necessary arrangements to protect the surveyors. Spanish officials, especially the commander at St. Marks, did nothing to make the survey a peaceful one, and because the bands in the Panhandle had been pro-Spanish for many years, Spanish gestures of friendship would have been most useful for Ellicott.[77]

During this period a series of minor incidents took place along the troubled and poorly protected Georgia-Florida border. When whites allowed their cattle to graze near Seminole and Creek towns and to invade their prime hunting grounds, conflicts developed. In March 1793 Seminoles broke into Robert Seagrove's store near Colerain, Georgia, and killed two whites. In retaliation, Creeks from the U.S. side of the river went into Florida, found the inhabitants had fled to safer spots, and stole all of the cattle, horses, and slaves they could manage. Because he knew that Payne controlled the bands in northeast Florida, James Seagrove, the American Indian agent in Georgia, wrote to "Payne, head-chief of the Seminole tribe of the Creek Indians at Sotchaway" (Payne's Town) requesting that the murderers be punished.[78] The letter was sent in vain, however, for the whites had been killed by warriors from the Seminole towns of Chiaha and Telluiana, who believed that a war had commenced. Payne (successor of Cowkeeper) and another leader nevertheless came to Colerain on May 18, 1793, for a conference with Seagrove that resulted in the Seminoles promising to remain peaceful and to move to their hunting grounds in southern Florida whenever troublemakers appeared. Their reaction to Seagrove's request showed that, while the Cuscowilla band was virtually free from Creek control, towns in the Chattahoochee-Flint area were still within the Creek Confederation.

Other Englishmen jealous of the successful activities of Panton, Leslie and Company made their move during these troubled times. William Augustus Bowles, who had come to Florida from Maryland for duty in a Loyalist regiment defending Pensacola, was dismissed by British military authorities for not following orders. Following his discharge Bowles went into Lower Creek country, where he acquired two wives, one Creek and the other Cherokee, and settled near his half-Creek father-in-law, Thomas Perryman, a leader of a town on the Chattahoochee.[79] When the Spanish forces lay siege to Pensacola, Bowles returned to his unit and fought well until the Spanish captured Fort George.

At the end of the Revolution Bowles fled with other Loyalists to the Bahamas, where he fell under the influence of John Miller, a prominent businessman. Because of Bowles's knowledge of the area, his ability to speak the native language, and his friendship with the Creeks, the Earl of Dunmore and Miller selected Bowles to lead a force to oust the Panton firm and sent him to contact McGillivray. When Bowles promised that the British navy would prevent the Panton firm from trading with the natives, McGillivray showed willingness to cooperate with him.[80]

It would take Bowles three attempts before he would succeed in this effort. In his initial attempt to capture the Panton stores located on the St. Johns and at St. Marks, Bowles landed with fifty men at the mouth of the Indian River in October 1788. Many Seminoles at Cuscowilla had migrated southeast to establish other villages along the banks of the St. Johns River. These wandering bands and the residents of one town gave little support and information to Bowles as he made his way from the mouth of the Indian River. He did not attack the lower St. Johns store, for the Seminoles told him that a large Spanish and U.S. force was searching for him; at this point some of Bowles's cold and hungry men deserted and fled to the Panton store. The Seminoles had lied to Bowles, for they did not want the store upon which they depended for trade items destroyed.[81] After this rebuff Bowles was repulsed when he tried to capture the St. Marks store, and he crossed into Lower Creek country, where he stayed for a few months. Finally, he returned to the Bahamas in the spring of 1789.[82]

After visiting England in company with a few Creeks and Cherokees, Bowles made a second trip to the Lower Creek villages via Nassau and the Indian River. On his visits to London and Nassau he had been assured of British support for his proposed independent state of Muskogee. On his way back to the Lower Creek villages he landed at Indian River, where he unloaded gifts for the Seminoles. He then headed for Apalachee Bay, where he made a short trip to join his father-in-law, Thomas Perryman. In a conference at Coweta in the fall of 1791, Bowles assured the Creeks and Seminoles that he and the British would protect them from their enemies and requested permission to establish two posts, one at the mouth of the Indian River for the Seminoles and the other at the Apalachicola or Ochlockonee River for the Creeks and Seminoles.[83] Perryman and another Seminole leader, Kinache, protected Bowles, and he also had the support of the Creek towns of Chiaha and Osochi; Eufaula and the towns around St. Marks were pro-Spanish and in the fold of McGillivray.[84] In January 1792 a party of whites and Seminoles under the command of Bowles seized the Panton store at St. Marks. When the Bowles force, commanded in the field by William Cunningham, moved into the Panton store, the Spanish garrison of less than fifty men in the nearby fort did not take any action. Yet the plan was once again destined to fail, for Bowles was lured by promises of negotiations by the Spanish and white Americans to New Orleans, where he was captured, sent to Cuba, and placed aboard a ship bound for exile in the Philippines.[85]

While being transferred from Manila to Spain Bowles escaped in Africa and made his way via Barbados back to Nassau, where he plotted yet another landing near St. Marks. On the way, he and his men were shipwrecked near the eastern end of St. George Island, recovered a few items, and made their way to friendly Seminole towns in the neighborhood.[86] To obtain as many deerskins as possible, Bowles again planned to seize the Panton store at St. Marks, and he bribed the neighboring Seminoles with trade items of little value and promises of more for their help.[87] At Mikasuki he was able to regroup, and with the help of 300 Lower Creeks and Seminoles and a few whites, he at last managed to capture St. Marks and the Panton store.

At a spot near the mouth of the Ochlockonee River, as the director-general of the state of Muskogee Bowles established the "free Port of Muskogee," from which ships flying the flag of the state of Muskogee sailed forth to engage in peaceful commerce and raids upon other ships. One of the ships flying the Muskogee flag was the schooner *Miccosukee* commanded by Richard Power. Bowles sent out parties of Seminoles to raid ranches and plantations along the St. Johns and to bring back slaves, but John Forrester, a Panton partner, negotiated a pact between the Seminoles and the Spanish government in 1802 by which the Seminoles returned some slaves.[88]

The climax of the Bowles saga came in May 1803 when the United States and Spain moved in separate operations to terminate Bowles and the state of Muskogee. The United States wanted Bowles out of Florida for two reasons: he had opposed Creek land cessions, and he planned to seize American Indian agent Benjamin Hawkins and try him under the laws of the state of Muskogee. The Spanish governor of West Florida, who wanted Bowles removed from the scene because of his raids against shipping and plantations, sent his son Estevan Folch to a conference of southern Native Americans at the Upper Creek town of Hickory Ground on U.S. soil. Folch was able to persuade some Upper Creek Indians to seize Bowles at the conference and to return him to the Spanish authorities, who shipped him to Cuba, where he died in the Morro Castle prison in December 1805.[89]

Kinache, as capable a leader as Cowkeeper, had come close to disaster when he supported Bowles's cause. Leader from 1770 to 1818 of the largest American Indian village in Florida, Kinache (Kenhagee or Cappachimico) was possibly of mixed white and Native American ancestry. He had previously lived above the forks of the Apalachicola but moved in 1783 with his followers to Lake Miccosukee. The villages controlled by Kinache and John Kinnard, a Lower Creek leader, at and near Lake Miccosukee prospered; their inhabitants farmed, herded cattle and horses, and traded deerskins, and both leaders owned large numbers of slaves. Kinache was determined to resist the efforts of the white Americans to seize the Mikasuki-allied towns in northwestern Florida and in later years eagerly sought the help of such allies as the Red Sticks, the British, and Billy Bowlegs, the leader of the Seminoles at Alachua. Unfortunately, he did not have enough warriors to make much of an impression.

To offset Bowles's destruction of the Wakulla stores and accumulated debts, on May 25, 1804, at Chiskatalofa (in present-day Henry County, Alabama) Creek and Seminole leaders ceded 1 million acres of land lying between the Apalachicola and Wakulla rivers to the Panton company. James Innerarity represented the company; William Hambly, a company employee, served as interpreter; and twenty-four Upper and Lower Creek and Seminole leaders from towns on the Apalachicola and Chattahoochee rivers signed the agreement. The demand that all bands pay for the damage to the Panton stores done only by Bowles's followers was rather unfair, but the Panton company, which controlled the fur trade, had a strong position and found some Creek and Seminole leaders willing to cooperate. Semathly and Kinache of Mikasuki, Tom Perryman and John Kinnard for the other bands, represented the Seminoles in the pact.[90]

Seminole resistance to the cessions developed almost at once. In August 1804 when James Innerarity met the leaders in a conference at Prospect Bluff on the Apalachicola River to mark the boundaries, he found some opposition from leaders who had not signed the pact. Additional opposition developed when news came that the hated backwoodsmen from Georgia would settle on the land, but Innerarity promised that all settlers would come from other countries and would be good neighbors.

James Kinnard, a mixed blood trader and leader, was afraid that the new Panton, Leslie store on the Apalachicola provided for in the pact would ruin his trade, but he could not prevent its acceptance by the others. The Panton representative and several Indian leaders were able to mark off a portion of the grant.

When the Lower Creeks and Seminoles went on to accumulate a debt of $19,387, Edmund Doyle, principal agent of John Forbes and Company (successor to the Panton firm), called another meeting at Chiskatalofa on April 10, 1810. Here the two groups surrendered title to three tracts of land adjoining their earlier grant. Having learned from past mistakes, the Forbes Company persuaded as many leaders as possible to sign the treaty, employed surveyors, and required a delegation of Creeks and Seminoles to observe the surveying.[91]

At the beginning of the nineteenth century approximately 3,000 American Indians lived in Florida. Although the first settlers in the former Apalachee region had been mostly Muskogee speakers, some of whom were Yamassee or Apalachee survivors, the later arriving Hitchiti (Mikasuki) speakers were in the majority. Most of them had come from towns along the lower Chattahoochee and lived in small towns or were part of migratory groups scattered along the upper portion of the peninsula. Chief spokesmen for the western bands were Semathly and Kinache, whose towns at Lake Miccosukee were regarded as the most important in Florida. By 1804 all the bands had become completely independent of the Creek Confederation. The efforts of agent Benjamin Hawkins kept relations with the Americans in Georgia good, and the Creeks made few raids across the borders.

The American Indian economy at this time depended upon their traffic in deerskins. The warriors made lengthy fall and winter trips to secure the hides, which were exchanged at the trading posts for guns, clothing, whiskey, and other commodities. The women stayed at home working the fields, tending the cattle and horses, and waiting for the males to return from their long jaunts.[92] After six months in the field, one such hunting party came into St. Augustine in 1818 to barter bear-, deer-, and pantherskins and bear fat.[93]

Gradually, the American Indians pushed deeper into Florida, although from available evidence it appears that before 1800 no permanent villages were located south of Tampa Bay. The Seminoles and Creeks used south Florida as a hunting ground, carrying with them "small bundles of sticks made of the sweetbay trees, which they used in roasting their meat" because it imparted "a pleasant flavour."[94] Sometimes scattered groups of Seminoles searched along the Atlantic coast for items washed ashore from wrecked ships.[95] In 1783 Joseph Antonio de Evia, charged by Spanish authorities to chart the Florida coastal waters, talked to some Yuchis, Tallapoosas, and Choctaws at Tampa Bay who said that they had traveled by horseback for five days to hunt deer in the area and that they hoped to exchange the deerskins for guns, powder, and dry goods with the English. The nearest English posts were at Nassau and Canada, so the hunters probably were referring to the Panton, Leslie firm at Pensacola.[96]

Ten years later Vicente Folch y Juan examined the same area in order to see if an outpost should be established. At Tampa Bay he explored the shoreline and found two American Indian villages, Cascavela and Anattylaica. The villages were apparently semipermanent in nature, and during part of the year the inhabitants hunted and killed the abundant wildlife found in the area. At the end of the hunting season they carried the skins to St. Augustine, St. Marks, or Pensacola, where they exchanged the hides for such items as blankets, shirts, beads, saddles, and flints.[97]

The greatest points of contact between whites and Seminoles were in central and southern Florida. During the eighteenth century fishing companies operating from Havana sent vessels to the lower Gulf Coast of Florida. The Cuban fishermen worked in the area from September to March, and they dried and salted their catch in semipermanent camps known as ranchos located on the coastal islands.[98] During the remainder of the year some fishermen preferred not to return to Cuba and instead cultivated vegetable gardens in Florida. It was not the custom to take white women to the ranchos, and the Cubans lived with women from the bands that roamed the area. These unions were regarded as legally binding in Cuba; the children were taken there for baptism and education.[99] In 1831 William Whitehead, collector of customs at Key West, visited Charlotte Harbor, the center of the fishing ranch activities. He found 134 men, half of them American Indians, 30 Seminole women, and 50 to 100 mixed-blood children.[100]

Relations between Seminole men and the whites living along the coast were congenial. Several Seminoles worked as crew members aboard the fishing vessels, others were employed as farmhands on plantations near Caximbus Sound, and some captured wild birds, which they put into willow cages and sent to Havana with the fishermen to be sold.[101]

2

Early Conflicts with White Americans

resident James Madison unwittingly ushered in the third phase of Seminole migration into Florida, 1812–20. On January 15, 1811, he was secretly authorized by Congress to negotiate a takeover of Florida to prevent the peninsula from being occupied by another power. President Madison commissioned seventy-two-year-old George Mathews, war hero and former governor of Georgia, to conduct negotiations by which West Florida might be obtained peacefully by the United States.[1] When Governor Vicente Folch y Juan of West Florida gave him a cool reception, Mathews decided to make a try for the seizure of East Florida, a separate province. Accordingly, he recruited a small army in Georgia and organized a government in exile under John H. McIntosh. The plan was to establish a foothold on the peninsula with the assistance of both a recruited force and the U.S. Navy and move quickly to seize St. Augustine, form a government in Florida to transfer authority to the United States, and insure quick acceptance of the territory by U.S. authorities.

The so-called Patriot Army composed of seventy Georgians and nine Floridians crossed the St. Marys River into Florida, seized and occupied Fernandina, and moved toward St. Augustine. Although white Americans owning large plantations in northeastern Florida supported Mathews, their numbers were not large, and other allies were needed. East Florida was not an easy prize for the taking—Governor Juan de Estrada would not listen to an appeal for a quick surrender, and lacking proper artillery support, the Patriot Army delayed an attack upon St. Augustine. As a result Mathews and General John McIntosh sought assistance from two groups—blacks and Seminoles. The blacks who had fled from slavery in the north and were living in villages near the Seminoles, however, had strong ties of loyalty to the Spanish government that had provided them with a safe haven. There was no chance that they would aid invaders who hoped to overthrow Spanish rule in Florida and make them slaves again.[2]

The Seminoles led by Payne proved equally stubborn in resisting white American overtures. (King Payne, having succeeded Cowkeeper in 1784, had moved his village from Cuscowilla to Payne's Town several miles away, where he had erected a European-style plantation house full of articles acquired from the traders. In 1793 he is reputed to have owned twenty slaves, 1,500 head of cattle, 400 horses, and many sheep and goats.) Mathews and McIntosh had no chance at all to secure Seminole help, for black messengers sent by the Spanish governor to Payne's Town told the Indians that the Georgians would seize their land.[3] At first Bowlegs, Payne's brother, wanted war because the Patriots were a threat to the deerskin trade, but Payne desired peace; when the young warriors refused to listen, Payne changed his mind.[4] Many of the Seminoles were eager to go on the warpath, for a reward of $1,000 had been offered by the Spanish governor for McIntosh's scalp and $10 for scalps of his followers.[5] The Seminoles hit hard at the invaders and the plantation owners who supported them, killing eight settlers and capturing from eighty to ninety slaves in one week. Soon they were driving cattle stolen from hostile owners' plantations into St. Augustine to help replenish the supply of food curtailed by the invasion.[6] They attacked the plantation of Zephaniah Kingsley, but the tough slave trader proved to be a good fighter and the raiders were forced to retreat, carrying away with them twenty-six slaves. Finally, under constant Seminole attack and with half of their men sick, the Patriot Army began a slow withdrawal from Florida.

A second wave of white Americans in the form of Colonel Daniel Newnan and 117 Georgia militiamen coming to the rescue of the Patriot Army fought three engagements in which eight men died, nine were wounded, and eight were missing. Newnan planned to make a quick attack on Payne's Town, burn or destroy food supplies, houses, and fields, and return with cattle and corn. It was a precarious plan, for he had only twelve horses and food for four days. The attack of the whites upon Payne's Town caught the Seminoles by surprise but the two leaders, eighty-year-old Payne on a white horse and Bowlegs on foot, directed fire that picked off the volunteers as they charged. The 200 Seminoles from the dispersed hamlets controlled by Payne and the 40 blacks from the neighboring village turned the tide of battle by a flank attack upon the rear of the men from Georgia. Finally, Newnan and his men retreated, carrying their wounded with them. This clash should have resulted in the killing and capture of more whites, but Payne was wounded and the Seminoles, having lost most of their ammunition reserves in the first engagement, had to restrict their fire.[7]

A major element in Newnan's defeat was the loyalty of the blacks to the Seminoles, who had helped them when they had escaped from plantations in the North. One white witness commented on the relationship between the two races:

> The Negroes uniformly testify to the kind treatment they receive from their Indian masters, who are indulgent, and require but little labour from them.
>
> Hence, though their number was, at one time, considerable, they never furnished the Indians with any surplus produce, for the purposes of trade; but, barely made them sufficient provisions for necessary consumption. The Negroes dwell in towns apart from the Indians, and are the finest looking people I have ever seen. They dress and live pretty much like the Indians, each having a gun, and hunting a portion of his time. Like the Indians, they plant in common, and farm an Indian field apart, which they attend together. They are, however, much more intelligent than their owners, most of them speaking the Spanish, English, and Indian languages. Though stouter than the aborigines, it is very singular to observe, how much they resemble the Indians in figure, being longer limbed, and more symmetrically formed than the Negroes of the plantations in the States. . . .
>
> . . . The partial union of wild and of social habits, as exhibited in the Negro settlements, presents a very singular anomaly, no where else, perhaps, to be met with. The gentle treatment they experience from the Indians, is a very amiable trait in the character of the latter.
>
> Whan, a very intelligent black interpreter, who had been one of the slaves of King Payne, on my questioning him upon this subject assured me, that his old master, as he called him, had always treated him with the utmost humanity and kindness, and often condescended to give him lessons for his conduct, instructing him to adhere to truth and honesty, and endeavor to act well in his course through life. Whan has profited by these inculcations, being remarkable for his good character and intelligence—the Indians reposing the utmost confidence in him, when making use of his services, in their dealings with the whites. This Negro mentioned to me, as a proof of the kindly feelings of his master, that the

latter, on announcing his will, a short time before his death, particularly directed, that his favourite horse should not be shot, (for it is a custom with the Indians, to destroy all the personal property of the dead) but, be well taken care of by his surviving daughter.[8]

After the defeat of Newnan, during the fall of 1812 the Seminoles held a general conference attended by most bands to discuss the next move. Having recovered somewhat from his wound, Payne told the group that a union of all the tribes in Florida plus black allies and supplies from St. Augustine would enable them to drive all undesirable whites from Florida. Wolf Warrior, a Mikasuki, said he had had enough of war, and the other leaders agreed with him, for virtually all unfriendly plantations on the mainland had by then been looted. Payne sent a messenger to American Indian agent Hawkins in Georgia promising that if peace were assured, all loot taken from Georgians would be returned, including slaves. While the messengers were talking to Hawkins, news arrived that Payne had died.

At the rites for the dead Payne, Bowlegs said:

Do not grieve, misfortune will happen to the wisest and best men. Death will come and always comes out of season. It is the command of the Great Spirit, and all nations and people must obey. What is passed [*sic*] and cannot be prevented should not be grieved for.

What a misfortune for me that I could not have died this day, instead of you. What a trifling loss our people would have sustained in my death; how great in yours.

I shall wrap you in a robe and hoist you to a slender scaffold where the whistling winds shall take your spirit to the happy hunting grounds.[9]

When people in Tennessee learned of the defeats inflicted by Seminoles and blacks on the Patriot Army and Georgia militiamen and of the Seminole counterattacks in Georgia and Florida, Colonel John Williams, adjutant general of the Tennessee militia, marched southeast from Knoxville on December 1, 1812, with 165 men armed at their own expense with rifle or musket, pistols, tomahawk, and butcher knife. In Georgia both Governor David B. Mitchell and Indian agent Hawkins tried to persuade the Tennessee force to return home, for Governor Mitchell wanted his home state militia to attack the Seminoles and receive full credit for protecting the frontier. Mitchell secured the approval of his legislature to mount a raid into Florida, but the details were to be kept secret for there was a good information flow from the Creeks of Georgia to the Seminoles in Florida. According to Mitchell, if Payne's Seminoles learned of an operation against them, they would hide their women and children, destroy all the food they could not carry with them, and either hide in the woods waiting to attack or run to safety behind the walls of the several Spanish forts.

General Thomas Pinckney, commander of federal troops in southeastern Georgia, believing that he had authorization from Washington, ordered Williams and his men to move ahead. Pinckney projected that the Seminole and black villages near Paynes Prairie would be attacked by two forces: the Tennessee force under Williams would move from the St. Marys River beyond the St. Johns, where it would meet a Georgia militia group commanded by Colonel Thomas A. Smith, and the two units would advance together toward the villages. The force was to attack the Seminoles, destroy their fields and homes, kill all blacks who opposed them, and return to slavery those who were taken prisoners.[10]

When the troops arrived, they found Payne's Town deserted and moved on to Bowlegs Town ten or twelve miles to the southwest. As the horsemen searched for them, the Seminoles fired from a hammock, and the skirmish continued until darkness obscured the field. A base was established in the center of the Alachua Seminole country at Bowlegs Town (two miles north of present-day Micanopy), and daily the troops moved out to kill as many Seminoles and blacks as possible and to destroy their fields and homes. The constant patrols of the soldiers turned up many houses, storage bins, and cultivated fields but few Seminoles or blacks. With the force from Georgia and Tennessee four times greater than their number, the Seminoles had decided to retreat from the villages into the swamps. A message from the Creeks had earlier informed Bowlegs's people that a white force was moving toward Florida, and some had found safe haven by rejoining the Creeks.[11]

After inflicting all the damage they could, early in 1813 the Georgians returned to Camp New Hope on the St. Johns and the Tennessee volunteers to Colerain, Georgia. In the three-week campaign, the soldiers had burned 386 houses, destroyed or consumed 1,500 to 2,000 bushels of corn, captured 300 horses and 400 head of cattle, captured or destroyed 2,000 deerskins, killed twenty Seminoles, and captured nine Seminoles and blacks.[12] When the U.S. troops were withdrawn from Fernandina in May 1813, the unprotected area between the St. Marys and the St. Johns rivers was overrun by bands of white American cattle thieves who stole cattle from the Seminoles and Spaniards and sold the livestock in Georgia.

After the destruction of their villages part of the band under Bowlegs moved from Alachua to Suwannee Old Town on the Suwannee River, where an Upper Creek settlement had been established at a much earlier time. The burning of the fields and villages and the migration were a serious setback to Bowlegs and the Seminoles, for he owned a large herd of cattle and horses, sold each year a thousand steers in northeastern Florida, and killed some cattle daily for the needs of his people. In the new locations such stock raising was limited, for the whites had carried away most of the stock and Old Town was located some distance from the markets. When Bowlegs moved to the Suwannee, he came near the domain of Kinache and had to deal with the Lake Miccosukee people for the first time.

Certain aspects of this initial clash between the Seminoles and the soldiers would continue to characterize the warfare between the races until 1858. The Seminoles were usually quick to detect the approach of the whites. They would typically flee to the safety of nearby swamps and hammocks, leaving the town's herds and fields for the whites to destroy. Finally, the whites seldom knew the streams and forests of Florida and rarely found their quarry until captured Seminoles and blacks led them to their hideouts.

Payne's death brought about a realignment of Alachua Seminole leadership. Payne was succeeded by the eldest son of his sister and, after the nephew's death, by her younger son, Micanopy. When Micanopy became chief, the neighboring black village moved to Pelaclekeha near present-day Center Hill in Sumter County and the Seminoles to Okehumpkee near present-day Leesburg.[13]

In 1813, the year after Payne's death and the year U.S. troops withdrew from Fernandina, the faction of Upper Creek Indians known as Red Sticks, influenced by the teachings of Tecumseh and of his brother Tenskwatawa, killed 500 whites in an attack on Fort Mims on the lower Alabama River.[14] This attack marked the beginning of the Creek War of 1813–14. In response Andrew Jackson assembled a large force of whites and friendly Lower Creeks that crushed the Red Sticks with a loss of 800 braves at the Battle of Horseshoe Bend in central Alabama on March 27, 1814.[15] After the defeat a few Creek leaders signed the Treaty of Fort Jackson on August 9, 1814, in which the tribe lost half of its territory—22 million acres of land in southern Georgia and central Alabama.[16]

Some of the Red Stick leaders had been killed. Others hid in the swamps and hills, some became friends with the whites, and others, including Peter McQueen and Josiah Francis, fled to Spanish territory.

Francis (Francis the Prophet), son of an Englishman and a Creek woman, and McQueen, son of Scots trader James McQueen and a Creek woman, and several thousand other Creeks headed for Pensacola in the Panhandle.[17] A smaller number settled in southeastern Georgia along the Flint and Chattahoochee rivers. The condition of the Creeks moving into Florida was pitiful, for under the teachings of Tecumseh and Tenskwatawa they had tried to eradicate all signs of white culture by throwing their axes and hoes into the rivers and killing their cattle, chickens, and pigs, domestic animals introduced by the whites.

When the English took time from events in Europe to pay attention to the U.S. conflict, they did their best to use the Red Sticks as allies in a campaign against ports in the South, but it was too late. Early in the fall of 1813, Red Stick leaders had written to Governor Charles Cameron of the Bahamas requesting that aid be channeled through the Apalachicola River entry, but six months elapsed before the British responded.[18] During the interval the refugee Creeks complained that they had been driven from their homes by a bitter foe, and the Spanish refused to help on the grounds that their own soldiers needed food and clothing.[19]

In March 1814 Earl Bathurst, British secretary of state for war, ordered Admiral Alexander Cochrane to coordinate a campaign in the coastal area, and as a result, within a short time aid was on the way to the Red Stick Creeks for their assistance in the coming offensive.[20] By May 1814 the British frigate *Orpheus* reached Apalachicola Bay, where muskets, ammunition, blankets, and presents were distributed.[21] According to American Indian agent Hawkins, fifty men were landed on Deer Island (St. George Island), and a British officer gave each Creek town in the neighborhood food, four large kegs of powder, some short muskets, and other articles. A colonel, nine other officers, and 300 men came ashore on St. George Island, where they erected a building to hold the supplies. When the ammunition and guns were distributed, the British told the Creeks that they were for hunting turkeys and deer and not for killing white Americans.[22]

The British viewed the Apalachicola River as a highway leading deep into U.S. territory and the well-provisioned Forbes store located at Prospect Bluff a strong defensive point. Lieutenant George Woodbine of the Royal Marines consequently led a small detachment fifteen miles up the Apalachicola to establish a base at the bluff. Seminole leaders Thomas Perryman and Kinache had listened to Tecumseh on his visit to Alabama and had tried to send warriors to assist the Red Sticks in the Creek War of

1813–14, but the Lower Creeks had prevented their passage through southern Alabama. When the two learned that the British had arrived at Prospect Bluff, they offered their services to Woodbine one or two days after his arrival. The British seized the John Forbes trading post at the bluff, with its stores of provisions and red paint, its ample housing and adjacent agricultural fields, and gave supplies to the destitute Creeks who had fled from Alabama and to the Seminole visitors from Lake Miccosukee. The British put the two caretakers found at the post, Edmund Doyle and William Hambly, to work as storekeeper and interpreter.[23] Woodbine was ready for action against Fort Mitchell eighty miles to the north, but he needed field pieces, more Creek recruits, and a British regiment to provide muscle for the attack.[24]

In organizing the Creeks and Seminoles for an offensive against the white Americans, Woodbine was successful in gaining strong support from Creek towns along the upper Apalachicola and the lower Flint and Chattahoochee rivers, but the Creek towns of Coweta and Cassita in Alabama remained only lukewarm. As a result of a message sent to Pensacola, former Red Stick leaders Francis and McQueen and their followers immediately set out in boats bound for Apalachicola to join the British.[25]

Two of Woodbine's enlisted men drilled the American Indians in firing procedures and military tactics, for the British believed that, given proper equipment, they would become a fearsome military power. Although British records do not reveal the type of training Sergeant Smith and Corporal Denny gave, white American observers claimed that it consisted of discharging a swivel gun, giving a war whoop, and firing small arms several times.[26]

As part of the plan to attack several cities along the Atlantic coast Major Edward Nicolls of the Royal Marines was selected to head a force of blacks, Loyalists, and American Indians in support of the British troops. Arriving at Prospect Bluff in August 1814 Nicolls met with those Creeks and Seminoles receiving food and arms and departed after several weeks' stay for Pensacola, where the Spanish offered little or no help. Nicolls nevertheless organized an attack near Mobile by a combined British and American Indian force that included some Seminoles under Thomas Perryman.[27] When the force attempted a landing at Fort Bowyer at Mobile Point without proper artillery preparation, however, it suffered severe losses of men and one ship and withdrew.

A second setback took place when Andrew Jackson captured Pensacola on November 7, 1814, and the Creeks and Seminoles camping nearby were forced to flee to Apalachicola. With the fall of Pensacola, Prospect Bluff became the only center supplying the Creek and Seminole Indians with food and arms. Perryman and Kinache and four or five other leaders visited several British ships when they anchored at Apalachicola Bay and were able to remain aboard in comfort for a month or more.[28]

By December 1814, nearly three thousand men, women, and children were assembled at the bluff.[29] Even shallow-draught vessels had trouble negotiating the river in December, and the food problem became so desperate that warriors were sent out into the woods to hunt deer. Yet, even with their large and fairly well-equipped force, Woodbine and Nicolls did little to harass the white Americans. The only other attack in which American Indians participated developed when a few Seminoles came along with the fleet in the British landing at New Orleans, a battle that ended in the overwhelming defeat of the British by Jackson.

Finally, the British troops were withdrawn in the spring of 1815 under terms of the Treaty of Ghent, leaving Nicolls as an American Indian superintendent without pay or official status, but with a desire to help. On March 10, 1815, a pact was signed by thirty leaders at a fort abandoned by the British at the juncture of the Chattahoochee and Flint rivers.[30] In the document the Creeks and Seminoles declared the Forbes Grant null and void and requested the English to send traders to establish posts at the mouths of the important rivers in northern Florida.[31] This land had been awarded by non-Muskogee Creeks to Bowles and later to Forbes to keep it out of white American hands. When a band of white Americans invaded Florida to attack part of the Bowlegs group of villages, Nicolls wrote to American Indian agent Hawkins pointing out that the Seminoles were keeping the peace by staying away from them. Nicolls tried to make a second point by insisting that land taken from the Creeks under terms of the Fort Jackson pact was a violation of the Treaty of Ghent and should be returned to them.[32] In reply Hawkins noted that Nicolls had no control over American Indian–white relations in the United States.[33]

When it became obvious to Nicolls that the white Americans would not honor article 9 of the Treaty of Ghent, which specified that the American Indians would not lose any land, and that England would not assist the natives in any way, he left a large supply of arms and ammunition at the fort that had been erected at Prospect Bluff and departed with an American Indian delegation that included Francis the Prophet to negotiate in England. So far as can be determined only a small amount of arms and ammunition were taken by the American Indians in the area; the larger amount was seized by black former British colonial troops. Although Francis and his son spent a year in England meeting with Earl Bathurst and the prince regent, the British leaders realized that signing the March 10, 1815, pact would perhaps cause the United States to resume hostilities. They were also still recovering from battling Napoleon, and thus they put the matter aside from further discussion.[34] To ease the pain, they gave Francis many presents and £325, a commission as brigadier general in the British army, and a splendid red-and-gold uniform. After leaving England on December 30, 1816, Francis remained in Nassau until the following June, when he was taken to Florida by Alexander Arbuthnot.[35]

When the British abandoned their fort at Prospect Bluff, the Red Sticks, mostly from Muskogee-speaking villages, moved deeper into Florida. Some moved into inhabited villages at or near Apalachee and the Suwannee, and others established new towns in the area towards Tampa Bay. Part of Peter McQueen's band moved toward the Suwannee River, and the other portion moved back to the neighborhood of Pensacola. It has been estimated that the Indian population of Florida increased from 4,500 to 6,000 persons by the Creek influx. Some established hunting camps that soon became permanent village sites, but others, especially those living in the area between Mobile and Tallahassee, wandered about in the swamps and remote hammocks where they farmed small areas, hunted, and stole cattle and hogs from the whites. Most of these refugees stayed for a brief time in the Florida Panhandle–Tallahassee area and then moved south into areas that had not yet been occupied by the bands that were longtime Florida residents.[36]

Once the Treaty of Fort Jackson had been approved by the Senate in August 1814, U.S. authorities had decided to assemble a sizable military force near the southern Alabama and Georgia boundaries as a show of strength to mark off the boundaries of the land that the Creek Indians had surrendered. With 1,000 men on hand and 5,000 more in reserve, Brigadier General Edmund P. Gaines had conferred with the Creek leaders, who promised not to interfere with the surveying team. As the surveying proceeded, however, a hostile force had gathered at the junction of the Flint and Chattahoochee rivers. When the Creeks saw the large number of soldiers, they dispersed.[37]

With the approval of Andrew Jackson, in the spring of 1816 Gaines erected Fort Scott on the west bank of the Flint River in Georgia to serve as an observation post for activities of both the Creeks and the blacks who had moved into the former British fort at Prospect Bluff, which had become known as the Negro Fort. He also built Fort Gaines on the east bank of the Chattahoochee River to serve as a supply post. The surveyors, meanwhile, observed large numbers of Creeks following them and ceased work until more protection could be given.[38] Much of the trouble at this time arose when the government failed to furnish food supplies promised in the Treaty of Fort Jackson, and the Creeks were starving. Some who had helped Jackson defeat the Red Sticks had not been paid, and annuities as promised in the treaty were not paid to either the winners or the losers in the war.

Acting under orders from Jackson, Gaines prepared for military action by moving along the Chattahoochee River, talking to Creek leaders and learning about the area. Although the orders from Jackson read "until murderers are delivered and the stolen property is returned no Creeks can remain in ceded territory except friendly parties . . . all others to be treated as enemies," the Creeks told Gaines that they were too poor and weak to oppose him, and he did not bother them.[39] Colonel Duncan Clinch, the commander for southern Georgia, went along with Gaines's decision until some friendly Lower Creek leaders fled to Fort Gaines for protection, and until two of Clinch's men were killed and thirty head of cattle stolen. At that point Clinch changed his mind and was ready for action against hostile former Red Sticks in southern Georgia. He proposed moving down the Flint River and destroying every village between Fort Gaines and the juncture of the Flint and Chattahoochee rivers, but Jackson and Gaines rejected such a scheme in favor of strengthening Fort Scott by moving provisions up the Apalachicola River from Mobile and New Orleans.[40] Jackson worked out a plan to supply food by water transport along the Apalachicola; if the Negro Fort impeded the passage of the food, the fort would be destroyed. A convoy composed of two gunboats and two schooners approached the Negro Fort from the south, and a force of regulars and friendly Creeks led by Clinch moved in from the north; a lucky shot from one of the gunboats landed in the fort's powder magazine and killed most of the 300 persons in the fort.

In 1816 several Creek leaders wrote to Governor Charles Cameron of the Bahamas requesting protection of their rights under the Treaty of Ghent but no answer was received.[41] Governor Cameron gave his reply to Alexander Arbuthnot to deliver when he landed at Ochlockonee Sound in the Florida Panhandle. Arbuthnot, a Scots merchant from Nassau, arrived at the sound in January 1817 in his schooner *Chance* to engage in the fur trade. An elderly merchant from the island of New Providence, he hoped to make some money by trading guns, calico, and other items for corn, hides, and beeswax. On his return to Nassau, Arbuthnot met Josiah Francis, who was returning to Florida after recently negotiating with the British in England. When Francis had arrived in Nassau in February 1817, Woodbine had invited the former Red Stick leader to his house, seized a gold-mounted tomahawk and a diamond snuffbox that Francis had been given in England, and charged him a high rent for the stay. When Francis asked for a detailed bill Woodbine replied that such was not needed for Francis could not read.[42] Francis traveled back to Florida aboard the *Chance,* arriving in Ochlockonee Sound in June 1817. The schooner was greeted by a large number of Creek and Seminole Indian leaders, who realized that Arbuthnot represented the final opportunity to secure English arms to help them in a probable conflict with the white Americans.[43] Accordingly, twelve leaders signed a paper on June 17, 1817, appointing Alexander Arbuthnot their agent and attorney with full power and authority to act for them and to write letters that were necessary and proper for the benefit of their bands.[44] By accepting this position Arbuthnot advanced from the status of trader to one of unofficial diplomat. At the request of the Creek and Seminole leaders Arbuthnot wrote letters to the governor of the Bahamas, the British minister at Washington, Colonel Nicolls, U.S. military officers, and the U.S. Creek Indian agent.

Francis wanted to return to Nassau, but Arbuthnot persuaded him to stay in Florida where he could keep the Indians at peace. Finally, Francis settled with his family in a village on the Wakulla, three miles from St. Marks, on what may have been the site of a large warehouse once owned by Forbes and Company. In the summer of 1817 a party of Seminoles captured Captain Duncan McKrimmon of the Georgia militia while he was fishing and took him to Francis's village to prepare him for torture and death.[45] Milly Francis, the daughter of the Seminole leader, saved his life by proposing to her father that McKrimmon should have his head shaved, dress like a Seminole, and live among them; McKrimmon would later betray the tribe's whereabouts to U.S. forces.

Arbuthnot and the Spanish commander at St. Marks got along well. As was the practice with other foreign traders, he was given a trading license by the government but in addition was allowed to keep his goods in the fort. In April 1818, he had stored at St. Marks 500 deer skins, dry goods, dishes, lead, molasses, gun powder, sugar, and forty barrels of salt. The price at this time for deer skins was twenty-five cents per pound, for raccoon skins twelve and one-half cents each, for fox skins eighteen and three-quarters cents each, for best otter skins three dollars each, for cow hides one dollar each, and for wildcat skins twenty-five cents each.

Arbuthnot's patriarchal but sympathetic attitude toward the Creeks and Seminoles and their problems was reflected in his journal.

> These men, are children of nature; leave them in their forests to till their field and hunt the stag, and graze their cattle, their ideas will extend no further; and the honest trader in supplying their wants may make a handsome profit of them. They have been ill treated by the English and robbed by the Americans; cheated by those who have dealt with them; receiving goods and other articles at most exorbitant prices for their peltry, which have been much under valued.[46]

Arbuthnot seemed unaware of the serious state of affairs augured by the buildup of white military strength in southern Georgia. In October 1817 he came to Florida on business, bringing with him George Woodbine and paving the way for the establishment of a trading post on the banks of the Suwannee River. Much of Arbuthnot's influence with the Creeks and Seminoles came as a result of his owning *Chance*, a schooner that offered the means of communication between the Florida Panhandle and the Bahamas. Yet with that power came obligations: he had to transport and feed Woodbine and his men for several months.[47] In fact, it may have been Woodbine who suggested the trip to the Suwannee River instead of a return to Ochlockonee. Woodbine and Gregory McGregor, an adventurer in both Florida and South America, had plans to seize Florida with the help of blacks, discharged British soldiers, and Seminoles.

At first John Fenix, the captain of Arbuthnot's ship, found it difficult to pass through the Cedar Keys into the Suwannee River but navigated the channel with the use of a small boat. While the schooner was anchored in the keys, five canoes approached the ship carrying Bowlegs, the principal leader of the Seminoles in the neighborhood, and Arbuthnot and Woodbine invited Bowlegs aboard with his black and Seminole followers.[48] Although the Seminoles and blacks talked all night with Woodbine, who wanted their assistance in overthrowing Spanish rule in Florida, the visitors did manage to exchange six deer skins, sixteen raccoon skins, and three pounds of wax with Arbuthnot for cloth materials. Within a short time Arbuthnot left the schooner and traveled up the Suwannee by canoe, where he met with Kinache and Peter McQueen and promised to write about Creek and Seminole problems to British minister Charles Bagot at

Washington and to send copies to officials in England. On November 10, 1817, the trader promised to return by December with articles Kinache and McQueen desired from Nassau, and sealed the friendship with presents of rum, sugar, coffee, and 100 cigars to each leader.[49] The separate conferences that Arbuthnot held with Kinache, McQueen, and Bowlegs indicated that the two Seminole bands were following separate paths and that Kinache was continuing his alliance with the Red Sticks.

While the Seminoles were establishing contacts with Arbuthnot, events that would soon disrupt their lives and his were developing to the northwest. When settlers began to move into the Fort Jackson cession, the whites and Native Americans stole each other's livestock, burned each other's houses, and murdered each other, with blame equally divided between the two races. Gaines lectured Kinache and Bowlegs in the following words: "You Seminoles are very bad people—I don't say whom. You have murdered many of my people and stolen my cattle and many good horses that cost me money . . . you harbor a great many of my black people among you at Sahwahnee [Suwannee River]. If you give me leave to go by you against them I shall not hurt anything belonging to you."[50]

Kinache hit back hard at Gaines with the following reply: "You charge me with killing your people, stealing your cattle and burning your houses; it is I that have cause to complain of the Americans. While one American has been justly killed while in act of stealing cattle, more than four Indians while hunting have been murdered by these lawless freebooters. I harbor no Negroes . . . I shall use force to stop any armed Americans from passing my towns or my lands."[51] Neamathla, a Red Stick and leader of Fowltown village located fourteen miles from Fort Scott, cautioned Major David E. Twiggs, Seventh Infantry commander of Fort Scott: "I warn you not to cross nor cut a stick of wood in the east side of the Flint. That land is mine. I am directed by the power above and power below to protect and defend it. I shall do so."[52]

Because Neamathla and his people were living in U.S. territory on land lost by the Creeks and refused to surrender alleged murderers of frontier people, Jackson gave Twiggs authority to remove the Red Sticks. Twiggs sent a note to Neamathla requesting a visit, and after he received a negative reply, Gaines authorized him to attack the village.[53] After an all-night march, Twiggs and 250 men attacked Fowltown at daybreak on November 21, 1817, killing four men and one woman; the remainder of the Seminoles escaped into a nearby swamp. This episode marked the first action in what has come to be known as the First Seminole War. When Lieutenant Colonel Arbuckle with 300 men moved through Fowltown several days later, the force was attacked by 60 Seminoles, who beat a hasty retreat after losing 6 to 8 men and inflicting a loss of 1 man killed and 2 wounded upon the military.[54] Within a short time the Fowltown inhabitants moved to Lake Miccosukee, where they joined forces with Kinache's villagers. (In 1819 before a Senate committee the Creek Indian agent David Mitchell testified that he saw no reason to attack the town, for Neamathla and his people had stayed away from hostile Red Sticks and tried to be friendly to the whites.[55] Mitchell believed that the attack took place because Neamathla would not visit Twiggs or surrender the murderers.)

A combined force of American Indians was able to avenge the Fowltown attacks on November 30, 1817, by ambushing on the Apalachicola an open boat commanded by Lieutenant Robert W. Scott. When a large boat bound from Fort Scott carrying forty soldiers, seven women, and some children came near the shoreline to avoid a strong current, gunfire from the heavily wooded banks killed all but thirteen of the people aboard. One of the women on the boat was captured and taken to villages to the southeast, but six of the soldiers aboard avoided death or prolonged torture and death by jumping into the river and making their way to Fort Scott to report the disaster.[56] Several days later a convoy of three boats commanded by Major Peter Muhlenburgh was proceeding up the same river carrying military supplies when heavy gunfire by concealed Fowltown Indians forced it to stop and remain anchored until a rescue party of troops from Fort Scott arrived.

In a related incident raiders led by Chenubby, a Fowltown Seminole, ransacked the Forbes store at Prospect Bluff on December 13, 1817, and carried off clerks Edmund Doyle and William Hambly. William Perryman, a Seminole leader friendly to the whites, had tried to protect the two men, but he was killed and his men forced to join the bands at war with the military.[57] Doyle and Hambly were first taken to Kinache's village at Lake Miccosukee, then to Bowlegs Town on the Suwannee, and finally to St. Marks, where they were placed under guard by the Spanish. The raiders attacked other plantations along the frontier, killing settlers and blacks, and taking cattle and horses. Creek and Seminole resistance was most determined in February 1818, when they lined the Apalachicola River firing at the boats carrying food to Fort Scott, forcing cessation of all traffic on the river and raising apprehensions that Fort Scott would have to be abandoned for lack of food.

When news of the Scott attack reached Washington, Secretary of War John C. Calhoun moved quickly. Because Gaines had been transferred earlier to Amelia Island, Andrew Jackson was directed to raise sufficient troops and proceed to Fort Scott.[58] Marching the 450 miles from Tennessee in forty-six days, Jackson arrived at Fort Scott on March 9, 1818, and within a short time moved down the Apalachicola to the ruins of the Negro Fort, where a fort that became known as Fort Gadsden was constructed.[59]

Once Fort Gadsden was completed, Jackson and his force of regulars and Georgia militiamen awaited the arrival of food so that they could go deep into Spanish territory. While Jackson was camped, General William McIntosh and Creeks friendly to the whites moved along the eastern side of the Apalachicola River, capturing 53 warriors, 180 women and children, and much-needed supplies of corn.[60] With the arrival of a large force of volunteers from Tennessee under Colonel Edward Elliott and with the addition of McIntosh's Creeks, Jackson's army numbered 3,500: 1,000 militiamen, 500 regulars, and 1,800 American Indians. Jackson's plans included attacks on the Seminole and black villages at Lake Miccosukee and the Suwannee River and the use of several naval vessels under Captain Isaac McKeever to carry supplies to St. Marks, where McKeever would wait for Jackson and capture any foreign vessels or American Indians in canoes that he might meet.[61]

Jackson's first objective was Lake Miccosukee, where ancient Kinache, a longtime opponent of the whites, was the leader of the Lake Miccosukee villages, whose population totaled 1,000 or more; Coche-Tustenuggee was the war chief.

At the end of March 1818, Jackson and his men met little resistance as they moved against the most populous group of Seminole settlements in Florida. Because Jackson's force outnumbered the Seminoles by at least ten to one, the Indians directed some scattered shots toward the advancing soldiers and then fled to nearby lowlands. The troops moving through the deserted village discovered a red pole standing near the council house from which hung fifty fresh scalps, including those of the Scott party. In revenge, Jackson's men seized the herd of 1,000 cattle and a large supply of corn and burned the village complex of 300 homes.[62] Military commanders were given the choice of either selling the captured cattle or distribut-

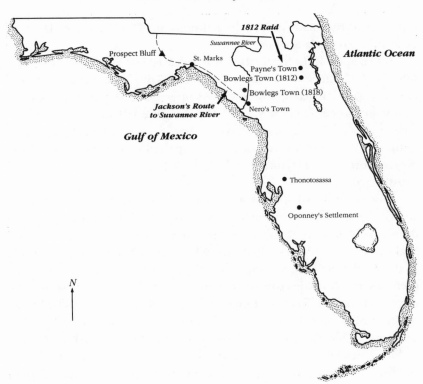

Battles and Events of the War of 1812 and the First Seminole War

ing them among the Creek allies. Kinache may have been killed in defense of his village, for it was at this time that Neamathla took his place as leader of the Seminoles in the Panhandle area.

Jackson's next target was St. Marks, where he believed the former Red Stick leaders Francis the Prophet and Peter McQueen and the Englishmen George Woodbine and Alexander Arbuthnot might be found. With no resistance from the Spanish garrison, Jackson and his men entered the fort at St. Marks and raised the U.S. flag on April 6, 1818.[63] Upon hearing in St. Marks of the approach of Jackson's army Arbuthnot wrote to advise his son and Bowlegs that Jackson was coming to attack the villages on the Suwannee and that if they simply fell back and let him have his way, he would soon move elsewhere.[64] Meanwhile, Francis and Himallemico, another Red Stick leader who had taken part in the Scott ambush, were decoyed aboard a U.S. ship flying the British flag commanded by Captain McKeever and hung without benefit of a hearing in the courtyard of the fort. It was McKrimmon, who, having been released from Seminole captivity, gave information that led to the taking of his captors.

The capture of Arbuthnot by the rapidly advancing U.S. Army took place under rather unusual circumstances. Arbuthnot had retired to the home of the Spanish commander within the walls of the fort, where he believed he could avoid the fighting between the U.S. soldiers and the Seminoles, but he had become alarmed and decided to flee for his life. Jackson captured him while he was attempting to escape, and he was held for trial at St. Marks.[65]

When the Negro Fort and later the Lake Miccosukee villages had been destroyed, a steady stream of blacks and Indians had fled deeper into Florida. Peter McQueen, the only former Red Stick leader who had eluded Jackson, had fled to the Suwannee River. Jackson decided to move against him and his followers, the black villages, the Arbuthnot trading post, and the town of Bowlegs, which were all located on or near the Suwannee and Econfina rivers. Abraham, a famous interpreter, was one of these black refugees who had been brought by the British from Pensacola to the Negro Fort, and after the destruction of the fortification Abraham fled to the town established by Bowlegs on the Suwannee.[66]

Near Bowlegs Town was the settlement of Nero, a mulatto who displayed considerable civil and military leadership. Nero's village and several other towns settled by 300 or 400 escaped slaves from plantations in Florida and Georgia were located on the west bank of the Suwannee thirty-five miles from the mouth of the river. The cabins, larger and better constructed than those of the Seminoles, were scattered along the bank of the river, and many inhabitants had gardens producing fruit, corn, potatoes, peas, beans, and rice, which were protected from roaming cattle and hogs by wooden fencing.

Arbuthnot's letter warning that Jackson was approaching St. Marks had been carried to the Suwannee River trading post and read to the assembled people. After deciding to resist instead of fleeing into the swamps, the Seminoles and blacks made themselves ready for the attack.[67] Nero placed his men in the village located on the western side of the river but moved the women and children to the east side where they could retreat for safety to the nearby swamps.

After capturing St. Marks Jackson moved 107 miles in a southeasterly direction to the Suwannee River. His campaign of the Suwannee was conducted in two phases—Creek versus Seminole (former Creek) and white versus black. The first phase involved Creeks and former Creeks from Alabama on both sides. On April 12 1,500 Creeks under McIntosh discovered near the Econfina River 200 Seminoles led by Peter McQueen hidden in a swamp and drove them into the open where a hit-and-run engagement took place. During the battle the Seminoles lost thirty-seven men killed and six men and ninety-eight women and children taken prisoner. In addition, they lost 500 head of cattle, many horses, and much corn; one white woman who had been captured at the Apalachicola ambush was taken.[68]

Jackson divided his force into three sections and moved against Nero's village on the late afternoon of April 16. The force of 300 blacks put up a spirited defense, but after realizing that further resistance was useless, they swam across the river to their families.[69] Nine blacks and two Indians were killed, two blacks were captured, and thirteen of Jackson's men were wounded in the brief engagement. Three hundred houses in the several villages scattered along the river were burned by the Creeks and whites.

At this juncture the unhappy fates of two Englishmen from Nassau, entrepreneur Alexander Arbuthnot and former British officer Robert Ambrister, came together. Arbuthnot's schooner *Chance* with a cargo of trade goods had arrived on March 19, 1818, at the mouth of the Suwannee and was seized the next day by Ambrister, accompanied by twenty-five blacks who had just come into the area. Ambrister was involved in the scheme to seize Florida under the direction of Woodbine and Gregory McGregor, and his appearance with the blacks appeared to be the first phase of the project.[70] During his brief stay at the trading post and Seminole village Ambrister was approached by Seminole leaders who wanted more ammunition and complained that Arbuthnot had not delivered the letters that they had dictated.[71] After seizing the *Chance* Ambrister ordered Captain John Fenix to sail for St. Marks, where he hoped to capture the Spanish fort. At St. Marks the schooner ran into a blockade by U.S. gunboats. The *Chance* then returned to the Suwannee, where it was run aground (probably by accident by a new pilot, as Ambrister did not trust Fenix), all of its cargo looted, and the booty taken to Bowlegs's village. After a short stay at the village Ambrister and his men took Alexander Arbuthnot's son John, who had been left in charge of the trading post, back to the schooner, refloated it, and prepared to sail for Tampa.[72] When Ambrister again went back to Bowlegs's village to obtain more food for the voyage, Jackson's men captured him and seized the *Chance* to carry supplies and wounded soldiers back to St. Marks. John Arbuthnot, who was taken into custody by Jackson's men, was later released and returned to the Bahamas, but the wealth of the family was dissipated by his father's Florida activities.

Alexander Arbuthnot, in a trial held in St. Marks April 26–28, 1818, before a board of thirteen officers ranging in rank from captain to major general, was accused of committing two crimes: (1) exciting and stirring up the Creek Indians to war against the United States and (2) acting as a spy, aiding, abetting, and comforting the enemy, and supplying that enemy with the means of war.[73] In the opening session on April 26 several witnesses testified against Arbuthnot, and evidence to support the testimony was presented in the form of letters, some written by the defendant and some dictated by Seminole leaders. Arbuthnot could not obtain any witnesses to testify in his behalf but defended himself by speaking in moving terms. He also pointed out that few original letters were produced in court and that rules of evidence dictated that proof of handwriting must be demonstrated before such letters could be admitted as evidence. In response to the second charge Arbuthnot claimed that he did not incite the Indians but tried to calm them. Further, the only supplies that he sold them were for two months of hunting. Finally, he pointed out, no Seminole witnesses were called or were available to support his defense.

At the conclusion of the trial Arbuthnot was found guilty on both charges and on the morning of April 29, 1818, the tall, white-haired man dressed in black was hung from the yardarm of his own schooner *Chance,* twenty feet above the water—an execution that most historians and attorneys would deem illegal. After the body had been hanging for thirty minutes from the yardarm, it was cut down, covered by a blanket, and buried beside Captain Robert Ambrister, who had been tried, found guilty, and shot by a firing squad of U.S. soldiers.[74]

After the trials and executions of Ambrister and Arbuthnot, Jackson and his men moved toward Pensacola, concluding the First Seminole War and leaving behind a Florida ripe for U.S. acquisition and filled with fleeing Seminole Indians and black allies, who hoped to protect themselves by moving deep into the peninsula.

The Fowltown Indians moved to the west bank of the Apalachicola. Part of the Lake Miccosukee bands moved to New Mikasuki west of the upper Suwannee, and others went to Alachua. Most of the Red Sticks migrated to the Tampa Bay area and Bowlegs's band moved from Suwannee to a point west of Lake Harris.[75] One of the most famous of the migrants to Florida was Osceola, or Asi-yaholo, who as a young boy fled from Alabama with Peter McQueen's band, was captured at the Econfina battle and released, and then moved to the Peace River and later to the area near present-day Ocala.[76] Peter McQueen and part of his band may have gone as far south as present-day Miami, where he died; his widow returned to Alabama. Captain Hugh Young, who was with Jackson, estimated a total of twenty-three Indian towns with a combined population of 4,685 in the area between the Apalachicola and Suwannee rivers.

By 1821, according to William Simmons, who did much traveling in Florida and was a "shrewd observer," the Mikasukis lived on the western side of the Suwannee, the Yuchis at Spring Garden on the St. Johns, the Ocklawahas at the shores of Lake Sennfky, Micanopy and his blacks and Seminoles at Pelaclekeha (thirty miles southwest of the ford on Ocklawaha River); there were also settlements at Chukochatty near present-day Brooksville and at Hitchepucksasa near present-day Plant City.[77] Included within the American Indian population of Florida at this time were also isolated bands of Choctaw and Yamassee Indians. Some blacks fleeing possible U.S. control of Florida made their way by canoe and visiting vessels from the Bahamas looking for wrecks to Andros Island in the Bahamas and introduced Seminole cultural traits to the islands.[78]

Muskogee-speaking bands had migrated into the region to the north and east of Tampa Bay between 1783 and 1821. Carrying with them skills learned in Alabama, these Seminoles established a series of plantations based upon cultivating the fertile soil and raising livestock. Simaka, leader of New Eufala near present-day Brooksville, had large herds of cattle and horses and many hogs. Twelve miles south of New Eufala lay Tomahitche, where corn and rice were cultivated.[79] Thonotosassa was founded between 1812 and 1820 a short distance northwest of present-day Tampa by Alachua refugees. At Oponney's settlement north of present-day Bartow were Red Stick fugitives from the Suwannee River battle. As had been the way of life in Alabama, most of the towns in northern and central Florida had square grounds, councils and officials, and satellite settlements. Some leaders, including Kinache and Bowlegs, were able to gain power during the early part of this period, when they took advantage of the prime locations to trade with the whites in cattle, horses, and grain, but events during the Patriot Army's invasion of Florida and the First Seminole War destroyed these advantages. Yet these bands deemed a move to central Florida necessary, for the area seemed to provide a safe haven several hundred miles distant from Georgia. When economic rewards were not forthcoming in central Florida, Seminole and black bands moved into the present-day Sarasota area, to the banks of the Manatee, and to the Peace River section, including Lake Hancock. The Seminole women gained in stature during this period, moving up from cleaners of deer skins to become small-time business operators by cultivating oranges, melons, corn, rice, and peaches and selling these products to the whites.[80]

3

Prelude to War,
1821–1833

n February 22, 1821, the United States acquired Florida from Spain, and with it guardianship of some 5,000 Seminoles. Even before he approved the treaty with Spain, President James Monroe appointed Jean A. Penieres as subagent for the Seminoles and Secretary of War John C. Calhoun appointed Captain John R. Bell as acting agent; within a short time Penieres died from yellow fever, and Bell was suspended from office for conduct unbecoming an officer.[1] Finally, when William P. DuVal was appointed governor of the territory of Florida in April 1822, Gad Humphreys became agent and Peter Pelham subagent.[2] Both were army officers released from service due to a shortage of military funds.

When the United States acquired Florida, the Seminoles in the territory represented a varied assortment of bands. One anthropologist who compared lists of leaders compiled at that time has concluded that in 1823, there were fifteen towns that had been established prior to 1812, eight towns composed of Red Stick migrants, two Yuchi towns, three black settlements, and two towns whose inhabitants were not identified.[3] Some twenty-nine independent bands were scattered throughout the peninsula from the Georgia border to Tampa Bay. It was said that the area directly south of Tampa Bay was used as a hunting zone and did not serve as a permanent home for any band at this time. Situated near the larger bands were villages of former slaves who paid tribute of horses, cattle, and produce to the Seminole leaders who had extended protection to them.[4]

Authorities began to consider the Seminoles living near white settlements a problem and to plan where they might be relocated. Governor

DuVal thought the area between the Suwannee River and Alachua, where most of the Seminoles lived, was one of the richest and most valuable in the territory and should belong to whites. He believed the Seminoles should be moved to join the Upper Creeks in Alabama or sent west of the Mississippi River.[5] Yet when Secretary of War Calhoun notified DuVal that unless Congress gave its approval and money, President James Monroe would not try to move the Seminoles from Florida, the governor tried to better their conditions. When, due to high water, the corn fields did not produce enough of a crop during the summer of 1822, he asked the secretary of war to increase their food allotment. In addition, he ordered that no whites could purchase their cattle, horses, or slaves or trade with them without a license from the American Indian agent Gad Humphreys or from DuVal. Any whites that settled near or at Seminole towns were liable to be removed by military force.[6]

On November 20, 1822, a council scheduled for the Seminoles at St. Marks fell through. Although the governor had planned the council with the Seminoles to explain the food situation to them, he left Tallahassee on a trip to Kentucky, the agent, Humphreys, did not appear, and the subagent, Pelham, was ill. Paymaster Thomas Wright, delayed by a storm, reached St. Marks on November 27, where he learned that after a wait of several days the Seminole leaders had returned to their towns. Wright arranged a meeting with several of them to explain the circumstances of the delay and prepared a distribution of food to them.[7] The Indians were apparently not angry at the cancellation of the council, and two leaders and eight warriors visited Pensacola on December 23 to determine if a council and subsequent treaty would be scheduled. Judging from cancellation of the council and the fact that the agent did not have a budget or even a base for his operations, federal Seminole policy was in disarray from the very beginning.

Under pressure by white settlers in Florida President Monroe recommended in 1824 that the Seminoles either be removed from Florida or be placed on a reservation. Because tribal relocation in the West had not yet been fully explored by the federal government, Secretary of War Calhoun in response to the urging of Joseph M. Hernandez, territorial delegate to Congress, proposed that commissioners be appointed to confer with the Seminoles and obtain their agreement for removal to the area south of Charlotte Harbor and Charlotte (Peace) River.[8] Should the lands south of the harbor be not sufficiently fertile, the commissioners were authorized to move the boundary as far north as Tampa Bay. Accordingly, Calhoun appointed James Gadsden of South Carolina, Bernardo Suqui of Florida, and DuVal as commissioners; Gadsden and Suqui were to be paid eight dollars a day.[9]

The spot selected for the negotiations was the north bank of Moultrie Creek situated some five miles south of St. Augustine. It was easy for some bands residing fairly close to the council site to attend the meeting, but those living in the Panhandle had to travel nearly 300 miles.[10] In fact, agent Gad Humphreys and interpreter Stephen Richards conducted a party of 350 Seminoles on a long trek from the temporary agency headquarters at St. Marks to Moultrie Creek. It was fortunate that they made the trip for they constituted the majority of the 425 persons that attended the meeting.[11]

On the day before the opening of negotiations the leaders of the various bands selected Neamathla, a Mikasuki and a hard-liner against white encroachments, as the principal Seminole negotiator.[12] Neamathla, a Red Stick whose village had been attacked by regular troops in southern Georgia in the opening battle of the First Seminole War and hit by Jackson near Lake Miccosukee later in the same war, had limited negotiating skills or advantages, but since their steadfast positions gave the Seminoles their only hope of remaining in Florida, the hard-line advocates would influence Seminole leaders for the next thirty-five years.

During the two weeks of negotiations held in a bark house constructed for the event, James Gadsden, briefed in advance for the meeting by his good friend Andrew Jackson, pointed out that a reservation was needed, for the Seminoles could not roam as they desired throughout Florida.[13] Neamathla responded that he was willing to accept a reservation but had doubts about the land to the south, for it did not have hickory nuts, persimmons, acorns, or much fertile land. As a result of Neamathla's remarks, the reservation area projected north of the Peace River was later enlarged by 15 percent in 1827 to 5,865,000 acres. An amendment to the original draft allowed Neamathla and five other important leaders and their followers to remain on separate reserves in north Florida and, according to the federal negotiators, had this amendment not been included, the treaty would not have been accepted by the tribe.[14] Finally, the ten-article Treaty of Moultrie Creek was signed September 18, 1823, by thirty-two Seminoles and three representatives of the government.

In return for relinquishing nearly 24 million acres of land that the government could sell at $1.25 an acre, the Seminoles received moving expenses; an annuity of $5,000 for twenty years; food for a year; payment for improvements left behind in northern Florida; provision for a school, blacksmith, and gunsmith; farming implements; livestock; and employment of an agent, subagent, and interpreter. The annuities promised in the treaty were withheld for a limited time to pay property owners for losses through Seminole thefts and runaway slaves. Since the commissioners were afraid that arms and ammunition could be supplied from Cuba, boundaries of the reservation were to be placed not less than fifteen miles from the Gulf of Mexico and not less than twenty miles from the Atlantic Ocean. A military post was to be established near Tampa Bay to make a show of military power and to prevent trade between the Seminoles and Cuban fishermen. Finally, the Seminoles promised to be "active and vigilant" in the return of escaped slaves and fugitives from justice.[15]

Once James Gadsden had selected the site for Cantonment (later Fort) Brooke on the northeast bank of the Hillsborough River where it entered Tampa Bay, four companies of the Fourth Infantry commanded by Colonel George M. Brooke and brought into the area by ships from Pensacola established the military post in January 1824.[16] The only Seminole town nearby was Thonotosassa, a village of two hundred persons twelve miles northeast of present-day downtown Tampa. After Brooke had assured the Seminoles that he came as a friend, they were regular visitors at the fort, which served as a subagency. The extent of these good relations was seen on the day Charles Cavallo, or Stout Chief, principal leader of Thonotosassa, was thrust into a campfire near Government Spring in present-day Ybor City by a drunken Seminole. When Brooke learned how badly the Stout Chief had been burned, he sent a wagon in which a bedsack had been placed to transport him to Cantonment Brooke. Two tents were erected near the hospital tent—one for Cavallo, the other for his wife, two sons, and a daughter—and the family remained in the compound until the military doctor certified that the patient had fully recovered.

The Treaty of Moultrie Creek also divided the Seminoles into two divisions, creating the northern division, the Apalachicola band, as a formal political unit. Neamathla, Yellow Hair, Mulatto King, and John Blount had conferred with Andrew Jackson as early as September 1821 and convinced him that the Apalachicola River valley was an excellent site for a Seminole reservation. Lower Creek leaders John Blount and Yellow Hair had been given favored treatment because they had been friendly with the Americans for many years, rendering valuable services during the Creek War, the assault on the Negro Fort, and the First

Seminole War. As stipulated in the treaty the reserves included the following areas:

> For the use of Neamathla and his connexions, two miles square, embracing the Tuphulga village, on the waters of Rocky Comfort creek. For Blount and Tuski-Hajo, a reservation, commencing on the Appalachicola, one mile below Tuski-Hajo's improvements, running up said river four miles; thence west, two miles; thence southerly, to a point two miles due west of the beginning point. For Mulatto King and Emathlochee, a reservation, commencing on the Appalachicola, at a point to include Yellow Hair's improvements; thence up said river, for four miles; thence west, one mile; thence southerly, to a point one mile west of the beginning; and thence east, to the beginning point. For Econchatomico, a reservation, commencing on the Chattahoochee, one mile below Econchatomico's house; thence up said river, for four miles; thence one mile west; thence southerly, to a point one mile west of the beginning; thence east to the beginning point.[17]

Persons belonging to the bands of John Blount and Yellow Hair were already living on the land set aside for them, but Neamathla, Emathlochee, and their bands were required to travel some distance from their former homes to the reserves. Since the migrating Seminoles had no chance to plant or harvest crops, they were supplied with rations by DuVal at St. Marks.

Although Seminoles and whites had signed a treaty of peace and friendship designed to endure for at least a few years, serious trouble arose within several months. Friction had developed between Neamathla and the territorial governor as early as January 1824 but DuVal, recognizing Neamathla's fine qualities, was reluctant to force the issue. As soon as the military units were removed from St. Marks, the Seminoles began to raid the herds of cattle grazing in the neighborhood, and the settlers complained about such activities to DuVal. It was apparent to Indian agent Gad Humphreys that a mistake had been made in placing Neamathla, the acknowledged leader of the tribe, on a reserve located some distance from the much larger reservation.[18]

By July 1824 DuVal's patience with Neamathla had worn thin, and he was forced to visit him to personally discharge him from his position as principal Seminole chief. Neamathla would not meet with DuVal and his followers but spent his time with his own followers clearing land, building homes, and showing little inclination to move to the reservation.

Actually, Neamathla never lived on the reserve on Rocky Comfort Creek near Quincy but probably remained near Tallahassee and St. Marks; he later claimed that money that should have been given to him for improvements was stolen. Another tense situation arose when the Seminoles, in a bold attempt to force white withdrawal from the area, killed some cattle and hogs belonging to settlers and threatened the whites. DuVal, moving quickly during this crisis, met with most of the Seminoles still remaining in the north in a session at Judge Benjamin Robinson's home some thirty miles from the Apalachicola towns. The next day DuVal visited Neamathla's town and told the three hundred armed warriors about a council scheduled July 26 at St. Marks. DuVal made certain that the meeting would be well attended—he informed the Seminoles that if his invitation was not accepted a military force would occupy their villages. Six hundred Indians showed their understanding of the situation by visiting St. Marks at the appointed time, where they learned that Neamathla had been relieved as head chief.[19] This news did not cause the Seminoles any distress, and within a short time Neamathla and his band had rejoined the Creeks in Alabama.

Lieutenant George McCall described the campaign for election of a new chief to succeed Neamathla and the inauguration of the executive.

The day appointed for the election was still some ten days off. During this time I had frequent opportunities of seeing and conversing with the chief of the Micasukies, the candidate chosen by the Micasukies and Tallahassees to run against Micanopy, the Seminole candidate for the supreme chieftainship of the consolidated tribes. "Tuko-see-mathly,"— meaning the "Ant-chief," in allusion, I suppose, to his industry in promoting the welfare of his people,—is a man of fifty years. He is known to the whites by the adopted name of John Hicks . . . his figure combin[es] strength with gracefulness; or, I might say, perfect ease in all his attitudes and gestures. The expression of his fine open countenance is habitually mild; but as he grows earnest in conversation, you see arise within him that glow of fervid feeling warming into the determined energy which characterizes the man. . . .

. . . [Micanopy or Pond Governor] is rather too indolent to rule harshly; and in fact he leaves official matters very much to the management of his Minister of State, as I may call him, a man who possesses great cunning and effrontery. This person, "bold in council, but cautious in the field," never distinguished himself by deeds of enterprise or courage, and has received the name of Hote-mathla, in English,

"Home-warrior;" he is known, however, more generally, if not exclusively, by the name of "Jumper."

I have remarked to you that the Seminoles, but particularly their chief, Micanopy, did not at all relish the idea of being incorporated with the Tallahassee and Micasuky tribes. Together, the latter were more numerous than the former; and as they would almost to a man vote for one of their own chiefs, Micanopy's chance for the office of principal chief was by no means flattering.

. . . The election of Supreme Chief of the three tribes, united under the name of the Seminole Nation, took place at the appointed time; and when the returns came in from the different bands, it was found to have resulted, as every one anticipated, in the choice of Tuko-see-mathla, by a decided majority. No disturbance had occurred anywhere; Micanopy, governed by the advice of the Agent and the presence of the troops, having wisely yielded to circumstances he could not control.[20]

The ceremony in which John Hicks assumed his position was indeed a most elaborate one, lasting for three hours from seven to ten in the evening in August 1826 in an open area a mile's distance from the agency at Fort King (present-day Ocala). Messengers were sent to all of the Seminole bands requesting their presence, and in the meantime a Mikasuki group constructed seats for 2,000 persons, a covering arbor, and a council fire site with a wide open area for dancing and an entrance march. Preceding the entrance and the speech by Hicks, 100 Mikasuki warriors performed the rattlesnake dance in honor of the clan of Hicks. In a speech translated by an interpreter for the benefit of the whites, John Hicks promised to enforce the laws in a manner that would be fair to all bands. McCall felt that in hearing the words of Hicks, he was listening to an enlightened and indeed a great man.[21] In the several conferences held with federal officials in 1826–32, John Hicks or Tuskalmathla was listed as the head chief, but others, including Micanopy and Jumper, did most of the talking at these meetings.

After the ratification of the Moultrie Creek treaty by the Senate, plans were made to move most of the Seminoles to the larger reservation in the south between the Peace and Withlacoochee rivers with a portion north of Ocala. When James Gadsden marked off the reservation, he concluded that its northern boundaries should be extended to include the settlements at Okehumpkee and Sitarky so that better grazing land might be secured. Gadsden noted that most Indian villages would be relocated to the northern and western portions of the reservation and that the southern portion would be used only during the dry season by hunting parties.[22] After Gadsden had marked most of the boundaries, he predicted that the land was of sufficient quality to produce good crops of rice and corn, provide grazing land for livestock, and provide good hunting. Gadsden believed that it was necessary to move the Indians to the reservation as soon as possible to quell all fears of possible attacks upon isolated white farms.

To comply with the treaty approximately twenty-three hundred Seminoles began to make plans to move to the reservations. Some were to travel westward to the Apalachicola River reservation, but the great majority were to move south to the central Florida reserve. In the spring of 1824 Governor DuVal awarded a contract to Benjamin Chaires to supply meat and bread to the Seminoles at 11.5 cents per ration at Tampa Bay and 14 cents at a distribution point at or near the fork of the St. Johns and Ocklawaha rivers.[23]

DuVal appointed John Bellamy to make a valuation of the Seminole improvements so that they could be reimbursed, but warned that the total figure to be awarded must not exceed $4,000. Accordingly, Bellamy, accompanied by interpreter Oren Marsh and two pack horses carrying their equipment, visited twenty-nine towns to evaluate homes, cultivated fields, and any other improvements—the town of John Hicks, which was known as Sam Paily, containing forty-three homes and 138 men, 118 women, and 62 children was valued at $430.00. After the appraisals were made and time of payment announced, $3,570.00 in silver coins was given to the leaders to distribute. Since silver was a most acceptable means of exchange, dozens of itinerant whiskey dealers hastened to the towns, sure of a ready market for their wares.[24]

DuVal decided that Seminoles who did not want to walk all the way to the reservations could use forty or fifty canoes made by the Seminoles under government contract. In November 1824 rations were distributed to the Seminoles, they were paid for their houses and improvements, and they began their trek. As they moved southward, agent Gad Humphreys was requested by Washington to select a site for his agency in the "center of the Indian population where good land and water may be found."[25] By January 20, 1825, the population from one town, Wakasassa, originally situated on the Gulf Coast east of the mouth of the Suwannee River, had reached the reservation and selected camping grounds.

The movements of two other towns to central Florida may be traced. One of the most well known Seminole villages was Thonotosassa, located near the hammock and lake bearing that name and some twelve miles from Fort Brooke or present-day Tampa. This village of two hundred persons was populated by Alachua refugees who either had come from the Suwannee River settlement or migrated directly from Alachua to Tampa Bay and settled there between 1812 and 1820.[26] A second town, Oponney's settlement, was located on a hill overlooking the southeastern shore of Lake Hancock in present-day Polk County. The settlement included a two-story home made of wood cut at a saw mill, a dairy building, corn storage bins, stables, and sheds—all evidence that Oponney tried to live in Florida in a fashion similar to his former style in Georgia. Near the buildings were an extensive peach orchard and corn, rice, and potato fields, and two miles from the plantation house were the homes of the twenty blacks who cultivated the fields. Three hundred head of cattle and one hundred head of horses grazed in nearby fields. When the rice was harvested it was sent by packhorse to St. Augustine for sale. Unfortunately, however, when Oponney died, his son Pulepucka followed the tradition of burning all of the buildings (except the black drink house) and moving with the livestock and inhabitants to a new home; he chose a place near the mouth of the Suwannee River.[27]

The recent identification of Powell's town, archaeological fieldwork, and the Henry Prince 1836 diary have given much needed information concerning Seminole life within the cove of the Withlacoochee River during the relocation period and time of warfare. Probably the band with which Osceola was associated moved into the cove a short time after the signing of the Treaty of Moultrie Creek. The settlements in the cove of the Withlacoochee were matrilineal clan camps composed of matriarch, husband, the families of the daughter, and the unmarried brothers of the matriarch. Although the homes were widely separated, these camps have been designated "towns."[28]

With a probable population of thirty persons, the town identified as Osceola's was located on a sandy incline in a dense oak scrub some twenty feet above sea level and one-half mile west of the Withlacoochee. Evidence indicated that garden crops, beef, and wild plants were important items in the Seminole diet, but with a plentiful supply of wildlife, the Seminoles probably ate much deer and fish. Food was cooked in clay vessels made by the women, but some iron cook pots obtained earlier from British traders were used.[29]

Federal officials had not planned well either the establishment of the reservation in middle Florida or the movement of the Seminoles into it. Virtually nobody knew the details of the territory or the fertility of the soil, and the boundaries would not be marked for several years. Since it took some time to establish an agency headquarters near Cantonment King, Cantonment Brooke served as the food distribution center.[30]

Food shortages and some starvation struck the Seminoles in central Florida between 1825 and 1827. A late rainy season resulted in poor crops, and the migrants who were dependent upon the government ration had insufficient food because many federal employees did not have the desire, skill, or experience to distribute enough. In addition the newcomers knew little about the best land available for cultivation or where to find either good hunting and fishing or growths of coontie or arrowroot, an essential Seminole food. Thus, both the newcomers and those old hands on the reservation were almost totally dependent upon the government handout of beef and corn.

For the weekly distribution of rations as stipulated in the treaty, cattle were driven from Georgia and turned loose at Alachua Prairie ten miles from the agency established in July 1825 at Silver Springs.[31] Seminoles drove them from the prairie to a gathering pen where the agent and Seminoles shot them; the bodies were carried to the Seminole camp for cutting and cooking by the women. When it was apparent that sufficient meat was not being provided, Colonel George M. Brooke, agent Humphreys, and George Walton, the acting governor, requested additional rations, and more money was allotted.

Colonel Brooke of Cantonment Brooke wrote in December 1825 to his commanding officer:

You will perceive by the ration returns for this month that more rations have been issued to the Indians than usual. This has been occasioned by a number of Indians (say from six to seven hundred) who were obliged to come to the sub-agency, near the cantonment, for the purpose of receiving their presents from the Government, agreeable to the treaty; most of them had traveled from eighty to one hundred miles, and were entirely without subsistence. The issuing of rations to the Indians under the treaty expired on the 10th of October. The major part of the nation are, and have been, suffering for some time in extreme want. Some have died from *starvation*, and many have lived upon the roots of the sweetbriar, as a substitute for bread. This is owing to several causes: 1st. The continued droughts, for two months, whilst their corn was tasseling; 2d. Those who removed within the new boundary line had to cultivate new lands which will not produce the first year of planting; and 3rd. Many did not come in until it was too late to plant.

I can assure you they are in the most miserable situation; and unless the Government assists them, many of them must starve, and others will depredate on the property of the whites in the Alachua and St. John's settlements. It is impossible for me, or any other officer who possesses the smallest feelings of humanity, to resist affording some relief to men, women, and children, who are actually dying for the want of something to eat.

I therefore wish that an additional allowance of rations may be made for the post; and I trust that, on your representation to the Secretary of War, partial rations may be given generally, through the Indian Agent.[32]

By now white political leaders too were recognizing that the reservation did not contain good agricultural land. The territorial governor, William DuVal, examined the land for thirteen days in January 1826 and concluded that "the best of the Indian lands are worth but little: nineteen twentieths of their whole country within the present boundary is by far the poorest and most miserable region I ever beheld."[33] James Barbour, the new secretary of war, agreed, saying that had the Seminoles known very much about central Florida they would not have consented to removal to the south. After reading DuVal's reports Barbour suggested in May 1826 that because of the many deaths from starvation on the central reservation, plans should be made to offer the Seminoles "a more congenial country west of the Mississippi."[34] In 1824 members of Congress seemed to agree that removal to the west would be better for when they were requested to add the fertile agricultural land at Big Swamp to the reservation limits, in the expectation that the Seminoles would want to leave Florida, they took no action.

As Brooke had predicted, the Seminoles began to roam beyond the borders of the reservation to kill cattle belonging to the farmers. Some moved back to their former homes. To monitor their movements Colonel Duncan L. Clinch, who succeeded Brooke in command of the Florida area, stationed one company near the Aucilla River to patrol the northwest boundary and two companies at Brooke to monitor the west side; he sent two companies to build Cantonment King in the center of the reservation.

By March 1826 DuVal discovered some serious problems: the construction of agency buildings in the middle of "Indian country" could not be undertaken with limited funds, and agency employees were more interested in defrauding the government than helping the Seminoles. Unless they were paid top wages, few workers could be enticed to travel some distance to work on the construction of the agency house, council house, and several outlying houses. With the exception of food distribution, of all the services offered at the agency the blacksmith shop managed by Thomas Ledwith seemed to be most appreciated by the Seminoles, and much repair work was done at the shop.

As early as 1792, American Indian leaders had been invited to visit the national capital, be impressed by federal power, and thus be willing to sign, at that time or some time later, documents giving away some land or rights. In line with this federal practice, John Hicks, Neamathla, and five other leaders accompanied by the agent, Humphreys, visited Washington in May 1826 to present their views to Secretary of War Barbour. In response to an initial lecture by Barbour it was John Hicks assisted by Abraham, a black interpreter, who did most of the talking. Hicks thought the Big Swamp should be added to the reservation area, but he and his people had no plans to leave Florida for they had suffered enough on their trek from northern to central Florida. He wanted the return of stolen or seized slaves and the end of education talk. Besides John Hicks and Neamathla, Micanopy (Alachua band), Holata Micco (Peace River band), Tulce Emathla, and Fuche Luste Hadjo (Alachua band) were signatories to a document that outlined their views.[35] If the seven Seminoles received the same treatment as Pushmataha the Choctaw who visited the capital at nearly the same time, they stayed at Tennison's Hotel and received much money for bar refreshments.

Settlers had protested the killing of the cattle by the starving Seminoles, and in 1827 the legislative council of the territory of Florida passed a law forbidding the Seminoles to cross the reservation limits; those apprehended would be given thirty-nine strokes of a whip on the bare back. The Seminoles did their best to adhere to the terms of the treaty, and often Seminoles who moved across the border were seized by other Seminoles, brought to the agency, and, with the agent standing by, whipped by the Seminoles.

In 1828 Gad Humphreys, who served as Seminole agent from 1822 to 1830, began to run into problems that would result in his removal from office by federal authorities. Humphreys believed that white intruders moving into the reservation had caused much of the trouble along the reservation borders. DuVal's opinion in the fall of 1828 was that sufficient food had been provided for the Seminoles but that they had developed a "wanton and insolent" way about them.[36]

As more whites demanded that escaped slaves be returned to the owners, under Humphreys's supervision the Seminoles returned many runaways to the U.S. marshal at St. Augustine. If a Seminole had any claim to a black, Humphreys was instructed by DuVal to defend the right of the Seminole to keep the black, but the Seminoles in a conference on April 17, 1828, showed little faith in the white system of justice.

Agent.—I understand you have come to have a talk with me: if so, proceed; I am ready to hear you.

Micanopy.—We are told there is a white man come into our country after certain negroes. I want to know what right he has to come after them; we have been told that white people should not come into our country; besides, these negroes are ours, and the whites have no right to them.

Agent.—This man has an order from the secretary of war to get the negroes, and I am directed to give them up to him, on his giving bonds, in the same way that Mrs. Cook got the negroes she claimed from Nelly Factor. Should the white woman who calls for these negroes, not prove her claim, the negroes will be returned to you. If you do not give them up, I shall have to send and take them by force.

Jumper.—This negro woman, who is now wanted from us, belonged formerly to a white man, who 'tis now said (by those who wish to get her and her children away from us) gave her to his daughter. May-be this is true, may-be not; but if he did give her to his daughter, for some reason, he took her away again and brought her and sold her to the Indians, who honestly paid for her, and are therefore the fair owners of her. It seems that the white people will not rest, or suffer us to do so, till they have got all the property belonging to us, and made us poor. The laws of the whites appear to be made altogether for their own benefit, and against the Indians, who can never under them get back any of *their* property; if it once gets, no matter how, into the white people's hands, we fear their laws will leave to us nothing. If we could see them work so as to restore the property that has been stolen, and otherwise unfairly taken from us, and not so as to rob us of the little we have left, we should have more reasons to believe them just, but as it is, the benefit to be had from them goes all to the white people's side.

It is well known that a great deal of our property, negroes, horses, cattle, etc. is now in the hands of the whites, and yet their laws give us no satisfaction, and will not make them give this property up to us. The property which this white man is after, we know to belong to our people, and we cannot therefore consent to give it up. If you send and take it from us by force, as you say you must, we cannot help ourselves, but shall think it very hard in the government to force from us that which we have purchased and fairly paid for, when it will not use the same means to make the whites return to us property of ours which they have *dishonestly* got in their possession. We were promised *justice,* and we want to see it! These negroes are ours, and we will not consent to surrender them.[37]

Although the Seminoles had delivered many runaway slaves to the whites, some owners claimed that the process was rather slow and that some slaves were being withheld with the help of Humphreys. Finally, after federal investigator Alexander Adair had failed to find any evidence to support such charges, Joseph M. White, delegate to Congress from Florida, and James Gadsden succeeded in influencing President Jackson to replace Humphreys with John Phagan, who had been a subagent.

President Andrew Jackson dedicated himself to removing the American Indians from the eastern portion of the country and settling them in Kansas and present-day Oklahoma. Northern tribes such as the Shawnees, Kickapoos, and Peorias signed agreements by which they surrendered their land and moved to Kansas; southern tribes such as the Creeks, Seminoles, Choctaws, Cherokees, and Chickasaws were taken to Oklahoma.[38] Only one-quarter of the Choctaws, a few Creeks, some Cherokees hiding in the mountains, and the Seminoles who concealed themselves in the swamps escaped the almost total relocation.[39]

Last to feel the effect of the creation of Indian Territory and the passage of the Indian Removal Act in May 1830 were the Seminoles. The act included a provision by which the American Indians could trade land in the west for their ancestral homes east of the Mississippi. In January 1832 James Gadsden was selected to conduct the negotiations for the trade of the land and subsequent removal of the Seminoles.[40] At first glance the proposition did not appear to be a hard sell, for whites were raiding camps in search of escaped slaves, hungry Seminoles were being whipped because they had crossed the reservation line to obtain food, and most important a long drought had dried up the corn fields and forced the Seminoles into the woods for three months in search of food. On May 9, 1832, in a meeting at Payne's Landing on the Ocklawaha River Gadsden and fifteen Seminole leaders signed an agreement. No minutes of the discussions were made, but sometime later Gadsden related that he told the Indians that the government could not continue to feed them and that life in the West would be much preferable to life in Florida under local rule. When the Seminoles protested that they did not have adequate clothing for life in the colder Indian Territory, Gadsden promised to provide each of them with a blanket and shirt upon arrival. The Seminoles believed that the treaty was binding only if a delegation sent to the West gave its approval and if the group's decision was accepted by the tribe. The whites claimed to the contrary that the delegation had full authority to make a binding agreement. There was doubt that the Seminoles fully understood this provision, and the black interpreters may have been bribed to mistranslate the terms. The Payne's Landing treaty stipulated that the Seminoles would leave Florida after three years from the date of ratification by the Senate, surrender title to the land in Florida in return for $80,000 in various services, and join the Creeks on their reservation in Indian Territory.[41]

As stipulated in the signed agreement seven leaders, accompanied by agent John Phagan and interpreter Abraham, made their way across the Gulf of Mexico, up the Mississippi and Arkansas rivers by steamer, and by horse from Little Rock to Fort Gibson to evaluate the land in the West. It was open to argument whether the delegation had the authority to make a treaty, but after Creek leaders invited the Seminoles to settle on their land, the Montford Stokes Commission, which was in the neighborhood negotiating a treaty with the Creeks, signed an agreement with the delegation on March 28, 1833. This pact, designated the Treaty of Fort Gibson, stated that the delegation was satisfied with the portion of Creek land that would be the new home of the Seminoles.[42] A different account of the proceedings in Florida and the Indian Territory was written by Major Ethan Allen Hitchcock, a respected military officer:

> When the chiefs were assembled [at Payne's Landing], with Abra[ha]m not only as sense-bearer but as interpreter, Colonel Gadsden disclosed the object of his mission, which was met at once by an answer that they had made a treaty with the United States, by which they were guaranteed certain interests in the country they occupied for a period of twenty years, several years of which remained unexpired; and they wished that time to be passed over, when they would be willing to talk about another treaty. Colonel Gadsden explained and talked with the Indians in that day's council, without making any impression upon them. King Miccanopy (*sic*) made but one answer, repeating again and again that the Indians had made one treaty, by which they were entitled to remain undisturbed in their country for twenty years, etc., etc. This first day's council was a pattern which was exactly followed through several days without making the slightest progress.
>
> But in these councils Colonel Gadsden fully discovered the character and influence of Abram, and he determined to confer with him privately

and see what he could be induced to agree to. It was finally arranged to add an article to the treaty prepared in Washington, to the effect that the Indians should appoint a delegation of six of their tribe, to be conducted to their proposed new country west of the Mississippi by an agent of the government, and it was agreed that if this delegation approved of the country, the treaty was to be made valid; but this could be secured only by means of another article which operated upon and was intended to be a bribe of the interpreter. Under pretence of providing compensation for the services of Abram, it was stipulated that, upon the ratification of the treaty, he should be paid $200, which was a large sum in the eyes of a runaway slave in a country where very little money was ever seen. That this was intended for a bribe became certain when, subsequently, Colonel Gadsden reported in person to President Jackson his efforts in securing the treaty and stated in the presence of Captain [Charles] Thruston of the army, who informed the writer of this article of it, that he never could have got the treaty through if he had not bribed the negro interpreter. But, precisely in connection with this bribe, there grew up a misunderstanding between King Miccanopy and the government agents.

Six of the tribe were deputed by the chiefs to go to the West, and examine the new country proposed for the tribe. They were placed under the care of a Major Phagan, who took them to the West, passing beyond Fort Gibson near the mouth of the Grand River; and having shown them the country, he returned to Fort Gibson, on his way back to Florida. While at Fort Gibson—and the authority for this statement is the officer at that post who affirmed the facts to the writer of this— Major Phagan submitted to the Indians a paper and asked them to sign it, expressing their approval of the country, with the design, by means of that paper, to complete the treaty according to one of the articles added by Colonel Gadsden, as stated above. The Indians refused to sign the paper, saying that they had no authority to do it, explaining that they had been ordered to go and see the new country, and then to return to their king and report their *opinion* about it, when the king and his chiefs were to decide whether they were to accept the treaty or not. Major Phagan would not allow them to take this course, insisting that they should sign the paper before he would proceed with them on the journey home; and under this duress they finally signed the paper, which was sent to Washington city as the evidence required that the treaty was now complete. The paper was not signed in the presence of commissioners, but was accepted by Governor Stokes and others, who had been appointed commissioners to execute some business with the Creek Indians already in the West, among whom it was proposed to incorporate the Seminoles.[43]

When the delegation returned from Indian Territory, the members wanted a general council convened to discuss the proposed treaties but agent Phagan, considering the matter closed, refused to permit the meeting to be called. A study of the two treaties led John Mahon to conclude that Phagan altered some words in the Treaty of Payne's Landing: "It is all but impossible to escape the presumption of fraud." [44]

Residents of the Apalachicola reservations were the first Seminoles to leave Florida. As early as July 17, 1828, Governor DuVal claimed that the Apalachicola leaders were willing to visit Indian Territory, and if they found the area acceptable, the band would probably move. It seemed to DuVal that the Seminoles were in a deplorable state—they were trading with river boatmen, and at least fifty were ill from a venereal disease: "Humanity demands removal of these unfortunate people as early as possible." DuVal's plan for removal included the selection of one Seminole from each town in Florida to form a party which would visit the country designed for them.[45] The reality was that the lands situated along the Apalachicola and Chattahoochee rivers had become too valuable to be retained by the Seminoles. Some way had to be found to remove them. Perhaps even more important was the feeling along the frontier that their presence posed a threat to the security of the pioneer families. In March 1830 John Phagan was promoted from the Apalachicola subagency to the position of agent for all of the Seminoles in Florida, and as a result the Apalachicola position was left vacant for several years.[46]

Although the Treaty of Moultrie Creek had stipulated that a reservation school be established, the Seminoles had not desired such an institution. Since President Jackson had endorsed a move to have Indian children educated at the Choctaw Academy in Blue Springs, Kentucky, a limited amount of educational opportunity was available outside Florida. It was suggested that eight Seminole boys between the ages of ten and fourteen be sent to the academy, and by December 1830 eight Apalachicola youngsters, including a son of John Blount, had enrolled.[47]

According to most observers the Apalachicolas were not doing too badly by 1832. As stipulated by the 1823 treaty they were paid an annuity of $1,000, and they had achieved a relative degree of prosperity, possessing many horses, cows, and hogs and even some slaves. "In the distribution of the annuity, some ten or fifteen of the head men of both divisions [Apalachicola and central Florida reservation] received from twenty dollars to seventy dollars each, the lesser chiefs from five to twenty dollars and the common Indian generally between two and four dollars." [48] Since the Seminoles had no bank accounts or a heritage of saving for a rainy day, they usually spent their money within several days upon hard liquor and goods purchased from nearby traders. The storehouse filled with corn from the fall harvest usually supplied them until February or March, when most were forced to support themselves by hunting or working for the white settlers. Some of the Apalachicola leaders had rented farm land to the whites, and others of the band were able to earn some money by selling hides at nearby settlements.

As early as July 1832 President Jackson directed James Gadsden to negotiate with the Apalachicola Indians concerning removal and authorized him to pay up to $30,000 for the land and complete removal expenses. Gadsden attempted to talk with Blount in August 1832, but heavy rain prevented him from meeting the Seminole. He sensed some problems at this time: "I fear, however, from information received that some attempts have been made by those who hope to participate in the plunder to induce Blount to be very extravagant in his demands." [49]

Gadsden's efforts were finally successful, and on October 11, 1832, in a conference at DuVal's house in Tallahassee, Blount and Davy Elliott (Osiah Hadjo) ceded to the U.S. government their Florida lands, were promised $13,000, and agreed to move west. [50] When neither Econchatimico and Mulatto King nor representatives of these two landed Seminoles appeared at the negotiations, Gadsden toyed with the idea of appointing younger and more compliant men to their posts as leaders. An exploring party, including two or three young leaders from Mulatto King's and Econchatimico's towns, was sent west to choose a site where Blount's and Elliott's bands could settle. [51] The Florida Seminole delegation visited Red Moccasin, an uncle of Blount who had migrated in the distant past to Texas, and obtained his permission to settle along the Trinity River. After signing the October 1832 agreement John Blount attempted to secure an advance of $400 from the amount due him, but the federal representatives refused to give him any money until he was ready to leave Florida. [52]

By October 1833 John Blount had undergone a change of heart and attempted to remain in Florida, but it was too late. He told the acting governor, James D. Westcott, Jr., and his newly appointed agent, Wiley Thompson (Phagan's replacement, a friend of Andrew Jackson, and for twelve years a member from Georgia of the U.S. House of Representatives), that "he had been deceived, trifled with and imposed upon but was willing to go if the white men did not want him in Florida." Westcott told Blount that he must leave during this winter, and that "the President of the United States had the power to drive him off and would do it if he violated the treaty."[53] The other Apalachicola bands were warned not to harbor any person from Blount's band who might try to escape the migration. Federal officials assured Blount he would receive his money in Texas, and Blount designated a fort near the Saline River that he might visit to obtain the funds promised him. The old chief had no choice but to leave Florida. He had an excellent record as a friend of Andrew Jackson, and he hoped that the president would give him and his people a yawl as a going-away present to carry them to Texas, but such hopes appeared to be in vain. In desperation Blount ordered his people to build fifty canoes to carry them west, but finally, in October 1833, Gadsden was notified to purchase a boat for Blount and to give it to him as a present from the U.S. government.

At first the fall of 1833 had seemed a good time for the removal, but such a judgment proved premature. The fall season had been selected because during this period cholera disappeared and the hurricane season had come to an end. After most preparations had been completed for the removal, someone recalled the eight boys, among them Blount's son, who were studying at the Choctaw Academy in Great Crossing, Kentucky, and Blount and his people refused to move a step until the youngsters rejoined the band. During November DuVal dispatched a letter to Richard M. Johnson, head of the school, complaining that no news had been received concerning the boys and some persons feared that they had died of cholera. He requested that the boys be immediately sent home by steamboat via Nashville, Huntsville, Columbus, and Mount Vernon, Florida, a route that would carry them within five miles of their homes. Not until late December did the boys, escorted by the assistant principal, James Henderson, return.[54] In order to ease the Seminoles through their period of waiting, $1,500 was paid to Blount and Davy Elliott.[55]

During 1833 and 1834 Blount's band was forced to endure a most difficult phase of their time of trouble in Florida. Three white men and a party of Creeks from Alabama seized a widow of a chief, three children, and cattle and hogs, severely beat Blount, and returned to Alabama with their spoils.[56] Warrants were issued for the arrest of the culprits and a $100 reward posted, but no one was ever convicted of the crimes.

The source of much of the trouble was that the subagent had previously lived on the reserve and had been able to protect the Seminoles, but when Phagan had been elevated to the post of agent, no subagent was appointed to replace him. In order to discourage other such disturbances William Pope was given a temporary appointment as subagent, but he was unable to prevent a robbery in May 1833, when Blount was absent from home hunting for some lost cattle. Three white men knocked down the door of his house with heavy logs, threatened his wife, and departed with $700 in cash.

One Apalachicola leader wrote to agent Wiley Thompson:

> I am induced to write you in consequence of the depredations made and attempted to be made on my farm by a company of men, negro stealers, some of whom are from Columbus, and have connected themselves with "Brown and Douglas." It is reported and believed by all the white people around here that a large number of them will very shortly come down here and attempt to take off Billy, Jim, Rose and her family, and others. These same men have been engaged in the same business up in the "Creek nation." I should like to have your advice how I should act. I dislike to make any trouble, or to have any difficulty with any of the white people; but if they will trespass on my premises and on my rights, I must defend myself in the best way I can. If they do make this attempt, and there is no doubt but they will, they must bear the consequences. But is there no civil law that will protect me? Are the free negroes and the negroes belonging in this town to be stolen away publicly—in the face of all law and justice carried off and sold to fill the pockets of these worse than "land pirates?" Certainly not. I know you will not suffer it. Please direct me how to act in this matter. Douglas and this company hired a man, who has two large trained dogs for the purpose, to come down and take Billy. The man came, but seeing he could do nothing alone, has gone off somewhere, probably to recruit. He is from Mobile, and follows for a livelihood catching runaway negroes with these large dogs.[57]

It was due to the hard work of agent Wiley Thompson that the bands of Blount, Davy Elliott, and Yellow Hair finally left Florida. The Indians paddled their canoes down the Apalachicola River to the bay where they camped at a place on the northwestern side known as Oat Point and were given passage to New Orleans.

When the bloody Second Seminole War broke out in December 1835, the Apalachicola bands gave full aid and comfort to the whites, but their efforts were not appreciated. In January 1836 Governor John Eaton requested David M. Sheffield to proceed to the Apalachicola River and persuade some Apalachicolas to join the militia companies being organized to wage a campaign against the warring Seminoles.[58] Eleven or more volunteered their services and were soon at the center of operations in Tampa. In an additional move to demonstrate their friendliness, most of the Apalachicola warriors surrendered their firearms, but this gesture was of no avail, for some whites from Georgia invaded the Apalachicola reserves in March 1836 and stole twenty slaves from defenseless Econchatimico.[59] In a meeting at Quincy on May 14, 1836, the citizens of Gadsden County resolved among various other matters: "Whereas there are some indications of a hostile nature among the Indians on the Apalachicola River, it be respectfully recommended to the Governor of the Territory to disarm those Indians and take such other steps as he may deem necessary to preserve their neutrality."[60] In June 1836 Archibald Smith, Jr., was appointed agent in charge of the Apalachicolas at $500 per year. In the letter of appointment he was "requested to use your best endeavors to keep these Indians friendly and to protect them from injury by white persons." The writer also suggested that Smith press for their speedy removal, for "circumstances will not suffer them to remain in Florida."[61]

By August 1836 the reserve Apalachicolas were in a desperate situation. Although they had assisted the military in operations against warring Seminoles, the whites had driven them from their homes and had stolen their slaves and property; as a result they had been unable to plant their usual crops and sought rations of corn and beef from the government. It was most discouraging to be attacked by both forces in the war; some of Osceola's raiders were able to elude the troops and inflict damage on the Apalachicolas.

By 1838 the federal authorities had begun their final drive to remove the Apalachicolas from Florida, pointing out that by remaining they would be subject to the laws of Florida "without annuity, without claim on the care and protection of the general government, with no means of support but the proceeds of the balance of their reserves and the residue of the annuity then to be advanced to them."[62] Econchatimico, Mulatto King, and other leaders signed on June 20, 1838, deeds that surrendered title to the reserves and agreed to move west by October. When Governor Richard K. Call needed men to drive the Alabama Creeks (who were fleeing removal themselves) from the swamps near Pensacola, the Apalachicolas volunteered their services. They spent several months tracking down the fugitives but never received any pay or other reward for their efforts.

In order to place the final touches upon the removal, Daniel Boyd, who had been placed in charge of surveying and appraising Apalachicola lands, visited Mulatto King's and Econchatimico's towns so that he could make a suitable census and appraisal of personal property and real estate. He experienced some difficulties. Although given two weeks notice, few people made themselves available for questioning—but most of the men could be found at nearby saloons.

Finally, on October 28, 1838, the entire group of Apalachicola Seminoles and a small number of Creeks departed from Florida for the West aboard one steamer and two schooners. The land they had left was surveyed and ready for sale by August 1839.[63] After 1838 no Apalachicola Seminoles remained in the Apalachicola valley. They had done their best to remain on friendly terms with the whites, but it was an impossible task, for the frontier folks wanted no American Indians in their neighborhood.[64]

4

The Second Seminole War, Phase 1, 1835–1838

f all the tribes living east of the Mississippi River, the Seminoles put up the most determined resistance to removal to the West. They forced the federal authorities to wage a seven-year war that cost the white settlers and their government an estimated $30 million to $40 million and, counting deaths from battle, disease, and accident, the lives of 1,466 regulars, 55 militiamen, and nearly 100 civilians. Yet despite the heavy casualties on both sides (the Seminoles had casualties of several hundred or more, and their black allies, at least 40), and removal to the West of four thousand or more blacks and Seminoles, four to five hundred Indians would remain in Florida.[1]

Events leading up to the war were rather casual. Federal authorities, feeling that the Seminoles were so few, did not apply much pressure for removal during the several years following the signing of the treaties of Payne's Landing and Fort Gibson in 1832 and 1833. With the dismissal of agent John Phagan, Captain William Graham, commander at Fort King, served as temporary agent until Wiley Thompson arrived. In his initial contact with the Seminoles, Thompson had helped remove some tribe members from the Apalachicola Reserve to Indian Territory. When he arrived at the Fort King Agency in central Florida, a log building with a high roof and long porches, on December 1, 1833, he found the building unlocked and only one employee, the handyman, available.

The major problem faced by agent Thompson, now fifty-two years old, would be planning the removal of the Seminoles from Florida as agreed in the treaties of Payne's Landing and Fort Gibson. Signs of the Seminoles' almost solid front against removal were already apparent when the members of the Fort Gibson delegation returning to Florida in April 1833 met a windstorm of ridicule and verbal abuse from both male and female members of the tribe for allowing the whites to outwit them. The only way that the delegates could live among their people was to label the treaties outright frauds. Charley Emathla, one of the delegation who opposed the treaty but was willing to leave Florida, had his life and the lives of his family threatened as early as October 1834.[2]

President Jackson had approved the Treaty of Payne's Landing and the additional Treaty of Fort Gibson on April 12, 1834, and the following year Commissioner of Indian Affairs Elbert Herring directed Thompson to make preparations for the removal of the Seminoles. At the October 23, 1834, agency meeting, after Thompson distributed the annual annuity to the assembled Seminoles, he asked them to gather in a council and to tell him their feelings concerning the following points: settlement with the Creeks or in a separate area in Indian Territory, the payment for cattle left behind in Florida, transportation by land or water to the West, and payment of the next annuity in money or goods. After Thompson had made his presentation, Holata Emathla, brother of Charley, who was eligible to speak for the tribe, announced that there would be councils held in the Seminole camp at Silver Springs two miles away on the same afternoon at four, again the following morning, and on the next day with the agent.

At the afternoon session Osceola spoke opposing emigration, although he had no authority to do so. Holata Emathla showed his desire to follow the provisions of the two treaties and the wishes of the Great Father at Washington.[3] In a surprise move Jumper, the former Red Stick and sense-bearer or speaker for the tribe, supported Holata Emathla.

The Fort King meeting may have been the first in which thirty-five-year-old Osceola demonstrated his powers of leadership to the other Indians. After the War of 1813–14 Osceola, who was born near the central border of Georgia and Alabama, had moved to Florida with the Peter McQueen band, which included his mother, and settled near the Peace River. After moving northward to the cove of the Withlacoochee, Osceola became leader or tustenuggee of a small band of Mikasukis and was infrequently employed by the agent and Mikasuki leaders to bring back to the reservation those who strayed beyond the poorly marked boundaries.[4]

When Thompson convened the council on the following day, Friday, October 24, 1834, two more leaders—Micanopy and Charley Emathla—stressed the fact that the Treaty of Moultrie Creek had guaranteed them seven more years in Florida. Having changed his mind during the night fifty-year-old Jumper summarized the views of most of the Seminoles:

> At the treaty of Moultrie it was engaged that we should rest in peace upon the land allotted to us for twenty years. All difficulties were buried and we were assured that if we died, it should not be by the violence of the white man, but in the course of nature. The lightning should not rive and blast the tree, but the cold of old age should dry up the sap, and the leaves should wither and fall, and the branches drop, and the trunk decay and die. The deputation stipulated at the talk at Payne's Landing to be sent on the part of the nation was only authorized to examine the country to which it was proposed to remove us, and report to the nation. We went according to agreement and saw the land. It is no doubt good, and the fruit of the soil may smell sweet and taste good and healthy; but it is surrounded with bad and hostile neighbors, and the fruit of bad neighborhood is blood that spoils the land, and fire that dries up the brook. When in the west, I told the agent [Major Phagan], "You say our people are rogues, but you would bring us among worse rogues to destroy us." Even of the horses we carried with us, some were stolen, and their riders obliged to return with their packs on their backs. The government would send us among tribes with which we could never be at rest. When we saw the land, we said nothing; but the agents of the United States made us sign our hands to a paper, which you say signified our consent to remove; but we considered we did no more than say we liked the land, and when we returned, the nation would decide. We had no authority to do more. Your talk is a good one, but my people cannot say they will go. We are not willing to do so. If their tongues say yes, their hearts cry no, and call them liars." [5]

Thompson, refusing to accept the Seminoles' views, called them fools and children and told them to come back the next day with a correct census of the population and a decision whether to travel by land or water.

On the final day of the meeting, Saturday, October 25, 1834, the council convened at eleven in the morning, and Thompson saw for the first time that the great majority of the Seminoles opposed removal. Holata Micco opened the meeting by pointing out that he never consented to go west, and Jumper followed, stating that he wanted to wait until the twenty years' stay in Florida guaranteed in the Treaty of Moultrie Creek had expired. When Micanopy claimed he had not signed the Treaty of Payne's Landing, Thompson retorted that he had touched the pen and that John Hicks had gotten out of his way so that he could do so. Thompson said that President Jackson would not allow the Seminoles to remain in Florida and that they had given their approval to removal within a short time by signing the treaty.[6] Osceola, unable to remain silent, replied that the feelings of the Seminoles had been expressed and that the situation was like the falling of hail to crush the flowers: it was destined to take place. Conflict was inevitable.

To avoid war and to leave Florida with its problems of slave hunters, trespass of reservations, and slow starvation, probably one-eighth of the Seminoles were willing to accept the terms of the treaties of Payne's Landing and Fort Gibson. Leaders of the proremoval group included the brothers Holata and Charley Emathla and Fuche Luste Hadjo. Aware that their lives were in danger, they sought and were given permission to move their bands to the now-deserted reservation on the Apalachicola River.

Acting under directions from Secretary of War Lewis Cass, Thompson called meetings at the agency during the next several months. In the December 26–27, 1834, session he explained to the assembled Seminoles that if they did not move to the ports of embarkation, sell their cattle and horses, and board the ships in a peaceful manner, the troops would use force against them. When a letter from President Andrew Jackson was read to a subsequent assembly of 150 Seminoles in March and a document agreeing to emigration was signed by sixteen leaders in April 1835, it seemed that some were willing to accept their fate. The absence of Micanopy from the meeting, however, coupled with the threat of Brevet Brigadier General Duncan L. Clinch that he had the men to enforce the treaties of Payne's Landing and Fort Gibson showed that matters were moving toward a climax.[7] When Osceola made some nasty remarks to Thompson in June 1835, he was placed in irons and confined within Fort King. After promising to sign an acceptance of the two treaties, he was released. He returned five days later to sign the statement accompanied by seventy-nine men, women, and children.

Probably the final council in which the Seminoles attempted to avert a conflict was held at Fort King on August 19, 1835. Some twenty-five leaders, including Osceola, requested a meeting to settle problems concerning the move to Indian Territory. Selected to speak for the tribe was Holata Emathla, who pointed out that the delegates in Indian Territory had told the Stokes Commission that they were willing to move from Florida if they had their own reservation separate from the Creeks. In addition they wanted Thompson to be assigned as their agent, for he was their friend and would take care of them in the West. The military officers who heard the talk endorsed this stand, and a letter supporting the view was sent to the secretary of war by Clinch, Thompson, and Lieutenant Joseph W. Harris.[8] In response, Secretary of War Cass stated that he preferred a "voluntary and peaceful removal to one effected by force," and the matter was left to the discretion of Clinch and Thompson. The additional time granted to develop a peaceful removal allowed the Seminoles planning hostilities to accumulate more powder and lead.

Another element that contributed to the tension was the fate of the blacks who were living with the Seminoles. Some had escaped from plantations in Alabama, Georgia, and Florida, and others had been captured by the Seminoles. Some of these highly acculturated blacks, having learned the Seminole dialects, served as interpreters at councils and, in addition, constituted a well-trained fighting force. A few had married Seminoles, and their fates were intermingled, for they dressed like the Seminoles, knew their language, and took part in the hunting and war parties.

With the permission of the secretary of war, whites had seized many blacks, claiming previous ownership, acts that aroused much bitterness on the part of other blacks and Seminoles. In the council that preceded the signing of the Treaty of Payne's Landing, the Seminoles were assured that the blacks would not be bothered by slave hunters, but some Seminoles suspected that Thompson was lying and would help his friends in Georgia who had lost runaway slaves. In addition Osceola opposed the surrender of runaway slaves, for much of his support came from blacks and from warriors who did not support the hereditary chiefs, and his band was recruited from among the blacks and Mikasukis. (In January 1837 his headquarters in a black village was raided and, of the fifty-five prisoners taken, only three were Seminole—fifty-two were black.) As late as October 1837 Osceola's band consisted of some fifty blacks and a few Seminoles.

Wiley Thompson, now superintendent of Seminole removal, and Lieutenant Joseph W. Harris, emigration disbursing agent, were directed by officials in Washington to work out the details for moving the Seminoles to Indian Territory. Thompson proposed on August 27, 1835, that the Seminoles should assemble either at the agency or Tampa Bay; those who came to the agency were to be taken by wagon to Tampa by January 15, 1836, and travel by steamer or schooner to New Orleans and thence by riverboat to Rock Roe on the White River.[9] Those who had signed the agreement on April 23, 1835, were directed to bring their cattle, hogs, and ponies to the agency before removal, and Thompson placed an advertisement in the territorial newspapers announcing the sale of the cattle on December 1, 1835. At Tampa, the designated port of embarkation, housing for the Seminoles and cattle pens for their animals were to be made available. While they were awaiting the ships, corn and fresh meat from the Seminoles' herds were to be distributed among them.[10]

The Seminoles saw that matters were approaching a decisive stage, and their leaders began to plan some action. The sale of ammunition had been forbidden by the agent, but illicit trade was carried on with whites in Georgia and the Cuban and U.S. fishermen operating from bases along the lower Gulf Coast. Only small parties of Seminoles visited the agency during July, August, and September 1835, and whenever the Seminoles met the agency employees, they were reserved in their conversation.[11]

In October 1835, agent Thompson and General Clinch, commander of federal troops in Florida, warned Secretary of War Cass that war was imminent. The country's army then consisted of 7,200 officers and men scattered among fifty-three posts under Cass's administration. Although federal officials occupied with such matters as the nation's growing pains, states' rights, slavery, and Europe could not spare much attention for a minor problem along the southern frontier, Cass ordered fourteen companies of regular troops transferred to Florida, but it would be some months before the first of them arrived.[12]

Upon deciding it would be best to leave Florida, Holata Emathla and four other leaders with 450 followers fled to Fort Brooke for protection. Charley Emathla had sold his cattle at Fort King and was returning with his daughter to his farm at Wetumka on November 26 when he met Osceola and a band of followers near the agency.[13] A violent discussion took place that ended in Osceola killing Emathla. Osceola threw the money paid for the cattle on the ground, where both the undisturbed body and the money lay for nearly two years. When the news of the Big Swamp council and the murder of Charley Emathla circulated, other Seminoles refused to bring in their livestock to Fort Brooke, and the proposed sale on December 1, 1835, was postponed indefinitely.

Minor clashes now occurred between Seminoles and whites. For example, when food was not furnished to the Mikasukis living in the Large Swamp and a drought ruined their crops, several who tried to steal cattle from a nearby farm were caught and tied in a barn without food or water for several days. Their friends were able to free them and upon seeing their pitiful condition set fire to the barn and prevented the owner from saving any of his possessions.[14]

Any council in which the tribe made a major decision usually took place in the fall. Following the killing of Charley Emathla on November 26, 1835, however, most of the Seminoles in the neighborhood of Fort King assembled at the towns of Big Swamp and Long Swamp and made a decision in favor of an attack upon the whites. Similar in style to those followed by the Creeks, councils were called by the leaders, who had great influence and who fixed the time and place of the meetings. All of the men of the tribe attended, but the only speakers were the leaders and the old men—young men were present merely to vote on the issues. Sessions of the council were held in the square of the village, where four cabins made of light material, elevated and open on the inner sides, had been erected. Each cabin was built to house a specific group: old men, young men, warriors, and women. At the opening session, the black drink was served to all according to rank from a large gourd, and pipes were lit. After the business of the council had been discussed and either approved or nullified, the discussants returned home without taking part in a feast or dance.

Once a decision for war was made, the war leaders assembled their men in a line and lectured them as a coach would do before a football game: "Don't be afraid. Something sharp will come. But the powers above will take care of you." On some occasions Arpeika or Sam Jones, shaman of the Mikasukis, planned the action, accompanied the war parties to the scene of battle, and from a distance encouraged them with his prayers.[15]

Before moving into the field the almost nude young men were painted red and black, the colors of war, and drank water in which the button or snake root had been placed. With each war party went a shaman or medicine man whose duty was to help care for the wounded. He carried a supply of parsley in the medicine bundle and, when a warrior was hit, chewed the heads of the plant and placed them in the wound.[16] Often, when the warriors had moved off to battle leaving behind the women, children, and very old men, the town was guarded by a fifteen- to seventeen-year-old male.[17]

When hostilities appeared imminent, the Florida militia was called into service. Although the men seemed ready for war, they were poorly prepared to meet such a challenge. Alarmed, the governor of the territory of Florida ordered the raising of a force of 300 men who would serve for at least one month, but federal officials found it difficult to supply General Joseph Hernandez with even 120 serviceable muskets, and no cartridges or musket powder were available.[18] In the first engagement of the war the baggage train of the militia commanded by Colonel John Warren was captured near Alachua on December 18, 1835, by a force of 80 Seminoles who killed 8 militiamen and wounded 6.[19]

The Seminoles' first two major attacks of the war were not difficult to plan. The lack of proper seaports, roads, and military posts meant that troops for the support of Fort King would either be landed at Tampa or Picolata and moved along the trails to the fort. All except one company of the troops at Fort King had been moved twenty miles away to General Clinch's plantation, where Fort Drane had been erected to serve as a base for a strike into the cove of the Withlacoochee. Accordingly, scouts kept a close observation upon this one-hundred-mile crude, sandy trail, and considerable numbers of Seminoles were ready to form an ambush whenever the proper time presented itself.

Company B, Fourth Infantry, under Major Francis Dade were the first U.S. troops to arrive in Florida, reporting on December 21 at Fort Brooke, where the company was attached to Company C, Second Artillery, and Company B, Third Artillery. A force of 108 men from the three companies, commanded by Dade, moved out three days later along the twenty-foot-wide sandy road that led to Fort King. They saw evidences of the Seminoles—a burned bridge, for example—but as they moved sixty-six miles in five days, fear of an attack ebbed.[20] About eleven o'clock on the morning of December 28, 1835, near present-day Bushnell, 180 Seminoles rose from concealment in the tall grass, pouring a murderous fire upon the blue-coated soldiers.

Forty-year-old Alligator (Halpatter Tustenuggee), who along with Jumper directed the attack, described the scene:

Just as day was breaking we moved out of the swamp into the pine-barren. I counted, by direction of Jumper, one hundred eighty warriors. Upon approaching the road, each man chose his position on the west side; opposite, on the east side, there was a pond. Every warrior was protected by a tree, or secreted in the high palmettoes. About nine o'clock in the morning the command approached. In advance, some distance, was an officer on a horse, who, Micanopy said, was the captain; he knew him personally; had been his friend at Tampa. So soon all the soldiers were opposite between us and the pond, perhaps twenty yards off, Jumper gave the whoop, Micanopy fired the first rifle, the signal agreed upon, when every Indian arose and fired, which laid upon the ground, dead, more than half the white men. The cannon was discharged several times, but the men who loaded it were shot down as soon as the smoke cleared away; the balls passed over our heads. The soldiers shouted and whooped, and the officers shook their swords and swore. There was a little man, a great brave, who shook his sword at the soldiers and said, 'God-dam!' no rifle ball could hit him. As we were returning to the swamp supposing all were dead, an Indian came up and said the white men were building a fort of logs. Jumper and myself, with ten warriors returned. As we approached we saw six men behind two logs placed one above another, with the cannon a short distance off. This they discharged at us several times, but we avoided it by dodging behind trees just as they applied the fire. We soon came near, as the balls went over us. They had guns but no powder; we looked in the boxes afterwards and found they were empty. When I got inside the log pen, there was three white men alive, whom the negroes put to death, after a conversation in English. There was a brave man in the pen; he would not give up; he seized an Indian, Jumper's cousin, took away his rifle, and with one blow with it beat his brains, then ran some distance up the road; but two Indians on horseback overtook him, who, afraid to approach, stood at a distance and shot him down. The firing had ceased, and all was quiet when we returned to the swamp about noon. We left many negroes upon the ground looking at the dead men. Three warriors were killed and five wounded. [21]

Osceola was not present at what came to be called the Dade Massacre; he and sixty warriors took part in killing agent Wiley Thompson and several others near the sutler's house at Fort King on the same day. As Thompson and Lieutenant Constantine Smith, Second Artillery, were taking an after-dinner stroll, Seminoles who had been hiding in the tall grass for nearly two days killed both of them. Thompson was hit by fourteen slugs and scalped by Osceola. The Seminoles set fire to the sutler's store and killed five other whites, including sutler Erastus Rogers. [22] Alligator claimed that the Seminole scheme to kill Thompson and to attack a moving military force had been planned for at least a year.

In order to celebrate the two victories a festival complete with dancing and drinks was held in Wahoo Swamp lying some eighty miles to the north-northeast of Tampa in present-day Sumter County. Liquor captured from the Fort King store was drunk in large quantities and a scalp dance was arranged by the medicine man, Hillis Hadjo, with Thompson's scalp mounted on a ten-foot pole given an honored spot in the center. Some Seminoles who had been forced to listen to Thompson's long talks imitated his gestures and mocked him in front of his scalp. On the next day scouts brought information that forces commanded by General Clinch were moving toward the Seminole villages along the Withlacoochee River.[23]

The cove of the Withlacoochee was a one-hundred-square-mile area of assorted swamp, hammock, and prairie formed by a big bend in the river. Before the Treaty of Moultrie Creek the blacks from Sitarky's village had moved into the cove on the banks of the river, where they established a village and cultivated rice and corn. The great bulk of the Seminoles migrated there after 1823, settling on the higher ground where they erected Creek-style villages with board houses sited about the town square. They cultivated crops such as corn, beans, and squash, and cattle, horses, and hogs roamed nearby fields.[24]

This cove and adjacent Wahoo Swamp made an excellent center of operations for the Seminoles who had established new towns to be near the agency. The whites knew little about the nature of the place for it was unmapped, and the numerous swampy islands and heavily wooded hammocks provided wonderful places of concealment. As soon as the fighting began the Seminoles transferred their homes to the small hammock islands of Lake Tsala Apoka. In order to attack a village the whites would have to wade through long stretches of marsh grass and bogs.

The largest number of troops in Florida were gathered at Fort Drane, a ramshackle fort on General Clinch's plantation, "Auld Lang Syne," thirty-five miles from the center of Seminole forces in the cove of the Withlacoochee. From Drane, Clinch organized a force of 250 regulars led by Lieutenant Colonel Alexander Fanning and 460 mounted militiamen commanded by General Richard Call with plans to drive through the hostile territory and end the conflict. When after three days' march the force made its way to the Withlacoochee River, the Seminole guide led the column two and one-half miles past the first crossing, where a Seminole ambush waited, to another crossing further downstream. The soldiers halted on December 31, 1835, near a portion of the river that appeared to be rather deep.

Since plans had been laid for an attack upon the settlements on the other side of the river, Clinch ordered the soldiers to cross. The regular troops crossed seven at a time using one old abandoned canoe and were relaxing on the southern side awaiting the volunteers, when 250 Seminoles opened fire on the resting troops. Osceola, easily visible in a blue jacket taken at the Fort King killing, fired his rifle and encouraged his warriors.[25]

The tide of battle turned when Clinch dismounted, carrying his sword, and moved into the field of fire, encouraging his men to make a stand. With the regular troops making successive bayonet charges and getting some help from the volunteers, the Seminoles were forced to retreat into the swamps, where the troops were too exhausted to follow. The hour and fifteen minute engagement cost the soldiers four killed and fifty-nine wounded, and the troops withdrew to Fort Drane. Osceola, slightly wounded in the conflict, sent word to Clinch that he was ready for another battle: "You have guns and so have we—you have powder and lead, and so have we—your men will fight and so will ours till the last drop of Seminole's blood has moistened the dust of his hunting ground." [26] General Clinch sent out a black man named Primus and two Seminoles to scout the area. They returned with the information that thirty-three Seminoles had been killed and many wounded in the fighting. Yet the Battle of the Withlacoochee was a Seminole victory, for they had stopped the advance of the troops against the villages.

The military philosophy that had proved effective in past wars against American Indians was not going to work in Florida. Standard procedure had been to bring in an overwhelming force of regulars, militia, and American Indian auxiliaries, build forts and roads leading into American Indian territory, and direct the main thrust of the army against the villages. After a decisive battle or two and destruction of their food supplies and village, most of the American Indians could be expected to sue for peace or to flee to neighboring tribes.

In Florida, however, the territory was unmapped, few whites knew much about the interior, and the swamps, hammocks, forests, and lowlands contained numerous havens from search-and-destroy patrols. Military leaders such as Winfield Scott and Duncan Clinch, with good military records in clashes against American Indians in other places, would fail utterly in Florida, unsure of how to handle their men and supplies in the harsh Florida environment. With no field training available in other parts of the East, troops would pay a heavy price during the period in which they learned how to counter the guerrillalike tactics of the Seminoles.

As was usual, large columns of men and supplies moved into Seminole country, and sometimes the Seminoles fought a delaying action until their women and children were able to move to another location, when the warriors dispersed to rejoin them. The deserted villages and fields could of course be burned or destroyed, but villages could be rebuilt and new crops planted. When a Seminole stronghold was discovered, it was easy for the troops to make an approach by night, for the Seminoles rarely posted night guards. Once daylight came heavy fire directed upon one flank followed by a bayonet charge usually ended the engagement. Yet such occurrences would be rare during the first year of the war, and not until prisoners were willing to guide the troops to the well-concealed villages would such attacks succeed.[27]

Although the Seminoles had the advantage in terms of environment and in their determination to remain in Florida, they too had their weaknesses. At the most there were 800 warriors to counter 5,000 or more regulars and militia available for the war. Agent Thompson believed that the Seminoles had bought from forty to fifty kegs of gunpowder from the Fort King agency and from traders at the beginning of the war, but once the war commenced, only captured lead and gun powder and an uncertain amount brought in from Cuba were available to them. There was evidence that some supplies were obtained from the Cuban fishing ranchos such as Bunce's, the Caldez operations, and others located along the southwestern coast of Florida. A rifle or musket that needed repair was thrown away, for few Seminoles knew the intricacies of the weapons. During one campaign the Seminoles kept their supply of ammunition and powder in a hole lined with bark; the powder was packed in a green hide container and the bullets or lead kept in a wooden box. Just before battle, all warriors gathered around the spot, the green hide bag and box were dug up, lead and powder were distributed in equal amounts, and they moved off to fight. One dead Seminole found by the soldiers in 1836 had an excellent supply of powder in his powder horn and a haversack full of bullets, gunflints, and flintlock-cleaning and -loading instruments. White observers believed that during the first year of the war the Seminoles' rifles were better weapons than the muskets supplied to the troops and their supply of ammunition was ample.

A dilemma during all three Seminole wars (1817–18, 1835–42, and 1855–58) was caring for the Seminole children, who suffered greatly. Some parents killed their infants when it was feared that their crying could lead the soldiers to their hiding places; some parents dug holes in the ground and placed their infants in the holes, shielded from the sun by palmetto fronds. Under cover of darkness mothers carried food and water to their babies.

Leadership posed another problem for the Seminoles, since the conflict represented a joint venture on the part of several diverse bands—the Alachuas, Red Sticks, Mikasukis, Muskogees, and blacks. Any massing of large numbers involved a group decision made by those leaders able to influence others among these diverse elements. So little is known of their councils, however, that it is difficult to determine the extent of leadership exerted by such men as Sam Jones (Arpeika), Wildcat (Coacoochee), or Osceola. Micanopy, descendant of Cowkeeper, had the best claim to authority but rarely gave directions, depending for advice upon his staff, which included Jumper, Alligator, Philip, and Holartoochee. Jumper, from the Wahoo Swamp, was a former Red Stick who left the Creeks to avoid signing the Treaty of Fort Jackson and, after he had married the sister of Micanopy, was considered Micanopy's sense keeper or private counselor. Philip was the war leader of the Seminoles living east of the St. Johns River, and his eldest son, Wildcat, became an outstanding commander in several battles.[28] Halpatter Tustenuggee, or Alligator, had great influence with Micanopy and did well in planning the first major Seminole victory in the war. Holartoochee had been banished from the tribe for adultery but, after a stay of four years with the Spanish Seminoles in the Everglades, became a war leader and warrior and speaker in the councils. Other well-known leaders included Sam Jones and a black man, Abraham.

Now that a full-fledged Indian war had begun, Congress voted funds to support military action, and Major General Winfield Scott, who was in charge of the Eastern Department, was directed to assume command in Florida. Authorized to call upon the governors of nearby states for volunteer troops, Scott dispatched letters to them requesting the services of 3,700 men. Scott's plan for conducting the war was to drive the Seminoles into the northern part of Florida where they could be more easily attacked. A column under Clinch would advance into the Seminole village area from Fort Drane, a second under Brevet Brigadier General Abraham Eustis would move out from Volusia, and a third under Colonel William Lindsay would march from Tampa Bay, with all three meeting at the cove of the Withlacoochee where they would crush the Seminoles.[29] Information obtained from prisoners indicated that the Seminoles had transferred operations from the cove and divided into three groups: one on the Ocklawaha, one on a tributary of the Peace River, and a third near the mouth of the Withlacoochee. The military commanders made little use of this information.

The three columns were never able to meet. After they had exhausted their ten days' supplies of food and ammunition, all three moved back to Fort Brooke. The Seminoles and their black allies, striking hard from their hideouts, were able to inflict damaging blows upon each of the military forces and return safely to the swamps. Scott later admitted that his men had killed less than sixty Seminoles, the horses had been reduced by hard use to pitiful beasts of burden, the men were weakened by lack of food and had suffered greatly from the ravages of measles and mumps, and he had known little about the topography of Florida. He tried to gain some measure of success by finally sending Colonel Perisfor Smith and the Louisiana volunteers in search of the Seminoles along Peace River, but by then few remained. One engagement was fought on April 27, 1837, by some of Lindsay's men under Colonel William Chisolm at Thonotosassa Creek near Tampa, in which Chisolm lost five men killed and twenty-four wounded. In revenge he placed a barrel of gunpowder in abandoned Fort Alabama that would explode when the Seminoles pushed open the gate.

The arrival of the commander of the Western Department, Brevet Major General Edmund Pendleton Gaines, at Tampa on February 10, 1836, with 1,100 men of the Fourth Infantry and Louisiana volunteers demonstrated that federal authorities were finally ready to pour larger numbers of men into Florida to quell the uprising. Within a short time after arrival by steamboat in Florida, Gaines and his force moved toward the area in which the Seminoles had gathered their forces. Advancing through the scene of the Dade battle on the eighth day of the march from Fort Brooke, the force buried the dead in two large graves and reached Fort King without seeing a hostile Seminole. With insufficient supplies of food available at Fort King, Gaines decided to return to Fort Brooke by a different route.

When the Seminoles learned that Gaines's men were moving near their stronghold, word went out to all nearby towns to send as many warriors as possible to the Withlacoochee area. Old men and young boys helped carry powder in bags and poured the contents into kegs and barrels set in the ground; women cooked the needed food and carried both food and bullets to the warriors. The time for the assembly of the force was fixed by the distribution of red sticks, which were discarded one at a time after the passage of each day.

After all of the preparations had been made, the Seminoles attacked Gaines at a crossing of the Withlacoochee. Although Gaines had with him 600 regulars of the Fourth Infantry and 500 volunteers from Louisiana, he decided to erect a log breastwork named Camp Izard and call for immediate help from Fort Drane. Besieged by 800 Seminoles and 170 blacks, Gaines and his men endured the smoke of grassfire and lack of food for eight days, losing 5 men killed and 46 wounded. To most observers it seemed foolish for Gaines with his superior force to build the entrenchment, where his men suffered the pangs of near starvation and a long siege.[30]

The sentries at Izard were startled on the night of March 5 to hear the voice of John Caesar, a black, requesting a talk with Gaines. Heartened by the success along the Withlacoochee and tired after three months of hard fighting, the Seminoles proposed a meeting during which suggestions for ending the fighting could be discussed. It appeared at this time that advocates of peace had influenced most of the tribe, and for the next several weeks not a single attack or hostile shot would be fired at the whites. It was agreed that a Seminole delegation bearing a white flag would be allowed to approach the military defensive line. At ten in the morning of March 6, six Seminoles and blacks including Osceola, Abraham, Alligator, and Jumper bearing a white flag approached the blue-clad troops, and Gaines directed Major Ethan A. Hitchcock and two others to negotiate with the delegation. Jumper as spokesman refused to enter army lines but from a safe spot claimed the Seminoles wanted peace, for they had lost many warriors. Osceola remarked that the Seminoles had been wronged but that they had gained satisfaction.[31]

In a second meeting on the afternoon of the same day, Hitchcock told the Seminoles that Gaines had no authority to end the fighting or even negotiate, but if the Seminoles moved to the other side of the Withlacoochee and refrained from hostilities, negotiations could be arranged. The arrival of Clinch's men from Fort Drane sent to assist Gaines and their discharge of rifles broke up the conference. The Seminoles did not resume hostilities at this time, but General Winfield Scott, who took command when Gaines was relieved, saw no profit in talking to them and he sent no envoys in search of them.

After the failure of the peace negotiations some Seminoles left the fighting force in disgust, for they had awaited the arrival of one hundred more warriors and with this addition were certain Gaines would suffer the fate of Dade.[32] When Clinch arrived, most of the large force scattered and returned to their towns. The number of Seminoles engaged in battles was determined by the sticks carried by each group and given to the leaders as they joined a force; during the assembling of warriors against Gaines, one black counted 700 sticks. The rapid dispersal of the large Seminole force showed a lack of effective military unity and a refusal to submit to the discipline that would enable them in large numbers to endure a long campaign. Persons like Osceola and Wildcat could only lead by example; they had little authority to impose discipline upon their followers.

In April 1836, while General Winfield Scott's men were searching for them in west central Florida, most of the Seminoles were attacking a small blockhouse that had been erected on the south bank of the Withlacoochee by the militia under Major John McLemore, some ten or twelve miles from the mouth of the river.[33] A garrison of fifty men and provisions of corn and pickled beef were left at a position that seemed to be secure, for it was some distance from the scene of fighting. Dr. Lawrence, a surgeon who was present during the attacks, has given this account:

> We had just completed building the block-house, and dug out a spring near the edge of the fort, when, on the morning of the 9th of April, at a little before dawn of day, we were attacked by the Indians, who had encompassed us on three sides, and were in number about 150 or 200. The engagement lasted one hour and three quarters, when they found out to their sorrow, that our reception was not only too warm, but that they had ventured too near us without due reflection. On the next day, we had one man killed on his post by an Indian rifle, fired from the opposite side of the river. On the 15 April, we were attacked by a body of the savages who had completely surrounded us, and whose number we computed at 4 to 500, though we have since heard that Powell had 1000 to 1500 of them. This was the hottest engagement we had during our stay on the Ouithlacoochee. They fired their guns by hundreds at the same moment at our block-house, and succeeded in taking our only means of escape, our boat—which they took down the river and destroyed after the battle. The engagement continued two hours and 45 minutes, and we had three men slightly wounded.
>
> On the 24th, we had a very severe battle, in which they displayed their ingenuity by shooting fire-arrows on fire upon the roof of the house, which destroyed the roof and left us exposed to the inclemency of the weather. This arrow-firing was performed by 26 of their men, whilst about 3 to 500 used their guns.[34]

After nearly two months of siege the men in the blockhouse believed that Scott had forgotten them. Three men were able to escape in an old canoe and notify the unresponsive outside world that they were still alive, and authorities at Tallahassee sent Major Leigh Read and a force of eighty militiamen to rescue the beleaguered garrison.

After the celebration of the Green Corn Dance at the beginning of summer 1836, the Seminoles, aroused by the dancing, spiritual awakening, and speeches by the leaders, moved against the weakened frontier settlements. The inroads of yellow fever, malaria, measles, smallpox, and diseases caused by food infection had caused many soldiers to become ill, and as a result, only a limited number of regular soldiers were available for duty that summer.[35] Striking at the plantation belt during the harvest season, the Seminoles destroyed many of the plantation homes and houses of the settlers east of the St. Johns River and south of St. Augustine and Picolata and, with the exception of Micanopy, Garey's Ferry and New-nansville, the central part of Florida was abandoned by the settlers.[36] In August, when news came that the Seminoles were gathering rice and sugar cane from Clinch's plantation, a force from Micanopy composed of 110 regulars under Major B. K. Pierce drove them away from the abandoned military post and plantation.

To guard against strikes by the military the Seminoles moved their camps to the edges of hammocks and pine woods where quick retreats could be made into the interior. They tied hogs and chickens so they could not roam, and planted corn fields on or near the banks of rivers so that crops could be silently gathered by canoe. One prisoner captured at this time claimed that all he had to eat was coontie and unsalted beef; the Seminoles' only garment was a shirt made of corn bags discarded by the military. Their limited supply of powder was a mixture of rifle and musket grains, and the bullets had been hand-made from sheets of lead.

In contrast, the soldiers at this time took little precaution to hold the noise in their camp to a wartime level, and the sounds of laughing men, of a daily discharge of artillery at eleven in the morning, and of bugles could be heard for several miles. Because few dependable scouts were available to move ahead of patrols, the Seminoles knew quite a bit about the whereabouts of the regular and militia soldiers, while the soldiers knew little about them.

When a war with the Creeks in Alabama broke out, Scott was transferred there, and General Abraham Eustis took his place until another successor could be appointed. Although Duncan Clinch was next in line to succeed Scott, he declined the nomination and resigned from the army in order to take care of his eight children. When Clinch had shown little inclination to take the place of Scott, Governor Call wrote a letter to President Andrew Jackson describing how the Seminoles should be beaten with use of the Withlacoochee as a supply line and avenue of attack. After some delay Call received his appointment and remained in command until General Thomas Sidney Jesup was named supreme commander of the

Florida militia, militia from other states, and units of the regular army by Secretary of War Lewis Cass on June 20, 1836.[37]

Andrew Jackson, perhaps the best of all the whites who fought the American Indians, could only watch from Washington what his generals were doing in Florida. The actions of Gaines disturbed him, for when Gaines should have attacked the Seminoles on their flanks, he ordered his men to build fortifications and to remain in the fortified post under siege. To Jackson, Scott was not much better, for he had not engaged the enemy to any degree, discharged the militiamen too soon, and moved into summer quarters too early in the season. It was obvious to both Jackson and the Seminoles that neither Scott nor Gaines understood the Florida environment or the determination of the Seminoles to remain in Florida. When Call assumed command, Jackson advised him to attack by moving deep into the cove of the Withlacoochee and waging an aggressive campaign.

Call formulated a plan that involved the use of volunteer troops, friendly Creeks, and regulars in a campaign against the Seminoles waged from four supply points, all accessible by steamboat. The opening phase of the campaign in the summer was not promising, for many soldiers had fallen ill and the roads were water-soaked and the temperature too high for constant campaigning. When the temperature had cooled by November, with a combined force of Creeks, Tennessee Mounted Volunteers, and Florida militia and regulars totaling 2,500 men, Call was able to come close to the center of Seminole activities in Wahoo Swamp. Hindered by limited supplies, inexperience in handling large groups of men, and a determined Seminole defense, however, this large force did not do well.[38] One camp four miles from the Withlacoochee was surprised, eleven Indian men killed, and twelve women and children captured, but a Seminole retreat through the swamp allowed Call and his force to gain only a few fruits of victory in the burning of several towns. Although large numbers of Creeks were used in operations against the Seminoles, they were not very effective, for their generation, like the whites, did not know Florida. After examining the cove of the Withlacoochee, Call concluded that corn could not be raised there and that the Seminoles in the area must have lived on beef and wild plants.

Next on the scene to challenge the Seminoles was forty-eight-year-old Brevet Major General Thomas Sidney Jesup. With little time left before their service terms expired, Jesup ordered the transfer of the Tennessee brigade from Volusia to Tampa Bay and construction of forts by the troops as they made their way to the docks, including Fort Armstrong at the Dade Massacre site and Camp Dade at the crossing of the Withlacoochee. Jesup and 8,000 of his men then moved into central Florida, where they achieved some minor victories with the capture of some blacks and a hundred ponies and the burning of some villages. As pressure mounted along the Withlacoochee River and the Wahoo Swamp, the Indian bands there divided into smaller units and moved southeast to the headwaters of the Ocklawaha to join Philip, Micanopy, and Jumper.

The first sign that Jesup was making progress in inflicting punishment on the Seminoles was the initiation and signing of an agreement to end the fighting. One of the black captives taken in a skirmish near the Great Cypress Swamp was released with an offer of amnesty to the Seminoles, contingent upon acceptance of the 1832 and 1833 treaties. The movement of the large number of troops into central Florida made it impossible to plant corn and other crops upon which the Seminoles' food supply depended, and after much debate, large numbers of Seminoles showed their inclination to cease all fighting and negotiate for a reservation in Florida. Some were even ready to go west.

In March 1837 some Seminole leaders gathered at Fort Dade to sign an agreement to cease hostilities. On March 6, 1837, Jumper, Davy Elliott, Cloud (a principal Seminole leader in the Dade Massacre), and Alligator, acting on behalf of Micanopy, signed an agreement at Fort Dade that stated that an immediate cease fire was in effect. The Seminoles gave their word that they were ready to move west and that they would deliver hostages to insure adherence to the agreement. Having promised to assemble for emigration near Fort Brooke by April 10, 1837, two hundred or more Seminoles, including Jumper, Micanopy, and other leaders, began to move toward Tampa Bay and were lodged in two camps eight miles from Fort Brooke. A much larger number of Seminoles under Osceola, Sam Jones, Philip, and Coacoochee gathered at Fort Mellon on Lake Monroe, a hundred miles from Tampa Bay, where relations were so friendly that Osceola slept in the tent of Lieutenant Colonel William S. Harney, the commander.[39]

The conflict was renewed with great distrust on the part of the Seminoles concerning promises made by Jesup and others. Two hundred Mikasukis, led by Osceola and Sam Jones, left Fort Mellon and made their way to Tampa, where they seized Micanopy, Jumper, Cloud, and their followers and fled into the interior of the peninsula with their captives. Micanopy was said to have refused to flee and to have been forced to mount a horse and leave with the others. Jumper, who had already sold his horse, walked back with the Mikasukis.

This sudden departure may have been caused by concern on the part of the Seminoles as to what would happen to their black allies. In the first meeting at Fort Dade the Seminoles refused to surrender to the whites any blacks, and Jesup agreed that the blacks would accompany the Seminoles in their move to the West. Yet after twenty-eight vessels had been assembled at Tampa Bay to remove the Seminoles and blacks, plantation owners began to demand their right to visit Seminole camps and remove any slaves that may have belonged to them. When Jesup insisted on the surrender of any blacks captured during the conflict, the Seminoles said that Jesup was not keeping his word, and all attempts toward a peaceful removal failed.[40]

The halt in the fighting gave the Seminoles a chance to recover from the hot pursuit, grow and harvest some crops, obtain more powder and firearms, and ready themselves to resume fighting.[41] By June 2, 1837, Jesup felt that he had failed to bring about peaceful removal and that the only solution was a war of extermination, which he did not desire.[42]

Jesup's request to be reassigned was refused by his superiors during the summer of 1837, and he strengthened his forces in preparation for the fall campaign. Seven hundred mounted militia soldiers were enrolled during the summer, nearly one thousand American Indians, mostly from the Middle West, were recruited to serve as an auxiliary force, and better equipment including the larger Dearborn wagons, Colt revolvers, and Cochran repeating rifles were secured for use by the regulars.[43] Although with insufficient regular troops, Jesup did not wage an active campaign against the Seminoles during the summer, he kept them off balance by using men mounted on horses in strikes against Seminole towns.

The peace movement that had ended with the sudden departure from the camps near Fort Brooke arose again during August 1837 when Seminole envoys visited Fort King. Jesup told the envoys that he would only negotiate with them when they were ready to leave Florida. At that time they could contact Jesup by the use of a white flag to protect them from the fire of the troops. According to Coa Harjo, one of the envoys and a signer of the Payne's Landing treaty, many leaders wanted to leave Florida, but when a council was held to discuss the matter, only a few leaders attended.

Both Osceola and Wildcat, who had led much of the fighting, believed that they could not endure another year of hostilities and were ready to begin negotiations with the whites.[44] Few Seminoles were ready to leave Florida, however; most wanted to be given a permanent reservation, probably in southern Florida.[45] Sam Jones would not consider negotiations with the whites under any conditions. At one council Wildcat talked from morning to night stating his views that the Seminoles could not endure one more year of hard fighting and made Sam Jones so angry that he left the meeting several times.

According to Titus, a black informant, Sam Jones replied in rebuttal to Wildcat that

> he would not give up as long as he had a single ball and a charge of powder—that when he could no longer shoot game, he would live on fish—when his lines are worn out, he will make others of horse hair—and when his hooks are broken, he will cut up his old tin pans and make others. He concluded by saying that he had 700 warriors, and that he would fight as long as they would stand by him; and that if every other Indian should leave Florida, he would find a retreat among the islands of the Everglades, remote from the face of white or red man. Sam Hicks, a son-in-law of old Sam Jones, advised contrary measures; but Sam Jones became exceedingly enraged—demanded back his daughter, and actually drove him from his camp. But Sam had another wife in three days.
>
> Titus thinks Sam Jones the only obstacle to the making of peace, and that he possesses a hundred time the power and influence that Powell (Osceola) did. He thinks that he has 400 men.[46]

In September 1837 the desertion of a slave from the camp of Philip brought about an unusual turn of events. When John Philip, who was Philip's slave, visited St. Augustine, he promised to lead the soldiers to the Seminole camp located south of the Tomoka River.[47] Guided by John Philip, 170 men, mostly regulars under the command of General Joseph M. Hernandez, on September 9 were able to capture Philip and his Mikasuki followers. Philip sent word to his son Wildcat (Coacoochee) to come in and talk, and when Wildcat and another leader, Blue Snake, strolled into Jesup's camp, they were captured. Since Philip was being held hostage, Jesup released Wildcat, who visited other Seminole camps and returned with two other Seminole leaders and the news that Osceola desired a meeting.[48]

When news came that Osceola and Coa Hadjo were willing to negotiate, Jesup gave orders to General Joseph Hernandez to arrange the conference at the Seminole camp, which was flying a white flag, and to seize the Seminoles as they came to meet the whites. On October 25, 1837, while trying to negotiate under the protection of a white flag, Osceola, 71 warriors, 6 women, and 4 blacks were captured within a circle formed by 250 soldiers. The opening contact between soldiers and Seminoles was brief, for the armed troops moved in quickly on all sides and showed that resistance was useless. The Seminoles' guns were collected, and everybody moved off to the old Spanish fort, Castillo de San Marcos or Fort Marion, at St. Augustine where the prisoners were lodged.[49] The first news brought to the Seminoles that Osceola had been captured was related by two that were able to escape. Showing terror and dismay on their faces when they stopped at a camp at Spring Garden, they told about the captives being bound with cord, the large force of horsemen that had surrounded Osceola's band, and the sound of heavy artillery gunfire that must have killed all of the captives.[50]

Throughout the eastern United States protests arose about the way in which Osceola had been captured, and for the rest of his life Jesup would try to defend himself. Sometime later Jesup claimed that the Seminoles knew very well that once they had begun their negotiations they could not leave, and that he had supplied the white flags to protect them from other troops. Although Wildcat and nineteen other Seminoles were able to escape from Fort Marion, Osceola remained in captivity and died several months later from quinsy aggravated by malaria at Fort Moultrie, South Carolina, where he was buried. Osceola had been ill for some time and may have acquired the disease when his band occupied Fort Drane which the troops had abandoned because of the climate and large numbers of sick soldiers.

Seminoles who surrendered or were captured were taken to Tampa or another port, where their livestock was sold and they were placed aboard steamers or schooners to be shipped to Indian Territory via New Orleans. One of the first groups to leave Florida were 407 friendly Seminoles under the leadership of Black Dirt; they left Tampa April 11 and 12, 1836, and arrived at Little Rock May 5. Of the 407 who started the trip, 382 were still alive at Little Rock and 320 arrived at Fort Gibson.

This deportation scene was to be repeated many times during the Second Seminole War.[51] Usually an army officer accompanied each group, but he had little control over conditions aboard the ships, land transport, food supplied by contractors at great profit, or medical care. Since the Seminole remedy for those who contracted measles was to give the patients cold baths and for all sick persons to apply great pressure upon the stomach, many died during the trip.

When they were captured, the black allies of the Seminoles were treated differently. The first group of ninety blacks taken by Jesup's command during the winter of 1836–37 and shipped to New Orleans on June 2, 1837, was captured by Creek warriors recruited by a promise of twenty dollars for each black taken.[52] Usually those blacks belonging to white U.S. citizens were restored to the owners, and the others were sent west to live with the Seminoles either as free persons or slaves. A breakdown of the first allotment showed that 103 blacks were sent west and 89 were restored to owners.

After the capture of Osceola Jesup began a late fall campaign with the more than 4,000 regulars and 5,000 volunteers assembled to terminate what was viewed as the Seminole problem. In Jesup's plan three columns sweeping through the Big Cypress Swamp and the Everglades would meet and defeat the fleeing Seminoles forced out by four other columns moving toward the headwaters of the St. Johns. Since over half of all the soldiers in the regular army at that time were in Florida fighting the Seminoles, it was necessary to call upon the militia to supply the bulk of the force needed, and numbers of mounted volunteers were summoned from other states, including Missouri.[53]

On Christmas Day 1837, when a force composed of 1,000 men commanded by Colonel Zachary Taylor engaged in combat a band of 400 Indians led by Wildcat, Sam Jones, and Alligator, the most impressive battle of the war took place northeast of Lake Okeechobee. Taylor landed at Tampa Bay with 1,100 men, mostly regulars but including some volunteers from Missouri and Native American allies. Jesup instructed him to destroy any Seminole force that he was able to meet, and following these orders, Taylor moved toward the Kissimmee River and Lake Okeechobee. When they saw the approaching troops, the Seminoles moved to a position protected by a swampy area of thick sawgrass and palmettos and prepared for battle by cutting the sawgrass, posting ten men in moss-covered trees to inform the others about progress of the troops, and placing marksmen behind the trees. With 380 warriors available to counter a force that outnumbered them three to one, the Seminoles formed a line of fire with Alligator's men in the center, Sam Jones and the Prophet, Otulke-thloco, a newcomer from Georgia, on the right, and Wildcat on the left. After the Sixth Infantry had left their horses and had advanced on food through the swampy area, they were met by a well-directed volley that killed or wounded all but one of the commissioned officers and most of the noncommissioned ones. The troops from Missouri, caught by the gunfire in the sawgrass between the Seminoles and the Sixth Infantry, began a retreat that could have resulted in disaster to the entire force, but a bayonet charge by the reserves stopped the Seminoles.[54] When the troops began to close in, Sam Jones and his men fled, but Alligator and Wildcat retreated only when the troops came close. On the following day the Seminoles gathered in small groups of ten to fifteen and scattered into the flat woods and lowlands. In this battle the soldiers lost 26 dead and 112 wounded; the Indians, 11 dead and 14 wounded.[55]

Another attempt at peacemaking resulted in the capture of many Seminoles during the late winter and spring of 1838. When Halleck Hajo and Tuskegee contacted Jesup in February 1838, he promised to request the government to allow the Seminoles to stay in Florida. When this request was turned down by Secretary of War Joel Poinsett, the troops under Jesup began capturing the Seminoles gathered near Fort Juniper who had been awaiting the outcome of the negotiations. More than 500 Indians were taken then; small bands later came in to surrender so they could join their friends, and as a result a total of 527 Seminoles, 156 free blacks, and 14 slaves were captured. When a delegation of Cherokees who had volunteered to help negotiate the Seminole removal brought in Micanopy and others under a white flag, Jesup acted as he had in the case of Osceola and placed Micanopy and his eighty-one followers in captivity. This act by Jesup disgusted the Cherokees, and they ceased their activities to help secure a peaceful removal. The number of Seminoles and blacks captured or surrendered during Jesup's command in Florida totaled 1,978 persons, and possibly 400 more were killed during that period. Since one-half or more of the total Seminole and black fighting force had been taken out of action by Jesup and his men, Jesup did more than any other general to end the conflict, but due to his methods, he deserves no praise.[56]

5

The Second Seminole War, Phase 2, 1838–1842

lthough the forces commanded by Brevet Major General Thomas Jesup during eighteen months of service in Florida had captured nearly 2,000 Seminoles and killed approximately 400, 1,000 or more remained, including sizeable numbers in the region between the Apalachicola and Ochlockonee rivers, in central Florida, and in southwestern Florida. The prime objective of Jesup's successors would be shipping the remaining Seminoles and their black allies to Indian Territory.

Due to Jesup's vigorous campaign the various Seminole bands had been scattered, and little communication took place between the widely separated groups. Those in northern Florida knew little or nothing about what was taking place elsewhere, and warriors from one band could not support another with assistance in the forms of warriors, food, and ammunition. The only area in which limited cooperation took place between the bands was in southwestern Florida where Sam Jones, Billy Bowlegs, and Otulke-thloco (the Prophet) met together in councils on a regular basis.

At this stage of the war the Seminoles were in rough shape. The soldiers had learned much about their hiding places and had attacked their camps, burning the houses, capturing the livestock, and destroying the fields of corn and melons. With the abandonment of the Cuban fishing ranchos and with frequent military attacks, arms and ammunition became scarce and supplies of clothing and food limited. Powder was allotted free to each warrior when he went with a war party, but for hunting game he was expected to pay for the powder. It was possible that during this period the Seminoles shifted from cabins to chickees, open-sided log shelters that were easily constructed, and to a new style of clothing made by sewing rags together.

When Jesup asked to be relieved of his command and to return to quartermaster duties, Zachary Taylor, now a brevet brigadier general, was assigned to replace him in May 1838. The fifty-four-year-old Taylor was sure that he could finish off the Seminoles by establishing many small posts throughout their territory from which frequent patrols could be made to harass them.[1] Fifty-three posts were established; many in service only for several months, new roads were built to carry supplies to the posts, but the plan, requiring the services of 30,000 men, had little chance of implementation and soon was cast aside. When Taylor decided to dispense with the use of the militia and use the twenty-six companies of regular infantry and four of regular dragoons to drive the Seminoles south of a line extending from St. Augustine to Tampa, he caused concern among the civilians of Florida about the lack of protection for their families. Finally the Territorial Council authorized the enrollment of twelve companies of militia, which Taylor accepted and placed in spots where the civilians could be protected. Taylor did succeed in removing 196 blacks and Seminoles from Florida to Indian Territory, but Old Rough and Ready was not a success against the Seminoles.[2]

In March 1839 Major General Alexander Macomb was placed in charge of the Florida command. While Macomb negotiated with the Seminoles, he allowed Taylor to continue construction of posts, roads, and bridges. In the spring of 1839 Congress appropriated funds for reopening negotiations with the remaining Seminoles in Florida, and Macomb was authorized to persuade them to move to a temporary reservation in southwestern Florida and remain there until they agreed to removal from Florida under terms of the treaties of Fort Gibson and Payne's Landing. Accordingly a meeting was held at Fort King May 18–22 between Chitto Tustenuggee (a Muskogee), Halleck Tustenuggee (a Mikasuki), and Macomb, at which a verbal agreement was made that hostilities would cease and at which the Seminoles promised to move to southwestern Florida by July 15 and remain there until other arrangements were made.[3] The sixty-six Seminoles who visited Fort King for the council showed signs of a harried existence, appearing in well-worn buckskins and grain sacks. Although this pact was hailed by some as the one that could end the war, four warring bands remained in southern Florida, and three of the four had made no contact with Macomb at all.[4]

As part of the Macomb agreement a trading post was to be established on the Caloosahatchee River to serve the residents of the proposed reserve. James B. Dallam, who had been appointed trader, erected a store some fifteen miles from the Gulf of Mexico, guarded by a detachment of twenty-eight dismounted dragoons. On July 24, 1839, bands of Seminoles led by Hospetarke, Billy Bowlegs, and Chakaika attacked the post and camp, killing thirteen soldiers and three civilians.[5] The attack succeeded because no ammunition was available for the dragoons' newly issued Colt rifles; as soon as the soldiers discovered their guns were useless, they threw them aside and jumped into the river, where Seminoles lined along both banks shot them. Lieutenant Colonel William S. Harney, in charge of the detachment, saved his life by wading into the river and paddling his canoe to its mouth. Harney would later gain revenge for this midnight swim in his underwear and for the oyster-shell cuts on his feet.

During Macomb's command the Territorial Council of Florida authorized the use of bloodhounds to track the Seminoles. Colonel Richard Fitzpatrick was sent to Cuba to purchase some bloodhounds that had been successful in subduing slave revolts in Jamaica and Cuba. Although several prisoners were released and tracked successfully by the dogs, their use in the field failed and ended with U.S. government officials refusing to pay the costs of procuring the dogs.[6]

Brevet Brigadier General Walker Keith Armistead succeeded Macomb and took command of the Florida theater on May 5, 1840. In an initial action Armistead divided Florida into two zones separated by the Suwannee River. He did his best to remove the Seminoles from each zone, but before he could place troops in the two zones the Seminoles began their attacks. On May 19, 1840, Wildcat, with nearly 100 warriors, ambushed a detachment near Micanopy, killing a lieutenant and five soldiers. When the Seminoles found several unprotected carriages and wagons traveling along the road from Picolata to St. Augustine, they killed most of the passengers, including several actors en route to an engagement. Aroused by these attacks the military searched through Big Swamp fifteen miles from the army's headquarters at Fort King. Other searches were directed at the Wahoo Swamp, Chocochatti hammock, and sites along the Ocklawaha River where a total of 500 acres of corn fields were destroyed.

Once troops had searched an area, destroying the villages, burning the fields, and taking away the horses, cattle, and pigs, the Seminoles moved back in. In June 1841 Lieutenant C. R. Gates of the Eighth Infantry, patrolling the Withlacoochee with fifty men in an area that had been searched many times, discovered several towns in the Wahoo Swamp that were well concealed by protective vegetation. Accessible only by canoes through winding passages of thick willow trees, these three villages contained twelve, thirteen, and three lodges. The patrol discovered fields of pumpkins and corn planted some distance from the villages and along the river small camps in which coontie was processed.[7]

The scene of warfare shifted to Indian Key midway between Cape Florida and Key West, where seventy persons lived, including Dr. Henry Perrine, a horticulturalist, and Jacob Houseman, a salvaging magnate. Chakaika, one of the leaders at the Caloosahatchee attack, led a band of the so-called Spanish Indians in seventeen canoes across thirty miles of water to Indian Key on August 7, 1840, where they killed thirteen settlers and destroyed most of the buildings.[8] The band could have killed more people but their noise as they attacked the two largest houses alerted the other inhabitants, who fled to their boats. Perrine saved his life for a short time by saying in Spanish that he would go with the attackers and help save the lives of their sick. The Spanish Indians had watched Fort Dallas at Miami for some time to make sure Perrine was outside the fort so that they could capture him and use his medical help, but they killed him. In this attack, they obtained four barrels of powder, which they sorely needed.

It took a year and a half for Lieutenant Colonel Harney to gain his revenge for the loss of thirteen men and the night dash in his underwear to the Caloosahatchee River, but he tracked down Chakaika and the Spanish Indians who had taken part in the attack. In December 1840 Harney and ninety men moved by canoe from Fort Dallas on a twelve-day trek deep into the Everglades in pursuit of those who had attacked Indian Key. They discovered the camp of Chakaika and killed the chief in an early morning attack that took the Spanish Indians completely by surprise. When two other Spanish Indians were captured and hung, Harney ordered the corpse of Chakaika to be hung alongside them.[9] Sam Jones reacted to the hangings with these words: "We have given them heretofore when prisoners a decent death and shot them instead of hanging them like a dog."

A short time after assuming command in Florida Armistead held a conference with Tiger Tail (Thlocklo Tustenuggee, a Muskogee) and Halleck Tustenuggee (a Mikasuki) at Fort King on November 10, 1840, at which he offered each leader $5,000 to bring in his band for removal to the West. After considering the proposition for two weeks and eating army food during that time, both leaders and their forty warriors said no and departed.[10] Following the failure of a peace delegation from Oklahoma Armistead ordered full mobilization of his military force of 4,500 regulars and 2,000 militiamen. Use of bribery, extensive scouting, and harassment helped Armistead remove nearly 700 Seminoles and blacks from Florida.

The final federal commander of the Second Seminole War was Colonel William Jenkins Worth. With nearly 5,000 regular troops at his disposal, Worth planned to clear the Seminoles from the frontier line above the Withlacoochee and to strike at Seminole villages in the south. When he found many local whites profiting from the war to such a degree that they wanted it to continue, he tried to save federal money by discharging four companies of Georgia militia and removing civilians from the payroll.[11]

Although approximately three-fourths of the Seminole and black population in Florida had been removed by January 1841, the Seminoles in central Florida remained a formidable fighting force. Halleck Tustenuggee and Wildcat stayed close to the white settlements, where they attacked isolated farms, unprepared military units, and unwary travelers. Their sanctuaries included the hammocks and riverbanks of central Florida, where some Green Corn Dances and councils were held. Corn fields, usually planted in the middle of hammocks, provided a food supply for the warriors and their families, and the network of swamps, lakes, and waterways served as gateways for forays. Wildcat and his band occupied the area of the headwaters of the St. Johns River along the east coast. Halleck Tustenuggee with thirty-five men operated in the central sections along Lake Monroe, the Ocklawaha River, Fort King, the Wahoo Swamp, the Withlacoochee River, and Micanopy. Tiger Tail, his brother Nethlockemathlar, and sixty warriors were to be found along the Suwannee, Homosassa, and Crystal rivers and the Chocochatti and Annuttiliga hammocks.[12]

When native peoples defeated by superior white firepower have grown hopeless and apathetic, they have often been vulnerable to messianic movements that promised victory in the face of defeat. Such movements have been inspired by such messianic leaders as Pope in the Pueblo Revolt in 1680, Tecumseh and the Shawnee Prophet in 1811, the Prophets in the 1813–14 Creek War, and the prophet Wovoka and the ghost dance in the late nineteenth century. The Messiah figure in the Second Seminole War was thirty-eight-year-old Otulke-thloco, the Big Wind or the Prophet, a former Creek who lived in the Big Cypress Swamp, where he dominated such leaders as Billy Bowlegs, Hospetarke, Assinwar, and Fuse Hadjo and their 160 followers.[13] Having escaped from a Georgia jail during the Creek War of 1836, the Prophet claimed that the Great Spirit had opened the jail doors, struck loose his chains, and told him to flee to Florida to continue the war against the whites. He controlled the activities of the Seminoles in southern Florida to a greater extent than Micanopy or Osceola had been able to do between 1835 and 1837. The Seminoles believed that he kept in constant touch with the Great Spirit by the continued practice of midnight fires, dances, and songs, and the use of roots to cure diseases. They were certain that he could hear the approaching troops before others, knew where the deer were hiding, and could cause the death of any person. He ordered two Seminoles put to death when he suspected that they were ready to surrender to the whites. Although he never took part in any of the battles as a warrior, the other leaders were so afraid of him that they dared speak no words of criticism. So greatly was his power feared that when the Seminoles surrendered, they held ceremonies to counter the Prophet's medicine. Military skill, however, was not needed in southern Florida, for various bands had withdrawn there to carry on their former life-style of hunting, fishing, cultivating fields, and gathering wild plants. With the exception of the raids at Indian Key and the Caloosahatchee River, they did not engage in offensive warfare.

In the extreme northern portion of Florida were several bands, including at least one that had fled from the Creek War in Georgia and Alabama. During the period 1837–42 many Creeks fleeing the forced migration to Indian Territory moved in small groups from Alabama and Georgia into Florida. Most walked along former American Indian trails, forded shallow river crossings, and waded through swamps to join the Seminoles. One of the first was Nokose Yahola, who had fought Jesup and Scott in Alabama and was captured by Jesup in Florida. Octiarche and some twenty warriors fought their way through southern Georgia and the Florida Panhandle to a hammock near the Steinhatchee River in northwestern Florida, where they settled and remained generally peaceful. Halpatter Tustenuggee and Mad Tiger headed a combined force of forty-two Creeks and Mikasukis located in the area west of the Suwannee River and along the Georgia border. Pascoffer, another Creek leader, with forty men occupied the land along the Ochlockonee River west of Tallahassee.

During the summer of 1841 the customary summer cessation of hostilities did not take place, no more passports to enter military camps were granted to Seminoles, and the military force of 4,200 men and 200 officers was ordered to "find the enemy, capture or exterminate them."[14] Day and night, parties of troops guided by captured blacks moved into known strongholds to capture Seminoles and destroy their homes and fields.

The relentless pursuit drove the Seminoles to new tactics of concealment. They avoided leaving footprints by jumping from log to log or destroyed them by crawling or walking backwards and crossing their tracks. Instead of large numbers tending the fields, only one or two took care of the corn and pumpkin plots. They traveled only at night and then in groups of four or five who met with the other bands at a designated spot. They said little concerning the whereabouts of other bands, for they knew that once captured a person became talkative, as had the mother of Coacoochee, who had led the soldiers to a spot where Cuban boats brought munitions to the Seminoles.

Finally, Halleck Tustenuggee, Tiger Tail, Nethlockemathlar, Octiarche, and 120 of their men met in council June 1841 at the Long Swamp near Fort King, where they agreed that no peace terms would be considered and that any Seminole or black who tried to deliver such terms would be killed.[15] In the same council defenses against the troops were revised. The warriors were advised to remain near their families so that if the troops attacked suddenly, they could put up a defense while their families escaped. Scouting parties of eight to ten men moved out daily to check upon the movements of the soldiers and to inform their leaders that night about what they had observed. Most of the towns of these Seminoles lay along the edge of a lake near hammocks where trees grew from eighteen inches to two feet in diameter and where unpenetrable scrub oak, palmetto, and grapevine underbrush concealed all signs of life.

In March 1841 Wildcat appeared at Fort Cummings (near present-day Lakeland) and Fort Brooke for meetings with military leaders. On May 1 he visited Fort Pierce (today south of Cape Canaveral) demanding and receiving a horse, food, and five and one-half gallons of whiskey and rode off to Tampa with a hangover. When it appeared that Wildcat would not keep his promise to surrender, he was seized during a second visit to Fort Pierce by Major Thomas Childs. With this outstanding warrior in their grasp, the military moved fast to ship him and his followers west.

On July 4, 1841, Wildcat and his men moved aboard the transport that would carry them from the land in which they had fought so hard to stay. John T. Sprague described the scene:

Coacoochee and his warriors came up slowly to the quarterdeck of the transport, their feet-irons hardly enabling them to step four inches, and arranged themselves according to rank. As they laid their manacled hands upon their knees before them, in the presence of so many whom they had so long hunted as foes, they hung their heads in silence. Not a cheering voice or expression could be seen or heard among the group.[16]

Colonel Worth spoke to the Seminoles, and Wildcat gave a most eloquent reply on this day of independence, July 4:

> I was once a boy, then I saw the white man afar off. I hunted in the woods, first with a bow and arrow, then with a rifle. I saw the white man, and was told he was my enemy. I could not shoot him as I would a wolf or a bear; yet like these he came upon me; horses, cattle, and fields, he took from me. He said he was my friend; he abused our women and children, and told us to go from the land. Still he gave me his hand in friendship; we took it; whilst taking it, he had a snake in the other, his tongue was forked; he lied, and stung us. I asked but for a small piece of these lands, enough to plant and to live upon far south, a spot where I could place the ashes of my kindred, a spot only sufficient upon which I could lay my wife and child. This was not granted me. I was put in prison; I escaped. I have been again taken; you have brought me back; I am here; I feel the irons in my heart. . . .
>
> It is true I have fought like a man, so have my warriors; but the whites are too strong for us. I wish now to have my band around me and go to Arkansas. . . . I never wish to tread upon my land unless I am free.[17]

In a rather strange turn of circumstances, the whites decided to make use of Wildcat's services to induce other Seminoles to surrender, stopped his ship in New Orleans, and had him and his warriors return to Florida. In a meeting in a transport anchored in Hillsborough Bay near Fort Brooke, Worth told Wildcat he could select several of his men to contact Wildcat's band on the Kissimmee and St. Johns rivers, but if they did not return within a selected time all of the Seminoles aboard the transport would be hung. Wildcat was able to induce a considerable number of Seminoles to surrender and return within the specified time. As a result of his efforts 211 Seminoles, including most of his band, were shipped out on October 12, 1841.

In an April 1841 council similar to that at Long Swamp in central Florida, the Big Cypress Seminoles, including the bands of Billy Bowlegs, Sam Jones, the Prophet, Hospetarke, Fuse Hadjo, and Parsacke, had decreed that anyone carrying a message from the whites would be killed. Hospetarke, an eighty-five-year-old leader, his fifty-four warriors, and seventy-three women and children nevertheless had been enticed with the assistance of Wildcat's brother to an August 1841 council at Camp Ogden near the mouth of the Peace River and captured by Worth.[18] Although his warriors had amassed a supply of food and powder and refrained from the use of alcohol so that they would not be captured, Hospetarke had grown tired of the long war and the tribulations connected with other leaders and was glad to leave Florida.

As the ships carried more and more Seminoles west, those remaining had a much better chance to remain hidden within the swamps and river edges; locating 500 persons in an area as large as central and southern Florida was difficult. Sampson Forrester, a black who lived with the Seminoles from 1839 to 1841, gave an excellent account of life at this time in the Everglades:

> In the center of the swamp, is the council ground. South of this, within two miles, is the village of Sam Jones. Otulke Thlocke [the Prophet] lives within two miles of him. Hospetarka's town was near the Everglades, twenty miles from the council house. Near him Passacka, his sub-chief, resided. Trails, or footpaths communicated with all these places. No trail whatever is visible outside the swamp, as such would guide their pursuers. Within the swamp are many pine-islands, upon which the villages are located. They are susceptible of cultivation; and between them is a cypress swamp, the water from two to three feet deep. The Indians rely principally upon their crops, which, though small, add much to their comfort. Corn, pumpkins, beans, wild potatoes, and cabbage palmetto, afford subsistence. The scarcity of powder deprives them partially of game; though bears and turkeys are frequently killed with arrows. Discharging a rifle was forbidden, as in a country so flat and wet the reverberation is in abundance; but there they apprehend discovery. A few ponies, cattle, hogs, and chickens are owned by the chief.[19]

In November 1841 Major William Belknap and soldiers of the Third Artillery moved into the Big Cypress and burned some villages. Although they captured or killed few Seminoles, the expedition succeeded in forcing them from the Big Cypress Swamp into the Everglades and Alligator Swamp west of Lake Okeechobee. When the Seminoles saw that the Prophet could not stop Belknap and his men from destroying his own village, two bands defied his authority by surrendering to the whites. After the Prophet had lost his power and Wildcat was captured, Billy

Significant Sites, 1823–1850

Bowlegs was recognized by the whites as the principal leader in the south, but Sam Jones continued to hold the most power as the leader of the hardliners.

In contrast to the tactics practiced in southern Florida, bands of Seminoles struck at the vulnerable area along the St. Johns River where no attacks had taken place for several years. Led by Halpatter Tustenuggee, Halleck Tustenuggee, and Chitto Harjo, they attacked Mandarin on the St. Johns River and other settlements. Although units of the Second Infantry pursued Halleck Tustenuggee, whose band had attacked Mandarin, the effort was fruitless.

One of the last engagements of the war took place on April 19, 1842, when a force commanded by First Lieutenant George McCall battled a band led by Halleck Tustenuggee. Accompanied by 200 men McCall moved into the Pelchikaha Swamp some thirty miles south of Fort King, a mass of grass ponds, pine ridges, and oak islands. When the Seminoles were discovered, they opened fire and then beat a quick retreat to a nearby hammock, where they lost their pursuers. The forty men had decoyed the

troops away from the women and children. According to the only prisoner captured, the Seminoles had no clothing, cooking utensils, other
articles, or food. After Halleck Tustenuggee had been detained during a
negotiating session at Fort King, Colonel John Garland finally seized part
of the band when they visited the army camp, and the remainder were
captured in their camp by McCall and his men.[20] Worth had done a good
job of capturing Seminoles; by February 2, 1842, he had shipped out 230.

The desperate straits to which the Seminoles had been reduced were
best illustrated by the account of a band that surrendered in northern
Florida in 1842:

> They are badly dressed, the blankets I have given them just covering
> their nakedness, and seem haggard and poor. Lieutenant Henry had
> issued a blanket to each and a shirt and turban to each man and a calico
> dress and handkerchief to each woman, food, & etc.
>
> [The next day they traveled on the *William Gaston* to the mouth of the
> Apalachicola River.] On nearing the wharf and seeing the people, the
> Indians had a revulsion of emotion and seemed to feel that they were
> now indeed in our power. The men became perfectly silent and se-
> rious—sad—while the women were nearly all in tears. I took occasion
> to speak to them, telling them not to lose heart, as they were coming
> among friends who would take care of them; that I was glad to see that
> they had tender hearts; but they would be treated well. The chief,
> Pascofa, himself was so much affected that his lips trembled and he could
> not say a word. A woman stood near with a little child in her arms, and I
> told her that they had been living more like wild animals than like
> human creatures, and she could now bring up her children in peace and
> safety. At this she dropped her head and burst into tears. There is a story
> current that at one period the members of this band put their children to
> death to avoid the chance of their exposing the hiding-places by their
> cries, and also to make flight easier. It is remarked that there is no child
> among them from four years old to about fourteen.[21]

Seven years of conflict came to an end when the military authorities
and President John Tyler realized that total Seminole removal was impossible. In October 1841 John C. Spencer replaced John Bell as secretary of
war and within seven months had ordered the termination of the Second
Seminole War. It is difficult to determine who influenced Spencer's decision most; probably it was the commander of all the troops in Florida,
Colonel William Worth, who recommended on February 5, 1842, that the
Seminoles be allowed to remain in peace in Florida, a suggestion rejected

by a council of officers. Regular regiments were withdrawn gradually, however, until only the Third, Eighth, and Sixth companies of the Fourth Infantry remained. Secretary of War Spencer was directed by President Tyler to authorize Worth "as soon as he shall deem it expedient" to declare that hostilities against the Seminoles in Florida had ceased and would not be renewed unless the Seminoles attacked. [22] Commanding General Winfield Scott notified Worth on the following day that he had the authority to determine the day and means by which the war could be concluded. When Worth was certain that no more hostile Seminoles remained in the area between the Peace River and Tallahassee, he could declare the conflict concluded. The Seminoles would be allowed to remain peacefully on a reserve in southwestern Florida. Since the policy of the federal government was that the remaining Seminoles should still be persuaded to migrate to Oklahoma, Worth was instructed that the bounds of their reservation need not have a permanent or exact marking.

The American Indians remaining in Florida in the spring of 1842 included a number of diverse bands. One large band led by Billy Bowlegs, a member of the so-called Seminole ruling family, had been leading a peaceful existence near Charlotte Harbor for some time. The Mikasukis led by Sam Jones resided deep in the Everglades near Fort Lauderdale. Somewhere in the scrubs and hammocks near Lake Istokpaga were the Muskogees led by Chipco. Two important bands were present in northern Florida. One was led by Octiarche, a Creek who had fled with his band from West Point, Georgia, to central Florida in 1836. This band would be a problem, for it was not regarded as Seminole. Another band, much smaller, was led by Tiger Tail, a Muskogee who had lived near Tallahassee. He had promised many times to leave Florida, accepted gifts, and then fled back to the wilderness.

Worth opened negotiations with the southern Seminoles through an ancient Seminole instructed to contact Billy Bowlegs. Bowlegs sent his sense bearer, Fuse Hadjo, back to Fort Brooke to ascertain if the accounts concerning peace negotiations were true. On July 21, 1842, a delegation of Seminoles headed by Fuse Hadjo arrived at Fort Brooke to negotiate an agreement concerning the reserve and peace terms. In a conference on the following day Worth told Fuse Hadjo and Nocosemathla that President Tyler desired peace between the whites and Seminoles and would allow them to remain in Florida, although it would be better for them to join their relatives in the Indian Territory. [23] Should they prefer to remain, they would receive no money or food but would be allowed to occupy land which they could not leave except to visit Fort Brooke, where a trading post would be established. The area designated for their reserve was the same as that stipulated in the 1839 Macomb agreement. Another meeting at the same place with Billy Bowlegs present was scheduled to take place in seventeen days.

Worth held conferences with Bowlegs and two other leaders of the southern Florida Seminoles on August 5 at Tampa and with the northern Seminoles and Octiarche's band on August 10 at Cedar Keys. Bowlegs accepted the terms given by Worth to Fuse Hadjo. (Since the Mikasukis and Muskogees were not present, it must be noted that this agreement was accepted only by the Billy Bowlegs band.) In the meeting on August 10 Worth informed members of Tiger Tail's and Octiarche's bands that every warrior who agreed to move west would be given a rifle, money, and rations for a year, but only a few accepted this offer. If they decided to remain in Florida, Worth explained, the bands were to move into the southern reserve as soon as possible.[24]

According to Worth, Octiarche's band was divided on acceptance of the peace terms. Some wanted to go to Indian Territory, others preferred to move to the reserve assigned, and still others could not believe that they would be absolved from punishment by the government. Since Billy Bowlegs, Tiger Tail, and Octiarche were the only parties to the agreement, the claim that the Seminoles never signed a peace treaty with the United States was probably true.

In his General Order 27 dated August 11, 1842, issued at Cedar Keys, Worth made two interesting points at variance with what the Seminoles understood. First, he claimed that his peace arrangement was made with the few Seminoles remaining in the southern portion of Florida; second, he claimed that they were to be permitted "for a while" to plant and hunt in the reserve.[25] If they had quickly moved into the reserve and had not delayed in making a decision, perhaps the northern bands could have remained in Florida under the terms of the Cedar Keys conference. Some citizens in central Florida began to attack isolated groups of Seminoles moving southward toward the reserve; Colonel Josiah Vose was ordered by Washington to take measures to prevent further such attacks.

Octiarche, a six-foot, forty-four-year-old leader, had left Georgia in 1836 with sixty men, thirty women and twenty children and settled eighty miles east of Tallahassee. From this place his band and the ones led by Halleck Tustenuggee and Tiger Tail had made a few raids. The soldiers recognized him in battle by his practice of painting one side of his face black and the other red, and of mixing both colors in markings on his chest. He wanted to live in peace in Florida, but forced by circumstances to take a stand, Octiarche was as good a leader as any of the Seminoles. Because a clash was sure to occur between Octiarche and Billy Bowlegs if Octiarche moved into the reserve, Colonel Worth directed Captain Washington Seawell to seize Octiarche and his band and send them to the prison at Horse Key, part of present-day Cedar Keys. On December 20, while the Creek leader and his followers were visiting Fort Brooke, they were captured and shipped to New Orleans.[26] Since Worth had given his word to allow safe migration south, the only defense for such tactics was that Octiarche had taken too long to move south and that he would cause trouble with the Seminoles already there.

In similar fashion Tiger Tail, a Muskogee from the area near Tallahassee, was captured. Named for the skin of a panther he wore attached to his belt in an 1823 ball game, Tiger Tail had moved with his band from the neighborhood of Tallahassee when fighting commenced and settled on an island in the Charlopopka Lakes. When troops discovered the hideout in 1841, he joined his brother Nethlockemathlar in the Annuttiliga Hammock. Since he spoke English well and had been a guest in fine homes in Tallahassee, Tiger Tail used his skill to delude the whites and boasted about it to the Seminoles. He had surrendered to the military three times, and three times he had skipped out after enjoying good food and lodging. Although he had promised to move to the reserve, he remained in his camp near Cedar Keys engaging in heavy bouts of drinking. A force of soldiers finally seized Tiger Tail's camp of six men and thirteen women and children and carried them to Cedar Keys.[27] Although some rationalizations could be offered for the seizure of Tiger Tail and Octiarche, their captures were violations of pacts accepted by both parties in August 1842.

By concluding a negotiated peace with the federal government, the Seminole Indians had accomplished something that many other larger tribes had not: they had fought a war with the whites during the nineteenth century in the eastern United States and under the peace terms had been allowed to remain in their own land. The Creeks had fought such a war in 1813 and were allowed to stay in Alabama, but they finally were removed in 1835–40 almost entirely, and only a few Cherokees escaped the Trail of Tears by hiding in the mountains.

The victory had been costly to the Seminoles. Of a population of 5,000 in 1835, 4,420 had been sent to Indian Territory. Approximately 600 Seminoles survived in Florida in 1842, and the whites would come back two more times to remove even these.[28]

6

A Period of Crisis

eace had finally come to the peninsula, and the territory of Florida was ready to back any federal legislation that would attract settlers to the subtropical land bypassed by the pioneers in favor of more peaceful locations in Alabama, Mississippi, and west. A May 1830 federal land law gave the settler who had built a home on land before it was surveyed the right to purchase 160 acres of land at $1.25 an acre.[1] This so-called squatters' sovereignty law was good, but a better one was needed to lure settlers into an area where they would serve as a barrier to Seminole raiders from the southern reserve. Accordingly, Senator Thomas Hart Benton of Missouri in June 1842 introduced a bill that, when signed on August 4, 1842, became the Armed Occupation Act. Under its provisions a head of family or single man over eighteen could file for 160 acres of land within the 200,000 acres available between Gainesville and the Peace River, provided the land was two miles or more from a fort and not near the coast.[2] The prospective settler was required to select the land and file for it at St. Augustine or Newnansville within nine months, erect a house, and cultivate five acres of land; after five years of living on the tract, the land was his. During the life of the Armed Occupation Act, 1,184 permits were issued for 189,440 acres of mostly unsurveyed land.[3] Although the specified land was some distance from the Seminole reserve, settlers used their tracts as springboards for movement further south. Unfortunately, the settlers did not form a protective barrier, for many of them did not have weapons. When Seminole threats developed, they ran to the nearest fort.

As squatters began moving closer to the reserve, President James Polk on May 19, 1845, set aside a twenty-mile belt to serve as neutral ground between the reserve and the white settlers. Under the terms of Polk's order no land could be claimed within the twenty-mile tract to the north of the reserve, but the surveyor-general of Florida made an agreement with John Jackson and John Irwin to survey the area near Charlotte Harbor, which included the reserve. When the secretary of the interior, Orlando Brown, protested to John Butterfield, commissioner of the Land Office, Butterfield replied that no titles would be issued for land within the belt and that the U.S. marshal upon request would remove any settlers.[4] The area of the reserve was 6,700 square miles or 4,288,000 acres, and the twenty-mile neutral zone, 5,400 square miles or 3,456,000 acres.[5]

After the Second Seminole War most of the Seminoles had moved into the reserve, and the warriors visited Tampa in groups of ten or more to trade and purchase needed items. Some visited the soldiers' barracks, pointed out their wounds and, if they knew sufficient English, exchanged war stories. Since most of them had come to Tampa for the whiskey available there, military authorities provided a house that served as a base of operations during their stay in which they could sober up, and they held their dances and ball games in its yard. Usually one man refrained from drinking so that he could safeguard the others.[6]

In September 1845 Thomas P. Kennedy, who had operated the sutler store at Fort Brooke, obtained permission to convert his fishing establishment on Pine Island (Caldez Rancho) to a trading post for the Seminoles. Articles needed for the post were carried in Kennedy's ten-ton sloop, *Julia Ann,* which left Tampa on September 20, 1845. Joab Griffin, employed by Kennedy as storekeeper, was assisted by Chai, a Creek, and his wife, Polly, who had served as guides during the Second Seminole War.[7] This business operation was not a success, for whites at McRaes, who sold whiskey to the Seminoles and wanted to keep them as customers, warned them that if they visited Pine Island, they could be captured and sent west to Indian Territory.[8] In 1848 Kennedy joined forces with John Darling in the trading post and mercantile store ventures, and the firm of Kennedy and Darling, located on Whiting Street next to the Palmer House, became one of the largest stores in Tampa. The firm advertised that merchandise brought by steamer from New Orleans could be traded for cotton, hides, and deerskins. When the trading post on Pine Island burned in 1848, Kennedy and Darling looked for another site.[9]

Under pressure by settlers in Florida, both the governor and the legislature did their best to restrict the Seminoles to the reserve and to secure their removal to Indian Territory as soon as possible. In 1848 Governor William D. Moseley wrote President Polk that "the Indians must be removed peacefully if they can, forcibly if they must." The governor approved a measure on January 13, 1849, explicitly stating that the Seminole agent could not give verbal or written orders for Seminoles to leave the reserve and that anyone, including the agent, selling liquor to them could be subject to a $100 to $500 fine.[10]

The Seminoles adopted a firm stand against negotiations with the whites. When Captain John C. Casey met Ishmatee's band near the mouth of the Peace River on July 6, 1849, he found them reluctant to accept any presents except tobacco and whiskey; they claimed that Sam Jones would kill them if they accepted other items.[11] Although allowing only limited contact with the whites, the Seminoles respected the terms of the 1842 agreement to the fullest extent. One clause, for example, stipulated that crews of vessels wrecked along the southwestern Florida coast should be taken by the Seminoles to the nearest settlement. Whenever wrecks took place and the survivors made their way ashore, the Seminoles treated them with kindness and assisted them to the nearest outpost.

In 1846 Captain John T. Sprague, a capable person who understood the Seminole character perhaps as well as any of the military men who had seen duty along the frontier, became the federal officer in charge of American Indian affairs in Florida. His duties were to lure the Seminoles from Florida and to arrange transport for them to Indian Territory. Captain Sprague served in Florida during the Second Seminole War and published in 1848 *The Origin, Progress, and Conclusion of the Florida War*, regarded as the best original account of the conflict for many years.

On January 8, 1847, Captain Sprague conferred with several Seminole leaders at Charlotte Harbor regarding a purported raid upon a farm. In his dispatch to the military authorities at Washington and the Florida governor reporting this meeting, he described Seminoles in detail:

> I have the honor to report that I met the Indians as anticipated at this place on the 8th instant. The chiefs Holatter [*sic*] Micco (Billy Bowlegs) and Assinwar [Bowlegs's father-in-law and a leader in his band], Echo-emathlar-Chopco [Chipco, leader of the Muskogees], Chitto Hadjo [nephew of Ismahtee, leader of the boat party Seminoles], Nub-cup-Hadjo, Subchiefs together with thirty four young warriors, well armed without women and children were present. I was disappointed in not meeting Arpeika or Sam Jones who sent a messenger stating that from age, indisposition and the extreme cold weather, he was unable to travel. My insisting upon seeing him tended to disparage the position and power of Holatter [*sic*] Micco, who, in all respects, is qualified for supreme command which he exercises with skill and judgement. He is

about thirty five years of age, speaks English fluently, active, intelligent and brave. Arpeika (Sam Jones) is ninety two years of age; without warriors, authority or influence. These chiefs and their followers express the strongest friendship and have adopted vigorous laws to punish those who violate the relation existing between the whites and red men but the young men, long accustomed to hunt the whites as they now do deer and turkeys, are ruthless, vicious and vengeful. To counteract this, I have enjoyed the necessity of prompt and severe punishment and shall see that they are executed. The Indians are timid and cautious. They came into my camp prepared to receive kindness and extend it, evidently determined to avenge on the spot any manifestation of a contrary feeling. Ten days elapsed before I succeeded in obtaining an interview with the chiefs who were deterred by the young warriors who, less credulous than the older ones, induced them to procrastinate until they reconnoitered the country as well as the coast. First a boy came, then a man departed, both to hear what I had to say. I demanded the promise of all and I should at once leave the country and they must be prepared for the consequences. This had the desired effect. Their scouts were extended ten miles around to announce the approach of soldiers, believing it to be my determination to surround them as they had been informed, vessels were on the coast for that purpose with troops. . . .

The Indians increase in number as well as improve in condition owing to partial intercourse with civilization. Their scattered condition, isolated camps and limited number, constitute their strength. One hundred and twenty men are capable of taking the field viz: Seminoles 70 [the Mikasuki speakers in Bowlegs's band], Mickasukies 30 [the Mikasuki (Hitchiti) speakers in the bands in Sam Jones's jurisdiction], Creeks 12 [Muskogee speakers, members of Chipco's band], Uchees 4 [Yuchi], Choctaws 4, for a Total of 120 warriors.

From observation and inquiry, I find seventy of this number grown from boyhood to manhood since December 1835, the commencement of the Florida War. The remainder excepting Sam Jones and Assinwar, the former, ninety-two and latter, sixty, are not over forty years of age. The women and children average about two to a man making two hundred and fifty, of this number, one hundred and fifty are children, thus making the total of Indians in Florida: men 120, women 100, children 140, for a total of 360.

The game of the country, climate and natural productions places them above sympathy or charity, every necessary want is supplied. Deer skins are the principal articles of clothing and trade for which powder and lead are obtained. Corn, pumpkins, potatoes, beans and peas are raised fresh and dried. Venison, turkeys and sea fowl, fish and oysters in abundance assure an independence the year round.[12]

Although federal and state officials wanted a speedy removal of the Seminoles, several factors prevented it. Among them was the Seminoles' distrust. At the commencement of hostilities the Seminoles had believed that military officers would keep their word in negotiations, but this faith had been badly tarnished by 1840 and destroyed with the seizure of Octiarche at Cedar Keys in 1842. When Billy Bowlegs expressed a desire to talk to Casey, others warned him in a council that he should not meet with the whites, for he could be seized under protection of the white flag and sent to Indian Territory.[13]

For the first time since the death of Wiley Thompson in December 1835, a Seminole subagent was appointed. Samuel Spencer, an attorney from Jefferson County in northern Florida, was hired in April 1849 at an annual salary of $750. He was not an effective agent, for he preferred to remain at Jacksonville with infrequent visits to the south.[14] When the secretary of the interior, Thomas Ewing, questioned Spencer's absence from Tampa, Spencer replied that the health of his family did not permit a move from Jacksonville and that suitable housing was not available at Tampa; he also noted that those seeking employment in the agency at Tampa and Enterprise could send reliable information to Jacksonville so that he could review their records before hiring them.[15] When a crisis developed during the summer of 1849, Spencer demonstrated little initiative and caused much dismay in Washington by visiting the capital at no one's request; as a result Ewing fired him and assigned his duties to an army officer concerned with Seminole removal.

Major William W. Morris, who was in charge of Seminole affairs at Fort Brooke, gave Kennedy and Darling permission in March 1849 to open another store on present-day Payne's Creek, a tributary of the Peace River.[16] After the firm had erected a combination store and dwelling, crude huts, a wharf, and a bridge, the Seminoles visited the store in greater numbers than had come to the earlier store. Articles stocked for trade with them included rifles, brass kettles, beads, blankets, tin cups and pans, calicos and cotton goods, powder, lead, flints, tobacco, broadcloth, spurs, bridles, saddles, mirrors, tools, shawls, hoes, hatchets, combs, salt, and whiskey. In a transaction on July 17, 1849, Chipco and three women came to the store with watermelons, deer meat, sweet potatoes, deer and other skins, and beeswax, which were purchased by Captain George S. Payne, proprietor of the store. He bought only nine or fewer of the watermelons, for he believed that they would not sell well in New York. Chipco remarked that he was going to return a pony recently acquired at the post, for it was not what he had ordered.[17] A disturbing fact was that within a period of eight months the Seminoles purchased one hundred pounds of rifle powder and a sizeable amount of lead, both far beyond their normal hunting requirements.

Most of the Seminoles now lived within the 6,700-square-mile reserve in ten or more scattered camps in the Big Cypress Swamp and south of the Caloosahatchee River, but a band of twenty under Chipco's leadership—five Muskogees, seven Mikasukis, six members of Bowlegs's band, one Creek, and one Yuchi—roamed beyond the reserve limits; they were called "outsiders." According to Casey they had been outlawed during the Green Corn Dance court day and forced to remove themselves from the tribe, at least for a short time.[18]

Some of the outsiders, including two sons of Chitto Tustenuggee, signer of the 1839 Macomb agreement, were angered by the 1849 law that restricted them to the reserve. Wanting revenge on traders who may have cheated them, they planned raids against isolated white outposts on both coasts of Florida.[19] On July 12, 1849, Holthe Mathla Hajo, Yahola Hajo (both sons of Chitto Tustenuggee), Panukee (a stepson of Kota Archelee), and Kota Eleo Kee (son of Eucha Kochakkner) visited a small town on the Indian River four miles north of Fort Pierce, where they were given food by the family of James Russell.

Upon leaving Russell's house they fired at Russell and inspector of customs William Barker, who were talking in a field, killing Barker and wounding Russell. Warned by Russell, who hobbled to the nearest house, the forty-four villagers fled in a boat but returned on the next day to find one house burned and two others robbed and vandalized. News of the attack caused most of the settlers on the coast between New Smyrna and Key Biscayne to move to St. Augustine, where federal troops stationed at Fort Marion could provide protection. The attack alarmed the Billy Bowlegs band as well as the settlers. Assinwar was sent to find out what was taking place, but by then the four Seminoles were moving toward another target on the west coast. Although the cause of the attack on the Fort Pierce settlement was not known, at least two persons speculated that Russell had been dishonest in trade relations with the Seminoles.

A second attack took place near sunset on July 17, when three of the Seminoles from the Fort Pierce attack and a fourth, Pahoy Hajo, appeared at the Kennedy and Darling store bearing rifles and requested the use of a boat to cross Peace River, where they had left a pack of skins.[20] Payne said they could use the boat but refused their request to sleep in the store. While the trading post employees were eating their evening meal, and the Seminoles sat on the porch near the door smoking their pipes, suddenly they took up their rifles and opened fire from the door, killing Dempsey Whidden and Payne and wounding William McCullough. When they paused to reload, McCullough grabbed a rifle from the wall and followed his wife, Nancy, and child, who were running to the bridge.[21] Both William and Nancy McCullough were wounded again by the Seminoles but were able to escape by hiding in the underbrush. The Seminoles took whiskey and merchandise from the store and set fire to the building and huts.[22] The McCulloughs made their way to a house along the Alafia River, where they told others about the attack and passed on the news that Nancy McCullough had recognized Yahola, who had been a frequent visitor to her home on the Alafia.[23]

Since the two active federal posts had limited manpower, a small supply of arms and ammunition, and no vessels capable of moving men quickly to the danger spots, Florida at this time was poorly prepared for a Seminole war. Captain C. F. Smith, commander of Fort Marion at St. Augustine, replied to a request for help, "If I had the means of transportation by water at my instant disposal I would at once send an officer and some men to Indian river to procure intelligence but the only boat we have at all fit for such a purpose is one of the Vera Cruz surf boats without mast or sail."[24] Abandoning their livestock and crops the settlers fled to the posts, ignorant of how poorly prepared the military was.

When he learned of the two attacks, Secretary of War George W. Crawford acted quickly and decisively. Major General David E. Twiggs took command of a force that would grow to 1,400 men, and the state of Florida called into service two companies of mounted volunteers to guard the frontier line of settlements.[25] Crawford told Twiggs that he should try to mediate with the Seminoles for a peaceful removal, but if negotiations failed, Twiggs should undertake forceful removal.

Two whites did not panic in this crisis and resorted to diplomacy rather than military action. Major Morris, commander of Fort Brooke, was quick to point out that his two interpreters—Sampson, a black, and John, a Cuban-American—could not give assistance because they had helped the whites during the 1835–42 war and now refused to venture into the reserve. Sending troops to capture the murderers without the services of an interpreter would be useless, for no one could talk to the Seminoles. Upon the approach of the soldiers they would retreat to the swamps to fight an indefinite defensive conflict, and only a war of extermination would bring about their forcible removal. Morris noted that "since the treaty made by General Macomb in 1839, there has been a great want of confidence in the government and its agents . . . and from that time to the 'patched up' peace made by General Worth in 1842 they were indiscriminately grabbed and under false pretenses shuffled off to Arkansas."[26]

The Seminole emigration agent, Captain John Casey, also did his best to settle the crisis in a peaceful manner. In a previous attempt to arrange a conference with Billy Bowlegs, Casey had left peace signs in spots along the coast where they might be found, and Bowlegs had responded by placing a white flag decorated with heron feathers on a tall pole from which a string of white beads and a twist of tobacco dangled. Felipe Bermundez, Casey's guide, found the pole left at the south end of Sarasota Bay near his deserted fishing hut.[27] When Bermundez informed Casey about his find, a white flag and message stating that the federal authorities wanted to meet with Bowlegs was left at the door of the hut. Bowlegs answered by sending three envoys carrying a white flag and an account of what actually had taken place.

Captain Casey traveled by boat to Sarasota Bay to meet with the Seminoles and to make arrangements for a parley between Twiggs and Bowlegs. Felipe Bermundez had left signals indicating that the message of the white flag would be answered by the time of the next full moon, and when Casey arrived on September 3, 1849, in a sloop, he saw three Seminoles signaling him to come ashore. The next day Casey learned from a runner, Fuss Escha, the names of at least five who had taken part in the attacks and that the killings had been committed without knowledge or consent of most of the tribe.

In a September 18 meeting arranged by Casey and Bowlegs, General Twiggs met with several Seminole leaders aboard the steamer *Colonel Clay* anchored in Charlotte Harbor. Bowlegs promised to deliver five renegades to the whites at another session in thirty days at the same place, and on the following day Kapiktoosootsee, representing Sam Jones, gave his approval.[28] A reporter described Bowlegs at the meeting with Twiggs: "His beard (head) was enveloped in a red shawl, surmounted with white feathers, encircled with a silver band, the crescents of the same material suspended from his neck, to which was appended a large silver medal, with brackets a likeness of President Van Buren on its face; his throat was thickly covered with strands of large blue beads and he also wore bracelets of silver over the sleeves of his hunting shirt."[29]

Almost a month later the *Colonel Clay* with Twiggs and Casey aboard arrived at Charlotte Harbor two days ahead of schedule and found that the Seminoles had been awaiting their arrival for nine days. On October 18 Billy Bowlegs came aboard and informed Twiggs that three of the murderers were being held, another had been killed while attempting to escape, and the fifth had made a successful escape.

The next day Bowlegs and twenty warriors boarded the *Colonel Clay* with the three prisoners and the severed hand of the fourth to prove that he had been killed.[30] Yo-ho-lo-chee, a member of Sam Jones's band who was identified by Mrs. McCullough as one of the attackers, had almost been captured while asleep, but he had heard the Seminoles' approach and fled with his rifle. One shot from the pursuers hit his right hand, wounding him and causing him to drop the gun. The damaged rifle with blood on it was brought back as evidence to show to the whites.

The three alleged murderers were chained and led away, and the other whites went below, leaving Twiggs, an interpreter, and the Seminole leaders together in a cabin.[31] Twiggs told the Seminoles that he had been ordered to remove them from Florida and would pay them at so much a head to leave the state. Assinwar was first to respond:

> We did not expect this talk. When you began this new [removal] matter, I felt as if you had shot me. I would rather be shot. I am old, and I will not leave my country. General Worth said he spoke for your President, too—that he was authorized to make peace and leave us quiet in our country; and that so long as our people preserved the treaty, yours would. For many years you have had no cause to complain; and lately, when a few bad young men broke the law, a thing that cannot be prevented among any people, did we not hasten to make atonement? We met you as soon as we could, and promised to give ample satisfaction; and from that day we have not rested. We have killed one of our people, and have brought three others to be killed by you, and we will bring the fifth. There has been much trouble and grief; but we have done justice, and we came here confident that you would be satisfied. Now, when you ask us to remove, I feel as though you had killed me, too. I will not go, nor will our people. I want no time to think or talk about it, for my mind is made up.[32]

Billy Bowlegs concluded the meeting with these words:

> We have now made more stringent laws than we have ever had before, and I have brought here many young men and boys to see the terrible consequences of breaking our peace laws. I brought them here

that they might see their comrades delivered up to be killed. This business has caused many tears, but we have done justice.

I now pledge you my word that, if you will cease this talk of leaving the country, no other outrage shall ever be committed by my people; or, if ever, hereafter, the worst among my people shall cross the boundary and do any mischief to your people, you need not look for runners, or appoint councils to talk. I will make up my pack and shoulder it, and my people will do the same. We will all walk down to the sea shore, and we will ask but one question: "Where is the boat to carry us to Arkansas?" [33]

It was emigration agent John Casey who was the prime motivator in assuring peace. When he came to Fort Brooke as an invalid in 1848, Casey found that no Seminole leader would trust the military officers. Casey attributed this lack of faith to past seizures under white flags and the influence of the whiskey dealers who wanted the Seminoles to have no contact with stores at Fort Brooke and Fort Myers. At great risk of life and health he was able to gain the trust of almost every Seminole leader who would come to the fort when he wanted their presence; the one exception, Sam Jones, met Casey in the woods. [34] Under Casey's influence the reserve was so safe that cattle could be driven by the cattlemen from the Alafia River to Fort Myers without threat of danger.

Casey tried to be truthful in his relations with the Seminoles. In April 1850, when Twiggs became tired of the fruitless negotiations and wanted to seize Bowlegs as Jesup had Osceola, Casey would decline to have any part in the seizure, warn Bowlegs about the danger, and finally convince Twiggs not to take such action. Lieutenant John Gibbon, who was present with Casey at Fort Brooke, described relations between Casey and the Seminoles:

There are no human beings on earth possessed of a quicker faculty for (in Western phraseology) "sizing up" a man placed in authority over them, than Indians. Innately honest themselves, they will detect in a very few days whether or not their agent is honest and disposed to fairness in conducting their affairs. He speedily finds out by observation, not only the honesty or dishonesty of an agent, but as to whether he is just, fair and zealous in his conduct of affairs.

When once his confidence is gained, he is as truthful and faithful as a little child. On the contrary, if the agent is not one calculated to inspire this kind of confidence, he can never gain it, and will always be looked upon with suspicion and fear; and when despairing of getting their rights in any other way, the Indians conclude to go to war, the first one on whom they wreak their vengeance will, in all probability, be the agent himself.

Casey early made it a matter of principle *never* to deceive them, never to promise a thing he was not able to fulfill, or never to allow them to first discover his inability to carry out a promise when circumstances took out of his hands the power to do so, but to warn them beforehand of his inability to do what he had promised. In this way he won their unbounded confidence in his honesty and integrity.[35]

Federal authorities had a threefold plan to remove all of the Seminoles from Florida that included large financial inducements, a strong military presence, and the negotiating skill of delegates from the West. Troops poured into Florida, and roads, bridges, and forts were constructed from the Manatee River to the Indian River. Twiggs listed the new and planned posts in an October 1849 letter: a post near the mouth of the Manatee; Fort Hamer on the Manatee; Fort Crawford fifteen miles from Hamer; Fort Myakka; Fort Chokkonickla on Peace River; Fort Gardiner on the Kissimmee; a post on Lake Tohopekaliga; Fort Gatlin; Fort Pierce on the Indian River; Fort Dallas at Key Biscayne; and two or three posts between Indian River and Kissimmee.[36] After the crisis had passed, almost all of these forts, with the exception of Fort Meade (not listed by Twiggs) would be abandoned by the military.

With $100,000 set aside for removal, army officers were able to offer as much as $10,000 to prominent leaders, $500 to each male, $100 to each woman and child, full subsistence for a year, payment for all property left in Florida, and proper clothing, food, and use of a physician for the trip.[37] It was the most ever offered to an American Indian tribe for removal to the West.

To impress the Seminoles with accounts of the good life in Indian Territory, a delegation of eleven Seminoles including Halleck Tustenuggee, two black interpreters—Jim Factor and Joe Riley—and Seminole subagent Marcellus DuVal made the trip from Indian Territory via New Orleans to Florida. In a council preceding the trip Wildcat tried to influence the members of the delegation to convey a secret message in which the Florida Seminoles were to be told to resist removal as long as possible so they could obtain land on the Rio Grande some distance from the Creeks.

In Tampa the delegation went into nearby fields to collect root medicines and to secure a supply of deer meat before traveling to the Peace River and meeting with the Seminoles. After a period of negotiations

Kapiktoosootsee, a Mikasuki subchief, promised to migrate with his followers but requested protection for his people, for Sam Jones and others threatened with death anyone who wanted to move west. Twiggs promised him that he and his people would be given protection and that they would be paid in gold as they came aboard the ships bound for New Orleans. On February 28, 1850, seventy-four Seminoles, including those in Kapiktoosootsee's band and the three that had been surrendered by Bowlegs, climbed aboard the *Fashion* at Fort Hamer on the Manatee River, where John Casey paid them for their personal surrender and for possessions left in Florida $15,953—$212.50 each.[38]

Meanwhile Bowlegs, the delegation from Indian Territory, and Twiggs discussed removal on January 21 and 22, 1850, at Fort Chokkonickla. During these discussions Bowlegs claimed that he wanted to leave Florida, yet after stalling for several months, he admitted to Casey in a meeting at Fort Myers that he had been afraid that if he objected to removal, Twiggs would have seized him.[39] By the middle of April Twiggs reported to Washington that there was no hope of further removal by peaceful means.

Two incidents led the Seminoles to break off all negotiations and flee toward the Big Cypress Swamp. In March 1850 Holahteelmathloochee, a Muskogee, and Is-haiah-taikee, a Mikasuki, came along to Fort Hamer with the Kapiktoosootsee emigrating party to trade with the whites but were shipped to New Orleans without Casey's knowledge. At the same time a detachment of mounted men commanded by Captain Britton of the Seventh Infantry moved into the reserve as far as Fisheating Creek before being stopped by order of Twiggs.

The people of Florida began to assess the work done by the federal and state authorities during the Seminole scare of 1849. Although the state of Florida could not afford it, $28,000 had been spent in putting state troops into the field. An editorial in the St. Augustine paper reflected the anger of some whites:

Last fall, one thousand five hundred troops were sent here against Indians to coax one hundred and thirty assassins to give up five of number and used two months to deliberate. Nine months time was wasted. Millions of dollars [were used] to bribe 70–80 old men, women and children and three murderers out of Florida. The murderers are set free in the west. We can expect nothing from a Federal government committed to peaceful removal and [look] only to our state legislature. Florida Indians should be outlawed and [a] reward [offered] of $1,000 for

[a] man dead or alive and $500 for [a] live woman and child. Thus, people could still hunt them . . . soldiers not worth $7 per month. We need thousands of . . . hunters.[40]

Another crisis developed on August 6, 1850, with the disappearance of Daniel Hubbard, an orphan who lived on the farm of Jesse Sumner near the boundary of Benton and Orange counties.[41] Although Sumner had seen and heard signs of Seminoles in the neighborhood—their fires and a gunshot—he had sent the boy to the nearby farm of Edward Crews to drive cattle to the Sumner farm. When Hubbard's horse returned to the farmhouse without saddle or bridle, Edward Crews, Wiley Mobley, Hiram Brick, and Sumner searched the area and determined the boy had been seized by the Seminoles.[42]

Several months later, after aroused citizens began to pressure their representatives in Tallahassee and Washington, Seminole emigration agent Captain John Casey received a letter from the secretary of war telling him to demand the surrender of all Seminoles who had taken part in the seizure of the boy. If this were not done, the president of the United States would hold the whole tribe responsible for the murder.[43]

By January 1851 Casey was able to contact Bowlegs and learn the names of three of the killers of Daniel Hubbard—Pahosee, Chiffu-Yahlosehee, and Kifsu Hajo—and arrange for a council with the Seminoles on April 13.[44] Casey demanded delivery of the three, and Billy promised to bring them to him as soon as possible. In the council on April 13, Casey, T. K. Walbridge, and interpreter Ben Bruno met with Bowlegs, Assinwar, and three others. Bowlegs was not able to deliver the three murderers at this meeting and indicated that if he were not careful in his approach, they would escape. He wanted another meeting ten or twelve miles away at Cabbage Key, but Casey told him that the Seminoles had failed to appear at two previous meetings scheduled there. In a conversation in English with Casey, Bowlegs suggested that at the coming Green Corn Dance, the three be given much whiskey so that they could be seized without much trouble.[45]

Bowlegs at this time was in a difficult situation, for he had promised to leave Florida if the three alleged murderers were not surrendered, and yet they probably were from Chipco's band—a group not under Bowlegs's control. Finally Iowaneah Hajo and Nokas Hajo, message carriers, reported to Casey that in a council held near Assinwar's home Chipco had decided to surrender the possible killers and that the three should be arrested when they came to trade.[46] The three visited Walbridge's store in Fort Myers and were finally arrested on May 17, 1851, nearly nine months after the murder. They were delivered by Casey to civil authorities in Tampa, and on May 19 the sloop *Kozak* carried them and six whites, including Walbridge, to Tampa, where the Seminoles were turned over to the justice of the peace, Simon Turman, the next day.[47] The prisoners, who were rather talkative, claimed that Chipco did not like them and that men from Chipco's band had murdered the boy. Casey believed that the three—Pahosee, 50; his son Chiffu-Yahlosehee, 19; and Kifsa Hajo, 20—were scapegoats and that Chipco and three of his followers did the actual killing.[48]

A terrible event brought an end to the affair. After the three had tried to escape from the Hillsborough County jail at the corner of Waters and Washington streets in Tampa, Constable William A. Campbell, using harsh language, chained them in their cell. At noon on May 23, 1851, the three were found hanging from the bars of their cell. One who was found to be still alive was not cut down until the next day, when he had died. According to Casey many citizens believed that the Seminoles had been murdered by Sheriff B. G. Hagler, Constable Campbell and James L. Whidden, Campbell's son-in-law and brother of Dempsey Whidden, killed in the Payne's Creek attack.[49]

After the tension had ebbed, Captain Casey proposed a plan for the eventual removal of the Seminoles from Florida. He urged meetings between leaders of both races so that each would fully understand the other's point of view. Most generous terms to leave the peninsula should then be offered. If they were refused, the military and Creek warriors should use force, with a large cash reward offered for each Seminole captured and removed.[50]

Before Casey's plan could be examined in detail, an "Indian removal expert" was hired by the federal government to bring a fresh approach to the problem. General Luther Blake was appointed by Secretary of the Interior Alexander Stuart to do with the Seminoles in Florida what he had accomplished with the Cherokees in Georgia—successful removal.[51] Authorized to offer $800 cash to each adult male and $450 to each woman and child who would emigrate, it seemed that Blake with his great self-confidence would accomplish the job. On May 8, 1851, he met with the commander of Fort Myers, Colonel John Winder, and Casey but decided that a trip was needed to Indian Territory where adequate interpreters could be secured.[52] He returned to Florida with a delegation of Seminoles by March 1852. The delegation was able to meet with many Seminoles, including Chipco and Sam Jones who lived in remote areas, and by July 1852 some sixteen who either were captured or had surrendered were sent to Egmont Key in Tampa Bay to await removal.

After conferring with Bowlegs at Fort Myers on July 17–23, 1852, and receiving the usual refusal to consider removal, Blake decided that a trip to Washington with the Seminoles would improve the situation. According to John Casey, Bowlegs went with Blake to Washington for two reasons: to have the Worth Agreement of 1842 confirmed so that it would serve as concrete evidence that the Seminoles could remain in Florida and to obtain payment for blacks owned by Bowlegs that were taken by Blake. Bowlegs had been given no authority by the Seminoles to sign any agreement, and few of his people knew that he had made the trip. Commissioner of Indian Affairs Luke Lea pressed Bowlegs hard for compliance with the Treaty of Payne's Landing with little success. When Lea asked Bowlegs to speak to a group of whites, he declined, saying that he had a bad cold.[53] President Millard Fillmore gave Bowlegs a medal, and perhaps in response to this gesture he and three other Seminoles, Nokose Emathla, Toslatchee Emathla, and Chocote Tustenuggee signed an agreement in which they promised to leave Florida and to persuade the others to follow their example.[54]

Blake took the Seminoles on an extended tour of the East that included visits to Baltimore, Philadelphia, and New York. The visit to New York City was described by a reporter:

> Our artist has presented us below a very fine and lifelike picture of an Indian party from the western wilds as they lately appeared in New York. The party consisted of the famous Billy Bowlegs, six Indian chiefs and an interpreter. Billy is himself a short, stout-built and quite ordinary looking man of about forty years of age and was clad in a calico frock, leggings and a belt or two and a sort of short cloak. On his head he wore a kind of turban enclosed in a broad silver band and surmounted by a profusion of black ostrich feathers . . . the whole delegation appears to look up to Billy Bowlegs as their leader and he is not at all modest in the matter . . . he now pretends that he is willing and in fact desirous to emigrate: he says game is getting scarce in Florida and he thinks he can do much better in the west.[55]

Later a reporter for the *Tampa Herald* interviewing Bowlegs found he thought that "steamboat travel was good, trains go very fast, the 'Great White Father' looked young and New York had many people."[56]

"Billy Bowlegs" and his Retinue, New York, 1852. Bowlegs is second from right. Courtesy of the Florida State Archives, Tallahassee.

Once the travelers had returned to Florida they repudiated the promises made in Washington. Casey accused Blake of making false promises to them and was fired as a result.[57] When it became apparent to all that Blake had failed in his endeavors, however, he was replaced by Casey in July 1853. Blake shortly presented the Treasury Department with bills totaling $47,797.39, or $1,405 for each of the thirty-four Seminoles he had lured from the Everglades; only part of the request was honored.[58]

Under authority of a measure passed by the legislature January 20, 1851, Governor Thomas Brown appointed Benjamin Hopkins commander of the Florida militia. As part of his duties Hopkins played an active role in Seminole removal, capturing both Seminoles and animals that had moved beyond the reserve's unmarked boundaries. In a January 1852 patrol Captain Aaron Jernigan and five men captured 120 hogs near the headquarters of the St. Johns River.[59] During the next month Jernigan captured a man, his wife and child, and an older woman near the south end of Lake Tohopekaliga, but the man, woman, and child escaped, leaving the old woman in a hut where she committed suicide. Accompanied by fifty men General Hopkins moved into the area between Lakes Monroe and Kissimmee, where he captured several women and one man.[60] After these patrols state authorities decided to furlough the militia on December 13, 1852. Hopkins's activities cost the state $40,000, sent some women and one man to Indian Territory, captured 140 hogs, caused the suicide of one woman, and made some militiamen very sick from diseases contracted in the swamps. The patrols of the troops may have forced the outsiders to move back into the reserve.

Florida's two senators and several representatives in Congress began to pressure federal authorities to secure removal. President Millard Fillmore, in his final message to Congress, recommended that more money was needed to survey Florida land and to remove the Seminoles.[61] Senator Stephen Mallory tried to obtain immediate federal funds when he attached an amendment to the army appropriations bill providing for active service upon presidential request by the Florida militia, but the amendment was defeated by western senators.[62]

After Casey regained his position as emigration agent, he secured the assistance of another delegation from the West. John Jumper, Tuliss Hadjo (Son of Sam Jones), Kapiktoosootsee, Jim Factor, George Factor, and nine others visited several camps but could not persuade a single Seminole to leave Florida. Still trying hard, Casey sent Billy Bowlegs and others on another trip to Washington and New York, but this time Bowlegs said that he would not leave Florida under any conditions.[63]

In August 1854 Secretary of War Jefferson Davis decided upon a program that forced the Seminoles to make a show of resistance and bring about the final conflict. Features of the plan, which was detailed in a letter sent to Senator Stephen Mallory, stipulated the imposition of a trade embargo, the survey and sale of land in southern Florida, and an increased military presence to protect the settlers. Davis concluded by stating that if the Seminoles did not present themselves for removal, the military would use force.[64] Within a short time new posts were opened, older ones reactivated, roads rebuilt, and patrols made their way from Fort Myers and Fort Dallas deep into the Everglades and the Big Cypress Swamp.[65]

7
The Final War, 1855–1858

y November 1855 there were 81 troops at Fort Capron (near present-day West Palm Beach), 247 at Fort Brooke, 168 at Fort Dallas and 217 at Fort Myers—a force that outnumbered the male Seminoles by at least four to one.[1] At a council held during the fall of 1855 on the east side of Taylor's Creek northeast of Lake Okeechobee, the Seminoles decided that whenever a suitable opportunity presented itself, they would attack. Probably the Sam Jones element took the initiative in this matter; according to one source, Chipco opposed the use of force.[2]

Military authorities ordered First Lieutenant George L. Hartsuff of the Second Artillery, who had led several patrols through the Big Cypress Swamp, along the Lake Okeechobee shoreline, and in adjacent areas, to move through the swamp. He was to take note of Seminole fields and towns but not to provoke any Seminoles he might encounter. The patrol left Fort Myers on December 7, 1855, equipped with two mule-drawn wagons and composed of one officer, two noncommissioned officers, and eight privates. It moved through a wide area that encompassed swamps, abandoned forts, corn fields, and three deserted villages, including the one inhabited by Billy Bowlegs and his band. When the troops left the Bowlegs village on December 18, a private may have carried along with him a bunch of bananas.[3] On the evening of December 19 the patrol made camp in a grove of pine trees near Bonnet Pond, where Hartsuff told the men that they would start their return to Fort Myers on the next day. Although no extra precautions were taken that night, the signs of abandoned and burned Fort Simon Drum and Fort Shackleford and deserted Seminole villages should have been cause for alarm.

Early in the morning of Thursday, December 20, 1855, while the men were packing and getting ready to saddle their horses and load the equipment into the two wagons, forty Seminoles led by Billy Bowlegs attacked the camp. Some of the men fled into the tall grass. Others were able to return the Seminoles' fire, but six whites were either killed or wounded. In his tent awaiting breakfast when the attack came, Hartsuff returned fire with his Colt revolver. Wounded in the arm, chest, and abdomen, he then crawled to a pond, where he was able to conceal himself.[4] When the return fire slackened, the Seminoles moved into the campground area, where they killed and scalped those still alive, cut the throats of the mules, looted, burned the wagons, and took away five horses. Four wounded and three uninjured soldiers made their way to Fort Myers sixty miles away and gave the alarm. Major Lewis Arnold and his men from Fort Denaud arrived at the scene on December 25 and buried the four bodies. (Recovered from his wounds, Hartsuff was able to lead a patrol by February 27 and would fight in several major battles in the Civil War. When he died in 1874, an autopsy revealed that the 1855 wound in the chest had been the major cause of the 1874 death from pneumonia.)[5]

When the news of the attack was carried to Tampa by persons aboard the *Texas Ranger,* citizens held a public meeting at two o'clock on December 24 in the frame Hillsborough County Courthouse where the militia was organized for action. There William B. Hooker, a prominent cattleman, was elected commander of the militia, and others were elected to posts as captains and lieutenants. Hooker with forty men from Tampa moved to the Peace River area, where volunteers were recruited and placed in various posts along the settlement line: twenty men at Fort Meade, twenty-five at Fort Hartsuff, sixteen at Fort Green, and twenty-four at Fort Hooker. A company commanded by Captain Leroy Lesley made its way to the mouth of the Peace River.

Acting under authority of an act passed by the Florida legislature in January 1853, Governor James Broome tried to organize as many volunteer companies as possible to defend the settlers. Because of the precarious condition of state finances, Broome had to check with federal authorities concerning expenditures for these forces. By January 12, 1856, he had accepted six companies and had ordered them to protect the frontier. Composed of citizens from Manatee, Hillsborough, and Hernando counties and armed, equipped, and rationed with the assistance of private funds, these units were offered to Secretary of War Davis, who accepted only three mounted companies and two infantry units.[6] Since Governor Broome believed that the number of men mustered into federal service was insufficient to meet the needs of a Seminole war, he retained in active service under state control the companies commanded by Captains Francis M. Durrance, Leroy C. Lesley, William H. Kendrick, and Abner D. Johnson and the detachment under Lieutenant John Addison—a total of 400 men.[7] On February 4, 1856, Broome appointed General Jesse Carter as "a special agent of the State of Florida without military rank" for service on the frontier.

With battlefield odds of fourteen to one, the outcome of the war never should have been in doubt. The federal troops in south and central Florida numbered 800; state troops accepted for federal service, 260; and state troops in state service, 400—for a total of 1,460. Yet the federal troops showed little interest in pursuing the Seminoles as they had done in the previous war, and the federal commander, Colonel John Monroe, had poor communication with General Jesse Carter, special agent for the Florida militia. Carter told half of the mobilized militia personnel in February 1856 to plant and cultivate crops while the other half pursued the Indians, cutting his fighting force by half.[8] In addition, the Florida cattlemen would not join the infantry or boat parties, preferring to serve in the mounted volunteers. The Tampa paper pointed out that mounted troops usually made their patrols in open country where it was easier to travel but where they could be seen by the Seminoles.[9]

Although Billy Bowlegs was present in the Hartsuff attack, it was Oscen Tustenuggee who organized many of the initial war parties. Oscen and his two brothers, Micco Tustenuggee and Old Tustenuggee, were Mikasukis who had married Muskogee women and consequently moved to the Muskogee villages along Fisheating Creek.[10] One of the first attacks that they or Sam Jones organized took place on January 6, 1856, and was directed at a farm on the Miami River six miles south of Fort Dallas. Peter Johnson and Edward Farrell were killed while digging coontie.[11] As a result of this attack all of the pioneer families in the neighborhood went inside Fort Dallas. When the fort proved crowded, some moved by boat to Key West.

The next attack took place near Fort Denaud on the Caloosahatchee River, where Major Lewis Arnold commanded a garrison of 150 men. Frustrated because they could not attack the well-guarded fort in retaliation for the burning of their village, Oscen and his warriors waited for another opportunity. Since fires were constantly burning inside the fort to ward off the mosquitoes and for cooking purposes, wood-cutting parties moved out daily from the enclosed fort. The Seminoles attacked one such party composed of a corporal and five privates on January 18, 1856, and killed all but one. They shot twelve mules but left the wagons and horses unharmed. The one survivor identified Oscen or Okchum as the leader of the twenty or more attackers.[12]

Defended by militia units that were almost totally unorganized during the first several months, the scattered settlements in the lower Tampa Bay area offered tempting targets for the Seminoles. One observer described Kendrick's and Johnson's companies in January 1856: "Just imagine if you please that you see 124 men dressed in common material of various colors and ages, long beards and smooth chins armed with a variety of blunder busses mounted on any sort of horse from the poor pony to the large old rip—a few mules and a few men riding on one side."[13]

Taking advantage of such poor defense, Seminole raiding parties killed George Owen and burned the William Whitaker home at present-day Sarasota, ambushed a boat patrol on Turner River, and attacked a settlement near present-day Miami. Another raid was directed at the sugar plantation home of Dr. Joseph and Hector Braden located on the banks of the Manatee in the center of present-day Bradenton. The large, square building made of tabby—a composition of shell, lime, and sand—was because of its sturdy construction a fire- and bulletproof fortress. Once Dr. Braden learned of the war, he followed a routine at sunset in which he warned the family, servants, and guests to stay within the house, closed the shutters, and barred the doors. On the night of March 31, 1856, with the family and guests seated for the evening meal, a maid heard a rap at the front door. When she peered at the door from the upstairs window, she identified the people at the door as Seminoles carrying guns. She warned Dr. Braden, who told his guests, Freeman Chaires of Tallahassee and Reverend T. T. Sealey, to move with him to the second floor, where he called to the Seminoles from the window. They replied by firing at the window, narrowly missing his head. Returning the fire with his shotgun, Braden was able to hit one Seminole on the porch.[14]

Driven from the Braden mansion the raiders looted the nearby slave quarters and began their return to their village through the thousand-acre Braden plantation toward a network of small streams. They took with them seven blacks—mostly women and children—and three mules to carry their captives and booty. The mules and captives rendered pursuit easy, and with such a burden the Seminoles could not make a quick return to their village. Not until early in the morning of the following day, April 1, did persons from Braden's plantation notify the people of Manatee that an attack had taken place. William Whitaker rode seventy miles in four days to notify the Florida militia unit at Peace River, where Captain John Addison gathered a small force and pursued the Seminoles.

The Seminoles usually looked good in offensive operations but sometimes were ineffective in defending against white attacks. During the Second Seminole War they had learned how to delay a pursuit by putting up a fierce counter fire or by moving to one flank so that the women and children could escape on the other. Yet few guards were posted around their camps, and dawn attacks by the whites usually resulted in the capture of some prisoners and the burning of homes and fields. Since a new generation of warriors had grown up since 1842, lessons learned during the conflict had been forgotten, and Oscen and his young warriors were caught napping.

Certain that no troops could be pursuing them, the ten or more warriors and their black prisoners had killed a stray cow and barbecued it on the banks of the Big Charley Apopka Creek. While the Seminoles and their captives were resting and eating barbecued beef, the militiamen were able to race along the damp sand that deadened the sound of hoofbeats and surprise them. The Seminoles lost two warriors, seven black prisoners, three mules, and one pony in the engagement, which was marked by sloppy tactics on their part and good pursuit by the militia. Oscen Tustenuggee, the leader on this raid, lost his pony but was able to escape.[15] Two scalps taken by the militiamen were placed on exhibition, one at Tampa and the other at Manatee. Dave Townsend, who captured Oscen's pony, rode the animal during the length of his service as a militiaman.

In April and May the Seminoles resumed their raids against the frontier people. In April they struck abandoned houses along the upper Manatee River and killed John Carney, a ferryboat operator, who was plowing in his field near present-day Bloomingdale. The homes of Hague and Whiddon on the Alafia River were burned, and Seminole tracks were discovered within a mile of Tampa. The people of Tampa and of neighboring areas became concerned; men began to carry guns as they made their daily rounds.

In May, when the Seminoles struck again at the scattered settlements, they traveled some distance northward of their previous raids. At the tiny outpost of Darby, in the central part of present-day Pasco County, lived Captain Robert Bradley, a veteran of the Second Seminole War, his wife, several children, and his slaves. On the evening of May 14, 1856, two of the younger children were playing in the passageway between the two sections of the log cabin house, when a band of fifteen Seminoles opened fire on them. The frantic mother attempted to save her screaming youngsters and became a target herself. Rising from his sick bed, Bradley was unable to join his older sons and return the gunfire before the two younger children were killed.[16] Although news of the attack was carried to a militia post and the militiamen hurried to the Bradley homestead, the Seminoles escaped, leaving behind the body of one of the band killed by Bradley. That they had attacked Darby while bypassing other more likely targets seemed odd, but a possible reason for the attack was that Captain Bradley had killed the brother of Tiger Tail during the Second Seminole War.

During the spring of 1856 patrols by the militia and the regulars made little contact with the hostiles. A combined force of regulars and militiamen under the command of Colonel John Monroe moved through the Big Cypress in April but saw no Seminoles. Militia companies in federal and state service searched the central and western sides of the peninsula without success, since they did not possess boats. During April Major Lewis Arnold found Seminoles near Bowlegs Town and fought a six-hour battle in which four regulars were killed and three wounded before the Seminoles withdrew to a nearby cypress area.[17] One young officer who fought in this battle noted that the Seminoles whooped and yelled loudly during the fray, came back twice to resume the fighting, and removed the roofs from the chickees in Bowlegs's village so that the buildings could not be easily burned.

On May 17 Seminoles who were probably from the band that raided Darby ambushed a wagon train on the road from Fort Brooke to Fort Fraser on Lake Hancock in present-day Polk County. While the mule-drawn three-wagon train stopped for water at a creek, the Seminoles fired from concealment behind nearby pine trees, killing three men.[18] As a result of this ambush, mail and stagecoach service between Tampa and other points was discontinued until military protection was provided.

A series of battles in June 1856 on and near the Peace River south of Fort Meade would bring an end to Oscen Tustenuggee's leadership and to the raids into Hillsborough and Polk counties. While their homes were being built, Willoughby Tillis, his wife and three children, and Thomas Underhill were living in a make-do house two miles from Fort Meade. At dawn on June 14 Mrs. Tillis, in the cowpen with one of her children, noticed as she began to milk one of the cows that the animals appeared frightened, especially near a pile of rails behind the cow pen. Mrs. Tillis then saw behind the rails a number of Seminoles crawling along the ground. When they opened fire, she raced to the house with her child and was able to close the door and alert the other members of the household.

The Seminoles now sent a heavy volley of gunfire against the house, which somehow did not kill or wound any of the persons within. Although the walls of the cabin were not plastered or sealed (such features being unknown in pioneer Florida), for once the gaps between the logs stood the inmates of the cabin in good stead. Safely barricaded behind the heavy logs, the defenders fired their rifles through the cracks and kept the enemy at bay.

A small militia unit composed of cowboys—Lieutenant Alderman Carlton and six others—which had been stationed at Fort Meade to guard the women and children, heard the sound of rifles. "Boys, there's work for us over in the woods," said their leader, and they mounted their horses and dashed full speed to the scene.[19] The Seminoles retreated to a nearby hammock, where Carlton and two of his men were killed in a skirmish and two others wounded.[20] More soldiers followed the Seminoles to another hammock but retreated after a sudden rain to obtain a supply of dry powder.

Two days later, on June 16, Lieutenant Streaty Parker and nineteen militiamen from Fort Fraser caught a force of Seminoles by surprise in the swampland along the Peace River, probably at a campsite on the banks of the river. Some were cut down by the gunfire, and others tried to cross the river, but most were able to return fire at the whites.[21] Oscen Tustenuggee was killed in the water. His brother saved his own life by diving into the water from a horse. When the skirmish developed into one that could have resulted in more serious losses to the whites than the two killed and three wounded, Parker ordered a pullback to Booker's Place. The militia estimated as many as twenty Seminoles killed, but the Seminoles admitted to a loss of only four warriors—two killed on shore and two in the water—and two wounded.[22]

At first most settlers believed that a white victory had been realized at Peace River, but after more serious thought they saw defects in the militia system. Captain William Hooker's unit at Fort Meade should have been at full strength, but most of the men were away hunting cattle and others were at Manatee and Horse Creek awaiting an attack that did not materialize. The undermanned militia detail led by Parker had been forced to withdraw under heavy fire, and the Seminoles had held the scene of battle. Captain Robert Bradley had stated the problem earlier in a letter to Jefferson Davis:

I am a citizen of Hernando County and am opposed to the manner and mode in which troops were mustered into service for protection of frontier. There are four companies in service. Troops are allowed to stay at home and work farms. Eight to ten men pretend to scout a day or two and then go home—no protection at all against Indians. It would be better if Col. J. Monroe did the defending and this class of citizens were out of the way.[23]

Davis later pointed out to Governor Broome that the volunteers in service took advantage of their position to become idle, to drink, and to steal from those they were supposed to protect.[24] Even the officers would not file reports concerning numbers, purchases, or services.[25] Yet in the Peace River battle the Seminoles had lost one leader who could lead his warriors against the settlements, and from this time to the end of the war they would fight a defensive battle, making a few attacks upon isolated homes and unwary persons and offering tough resistance to the militia and regulars who moved into Seminole land.

In September 1856 Brevet Brigadier General William S. Harney was appointed commander of federal troops in Florida. Harney had learned about Seminole tactics, having fled for his life in his underwear when in 1839 Seminoles attacked his camp during the Macomb truce and having later tracked one of the bands into the Everglades and hanged Chakaika, the leader. When he assumed command in Florida, Harney wanted a manned line of forts across Florida; troops moving deep into Seminole country from these forts would force the Seminoles either to surrender or to fight.[26] Before launching an offensive, however, he tried to negotiate. This attempt failed, with no contacts at all made. He finally ordered active pursuit on January 5, 1857.[27] Although Harney's men captured or defeated few Seminoles, he established an efficient military organization that would benefit his successor, Colonel Gustaus Loomis, when Harney was transferred to Kansas thence to Utah in April 1857.

Harney planned a full-scale campaign in which the Seminoles would be constantly harassed by patrols that would move deep into their country. These plans were outlined in a memorandum sent to Washington in March 1857:

1. Confine Indians to Big Cypress Swamp and Everglades where it will be impossible to live during wet seasons. They will try to occupy islands of coast and high country to north and east of Lake Okeechobee. They can be captured at those positions. Disposal of troops should be as follows: Six companies in boats on Gulf Coast from

Cape Sable to Punta Rassa. They can examine whole area and go into interior.

2. On Atlantic Coast. Two companies at Fort Dallas in boats move from Cape Sable to Fort Dallas. Enter Everglades when water rises.
3. Company at Fort Jupiter guard coast from Dallas to Capron in boats visiting islands and rivers.
4. Company in Indian River using boats moved as far up as Smyrna.
5. Two companies on Kissimmee River go to the area south of Lake Okeechobee and enter the Everglades. If Indians are on Kissimmee send only one company.
6. Keep Company of F.M.V. at Fort McRae.
7. Depot One be kept up.
8. F.M.V. troops be kept scouting on way from Fort Brooke to Fort Capron.
9. Indians will endeavor to reach islands of Lake Istokpoga and cultivate crops. One company in boats will render good service there.[28]

Boats for use in Florida inland waters had been planned as early as 1854, when General Thomas S. Jesup had ordered the construction of metallic barges and whaleboats, but it was Harney who made use of the boats. The whaleboats used in Florida were thirty feet long, pointed at both ends, and flat bottomed; they could operate in water twenty-four to thirty-six inches deep. Some persons referred to this type of boat as a gondola or alligator boat, because of its strange shape. Fort Myers, which was the center of operations, had by December 1856 sixteen metal whaleboats and barges, twenty-three Dunham boats, and twenty-four wooden skiffs.[29]

The increased pressure on the Seminoles forced them to make adjustments in their way of life. As in the Second Seminole War their clothes became tattered; their firearms were less accurate, and for ammunition they were reduced to cutting lead pellets from the trees used by the troops for target practice. As one captured woman claimed, surrender was better than fleeing from one swamp to another, but the leaders had decreed death to those who would negotiate with the whites. Chipco's band of Muskogee-speaking Seminoles was most vulnerable to the patrols. Concealment was more difficult along the shores of Lake Okeechobee and the banks of several rivers, including the Kissimmee and the St. Johns. The troops captured Seminoles from these bands living in south central Florida and took them to Egmont Key. (At first Fort Myers served as a detention post but strict control of boats made Egmont Key, an island at the mouth of Tampa Bay, an ideal prisoner-of-war camp.) Rarely would a member of Billy Bowlegs's band be captured, for the Big Cypress Swamp and adjacent coastal islands offered excellent hiding spots.

Whites knew little concerning the location of Sam Jones (Arpeika) and his Mikasuki band during the final years of the Second Seminole War and during the period 1842–60. The small band could move without fear of detection from one camping ground to another in the neighborhood of present-day Miami and Fort Lauderdale. One such camping ground and garden was located along the west bank of Allapattah Creek in Miami; a second camp and adjacent corn fields were located in a hammock six miles northwest of Fort Lauderdale. The headquarters of Sam Jones appear to have been at the ruins of Sam Jones' Old Town on a pine ridge fourteen miles south of Lake Okeechobee, where councils and other meetings were held.[30] So far as can be determined Sam Jones played an important role during the 1842–55 period, but once the war had commenced, little was heard of him or his band.

The withdrawal of Harney and the Fifth Infantry to Utah reduced the federal troops available in Florida to ten companies of the Fourth Artillery and later cut to four companies. Loomis made more efficient use of his remaining manpower by moving units from other forts to Fort Myers; this force was supplemented by guides and boatmen. Loomis organized three forty-five-man companies of volunteers known as boat companies and gave each company flat-bottomed metallic boats that could carry as many as sixteen of the experienced frontier men deep into the shallow swamps, bayous, and creeks of the Everglades and Big Cypress.

During the summer of 1857 the most successful commander of the boat companies was Captain Jacob E. Mickler, who made two trips to Lake Okeechobee in search of Seminole encampments. Mustered into service at Fort Brooke, on the first trip the company carried their boats by wagon to the Kissimmee, where they were launched.[31] Upon arrival at Lake Okeechobee Mickler allotted thirty men among the six boats to search the nearby islands and shores of the lake for Seminole signs. They found shells of freshwater turtles that had been roasted, Seminole tracks, and a large canoe taken from the military.[32] When Mickler climbed a tree to observe the neighborhood, he saw that the leaves of a tree in a nearby hammock had been blackened by smoke from a campfire. Certain that Seminoles were near the camp, he ordered his men to approach the hammock through the tall saw grass. Jim Cook selected ten or twelve men, who moved quickly upon the unsuspecting Seminoles. At this point the rest of the men moved into the camp.

Hastening forward, we found the doughty James Cook standing guard over a half dozen squaws and "pickaninies." He had surprised and captured them, as they were preparing dinner. After hanging the venison pots over the fire, they had taken a rest, and were lounging on a rude scaffolding of poles and cabbage-palm leaves. Some of the squaws attempted to escape by hiding in the tall saw-grass, but a few shots from our rifles soon brought them to terms, and it was an easy matter to find and capture them. The women, although badly frightened, remained sullen and silent, but the "pickaninies" set up a howl that would have done credit to a herd of young hyenas. The poor creatures had been fearfully cut and lacerated, by running through the tall saw-grass, and their faces were, as Jim Cook said, "a reg'lar sight."

Hung over the fire were some brass kettles, in which they had been cooking dinner, when we surprised them. Near by were several baskets woven of wire-grass, full of huckleberries and other wild fruit. Hanging in one of the wigwams were two chiefs' costumes, richly embroidered with beads. Some breast-plates, hammered out of silver dollars, were also found. We made a dash for these, and I was fortunate enough to secure one of these costumes. This consisted of a sort of a waistcoat, a pair of leggings and moccasins, and a sash. Each article was covered with elaborate designs, worked in beads and silk, representing birds, fishes, etc., and must have cost much time and patience.

We were again put on our guard by the sound of defiant yells, coming from the distance, and put ourselves in readiness to withstand an attack, as it was natural to suppose that the warriors, who had left this camp, were returning, and that they would be ready for battle when they came. They did not put in an appearance, however, during our stay.

This island was circular in shape, and contained about an acre. It was surrounded by a belt of timber, which completely hid its occupants from the sight of enemies approaching from the outside. Within this circle, all the timber, with the exception of a few large live oaks and cabbage-palms, had been cleared away, and the ground was in a high state of cultivation. Fine corn, beans, and pumpkins were growing underneath the live oaks; the vines had climbed the trees, and the immense pumpkins hung from the limbs, presenting a strange appearance.

Among our prisoners was a boy about twelve years of age, named E-chepko, whose duty it had been to post himself in a tall hackberry tree, and gave warning, in case of the approach of an enemy. A feeling of complete security had caused him to neglect his duty on this eventful morning, and a surprise and capture was the result.

After satisfying ourselves that the warriors were not coming, as we had expected, preparations were made to carry our prisoners to the boats.[33]

The prisoners were taken to Fort Centre, thence to Fort Myers, and finally to Egmont Key.

Polly, a Seminole woman, served as a guide for Mickler and other patrols moving into the Everglades. Both she and her husband, Chai, had assisted the military during the 1835–42 conflict and had been allowed to remain near Bradenton after the war for their own safety. When the 1855–58 war broke out, Chai committed suicide rather than face the Seminoles again. Polly, however, usually mounted herself at the bow of a boat as it moved through the waterways, enjoying her work as guide; she later married a Cuban-American fisherman from Charlotte Harbor.

In contrast to the relentless pursuit of the Seminoles by Mickler and his men, which was stimulated by large rewards offered for each live Seminole, the regulars did not have their hearts in the struggle. During the summer of 1857 few engaged in combat or captured any Seminoles. Lieutenant Oliver O. Howard noted the peculiar situation in his autobiography:

> Our new department commander in Florida was very active in his operations with a view to close out the war with the Seminoles, but there was no great battle. The regulars had little faith in the war itself. It was frequently remarked by our regular officers: "We haven't lost any Indians." Of course, however, they did their duty, but without much ardor or enthusiasm. It was not the case with the volunteers. They usually had well-selected officers, but the majority of the companies were made up of the roughest element. Very often they would involve in their attacks Indian men, women, and children and take very few prisoners. As far as the Indians were concerned, they behaved very much like the Bashi-bazooks of Turkey. Our department commander did not like the reports that came from this rough campaigning and he made up his mind to try hard to secure some sort of peace with the few remaining Indians in Florida.[34]

The same type of observation was made by Captain Abner Doubleday (of baseball fame), who observed that the Seminoles kept out of his way and allowed him and his men to wander around: "There were only 150 warriors in the whole vast peninsula and it was impossible to surprise them with the material we had principally as I stated German or Irish emigrants who finding themselves penniless in our large cities had enlisted to get bread. The men were wholly ignorant of woodcraft and consequently were no match for the savages." [35]

In another futile attempt to lure the Seminoles from the Big Cypress Swamp, the federal authorities brought Jim Jumper and some other western Seminoles to negotiate with Billy Bowlegs. In August 1857 the steamer *Texas Ranger* carried the group from Tampa to Fort Myers and on to Marco; other boats were able to carry the envoys from Indian Territory several miles along the Caxambas River. The effort was of no avail, however, for Billy Bowlegs was not ready to talk terms. [36]

John Floyd, who had succeeded Jefferson Davis as secretary of war in March 1857, cooperated with Governor Broome to bring about an end to the war by calling into federal service a large enough number of militiamen to saturate southern Florida. Ten companies organized in central and northern Florida joined the regulars, ready for thrusts into Seminole country from Fort Myers and Fort Denaud. By September 1857 Colonel S. St. George Rogers of the Florida militia had under his command 93 officers and 700 men. [37]

In November some progress was reported west of the Okaloacoochee slough with the capture of five women, thirteen children, and assorted items belonging to Billy Bowlegs. [38] Late that month Captain John Parkhill with seventy-five men found a principal stronghold and food supply center of Billy's band near Royal Palm Hammock. Following several trails through cypress forests and prairies, the force discovered a settlement of thirty dwellings and a nearby agricultural tract of forty acres of land, which had been cleared and planted in rice, peas, pumpkins, and potatoes. So thick was the crop of pumpkins that they covered the ground and the nearby trees, but the militiamen destroyed the homes and much of the crops. Nearby were two other settlements containing fifteen and ten or more dwellings and adjacent fields.

The discomforts faced by the militiamen under Colonel Rogers as they moved into the area controlled by Billy Bowlegs were discouraging.

> It was in a field of dense sawgrass about four miles wide. The grass was two feet higher than our heads and was so dense that we could not see a foot ahead of us. One man was selected to break the road so others could pass. No man could endure this task more than five minutes and first one and then the other took turns at pushing in front; the side and shoulders were used in this laborious and painful work. To add to our misery the

sun shone with a terrible force upon us and not a breath of fresh air could reach us. Worse than all, the water was poison and our feet soon felt the effects of it. The men who were grumbling before, lifted their voices and gave vent to some hair-lifting expressions. The volunteers from middle Florida who had never experienced the like before were almost furious. But in time we emerged from the dreadful Ock-Kallowshsootchee and reached Fort Simon Drum.[39]

New Year's Day saw Colonel Rogers moving the healthy men from his regiment plus 192 from several independent companies into the Big Cypress. He divided his little army into three detachments commanded by Major J. L. Dozier, Lesley, and Simeon Sparkman, with Major Dozier directing the entire operation. Several villages and large areas of cultivated fields were discovered and destroyed by the walking and rowing Florida mounted volunteers and U.S. Army artillerymen. The extent of the damage inflicted can be seen in a summary of the drive southeastward from Camp Rogers:

Sparkman finds fields of pumpkins—half roasted, next day discovers 7 horses, boat-tracks, 2 ponies captured. On 31 (Dec.) found another field. Jan. 1 large fields, pumpkins, potatoes, beans, 50 bu. corn, pumpkin and melon seeds, all destroyed. Jan. 2 eight horses, 7 houses, 8–10 bu. corn, 12 houses, 6 houses, fields, 5 houses (Stephens encounter). Village of 40–50 houses which had been burned by Indians themselves. Another village of 50 houses discovered and burned. 10–15 bu. corn, 4 boats destroyed, go to Prophet's Landing 4 mi. N. of Falso Hadjo's Town.[40]

At the same time the militiamen were hitting Bowlegs hard for the first time, negotiations were under way that would end the struggle. On August 7, 1856, representatives of the Creeks and Indian Territory Seminoles signed a treaty in Washington by which the Seminoles were given their own 2,170,000 acres of land in Indian Territory separate from the Creeks', $90,000 for costs of removal to the new reserve, annuities of $3,000 for ten years, and $2,200 for blacksmiths. The sum of $250,000 was to be invested, and 5 percent interest should be paid on an annual per capita basis. The same amount in addition would be invested and distributed in a similar manner when the remaining Seminoles in Florida joined those members of the tribe in Indian Territory.[41] Consequently, another delegation composed of forty Seminoles headed by John Jumper; six Creeks;

Young wife of Billy Bowlegs, 1858. Courtesy of the Florida State Archives, Tallahassee.

Elias Rector, superintendent of Indian affairs for the Southern Superintendency; Samuel Rutherford, the Seminole agent; and William Garrett, the Creek agent, arrived in Florida on January 19, 1858, for negotiations. A niece of Bowlegs released from Egmont Key joined the group at Fort Brooke, where they moved southward by steamer to Fort Myers. Loomis ordered all military action at this time discontinued; patrols ceased, and white flags were posted.

Once at Fort Myers the delegation divided into three groups to move into the interior; one made contact with Bowlegs, as Superintendent Rector reported:

> Yesterday evening about 5 o'clock we were agreeably surprised at discovering a white flag about a mile from us in the edge of cypress [trees]. Upon approaching it we found an Indian of Bowlegs' party and a Negro belonging to Bowlegs. They came into our camp, remained awhile and left this morning. They returned with another Indian, a brother-in-law of Bowlegs and have made an appointment to meet with Jumper bringing Bowlegs with them in four days. I want to move within 12–15 miles of Fort Myers and want all volunteers withdrawn. We will try to meet some of Jones' men before I leave.[42]

By February 27th, Rector had conferred with three other Seminole leaders and matters seemed to be moving along in good fashion.

In a meeting on March 15 thirty-five miles from Fort Myers, Bowlegs, three of his warriors, and five representatives from Assinwar's band listened to the terms offered by Rector: $7,500 to the chief, $1,000 to each of four other leaders, $500 to each warrior, and $100 to each woman and child, paid when the Seminoles boarded the ship at Egmont Key.[43] The Seminoles accepted the offer in a council on March 27 at the same site.

On May 4, 1858, thirty-eight men and eighty-five women and children boarded the *Grey Cloud* at Fort Myers and proceeded to Egmont Key, where forty-one prisoners were moved aboard and sailed for New Orleans; a few escaped when the ship stopped at St. Marks for wood. While awaiting the river steamer that would take him to Indian Territory, Billy Bowlegs enjoyed exploring New Orleans while the rest of the band was confined to a barracks. On May 8 Colonel Loomis issued an order proclaiming the end of hostilities, for he and the other whites believed that there were only 100 Seminoles remaining in Florida, and they had not committed any hostile acts for some time.

In December 1858 Rector, after acquiring the services of Billy Bowlegs for $200, returned to Florida for a final attempt to contact the bands that may have eluded the spring removal delegation. Two bands were contacted and persuaded to remove; on February 15, 1859, seventy-five Seminoles left Florida for the West.[44] A period of uninterrupted peace had finally come for the followers of Chipco, Sam Jones, and isolated families remaining in Florida within the Ten Thousand Islands, the Everglades, and Big Cypress Swamp.

8

Early Contacts and Establishment
of a Reservation

ecuring the surrender of all the Seminoles was an impossible task. The fighting had scattered other bands to the more remote southern parts of the peninsula, and Billy Bowlegs's control was not absolute. Chipco's band of Muskogees, hiding north of Lake Okeechobee, could not be located at all. Ancient Sam Jones, leader of the Mikasukis, refused to negotiate and remained deep in the Everglades. As soon as the *Grey Cloud* had moved into the blue waters of the Gulf of Mexico, the white military organization was rapidly disbanded. The militiamen returned to their homes in the northern part of the state, and the federal forts that had been bases for the troops were closed. Troops from Fort Brooke were sent to Key West and other posts. Fort Myers, Fort Centre, and Fort Denaud were decommissioned. Settlers carried away windows, doors, and other post items for their homes. In March 1862 Governor John Milton appointed Joab Griffin to visit the Seminoles and tell them that Florida and the Confederacy would fully cooperate with them. Griffin was a good appointment, for he had lived at Charlotte Harbor and accompanied Billy Bowlegs on his 1852 Washington visit. It was important that friendship be maintained with the Seminoles, for the cattle upon which the Confederate army depended for food grazed near their camps, and due to good contacts, the Seminoles gave the cattlemen little trouble during the conflict.[1] In December 1862 the legislature passed a measure that provided farming tools and ammunition to the Seminoles and that recommended that an agent and interpreter be appointed for them. After some delay agent Henry Prosens and interpreter John Montes De Oca met with Sam Jones and his followers and were convinced that the Seminoles would remain neutral. Yet, the agent rendered little or no service to them, and Confederate Florida gave them none of the supplies that they sorely needed. When Major Pleasant W. White, the chief commissary of Florida, became worried that his supply of beef might be threatened by the Seminoles, he visited them in late 1863 and found them to be destitute of ammunition and supplies but not in a mood to steal Confederate cattle.[2] At the war's end the Republican party did not attempt to register the Seminoles as voters but did grant them one concession. The 1868 Florida Constitution allowed the Seminoles to place one representative in the house and one in the senate, but as no representative from the tribe appeared, the provision was dropped in the 1885 version.[3]

The widely scattered bands gradually adjusted to peace, although not for many years would the Seminoles lose their fear that the whites wanted to take them away to join their relatives in the West. In 1872 Charlie Tiger, while drunk, told Captain James Armour that Big Tommie had taken part in the killings of four settlers at the home of Peter Shives, eight miles south of New Smyrna, on December 17, 1856. The members of Tiger's and Big Tommie's bands were afraid that the disclosure would lead the federal troops either to kill them or to ship them to Oklahoma, but finally Captain Armour, who was in charge of Jupiter Lighthouse, assured them that he would not tell anybody what he had heard. When the Seminoles were able to hold a council, they banished Charlie Tiger from the tribe for a year and cut the lobe of one of his ears; as a result he was known by the whites as Crop-Eared Charlie.[4] There remained among the Seminoles a sense of fear and dislike for the whites. Children were taught to turn their backs to the whites and to ignore any attempts at friendship. The women were not allowed to talk to white people or even to look at them directly.

Throughout the latter part of the nineteenth century the Seminoles relied upon friendly ranchers to warn them if troops were moving into their neighborhood. Between 1884 and 1900 Mr. and Mrs. Curry, living in present-day Immokalee, earned their livelihood in the cattle business. Each time that a white person traveled through the section, the neighboring Seminoles checked with the Currys as to the visitor's destination and business.[5] As late as the 1920s a virtual riot took place at Madison Square Garden when a speaker joked with a visiting group of Seminoles that they were being moved to Oklahoma. And finally, in 1933, some Seminoles attending a festival in Sarasota panicked when a fleet of boats, including

Coast Guard cutters, approached their camping ground along the bay front.

The largest camp at this time, composed of eight to ten families, was located at Pine Island near present-day Hollywood Reservation. The other camps, scattered throughout interior southern Florida, were much smaller, consisting of extended families whose members cultivated small plots during the summer and hunted from temporary camps for skins and meat during the winter. To prepare the fields the oak trees were girdled to kill them, underbrush cleared, and potatoes, corn, and bananas planted in the rich hammock soil. The Seminoles planted pumpkins at the foot of the girdled dead trees, and the vines climbed to the branches so that yellow and green pumpkins dangled from the limbs.

Chipco's band did a considerable amount of moving about the Florida wilderness during this period. The group lived in the cypress swamps north and east of Lake Okeechobee until 1866, when it moved to the Kissimmee River Valley. The band moved again in 1872–73 to Catfish Lake (Lake Pierce), northeast of Lake Wales in Polk County but migrated from there in 1885 to Lake Rosalie.[6]

Lewis "Grandpa" Griffin, who lived near Chipco's camp in 1880, gave the following account of the Seminoles, retold by his grandson:

> Grandpa says in those days it was not uncommon for a small number of Indians to bring home 10 to 20 deer and 40 to 50 wild turkeys as a result of a day's chase, and invariably his family were included, and received a share of the hunt.
>
> This tribe had their home on the Elisha Davis tract. They planted "wampe" in the low places and raised hogs that compared with those of the best breed today; their sugar cane was planted only once, the roots not dying, and year after year unbelievable crops were cut, stalks averaging in weight over 11 pounds.
>
> Their pumpkins, too, were different from the white man's variety, being planted in low shady places alongside of immense trees, and allowed to run up the trees, where, 50 to 60 feet from the ground, they ripened. These pumpkins were small in size, and very sweet, having taste and flavor of the present Florida yam, and were cooked by the Indians just as potatoes are cooked today.
>
> Corn raised by the Indians was immense, having three or four ears on each stalk, the stalks being 15 to 20 feet high. The Indians made "safky" from the roots of the young palm trees growing in the wilds around the lake. The outer skin was peeled, softened by water, and then rubbed by

hand by the squaws, strained through cloth in barrels, and allowed to
dry. A substance similar to flour resulted, from which the Indians made
a most nutritious and pleasing drink, and also made food balls, or
biscuits, frying these balls.[7]

Corn, a basic food, was purchased from the trader in the form of grits,
but when a Seminole woman had no money she gathered the corn from
the field, dampened the kernels, and placed them in a hollowed-out tree
stump or log. Next, she used a pestle or stick to pound the corn to a
powder, which was sifted through woven palmetto fibers and placed in a
kettle of boiling water. The resulting porridge, known as *sofkee*, became
more palatable when coontie, venison, pork, or even alligator meat was
added.[8] Sometimes coontie was mixed with wheat flour, made into cakes,
and fried.

The larger portion of the tribe, the Mikasuki speakers, lived to the
south of Lake Okeechobee in the Devil's Garden, Big Cypress Swamp,
and Everglades areas. A visitor described a camp near the Caloosahatchee
River in southwestern Florida:

> The form of this camp was in a semi-circle fronting on a "slue" as they
> call it (we would call it a canal). This camp consisted of three huts, built
> square and roofed in with palmetto fans, four upright pineposts,
> planked in roughly—and the home was complete. The other two shan-
> ties were simply covered with canvas stretched over four straight oak
> poles.
>
> When we arrived they were fixing their camp. One swarthy looking
> Indian was busily engaged cutting a young pine in the requisite size for a
> tent pole, another was digging the hole for the post with a large butcher
> knife . . . all the women go bare-headed and bare-footed and wear their
> hair down their backs. Usually it grows thick and silky and long. They
> raise magnificent hogs and their flesh is rich and good. Their houses are
> about ten feet long by eight wide and have a platform running the length
> and breadth, about three feet from the ground, there the families eat,
> sleep and live . . . they live chiefly by hunting and fishing both of which
> they excel in. The chief trade with them is in March and April when the
> plume birds are in fine condition. They travel from place to place in
> canoes about fifteen feet long and three feet deep and one foot wide,
> made of solid tree and propelled by paddles.
>
> The staple food of the Indians is corn but they eat hominy and pork to
> a large extent as well as turkey and venison. Sugar cane is consumed by
> them very largely in the camp and it is rarely that you see the squaws
> without a piece between their teeth.[9]

During the Second Seminole War clan camps had developed in which all members of a clan lived in the same camp, except the married men who had come to live in their wives' camps. (All women and unmarried men in the camp belonged to the same clan but, since residence was matrilocal, the married men came from different clans.) A typical camp consequently included one or more women in their twenties, perhaps an elderly woman or two, some children, and the husbands of the younger women. The pattern of the clan camp continued through the Third Seminole War and the long period of peace that followed. Among the Muskogee speakers in 1943 were eight Bird, six Panther, three Talahasee (Old Town), and two Snake clan camps. The Mikasukis had nine clans: Panther, Bird, Wildcat, Tiger, Otter, Wind, Wolf, Snake, and Big Town. The only time these isolated camps came together was for the Green Corn Dance or busk in June or July and the Hunting Dance in the fall season.[10]

Hunting occupied much of the time of the men. One band residing along New River hunted the manatees who lived in great numbers near the mouth of the river. Approaching the sea animals in their canoes the Seminoles harpooned the manatees as they rose to the surface for air. When harpooned, the animal sank; when he rose to the surface again, the Seminole shot him in the head and towed him to shore. The Seminoles were fond of the flesh, which resembled coarse beef; any surplus meat was sold to the whites. Alligators were "fire hunted"; that is, they were dazzled by the light of a burning torch and, while in that state of bewilderment, shot by a Seminole standing in a canoe, speared, and towed to the canoe. Alligators were hunted in the Everglades, where the animals tended to gather in great numbers in deep holes. After killing the gators the Seminoles placed the hides on a scaffold to dry and gathered them during the rainy season. Each kept the hides of the alligators that he had killed. When hunting deer, the Seminoles divided into parties of two or three men and their families and moved into areas deer were known to frequent. After making camp the men moved out into deer country during the early mornings and late evenings. The deer meat not sold to the whites was smoked and dried for future use. Every spring the Seminoles set the dry grass and trees on fire so that new growth would attract the deer and turkeys.[11]

The Seminoles used their traditional customs during this period to handle all cases of murder, robbery, and general misconduct. They believed that a person must pay for the advantage of group membership by obeying the regulations established by the group. Those who broke the laws were acting against their own good and must be insane. Therefore they were excluded from all social functions until they had demonstrated to a shaman that they were willing to adjust to the rules. If they had committed a serious crime and showed no chance of being reformed, they were considered outlaws and might be killed by Seminole, white, or black.

The Seminoles handled most criminal cases in their traditional manner at the annual Green Corn Dance or busk. On Court Day all of the males gathered in a meeting place where the medicine man or shaman and his several assistants were seated in a small open structure. To some white observers the grouping of the shaman and his several assistants represented a political and judicial council with the shaman acting as chair. Elevation to the council was by selection by council members; shamans came from the ranks of those who had taken a prescribed course of training as boys. At this time problems confronting the group or the tribe were discussed, and charges were brought against those who had committed crimes. All males were encouraged to speak on any matter considered, but the opinion of the shaman, council members, and the oldest member of each clan present seemed to carry the most weight.[12] The members of the council acted in conservative ways and did not oppose the whites; when a conflict developed, the Seminoles retreated.

In 1879 Billy Konipatci went to stay at the home of Francis A. Hendry in Fort Myers and received the elements of an education. A council was held and a messenger sent to Hendry telling him that the Seminoles wanted the boy back. If he was not sent home, they would take him by force. Hendry replied that it was up to the boy, and Billy answered that he wanted to stay with Hendry. After the messenger threatened to seize the boy, Hendry replied that he would kill the first Seminole who entered his house. After a stay of several years with Hendry, Billy went back to his home in Big Cypress and stated the reasons for his stand to a council; some wanted to ban him from the tribe, and others wanted to kill him. One of the oldest counselors rose to his defense, stating, "Some day we may need him and his education." At the end of the council they decided to let Billy live among them, on the condition he would not teach his children or anyone else to read and write. This he agreed to. When Josie Billie, his son, grew up and like his father wanted to learn to read and write, his father told him to not become literate, for the Seminoles would kill him and "me too."[13]

During the 1880s when justice was rendered to those who had broken the code, women lost their ears for adultery, and men were sent into exile for being too friendly with the whites. Phillip Youmans learned that some Seminoles who had committed serious crimes and did not abide by the decision of the council fled into the Big Cypress Swamp. If they escaped being caught by their own people, and if they could sneak back into the camp at the next Green Corn Dance, they went unpunished.[14] (Fifty years earlier, in 1837, a widow who should have waited four years remarried; both she and her husband had their ears cropped and their noses clipped, but with her hair concealing her ears and a handkerchief her nose, the woman walked about proudly displaying her pregnancy.) No white official objected to the Seminole style of justice; it was a case of Seminole dealing with Seminole.

When punishment other than treatment by the shaman was required, the male members of the clan of the wronged person met and decided upon a proper penalty for the culprit. During the 1890s Charlie Dixon, half-black and half-Seminole, was alleged to have executed Charlie Billie because the council had found Charlie Billie guilty of having sexual relations with his sister.[15] Josie Billie, one of the most important medicine men and shaman of the Mikasukis, presented a difficult problem in social control. He was often drunk and violent, but since he was a shaman, his misdeeds were overlooked. Finally he was ostracized and threatened with death by the Trail Indians and moved to the Big Cypress Reservation.

During the 1930s Johnny Billy killed two members of the Tiger clan on different occasions when he was drunk. Nevertheless the clan took no drastic action except to prohibit him from taking part in ceremonies, for it was hoped that he would be rehabilitated. In 1938, after he had beaten a pregnant woman, the clan met and decided that reform was impossible and that Johnny Billy should be executed. The oldest member of the clan, John Osceola, was given a gun and driven in a truck by his son to Musa Isle where John Billy worked. Osceola killed Billy with a blast from a sixteen-gauge shotgun.[16] Arrested by the Miami police, Osceola was given a hearing by a justice of the peace and a coroner's jury. Lawyer O. B. White's defense impressed the jury, who voted for justifiable homicide and freed Osceola after ten minutes of deliberation.

Besides his important role in the Green Corn Dance, the medicine man or shaman had another specialty—medicine. Josie Billie, for example, a prominent Seminole born in 1885 who became the chief medicine man of the Mikasuki, received four years of training and instruction under Billie Motlow, according to an anthropologist who interviewed Billie:

The preparation of the medicine man advances by degrees. The respective degrees are named after the months in the Indian lunar calendar. Thus during the first month *(fubli hasi)* "wind moon" of his preparation a prospective medicine man is given the "black drink" which acts as a purgative. Herbs and medicine are then given him for eight additional days. After this the "medical student" is allowed to study on his own but he is expected to return to the medicine man who is in charge of his teaching on the first month of the ensuing year for further instruction and to ask questions. In order to cure one must learn the proper magical chants and formulas. Hence the teaching of the songs in connection with each one of the various types of disease undoubtedly forms a significant part of the training of a new medicine man.

. . . A most common cause of disease is the loss of the ghost or soul. The Seminoles believe in the existence of a double soul. One soul may leave the body in sleep and wander far afield while the other leaves the body only at death. The nightly adventures of the first soul are revealed in dreams. To discover the cause of sickness a medicine man must analyze dreams.

. . . His informant explained that sometimes the ghost enjoyed his nocturnal adventures so much that it did not come back at dawn. When this happened the person who had dreamed suddenly found that his body became sick. Hence a medicine man always asks his patients first about their dreams. Upon learning from the dream how the soul has been detained the medicine man obtains the proper herbs, mixes them in a pot, and sings the proper chants beseeching the soul to return. It was important to blow his breath through the medicine pipe, "his ammunition," as this power of breath is quaintly called. The medicine man believed that certain magical power comes from himself through the pipe and that this power is sufficient in most cases to retrieve the wandering soul.[17]

Only a few Seminoles became advanced medicine men—shamans and guardians of the sacred bundles—but others, including women, were counted as doctors who treated the sick with herbs but have not undergone detailed training. Since these doctors were believed to have communication with the spirits, some of their followers were certain that they could change the weather, guarantee better hunting, and give success in obtaining sexual favors. Payment for services performed by the medicine men and doctors was through gifts of deer meat, pigs, cloth, and skins.

During the postwar period of consolidation and migration some contacts were made with the neighboring settlements of Kissimmee, Sand

Point (Titusville), Bartow, Fort Ogden, Fort Meade, Tampa, and Fort Myers to trade and sell skins and feathers.[18] One example of such traffic took place in 1889, when three male Seminoles carried a load of alligator skins by canoe from the shores of Lake Okeechobee along the Caloosahatchee River to Fort Myers, where Charley Tommie sold 84 skins, Billie Motlow 75 skins, and another Tommie 88 skins at Blount and Company.[19] Besides alligator hides, the plume or feather trade proved most profitable to the Seminoles. Women's hats decorated with the white plumes or feathers of the American egret and snowy egret became popular throughout the United States, and the egret rookeries in Florida were a major source of supply.[20]

Many of the camps were equipped to be self-sufficient for many months. The gardens produced enough food to supply the wants of the camp, and the surplus corn, pumpkins, and potatoes were kept in the storehouses. When hunting alligators in an area where little wild food was to be found, Seminoles carried along coontie flour and dried cabbage palmetto buds, which they placed in boiling water to restore their natural flavor.

During this period the Seminoles developed a special relationship with whites whom they knew they could trust. Some whites found the Seminoles a strange group in which trust had to be developed over a long period of time. The initial contact could be rather rough. Dora Doster Utz recalled her early experiences:

The afternoon we were sitting quietly in front of the cabin taking the breeze from the river, Mama's attention was caught by a movement over the rise of the hill towards the river. It looked like a plume stuck in the turban of an Indian. It was! Then she saw another, and another, and soon the whole file of them were coming up the trail from where they had beached their canoes. She was terrified, and grabbing us children, she raced into the house and bolted the doors. They filed silently by and headed for the trail to town. Then, to her consternation, she saw they were preparing to camp along the trail for the night on our ground, practically cutting us off from town. To increase her further fears, she saw them come up to the back yard pump with their pails and buckets for water. She remained indoors. When Papa came home along the trail that night from the store, he saw the Indians at their evening meal. The men were sitting about a large pot in the center of the circle while the women remained at one side, cooking and occasionally replenishing the pot with meat. Papa paused to address them, but they paid him little attention until the Chief spoke. Nodding his head in the direction of the cabin, he said, "Humph, white squaw scared." [21]

Although the Seminoles did their best to remain within the sanctuaries of the Everglades and Big Cypress Swamp, they also made certain accommodations to white culture. No longer did they use the bow and arrow, pottery, and deer skins but now depended upon modern .38- and .44-caliber breech-loading rifles, iron pots and pans, and calico, cotton gingham, and flannel materials. Whenever these items needed replacing, the male Indian had to kill enough deer, mink, or alligators to exchange the skins and pelts for the needed items. It would have been much easier for the Seminoles to use the bow and arrow and clay pottery, but the white culture's articles were so much better: more game could be killed with a rifle; iron pots did not easily crack; and everyone liked to wear the brightly colored calicoes. Rarely were the articles of clothing made by the white man worn in the camps, however, for the older Seminoles did not like the younger ones associating with or adopting the customs of the whites.

Before 1890, clothing for a Seminole man consisted of a striped or figured cloth clout covered by a shirt that fell halfway between the waist and the knees, a beaded belt or cloth sash about the waist, and no moccasins. Several red and yellow bandannas were worn about the neck, and a brightly colored turban was usually worn upon the head. Buckskin moccasins and leggings were infrequently worn. With no pockets in his shirt, a Seminole carried all of his necessary articles in the several pouches that hung from the belt about the waist.

The women wore short jackets or shirts with a low neckline, bare midriff, and narrow collar or cape and long, full skirts made of dark-colored calico or gingham with a cord tied about the waist. They piled a large amount of beads in all colors about their necks. In 1881 Clay MacCauley noted one woman who had at least 200 strings of beads about her neck. The women wore no shoes. The children generally went about naked, but a few female babies wore beads. [22]

Between 1875 and 1879 seventy-two Cheyenne, Arapaho, Kiowa, Comanche, and Caddo warriors had been held as prisoners at Fort Marion in St. Augustine under Lieutenant Robert H. Pratt, who hoped to transform them into men who could enter the white world. He hired persons to teach English, and the prisoners were encouraged to develop any usable skills. [23] Within a short time so much progress had been achieved that Pratt was encouraged to establish at a later date Carlisle Institute, a boarding school for American Indians in Pennsylvania.

The transformation of the western tribesmen caused some Florida people who had contact with the St. Augustine experiment or who were interested in American Indian education to think that the Seminoles might benefit from such an experience. L. B. Darrell, who operated the Cookman Institute at Jacksonville, suggested to the Indian Bureau that some Seminoles could engage in learning mechanical arts or agriculture at his institution.[24] The suggestion received serious consideration at Washington until it was ascertained that the eastern Seminoles had no rights specified in treaties and that Cookman Institute was neither an agricultural nor an industrial school.[25] Henry Caruthers, M.D., had observed the work of Pratt at St. Augustine and had been so impressed that he invited one Kiowa to stay at his home. When the Kiowa returned to Oklahoma, Caruthers followed his progress with great interest. Mrs. Caruthers had taught a class for two years at the fort and was certain that such a school would be beneficial to the Seminoles.[26] Caruthers offered to take ten or twelve Seminoles to his summer home on the Hudson River at no expense to the government and educate them, but no action was taken regarding his suggestion.[27]

Pratt, who has been called "the Moses of Indian education," requested the acting commissioner of Indian affairs in 1879 to investigate the state of the Seminole Indians in Florida and to see if they could be persuaded to move to Oklahoma.[28] He then made an extensive trip into the interior of the state. On June 29, 1879, Pratt visited Chipco's village thirty miles northeast of Fort Meade in the vicinity of some beautiful lakes. He found in the village ten chickees and an adjacent fifteen acres where sugar cane, sweet potatoes, rice, corn, and melons were cultivated in separate family patches. The thick underbrush on all sides of the agricultural site served as protection against roaming cattle and pigs and white intruders who could seize the property as their own. Pratt observed numerous skins of otters and deer near the chickees, but Chipco complained that the game supply had been greatly reduced. Three blacks, unprotected by the Thirteenth Amendment, were living in the village. Chipco considered them slaves valued at $800 apiece.

On July 11, 1879, Pratt met at Fort Myers with a delegation of seven men from Big Cypress Swamp. These Seminoles showed a reluctance to shake hands and would not accept gifts of tobacco or food. Pratt learned from white informants that the Seminoles had no problems in securing ample supplies of liquor when they visited towns to trade their pelts. White neighbors claimed that 150 to 200 head of cattle owned by cattlemen were killed by the Seminoles each year and that when the Seminoles visited white homes, they stole pots and pans from the kitchen.

Believing that removal to Oklahoma would be best for the Seminoles, Pratt recognized that such a removal could not be accomplished without war or great deception. He suggested instead that an agent be appointed who would stress the value of education and help establish a boarding school in Florida where manual labor would be the central theme.[29] A census of the several bands included the following estimated figures:

Chipco (near Fort Clinch)	26
Tustenuggee (near Fort Centre)	90
Old Tiger Tail (near Fort Shackleford)	80
Young Tiger Tail (near Miami)	20
Possible oversight	20
	236[30]

At this time the federal government considered moving the Seminoles to Oklahoma and in 1881 directed Clay MacCauley to visit Florida and to make a report of what he had found. MacCauley uncovered enough information to write what has become a classic account of Seminole life. MacCauley found that the Florida Seminoles were composed of thirty-seven extended families living in twenty-two camps grouped roughly in five distinct areas—Big Cypress Swamp, Miami River, Fisheating Creek, Cow Creek (since some Muskogees lived on Cow Creek at that time, they became known to MacCauley and some subsequent writers as "Cow Creeks"), and Catfish Lake.[31] He discovered, as so many federal investigators were to do, that the Seminoles did not want to leave Florida or have anything to do with whites. As a consequence of MacCauley's report, any talk of moving the Seminoles to Oklahoma ceased, and on July 4, 1884, Congress began appropriating the annual sum of $6,000 to purchase homestead tracts of land for them.[32] Since interpreters used only Muskogee, and the Mikasukis spoke Muskogee to communicate with outsiders, both Pratt and MacCauley recorded that the Seminoles spoke Muskogee. Neither understood that two-thirds of the tribe spoke Mikasuki.[33]

One large center of Seminole settlement was at Pine Island at the headwaters of the New River in present-day Broward County. Pine

Seminole dwelling, 1880. Courtesy of the National Anthropological Archives, Bureau of American Ethnology, Smithsonian Institution, Washington, D.C.

Island, which had been a refuge for the Seminoles during the Second Seminole War, probably served as a Mikasuki ceremonial center for the Green Corn, Hunting, and Snake dances. Some time later the Seminoles would go to selected Green Corn Dance sites and erect temporary housing where no previous housing had existed or in some cases where no dances had been previously held. A visitor to the Pine Island complex described it as a cluster of twenty-five to thirty huts on the edge of a grove of pine trees containing at least three clan camps—Panther, Big Town, and Bird. Agricultural fields were located on nearby islands. Communication with traders and other bands was by cypress dugout canoes, some equipped with sails. With the drainage of the Everglades and the influx of white settlers into the area, the problems of feeding such a large Seminole population caused the Seminoles to leave Pine Island by 1910.[34]

In December 1884 Special Agent Cyrus Beede was ordered by the commissioner of Indian affairs to determine the number of Seminoles who would be willing to take a homestead tract and become "farmers." Beede was able to interview a few of the Seminoles living at Big Cypress, the Miami River, and Lake Rosalie, and found them highly reluctant to have anything at all to do with whites. He discovered that it was difficult to secure suitable vacant land, for the agents of the state of Florida were continually making selections under provisions of the Swamp and Over-flowed Land Act.[35] Tallahassee, who had succeeded Chipco as leader of the Muskogee band, had consented to take homestead land, and three Seminoles went with Beede to file a claim for land. When Beede was able to reach a telegraph office, he found that the desired land had been taken by other parties. Beede recommended to the commissioner that the U.S. government purchase for Tallahassee and his band of twenty persons the land on which they had lived for some time.

With the white settlement of areas on the eastern and western limits of their range, the Seminoles were pushed away from the Atlantic coast and Polk County into more undesirable tracts further south. Accordingly, their visits to Tampa and Bartow became less frequent, and enterprising persons established posts in the south where transactions could be made during the fall and winter seasons. Such outposts included the stores of George W. Storter at Everglades City, Ben Hogg at Fort Pierce, Ben Hill Doster at West Palm Beach and Jupiter, Ted Smallwood at Chokoloskee, Bill Brown at present-day Immokalee and later at Boat Landing, Frank Stranahan at Fort Lauderdale, and the Girtman brothers, W. M. Burdine, and William Brickell at Miami. In addition to the plumes, which sold for thirty-five cents, and the alligator skins, which sold for fifty cents, the Seminoles traded sweet potatoes, melons, chicken, deer hams, bananas, and starch made from the coontie root.[36]

The traders had developed a system that worked well to the benefit of both themselves and the Seminoles. The trader advanced a sum from $10 to $25 to each Seminole to purchase enough supplies for a hunt. When the Seminole returned from the field, the trader paid cash for the hides, and the hunter settled all or part of the amount owed. The Seminoles knew the price of hides, and when they felt they were being taken advantage of, they went to another store. Because they refused to accept shoddy merchandise, they purchased only the best products available. When hunting was poor, some traders advanced credit from $350 to $800 to each Seminole, with his personal honor as security. Should a Seminole die with substantial debts, the trader marked the account closed and made no effort to collect the money from his family. When one of the Girtman brothers closed his doors, he had $6,000 in unpaid accounts.[37]

The leader of the band usually came first into the store, followed by the other men, with the women and children bringing up the rear. While they moved behind the counters and made their selections, limited conversation was held with the proprietor. After the desired articles were gathered, the Seminole men and the storekeeper began to bargain for the proper amount of venison, meat, and skins to be exchanged for each item from the white world.[38] At first the women used natural dyes, but later they purchased dress materials and dyed them with manufactured dyes in their copper and iron kettles. Finally, when cotton goods were produced in fast colors, they bought this material by the yard and within a short time did not dye any materials.[39]

Ever since the Seminoles had entered Florida in the eighteenth century, the consumption of hard liquor had been a problem. During the 1890–1910 period according to one observer they were allowed to be drunk and disorderly in the southeastern Florida towns, for if such "disgraceful scenes of drunkenness and brutality among both Indian men and women" were prohibited, they would go elsewhere and deprive the towns of a considerable amount of business.[40] Whenever they could not obtain liquor at Fort Lauderdale, visiting parties of Seminoles would travel by train to West Palm Beach where a sufficient supply could be obtained at Zapp's. According to one witness, a drink blended in the black section of Miami composed of red pepper, whiskey, and a drop of cocaine to a quart of whiskey was most popular with the Seminoles. When a group visited Miami, Fort Lauderdale, and West Palm Beach, one Seminole stayed sober to protect his friends, but the others spent most of their hard-earned money for liquor.

M. C. Osborn, a white who owned a plantation at Kissimmee, was concerned about the liquor problem and together with Chief Tallahassee was able to stop the sale of liquor to Seminoles in his town. Consequently Seminoles from this band bypassed Kissimmee and traded at Bartow and Titusville, where they were able to obtain all the liquor that they desired.[41]

In January 1887 Lilly Pierpont of Winter Haven wrote to the wife of President Grover Cleveland about the problems of the Seminoles, and in consequence the president appointed her in November 1888 to a position that might be called "honorary Seminole agent." In her letter to Mrs. Cleveland, Pierpont told about the visits of the Seminoles to Winter Haven and suggested that a consequence of the settlement of the country would be to drive the Seminoles into the Atlantic Ocean or Gulf of Mexico. She related how a band of desperadoes was killing hogs and cattle belonging to the Seminoles, but instead of resorting to warfare, the Seminoles protested these acts to the mayor of Titusville. When Seminole Streaty Parker purchased fifty head of cattle from a white man, the cattle were found to be stolen, and Parker, without a promise of restitution, surrendered them to the owner. In response to protests by white friends of the Seminoles, authorities claimed that only an act of the legislature could protect the Seminoles in such matters.[42] Pierpont served until July 1889, but little is known concerning any lasting contributions she might have made or whether she received any federal funds at all.

Although since 1884 the U.S. government had appropriated the annual sum of $6,000 to place the Seminoles on homestead tracts, little interest was expressed by either federal representatives or the Seminoles in the money, and it reverted to the Treasury. In 1887 E. M. Wilson, appointed special agent by the commissioner of Indian affairs, made two trips to Florida to determine the readiness of the Seminoles to accept a homestead arrangement. Although Wilson made a great effort to meet the leading Florida Seminoles in his May and October visits, he found them uninterested in having anything to do with whites. Wilson concluded his report:

> This was the most tedious, laborious and disagreeable trip that has ever been my lot to make and I fear has not been very fruitful of results. I talked with many Indians upon the subject of homesteads; most of whom expressed a willingness to locate provided always that other and older ones would do so themselves. . . . I met two Miami Indians who stated that if their people would secure the lands upon which they live, they thought then there would be no trouble about locating them. And I think according to the maps, their lands are embraced in an unsurveyed territory in which case I presume there would be no trouble because of the present proprietorship of the land.[43]

In 1891 the Missionary Committee of the Women's National Indian Association (WNIA) under the leadership of Amelia S. Quinton of Philadelphia purchased 400 acres located forty-five miles southeast of Fort Myers for $2,000 with the objective of dividing the land into small tracts, each with a home for one Seminole family. The association, composed mostly of eastern women, had the policy of erecting chapels and missionary stations at the various reservation areas and of presenting the going establishments to one of the several denominations that carried on missionary work among the American Indians. In March 1891 Quinton and two other women, accompanied by Francis A. Hendry, a trusted friend of the Seminoles and veteran rancher, visited one Seminole village and several prospective sites for the enterprise and selected 400 acres known as the William Allen settlement.[44] William "Billy" Allen had been a Confederate veteran from Arcadia, Florida, who had erected a log house on the land and lived there for over twenty years. The U.S. government purchased 80 acres of the tract and assigned a special agent, Robert W. Chapin, to a project that involved the erection of necessary office and storage buildings, a school building, and living quarters. Although the site was twenty-five miles from the nearest camp and most supplies had to be hauled forty-five miles from Fort Myers over sandy trails, the general location seemed to be suitable for the purpose.

The William Allen settlement, known today as Immokalee and located in the north-central section of Collier County, was on a hammock forty feet above sea level that included a considerable amount of excellent land suitable for farming, provided the water level was controlled. Early white settlers preferred to use the land for cattle ranching and subsistence farming; not until the twentieth century were large-scale agricultural ventures begun. The Seminoles used the place as an occasional camping and resting place from which smaller groups would move into the nearby forests in search of game. Since a large number of land turtles were found in the higher ground and were used by both the Seminoles and settlers for food, the hammock became known to the Seminoles as Gopher Ridge.

During May 1891 the WNIA appointed Jacob E. Brecht, M.D., of St. Louis, Missouri, Seminole agent. The Seminoles were friendly but untrusting, and living in the rough two-room pine-log house erected to house the employees and the agent was described as being "in greatest discomfort."[45] A sawmill, ten mules, a wagon, two oxen, a cart, two logging carts, and assorted farm implements were purchased for use at the agency. Brecht left the employ of WNIA in the spring of 1893 to become industrial teacher on the reserve for the Bureau of Indian Affairs.[46]

By September 1894 one hundred rods of fencing had been erected on the hammock, the land cleared, and pineapple slips and fruit trees planted. In initial contacts the agency staff found the Seminoles reluctant to hold any meetings with them. Some whites, resentful of Brecht's attempts to reduce the traffic in rum, spread stories that he was encouraging the Seminoles to kill deer. The Seminoles would not accept gifts of nails or shingles made at the sawmill, nor would they haul sawed wood to settlers. Clara Brecht opened a school for the Seminole children, but when the only ones who enrolled were the children of nearby white settlers, it became part of the Lee County system.[47]

Brecht realized that in order to win friends among the Seminoles he had to make some services available for them at the reserve. Accordingly, a store was established in which groceries were sold to the Seminoles at cost and dressed deer skins were accepted as payment for the supplies. Brecht's efforts bore fruit, for on Christmas Day 1894 a large number of Seminoles came to the agency to hear the agent tell about the origin and meaning of Christmas and to receive presents of combs, mirrors, soap, knives, saws, and assorted items of apparel.[48]

Despite the success of the Christmas Day event Brecht experienced difficulty attracting Seminoles to the reserve. The children would not attend the school, and without gifts as lures the adults would not make use of available services. When Brecht visited the camps he found that the death rate as a result of the "eating of trash and exposure to the elements" was the greatest among children under six; once past that age the Seminole had a good chance of living until seventy.[49] Liquor traders did their best to discourage Brecht's visits to the camps by telling the Seminoles that the steam engine of the sawmill would be used as a signal to call the soldiers to capture them and carry them to Oklahoma. By 1896 Brecht was nevertheless making limited progress by employing Seminoles in the sawmill and in planting pineapples.

One well-known visitor, writer Kirk Munroe, described the so-called Indian Station:

> Besides a dwelling for the instructors have been built a large house especially for visiting Indians, a blacksmith shop, a sawmill, operated for Indians exclusively, and needful outhouses. A large garden is cultivated, wagons and horses are kept for use, and, whenever possible, or practicable, the Indians are pressed into service that they may have the benefit of the experience. At first they were very shy, refusing even to cross the grounds of the agency, but now they will frequently come in to 'help.' They buy of the agents and agency institutions things useful and convenient; several have bought wagons and when these are out of repair they bring them in to the blacksmith and intelligently assist him in the work of mending. They also use garden tools and they seem to like the buzz and whir of the little sawmill, and are becoming helpful in its operation. The hope is entertained that by first teaching them useful methods of self-help they may be gradually approached for other purposes. Indeed, the workers have had to take hold where they could; the Indians are attainable only in this way, for they have and continue to resist strenuously all school and church instruction.[50]

Although the efforts of Brecht and the Women's National Indian Association were doomed to failure, they laid the foundation for later successful religious and governmental activities. On August 15, 1894, and in subsequent years for some time, Congress authorized one-half of the annual $6,000 appropriation to be spent for land for Seminole homes and farms. Brecht was in favor of the measure, for he realized that much of the Everglades had been purchased by the land companies or acquired by the railroads, and that streams of settlers were moving southward along both coasts to occupy any overlooked land. Unless some lands were reserved for the Seminoles, they were in danger of being driven from their homes in Florida. In fact, settlers were already moving onto the camp and cultivated grounds of the Seminoles and warning them not to return to the area. Accordingly, much of Brecht's effort was shifted to the purchase of land. He felt that if the Seminoles would not come to the reservation, the government should purchase the land on which they lived. Brecht chose tracts already occupied by the Seminoles or for which they expressed a preference. As a beginning he purchased 644 acres from Hamilton Disston for $418; 1,920 acres from William Brown for $1,344; and 640 acres from Brown for $448. In the following years tracts were purchased from the Florida Southern Railroad and the Plant Investment Company at an average of less than a dollar an acre.[51] Buying parcels of land at various times resulted in the reserve being composed of five separated parcels of land. By 1909, 23,040 acres purchased by Brecht and others for $15,265.75 was situated about seventy-five miles to the south and east of Fort Myers and extended to the Everglades. The largest portion of this land would be developed later into the Big Cypress Indian Reservation.

Some white friends of the Seminoles tried to help them at this time by attempting to establish a state reservation. The Florida legislature on June 8, 1891, authorized the trustees of the Board of Internal Improvements to set aside a tract of land no larger than 5,000 acres for their use.[52] Commission members for the selection of the proposed State Indian Reservation included James E. Ingraham, chair, Francis A. Hendry, and Garibaldi Niles. The commission agreed that any attempt to force the Seminoles onto a reservation would be foolhardy and decided to select an area where they had already settled; however, no funds were available for location and survey of the needed land.[53] On April 27, 1897, the commission met in St. Augustine and voted for the acquisition of 5,000 acres at Long Key in the Everglades, but the legislature took no action. During the same period Dr. Jacob Brecht and others tried to reserve some land for the Seminoles before it was transferred to the state of Florida, but authorities ruled that the Seminoles had no rights to the land.

In 1899 an organization known as the Friends of the Seminole Indians was founded at Kissimmee by Bishop William C. Gray, Francis Hendry, P. A. Vans Agnew, James M. Willson, Jr., Minnie Moore-Willson, C. A. Carson, and George Wilson. With the assistance of the editor of *Harper's Weekly,* the Friends of the Seminoles were able to raise forty dollars in 1899 to purchase eighty acres in Brevard County, but no Seminoles would move to the tract, and it was sold for taxes in 1926.[54] When the group tried to purchase the actual camping sites of the Seminoles, they found the price asked by land companies prohibitive.

Acting under pressure from the Friends of the Seminoles, the Florida legislature on May 29, 1899, set aside a large tract of land for the use of the Seminoles, but since practically all of the land had already been deeded to corporations and individual citizens, the action was fruitless.[55] Several days later, on June 1, 1899, the state appropriated $500 to establish an industrial school for the Seminoles in Brevard County; the school never progressed beyond the planning stage.[56] Although the passage of these two measures was intended to satisfy persons interested in the Seminoles that the state of Florida was doing something for them, they were of no benefit. In a third action the Friends of the Seminoles assisted Tom Tiger in his attempt to regain possession of his horse from a white trader, but when some vital evidence turned up missing, Tiger lost his chance to regain his steed.[57]

Over a short span of years the combined efforts of private and governmental agencies to aid the Seminoles were doomed to failure, for the Seminoles did not want to learn English or to farm extensively when they were free to roam throughout southern Florida. Brecht had failed because he was dealing with hunters, not farmers or ranchers. The Seminoles came to the agency mostly from curiosity—to saw a board, pull a steam whistle cord, or trade a few items at the poorly equipped store—but they refused to budge an inch from their stand. Only when the land developers had taken over most of the available land and the drainage experts had changed the water levels would the Seminoles realize that changes were necessary in their way of life, an awareness that would not come during the nineteenth century.[58]

9
Missionary Efforts and New Federal Reservations

hen Brecht resigned as agent for the Women's National Indian Association in 1893, Amelia Quinton wrote to a man the Seminoles would come to call Straight Tongue, an Episcopal bishop of the Missionary Jurisdiction of Southern Florida, requesting that his group take charge of the Seminole Indian project.[1] This was the usual practice of the Women's National Indian Association— to purchase some land, hire a vocational worker or adviser to work with the tribe, and then pass the project on to a religious group. The Right Reverend William Crane Gray of Orlando, inspired by the missionary work of Bishop Henry Benjamin Whipple, decided to investigate the offer. Traveling to the Allen Place by train, boat, and finally pony cart, Gray found a house, school building, and stables, fenced land, and the nearby federal agency. He and Quinton met in Chicago in June 1893 to sign the necessary papers for the transfer of the property.[2] On the advice of Whipple, Gray attended a session of the Lake Mohonk Conference where concerns regarding American Indians were discussed.[3]

In order to understand the problems connected with the mission, Bishop Gray accompanied Jacob Brecht on an excursion to the camps scattered about Big Cypress Swamp, assisted as guide and interpreter by Billy Konipatci, who had helped Clay MacCauley in 1880–81.

With the missionaries in charge, the Allen Place went through a few changes. Among them was a determined effort to convert the Seminoles to Christianity. The residence building became known as Immokalee, "his home" in Mikasuki, and Christ Church was erected nearby.[4] A beef and pork barbecue was held on July 4, 1896, to launch the mission, with the

Seminole guests showing their appreciation by singing songs in English. On the following day the opening services were held at Christ Church, and Rose Brown, the daughter of a trader, was confirmed.[5]

Although English-born Reverend and Mrs. Henry O. Gibbs, the resident missionaries recommended by Brecht for the positions, worked hard at Immokalee, few Seminoles regularly visited the place, and it became evident that a change of mission sites was needed. William Brown had established a store in 1896 in the Big Cypress where the Seminoles frequently visited to trade hides for needed articles. In 1898 the second mission was established three miles from Brown's store. Placing a cypress beam across a palmetto tree, Bishop Gray fashioned a crude cross, the signpost for the new venture. After religious songs and prayers, the missionary christened the outpost Everglade Cross. Everglades Lodge, a housing unit for the missionaries, was erected along with a store, hospital, and outbuildings; corn, potatoes, bananas, and citrus were planted on the higher ground.[6]

Brecht had served the Seminoles for eight and a half years when he resigned on January 1, 1899, and moved to Fort Myers.[7] The physician claimed that he could have made four times as much in private practice but that he had wanted to help the Seminoles. The entire station was shut down seven months after Brecht's departure. The sawmill was sold to Witt Tolles, who transferred the equipment to another site where it became a profitable venture. The federal government sold all of the improvements by 1900, and they were moved elsewhere; in 1904 the eighty acres that were owned by the federal government were sold.

Reverend Gibbs and his wife usually spent part of the year at Immokalee and the remainder at Everglades Lodge, moving from one to the other by horse and buggy. As the congregation of fourteen on April 27, 1903, indicated when Bishop Gray visited Everglade Cross, few Seminoles made use of the mission's services. Problems connected with Everglade Cross included its being 80 miles from Fort Myers, the nearest town, and 150 miles from the nearest railroad. Whiskey dealers also spread rumors among the Seminoles that the missionaries were government agents, and in addition a penalty of death was decreed by the tribe to any Seminole who took whites to permanent Seminole camps.

In 1901 William Brown, who had earlier owned a store at Immokalee, purchased the holdings of J. A. Wilson, thirty miles southeast of Immokalee, and, to make sure that the Seminoles could pole their dugouts to his store, dug a canal from the front of the store to the deeper water in the

Everglades. Boat Landing became extremely popular with the Seminoles, for now they did not have to travel to Fort Lauderdale, the Everglades, or Miami to trade. Brown purchased alligator hides at 10 cents a foot and otter skins at eight dollars apiece and sold the Seminoles sugar, flour, grits, rifles, shotguns, ammunition, canned goods, beads, derby hats, sewing machines, cloth, pots, pans, and knives.

By the turn of the century Seminole women were able to obtain hand-operated sewing machines at the trading posts, and distinct changes took place in both male and female attire as a result. The men's shirts were extended to a point several inches below the knees, and buckskin leggings were cast aside by some men in favor of trousers. The women enlarged the small cape attached to their blouses, and the sleeves of the blouses were gradually shortened.[8]

In 1905 William J. Godden, an elderly English pharmacist who had moved to St. Petersburg, approached Gray requesting ordination and offering to spend the rest of his life in service to the Seminoles. Gray quickly accepted the offer. Before his move to Everglade Cross, Godden received a brief course in practical medicine from Dr. R. F. Altree of Tampa. At first Godden had little success, but an outbreak of measles with attendant pneumonia caused the Seminoles to turn to anyone who could help them. With little or no assistance from others Godden took care of twenty-seven patients, giving medicine and preparing meals; he lost only two patients, both as a "result of their own neglect."[9] As Bishop Gray said, "The Indians were at last convinced that some white men did not come to them merely for what they could make out of them."[10] In March 1910 Godden reported to Gray that the services at Immokalee were well attended, two communicants held Sunday school services for interested persons, some Seminoles were using a toothbrush regularly, and most men possessed at least one suit of "civilized" attire.

In December 1907, when the Gibbses retired, Reverend Irenaeous Trout, a missionary stationed at Punta Gorda and Fort Myers, was placed in charge of the missionary work for the Seminoles. Trout showed some skill in learning the Seminoles' dialects and in cultivating their friendship. In October 1908 Ho-tul-ca-hat-sie, a leading Seminole who belonged to the Tiger clan, was baptized, and on August 4, 1909, Charlie Osceola, an important medicine man, went through the same ritual. It is doubtful, however, that they understood fully what baptism meant. Until Godden was ordained, Trout taught the Seminoles to write their names, to sew, and to use hand tools.

In February 1908 William Brown, the trader at Boat Landing, decided
to return to a homestead forty miles distant and to sell his store to the
missionaries. He offered Bishop Gray the house, store, stable, and six
yoke of oxen and wagons at a figure between $1,500 and $2,000. Since
Gray did not want another trader who had fewer scruples than Brown to
purchase the place, he borrowed the necessary money and bought Boat
Landing.[11] The former trading store served as joint chapel and recreation
center; the missionaries concealed the altar and organ when not in use by
drawing a canvas curtain that served as a screen for showing magic lantern
pictures.[12] Another building was erected at Boat Landing in July 1909 to
serve as a store and home for Godden, and a hospital was scheduled to be
erected in 1910.

In March 1909 the Reverend Irenaeus Trout offered the commissioner
of Indian affairs his observations concerning the Seminoles at Everglade
Cross Mission and Boat Landing:

> They are *hunters*. During the months when they can market their skins
> they flourish and have plenty of money but during the forbidden months
> when there is no market they do anything they can and at such times will
> perform labor when they can get it to do at $1 to $1.50 per day. The
> women do some bead work which the merchants at the coast points sell
> to tourists, make moccasins, sell a few chickens. They are improvident
> and either have plenty or nothing, like the negro, except for a few cases
> where they have been known to accumulate several hundred dollars, and
> one of them has a very creditable store near the East side.
>
> They are not inclined to work as a rule, but only when necessity drives
> them and they can get the work to do; they do it well. They build canoes
> very gracefully and possess artistic taste in decorating them—paint and
> oil sells freely among them for such purposes. They build well-
> constructed shacks "tho crude and primitive." They would doubtless be
> more industrious did they not fear and distrust the white man so. Frank
> Tiger (a man 25 years old) went out to Fort Myers to work on the sea
> wall last summer, but the tribe compelled his return in 60 days. . . .
>
> The Indians are very much afraid of and distrustful of the Govern-
> ment. Anyone professing to represent it, they would flee from in fear.
> They have confidence in the church as represented by Mr. Gibbs,
> Bishop Gray, Dr. Godden and myself, and are fully assured that we are
> not Government people, and are looking only to their welfare. They
> come about us and talk freely to us, sometimes even telling us of their
> plan for a big hunt, etc., etc. They would not be averse to accepting aid
> from the Government if they were assured that there was not some

sinister motive behind it. They fear deportation to the west. . . . It has been objected to that the Indians will not work. Certainly not, they get 70 cents, 90 cents, $1.00 and $1.15 for alligator hides, and they can catch 40 or 50 per week, and they get $5.00 to $7.50 for otter skins, and they can trap 1 or 2 per week, so there is no need for it, but the game is disappearing. The plume birds are practically extinct already. And then there are several months in the year when the game is protected and they cannot market their hides. Then they will work. They have worked for Godden and me and they are glad to do it. It will not do to look back at past failure, and judge the future by it. The conditions now are different. So if the Government can secure lands and help Bishop Gray and myself to train the Indians, we can do it and the Indians can be saved.[13]

A reporter from the *Tampa Tribune* visited Godden at Boat Landing and Everglade Cross in the fall of 1909. Godden met him at the Palmetto train station near Bradenton and took him the rest of the way by oxen-drawn wagon. Christ Church at Immokalee, a mission church, was deserted, for the resident missionary family was away, but near Boat Landing the Seminoles were cultivating corn, pumpkins, and other crops in nearly every hammock and as many as thirty had been patients at the Everglade Cross hospital at one time. Seminoles identified by the reporter as being at Boat Landing included Willie Willie, Tommie Doctor, Charley Fewell, Henry Clay, and Water Turkey, accompanied by their families.[14]

Despite the optimistic picture presented by the missionaries and the number of Seminoles using the hospital and trading post, a line here and there pointing to probable failure appeared in the letters sent from Boat Landing. One observer noted that "a few Indians have united with the church, but progress in this direction is necessarily very slow, as actual contact with the Indians is so irregular, although the work is in the hands of noble, devoted and self-sacrificing men, who are spending their lives in this work and are receiving only a bare subsistence."[15] On June 11, 1910, Godden reported that he was $130 short of the amount needed to move the hospital from Everglade Cross to Boat Landing. He also regretted "to say that business had been very slack in the store this spring, and we have really not been paying expenses."[16] In 1910 Lorenzo S. Creel, special agent to the Seminoles in Florida, made a detailed examination of Boat Landing and found the location "difficult to access, extremely, and remote from the nearest Indian camp. . . . it is a most forlorn, dreary and unattractive spot and I believe it will grow more and more unhealthful as the Everglade region is dug up and disturbed."[17] He concluded:

Commissary building at Everglade Cross or Boat Landing, c. 1910. Courtesy of the National Archives, Washington, D.C.

I regret to say that the deeper I probe into the matter the more hopeless it seems. The Mission itself seems the forlornest of forlorn hopes. Everything that Bishop Gray, who seems one of the most noble and devoted men, is trying to accomplish through Dr. Godden and the Mission seems to me to be done under the most trying conditions and unfavorable and unsympathetic environment and calls for such an extravagant expenditure of means, effort and energy wholly out of proportion to the ground gained that is speaking from a human point of view that the whole occasion would seem to me from a business standpoint to be an absolute waste of life and money.[18]

Since Boat Landing was situated on land acquired by Brecht for the Seminoles, the missionaries actually were squatters and needed some legal protection for their work. In view of the failure of the Brecht venture and subsequent pullback, federal officials were reluctant to initiate a similar program and were eager to encourage the Episcopal Seminole Indian mission in its work. Secretary of the Interior Ethan A. Hitchcock summarized the situation in 1904: "It is deemed unwise for the Government to contemplate any further purchases of land for these Indians or to attempt to aid them in any way at the present time, owing to their fear and lack of confidence in State and National Government on account of past injustice." [19] When Bishop Gray disclosed the difficult situation faced by the missionaries, the commissioner of Indian affairs, Robert G. Valentine, promised him that the mission site would be reserved for the religious organization. [20] Finally on July 13, 1910, Section 15, Township 485, R34 E, was set aside for use of the Episcopal mission among the Seminoles. [21] Gray answered the award letter with "thanks, God's blessing from every effort," and a store, chapel, and hospital were erected at Boat Landing. [22]

With the lowering of the water table by drainage operations, Boat Landing became more difficult for Seminoles to reach. When a hurricane in October 1910 demolished the hospital and other buildings, Godden recommended that the mission be moved to Everglade Post Office or to the store of George W. Storter, Jr., on the Allen River (now Barron River), and in 1911 special agent Lorenzo Creel recommended that twenty-eight acres be purchased at Everglades City for the Seminoles' use but nothing came of Godden's or Creel's suggestions. [23] Instead, the Seminoles used the material from the hospital to build a camp house under the direction of Godden. Since Godden could handle only minor ills, more serious cases were sent to the church's home hospital at Orlando.

A letter dated March 1914 from the commissioner of Indian affairs informed the secretary of the interior that Bishop Gray had relinquished the 640-acre tract in September 1913 as too low and swampy for missionary work; in return he wanted a grazing permit to raise hogs on 720 acres plus use of 120 acres for the mission. [24] Several days later a note from the Interior Department stated that the request was approved, and with funds obtained from various sources, the venture known as Seminole Farm began operations. [25]

The Seminole Indian mission seemed doomed. Bishop Gray resigned in October 1913 at the age of seventy-seven, and Bishop Cameron Mann took his place. [26] One of Mann's early acts was to travel by automobile from Orlando to Everglade Cross in March 1914 and announce that he was "studying business affairs of this part of the diocese." [27] The proposed move from Boat Landing to Seminole Farm was costly, but Godden was promised $400 if he could raise a like sum. Before Bishop Mann took any action concerning the mission, the matter was unexpectedly settled when Godden was found dead in bed on September 29, 1914. The body was taken to Fort Myers and then to St. Petersburg, where it was interred in the Episcopal cemetery on Lakeview Avenue.[28] When W. Stanley Hanson from Fort Myers, friend of the Seminoles and Godden, visited Everglade Cross after Godden's death to dispose of the livestock and perishable items and to store the rest, looters had already removed most of the tools that could be carried away. The mission was closed, and Episcopal missionary efforts in Florida ceased for nearly two decades.

The Baptists also made some attempts to convert the Seminoles to the Christian faith. In 1907 Andrew J. Brown and W. F. Joseph, Seminole Baptist ministers from Wewoka, Oklahoma, had only limited success in Florida.[29] Two years later another Baptist missionary, George Washington, not only failed in his mission but received a rebuke from Washington for not informing the Bureau of Indian Affairs in advance about the visit.[30] A full-blooded Oklahoma Seminole, Washington decided to remain in Florida and found work at Bower Brothers' store and citrus groves at Indian Town; he preached in the Muskogee dialect when he was not working.[31] Brown returned to Florida twice again in 1912 with a group composed of three other ministers, their wives, and Brown's wife, sister, granddaughter, and niece. The group had a difficult journey, traveling by train from Wewoka to Fort Pierce via Memphis, Birmingham, and Jacksonville, but unfortunately the Florida Seminoles regarded the Brown group as whites and did not receive them as fellow Seminoles.[32] Still, the Florida peninsula was regarded as a fertile missionary site. In 1912 a federation of twenty-six Baptist churches, the Creek Seminole and Wichita Baptist Association, decided to sponsor the missionary project and began to send missionaries at regular intervals to Florida over the next thirty years.[33]

While the Women's National Indian Association, the Bureau of Indian Affairs, and the Missionary Jurisdiction of Southern Florida—Protestant Episcopal churches were failing in their efforts to lure the Seminoles onto a reserve where they would permanently settle, most Seminoles were doing too well in their hide trade to consider being confined within one area. A typical migratory Seminole group was Water Turkey and his family, who lived in a village at the southwestern side of the Big Cypress Swamp, visited Godden's store, where they obtained supplies on credit, and then canoed across Lake Okeechobee through Lake Hicpochee and the Caloosahatchee River to LaBelle where they boarded a steamboat and paid for passage to Fort Myers. At Fort Myers Water Turkey and his relatives sold their otter skins and alligator hides and returned by steamboat to LaBelle, where they purchased needed items of food and clothing.

Not until the fall of 1910 was special agent Lorenzo Creel directed to take a careful look at the real estate in Big Cypress Swamp that had been acquired between 1895 and 1900. According to Creel the major part of the land was "low, wet prairie with a few small, low islands scattered over it. The soil is sandy and infertile, sour and unproductive."[34] Soon after the land was purchased the Seminoles had left the area, and by 1911 none were living within the so-called reservation. In addition, the acquired area was not suitable as a reservation because thirty-three sections of land were scattered in five adjacent townships, and only twenty-five sections were included within one tract in Township 48, Range 34. Sooner or later someone would have to make trades or additional purchases to create a suitable reservation composed of a solid block of land.

Since the Seminoles only used the land for occasional hunting and lived further south, some persons wanted Congress to set aside its obligation to obtain lands for the Seminoles and to sell the tracts to whites. Dr. Jacob Brecht, the former federal employee who had purchased the lands and now lived at Fort Myers, was requested by several persons to use his influence to have the government open the lands for settlement, but he declined to cooperate with such schemes. Misfortune continued to plague the land acquisition; Lee County seized part of it for nonpayment of taxes and began selling the tax certificates.[35] Of course, such action was illegal and soon came to a halt.

Alanson Skinner, assistant anthropologist in the American Museum of Natural History, took a trip in 1910 to collect specimens for the museum that led him into regions not penetrated by whites since the final Seminole War in 1858. He reported a view of Seminole life that few whites had observed at that time:

> When we got to Fort Myer, we were told we were attempting the impossible. The Everglades have only been crossed five times in all at any season of the year, and in the height of summer the obstacles are held to be insurmountable. Many of the waterways are then dried up, or nearly so, and we were to travel by canoe. Lines of travel in the Everglades are waterways artificially deepened by the Indians. The depth varies from a few inches to thirty feet, though the general depth is under two feet. Where the water was not deep enough the canoes had to be hauled.
>
> Our first step was to enlist the services of competent guides, and in this we were fortunate. We succeeded in obtaining Frank Brown, a cracker, who with his father has the reputation among the Indians of

never lying to them. This reputation stood us in good stead, as the Indians on many occasions received us on our guide's say-so. The crackers, you understand, are the poorer whites in the southern South. Our party at the start was made up of myself, Mr. Julian A. Dimock, Frank Brown, another cracker, and a Seminole. The latter, however, had to turn back when he reached more uncivilized Indians. We afterward learned that they severely punished him for guiding the white man to their domains. . . .

The most interesting experience came when we had penetrated into the heat of the swamps. There we found villages to which the white man had never penetrated and Indians who had never before seen our race. These were squaws and children, for although civilization has never reached the interior, the men had all been out.

The Seminoles are hostile to the whites and still have a horror of them. The memory of the capture of Osceola, their chief, is very much alive. Since the close of the Seminole War the government has done nothing for them. It ignores them. They are neither wards nor citizens. Theoretically they do not exist. There are only about three hundred of them.

We were allowed to enter only the remote villages on the word of Cracker Brown that we did not lie. At most villages the Seminoles were afraid to let us in, believing we were government spies come to arrange for their removal to Oklahoma. At one camp seven armed warriors appeared, insisting that "white men were no good." [36]

Pressure was constantly mounting on the Seminole camps near settlements or on tracts that were desired by the whites. In 1899 there had been three camps at Long Key in the eastern Everglades, but by 1902 whites had driven the Seminoles from the key and had taken the harvest from the cultivated fields. When drainage operations began in the neighborhood of Pine Key, the dredgers, knowing that the Seminoles were fair game, carried all they could carry of the produce from their fields and camps and destroyed the rest. According to author Kirk Munroe, the whites living on New River boasted that they had driven the Seminoles from the high land and would chase them away from any land that could be cultivated. The Seminoles were most unhappy, for they had been forced to retreat to places where the drinking water was bad and where it was difficult to find a dry spot where a home could be erected. [37]

On November 22, 1907, a tract of 520 acres of federal land was withdrawn from settlement by the Interior Department and held for the use of the Seminoles. [38] The land situated near the town of Dania on the east coast was covered in most spots with pine trees, including an area of soil suitable for agricultural purposes. Although the acreage had been held in reserve by the U.S. government, J. M. Bryan, Jr., moved onto the most fertile land—a forty-acre tract—planted grapefruit and orange trees, erected a house and outbuildings, and considered the property his; in addition, he planted twenty-five to thirty acres of tomatoes on adjacent tracts.[39] Although the Seminoles had lived on or near the land and called the place "old city" for many years, and although fencing government land was illegal, Bryan held a strong hand, for his brother would soon be sworn in as U.S. senator from Florida.[40] Having failed to obtain the land from the state of Florida, Bryan sought the aid of Congress, which on March 4, 1909, acknowledged that he had made substantial improvements on the forty acres and gave him title to the land for fifty dollars.[41] Perhaps in compensation for such action, Congress passed on April 4, 1910, an act that appropriated $15,000 to aid the Seminoles, and the subsequent Indian Appropriation Act of 1911 that provided an additional sum of $10,000.[42]

In an executive order dated June 28, 1911, President William H. Taft set aside lands in Collier, Martin, and Broward counties for the Seminoles. Although the land in Collier and Martin counties was later released or traded, the 480 acres in Broward County became the agency headquarters fifteen years later and still serves as a center of federal operations. Acquisition of the Broward County land was a good move, for the land was convenient to the Seminoles, but more land should have been acquired.[43]

Since every acre of Florida represented a chance to realize some profit, land speculators were reluctant to have land reserved for the Seminoles. While in Florida, Lorenzo Creel had met with former Governor William S. Jennings, who was then attorney for the Everglades Land Sales Company and who did not want any more land preserved for the Seminoles. The land in alternate sections lying to the north of the Hendry County reservation had been sold by the state to land companies that had subdivided the property in five- and ten-acre tracts to sell to individual owners at prices ranging from $24.00 to $60.00 per acre. Jennings believed that the Seminoles, who had signed a treaty to go to Oklahoma, had no rights in Florida either as citizens or as wards of the government.[44] With the digging of drainage canals near Fort Shackleford, the lands were expected to double in value and from the white viewpoint would be too valuable to use for reservation.

Other persons living in Florida believed that the state should donate some land for the use of the Seminoles. A bill providing for a reservation of 100,000 acres that passed the Florida house on May 23, 1913, by a vote of 45 to 1 and the senate on June 4 by 23 to 0 was vetoed by Governor Park Trammell on June 5.[45] The governor gave as his reasons for the veto the unfairness of an outright gift of land to 400 Seminoles when there were 800,000 persons living in Florida and the need for private ownership of land so that drainage taxes could be collected. If the Seminoles needed a reservation, the federal government should relinquish part of the 350,000 acres that it owned in Florida.[46] The veto was sustained by a vote of nine yeas to forty-three nays. In 1915 Augustus M. Wilson of Myakka proposed a similar measure, but it never received enough support to reach the floor of either the house or the senate.

Both the missionary efforts of the religious groups and the attempts to place the Seminoles on a reservation by the Friends of the Seminoles were bound to fail. The Seminoles were antimissionary and antireservation, preferring to practice their traditional religion and to migrate during the hunting, trading, and planting seasons. The sites selected by Bishop Gray were good ones until the Seminoles moved away. Indian trader Brown made better choices because the Seminoles had to come to him for trade articles, but no permanent installation had any chance of success at this time.

10

Lucien A. Spencer and His Work, 1913–1931

n March 1, 1913, Lucien A. Spencer, a man whose life had been dedicated to the service of the Protestant Episcopal Church and the American Indian, became special commissioner in charge of the Seminole Indians.[1] In 1897 he had been a missionary among the Chippewas at the Whiskey Bay Reservation in Minnesota. He had then served as dean of St. Luke's Cathedral at Orlando for many years, and after the retirement of his superior, Bishop William Crane Gray, he decided to work among the Seminoles with the backing of the U.S. government rather than of the Protestant Episcopal Church.[2] When Spencer took charge of the Seminole agency, he was told by Abbott, the acting commissioner of Indian affairs, to do his best to persuade the Seminoles to locate on the reservation land so that they could be instructed in modern farming methods and become educated.

Spencer faced enormous obstacles. He had no agency in which to base his operations and was forced to operate from temporary quarters in Miami. Few Seminoles lived on the widely scattered, unsurveyed reservations that the U.S. government had acquired for them, eighteen separate tracts ranging from 40 to 16,000 acres; only one group, the Billy Fewell camp, had settled on the reservation lands, and they had probably not known that the land had been designated a reservation. The other Seminoles lived in twenty-eight camps scattered over 9,000 square miles.

The special commissioner to the Seminoles had selected Miami as his base because most of the Seminoles came there by canoe at least once a year. Once in Miami Spencer saw the need for better office quarters, a hospital, and a garden on the Miami River. Since they could not endure a bed or mattress, confinement at Miami City Hospital was not satisfactory for sick Seminoles, and Spencer suggested that galvanized sheds and latrines be erected at a proposed Miami River site to provide hospital facilities.

Ever since the end of the Second Seminole War, the Seminole Tribe had maintained a determined stand against their young people attending school. As many as 6 Seminoles in the population of over 500 had gained some knowledge of reading and writing, but without the approval or perhaps knowledge of the leaders. The opposition to education rose from their observation that an educated Seminole was a changed person. As one old Seminole said: "As soon as an Indian learns to read and write, he learns to lie."[3] Nevertheless, the Jim Gopher band at Stuart, according to Spencer, had set aside all objections to education, assumed white styles of dress, and was willing to move to the reservation and learn how to cultivate crops in the whites' style.[4] The members of a nearby band gave rough treatment to the Gopher band, however, whenever its members were seen wearing articles of white clothing.

With his clan leader's permission Tony B. M. Tommie was able to enroll in the Fort Lauderdale school in 1913. Wearing shoes, pants, and a Seminole shirt, Tommie was probably the first eastern Seminole to enter school since one of the Apalachicola leaders had enrolled his son in the Choctaw Academy in Kentucky during the 1830s.[5] The Seminole boy passed the first two grades in the 1913–14 term and the next two in the 1914–15 term. So that he would adjust more readily to the white environment, Tommie was boarded at government expense with a white family during the first school year, but the next year he lived at his Seminole camp.[6] Through the efforts of Frank Stranahan, the trader at Fort Lauderdale, Tommie was sent to the Carlisle Institute in Pennsylvania but because of illness had to drop out and transfer to Tuskegee Institute in Alabama. In 1917 as a result of Tommie's influence six Seminole boys and girls were enrolled in the Fort Lauderdale public grade school, and whites provided them with food and clothing. The venture was a failure, for within one month all had quit school and returned to their camps.[7]

Four months after his appointment, Spencer was obliged, like the other Seminole agents, to make a census of his charges. Compared to more exacting ones compiled in recent years, this census completed during July 1913 was inadequate. Spencer counted all of the Seminoles and blacks living with them for a total of 567. Adult males' names and, if known, ages were noted. Of the female adults, approximately ten names were listed; the rest were designated as squaws. Children were listed as "child," with no designation of sex.

The Seminoles had a problem with the English-speaking frontier people regarding their names. The most famous example was Asi-yaholo, or "Shout given when drinking the black drink," whom the whites named Osceola. The Seminoles adopted the name to such a degree that in 1913 there were nine Osceolas. According to William Sturtevant, all of the living Florida Seminoles surnamed Osceola, both Mikasuki and Muskogee, were descended from Charlie Osceola of the Bird clan and his wife, Nancy, of the Tiger clan.[8] Sturtevant also stated that the literal meanings of Seminole adult male names have nothing to do with the personal characteristics or experiences of their owners.

Of the men who submitted names to Spencer, only two—Fi-lan-a-hee (Spencer list item 226) and Hautlee (247)—had neither a western first or second name. Some bore both a Seminole name and a white one, such as Billy Conepatchie [Konipatci] (43), E-faw-le-harjo Charley Osceola (126), and Billy Buskenuggee (90).[9]

The adult male Seminoles reflected a variety of names. Forty-four bore the first or second name of Billy; nineteen, Tiger; twenty-two, Charley; six, Tommie; and twelve, Doctor. Three were named in honor of Seminole traders: Joe Bowers (257), Frank Stranahan (224), and Girtman Billy (231). Several bore the names of outstanding Americans or white Floridians: Ben Franklin (78), Jackson Charley (302), William McKinley (79), Charley Ingraham (167), Billy Harney (64), George Hendry Jim (234), Ingraham Tiger (282), Ingraham Billie (281), and two Henry Clays (275 and 279).

Some names indicated geographical areas, such as Lake Wilson (375), Miami Billy (418), Miami Charley (419), Miami Jim (420), Miami Jimmy (425), Tallahassee Chipco (470), John Miami Tiger (330), and Tom Devil's Garden (481). Others indicated physical structure, age, or illnesses: Blind Tom (36), Little Doctor (396), Tom Smallpox (492), Smallpox Tommie (469), Old Jumper (443), and Old Polly Parker (424). Two rather unusual names were Henry Homespun (250) and Ginger Snaps (233). Of the men, 5 were born in the 1830–39 period; 7, 1840–49; 6, 1850–59; 7, 1860–69; 17, 1870–79; 29, 1880–89; and 34, 1890–99. Certainly these ages are suspect, but one instance has been confirmed. Billy Konipatci told Robert Pratt that he was born in 1860, the date also given in the 1913 census next to his name.

Spencer often listed women in terms of a male relation: Billy Smith's daughter (26), Charley Tigertail's mother (156) and sister (157), Little Jim's squaw (401), Dan Parker's mother (207), Nellie, daughter of Willie John (514). A few were listed by both first and second names: Lucy Bowles (288), Old Polly Parker (424), Ruthie Parker (449), Nancy Tiger (423), and Etta Tiger (211). Three were listed by white name alone: Morilee (517), Marrylee (518), and Old Pinty (439). Five were listed by Seminole name alone: Tehim-cha (463), Bi-san-gee (464), Matottnee (516), Stem-l-h-eel (465), and Sho-y-o-chee, a widow (461). At the end of the list Spencer listed ten widows and orphans, supplying no names. He seldom listed ages for the women.

Spencer was probably the first census taker to indicate the number of blacks living within the Seminole community. They included Charley Dixie Hall (115), a half-black born in 1870 who married a full-blooded Seminole and had three children. Dixon's black mother was listed (120), as was Funke (217), another black woman.

When Spencer learned that one band was willing to move to the reservation to try farming, he made plans to fence one agricultural tract and to hire a Seminole husband-and-wife team: the man would teach agricultural skills and marketing and the woman would instruct the women in sewing. In his justification statement submitted to the commissioner of Indian affairs on September 9, 1914, Spencer appealed for $3,000 to start the work in making the Seminoles self-supporting along agricultural lines and a total of $10,000 for the project. His request was approved and included in the appropriation bill, but it failed to be passed by Congress.

After working two and a half years in the job Spencer began to sense the obstacles he faced and the difficulty of removing them:

> The work is most difficult and discouraging and I should feel that my time was wasted and ask to be relieved, were it not for the fact that I *know* these people, know their heroic struggles, suffering and hunger which are borne without a complaint, and although the white man has taken their all, they treat him as a honorable victor and try to learn and abide by his laws. When I see all this and their great need for a white friend, I am determined to stay with them just as long as the Office will accept my services.[10]

To make his annual visit to the camps in the Big Cypress Swamp, Spencer had to proceed by launch from Miami via one of the drainage canals to Okeechobee, cross the lake in a westward direction, go down the Caloosahatchee River to Fort Myers where he left the boat, and then travel by ox cart to the twenty-one Mikasuki camps located in Dade, Lee, and Monroe counties. Actually these 400 Mikasukis, two-thirds of all the Seminoles in Florida, needed little aid from the government. No whites lived within fifty miles of their camps, game was plentiful, and their life was good. The only problem developed late in 1914 when World War I closed off their fur markets and made it difficult for them to purchase the much-desired calicoes and coffee.[11] Sometime later, when the war curtailed the supply of tin cans, the Mikasukis could not sell their crops to the canners. Probably the cruelest blow came when whites stole the hogs that the Mikasukis had hoped to sell on the war-inflated market.

The seven Muskogee-speaking camps in Palm Beach, St. Lucie, and Okeechobee counties required much of Spencer's attention. This area had seen much land speculation and development. Whenever a Seminole cleared an acre or two to plant garden crops, citrus trees, or banana plants, his farm was taken over by a white who had obtained legal title to the land. Usually the whites burned the chickee, erected a shack, and planted crops in the former Seminole field. To protect these Seminoles, Spencer hoped to purchase some land from the Florida East Coast Line, which was willing to sell tracts for as little as three dollars an acre.[12]

Spencer's letters to the commissioner of Indian affairs in 1915 and early 1916 reveal some of the problems he and the Seminoles faced. On July 27, 1915, Spencer visited Billie John's camp and found he had quit hunting to devote all of his time to farming, but Billie John was a squatter on the property and would have to leave when the white owner wanted to use the land. Billy Bowlegs had cleared a large field, fenced it, and planned to plant three hundred orange trees but he, too, had no legal title to the land that he occupied. In December Spencer went to Stuart to confer with the Seminoles and furnish clothing to those children attending school at Annie, Florida. In January 1916 he visited the Twentieth Street Miami camp to adjust differences in the otter skin pay scale between the Seminoles and the traders.

In 1917 a move by the Friends of the Seminoles to obtain a state reservation for the Seminoles succeeded. Principal figures in the project were James Willson, Jr., a Kissimmee real estate man, and his wife, Minnie Moore-Willson, who wrote the popular *Seminoles of Florida* published in 1896. Some Muskogee speakers were frequent visitors to their home in Kissimmee, and the Willsons were willing to devote time and

Lucien Spencer in the field, c. 1910. Photograph from National Archives, Washington, D.C.

money to aid their friends. In 1916 the Willsons secured the help of the Philadelphia-based Indian Rights Association established in 1882.[13] Herbert Welsh was the leader of the organization, which would become the major nongovernmental unit dedicated to helping the American Indian. Welsh's assistant and recording secretary for many years was Mathew K. Sniffen, who spent much of his time working in the field. The Indian Rights Association was mainly a lobbying instrument, and in many cases government officials turned to the association for advice and for recommendations for jobs in the Bureau of Indian Affairs.

In 1887 the Indian Rights Association had helped write and lobby through Congress the General Allotment or Dawes Act, which provided for the division of reservations into 160-acre tracts and for the sale of some land to white purchasers. Under its terms many reservations were dissolved, and Commissioner of Indian Affairs John Collier later said the act

Aerial view of Seminole Camp in the Big Cypress Swamp, c. 1920. By permission of National Anthropological Archives, Bureau of American Ethnology, Smithsonian Institution, Washington, D.C.

had deprived the American Indians of vast quantities of property and created a class of landless paupers who depended upon the government.[14] By 1916 the Indian Rights Association realized the folly of its 1887 work and was trying to create reservations instead of destroying them. While on a field trip that year to investigate conditions there, Sniffen met many of the Floridians who wanted to help the Seminoles. He and his companions, Lucien Spencer, Joseph Elkington, and Billy Bowlegs III, went into the Big Cypress Swamp in search of the camps but fleas, red bugs, and high water kept them from meeting many Seminoles.[15] Sniffen reported that the 600 Seminoles scattered in thirty-two camps were in a precarious economic situation, for there was little demand for either alligator hides or bird plumes.[16]

In planning her campaign to secure a state reservation for the Seminoles, Minnie Moore-Willson feared opposition from some prominent people including May Mann Jennings, president of the Florida Federation of Women's Clubs and wife of the former governor. Moore-Willson alleged that Governor Jennings had acquired 100,000 acres of land at thirty cents an acre and that, if the Seminoles left Florida, lands designated for them could be made available to land companies in which he had an interest.[17] In 1915 when Moore-Willson had criticized the state's position on Seminole policy in a publication of the Florida Federation of Women's Clubs, she was told that henceforth all statements on the Seminoles would have to be cleared by Ivy Cromartie Stranahan, chair of the club's Seminole Indian committee.[18] Despite pressure to resign from the Indian committee, Moore-Willson remained a member but directed the main thrust of her views to areas where she could not be controlled by Mae Mann Jennings or Ivy Stranahan.[19] Actually, Jennings testified before a congressional committee in 1917 that she was angry that Governor Trammell had vetoed the bill and that she supported a state reservation. She did admit that some Floridians felt that "some of the large land interests in the State are involved in the non-passage of the bill."[20] Moore-Willson seemed to see another foe in Congressman William J. Sears, a member of the House Indian Committee, who was eager to support a bill providing for another federal reservation in Florida. She should not have regarded him as an enemy, however, for he gave her full support and cooperation.[21] Moore-Willson believed that there were others on the state level who pretended to be friends of the Seminoles but who either lost bills in committee or helped push measures that really gave the Seminoles nothing.

Moore-Willson's first and perhaps most important goal in the preliminary planning stage in 1916 was to obtain the support of Governor-elect Sidney J. Catts. Representing almost a complete break with past political policies, he seemed to be a most suitable official to help the Seminoles.[22] Since Catts showed great loyalty to those who had helped him get elected, and since James Willson, Jr., had worked in his campaign, Moore-Willson suggested that Sniffen write Catts a letter.[23] In reply Catts informed Sniffen that "we need to do something about these Indians."[24] Catts planned to take the matter up with the Willsons, who, according to Sniffen, hoped to have a bill introduced in the 1917 legislature. Catts asked for more information from Sniffen and promised to study the matter. At this point Catts was in favor of either a federal reservation or federal assistance, as he stated in letters to Welsh and Sniffen. After a conversation with James Willson, Jr., on February 21, 1917, the governor seemed ready to release land for the reservation when it was approved by the legislature and would call a meeting of the Internal Improvements Board for approval of this action.[25]

The measure worked its way through committees in both houses and was passed by the house 47 to 0 and by the senate 27 to 0. Little opposition had developed to the bill, for in a hearing before the Internal Improvement Board it was pointed out that, outside of hunting and fishing activities, the land had little value for the whites and that nobody had plans for its use except as a Seminole reservation. A day of celebration took place on May 9, 1917, when Governor Catts signed the measure into law. Sniffen, Willson, and Spencer were present at the signing ceremony, and in recognition of her perseverance during the past twenty years Moore-Willson was presented with the golden pen that Catts had used.[26] The success of the operation was due to the dedication of the Willsons, the political astuteness and personal charm of Sniffen, and Spencer's knowledge of state and national politics.

The trustees of the Internal Improvement Board transferred 99,200 acres in Monroe County to the Board of Commissioners of State Institutions (the Florida cabinet) for the perpetual use and benefit of the Seminole Indians. Roy Nash, visiting the reservation in 1930, saw little agricultural value in the site, for excessive rainfall flooded the area, but found it fine for hunting and fishing.[27] Few Seminoles took advantage of the state land reserved for them, for they did not want to be confined to a reservation, and the state was not willing to spend much money on it. When the Everglades National Park was created in 1935, the land contained within the original tract was exchanged for 104,000 acres in Broward and Palm Beach counties. In addition to limited grazing and hunting activities, the reservation land rose in value as a result of oil and gas leases granted in 1938 but declined during the 1950s when the release of water from flood control areas to the north caused much loss of life for the deer and other wildlife.[28]

Nowhere during the entire proceeding had the Seminoles been consulted as to the value or use of the proposed reservation. White friends thought they could help by providing a reservation, but local opposition caused it to be placed in an area thought to have little value to the white man, and no money was provided for improvements. Had either the federal government or the state of Florida been willing to purchase good agricultural land for a reservation, a site with such assets would have been more suitable. The white friends of the Seminoles had accepted land good only for hunting and fishing, and the Seminoles refused to live there.

After a leave of absence Spencer served as chaplain (July 1, 1916, to March 19, 1917) with the Second Florida Infantry in service on the Mexican border with General John J. Pershing, and Inspector W. S. Coleman took his place as Seminole superintendent. His tenure brought renewed interest in the western reservation in Hendry County seventy-five miles from Fort Myers on the western side of the Everglades.

Coleman visited the reservation and offered the following plan for its use: (1) Move the agency headquarters from Miami to the largest Hendry County reservation tract and place a store there where hides would be purchased at top prices from the Seminoles and items sold to them at cost; (2) locate at the headquarters a farmer, school, post office, and hospital with a staff of a nurse and doctor; and (3) fence and ditch the best lands and construct a road system on the reservation. Cutting fence posts, erecting fences and shelter houses, and cultivating land would be performed by the Seminoles. After all of these provisions had been completed, Coleman believed, the Seminoles would move in gradually increasing numbers to the reservation.[29]

Spencer served with Pershing in the pursuit of Pancho Villa, returned to Florida and the Seminoles from March to August 1917, and resigned to serve with the army in France. His replacement, Frank E. Brandon, was given approval and funds amounting to $20,000 to purchase wire for fencing and lumber for buildings to be erected on the largest tract of the Hendry County reservation, which was to be known as the Industrial Station. In fall 1918 work at the Industrial Station was placed in charge of W. Frank Brown, a white man who knew the Mikasuki dialect and had been in contact with the Mikasuki-speaking Seminoles for many years when his father, William Brown, operated a trading post. Daily wages were paid to Seminoles who helped place the Industrial Station in operating order, but as the white administrators were to find out, they needed to be instructed in basic techniques in all phases of ranch work, including digging post holes and wells and stringing wire.

The influenza epidemic that swept the nation and Florida in fall 1918 and spring 1919 resulted in twenty reported cases and three deaths among the Seminole children and forty-six cases and seven deaths among the adults, with more deaths proportionally among the Seminoles than among any other group. According to one witness dozens of Seminole deaths went unreported near Turner River, Allen River, and the Hendry County reservation.[30]

In November 1919 Spencer returned from military service in France to devote most of his time to improving the Industrial Station. By that year, when the work was completed, 12,800 acres were fenced for use as a cattle range and 1,280 acres enclosed as a hog range. Although hauling lumber for buildings had been difficult over the eighty miles of sandy road and muck stretching from Fort Myers via Immokalee to Brown's Store and Everglade Cross, a caretaker dwelling, council house, office, warehouse, stable, and garage had been built. When evidence indicated that the major portion of his work would be at or near the Hendry County reservation, Spencer shifted operations from Miami to a small rented office in Fort Myers, where he awaited the opportunity to move to larger quarters in the soon-to-be-constructed Federal Building.

When Congress appropriated $5,000 instead of the $45,000 needed to continue work in 1921, all activities ceased at the Industrial Station. Cattle raising had been regarded as the centerpiece of the program, but without sufficient funds all hope for the enterprise faded away. Spencer had purchased some hogs, but in two nights forty were killed by panthers. To observers the work done at the Industrial Station was a tragic comedy of errors. Wire for twenty miles of fencing was hauled over eighty miles of bad roads during the rainy season. A complete set of ranch buildings was constructed but used only by a caretaker. Instead of purchasing the cattle that would have been suitable for the reservation, hogs were purchased and placed unprotected within an enclosure until killed by natural enemies. It was a waste of federal funds and of the hard work of those who carried the fencing and building materials over the terrible roads.[31]

Many Seminoles wanted to settle on the reservation, but when funds were not available, they preferred to remain in their camps. The year 1921 was a bad one for the 115 Muskogees and 339 Mikasukis, for there was little demand for furs or alligator hides. Since they could not trade their furs for commodities at the local stores, they were forced to move into the lowlands where they could obtain an adequate supply of their traditional foods.

Although the Seminoles had been promised that they had full rights on the Hendry County reservation and had been encouraged to raise hogs, cattle, and horses, the exclusive grazing rights on the reserve were sold to a white.[32] Three Seminoles were able to begin farming at Dania, but a late summer 1921 tornado and early spring 1922 drought ruined their crops, and the agent tried to find jobs for them with nearby ranchers and farmers so that they would not starve.[33] Employees of the agency at this time included Spencer at $2,000 a year, Trezevant Williams, clerk, at $1,200, and W. Frank Brown, laborer, at $900.

The migration of homemakers, real estate developers, and farmers into Broward and Dade counties brought the white population into contact with the Seminoles, and friction developed. In May 1919 federal game wardens and the U.S. deputy marshal arrested Willie Willie, a Seminole, and J. G. Truitt, a white man, on charges of violating the migratory bird treaty by having migratory bird plumes in their possession.[34] On April 19, 1920, Lake Wilson, an Indian, was arrested on the same charge, pleaded guilty along with Willie, and was fined ten dollars; Willie was fined five. In March 1920 Ingraham Charley was arrested in Fort Myers, charged with drunkenness, and after pleading guilty fined five dollars. In March 1922 Jack Tigertail was killed on a wharf in the Miami River at Miami by Charles Vebber, a trapper and trader. The concerned citizens in Miami raised a fund, which was placed in trust for Tigertail's wife and child, and provided a lawyer to assist the state attorney. In Dade County Circuit Court Vebber was found guilty by the white jury, but the verdict was set aside on a technicality.[35] In contrast to the Vebber decision, a case arose in December 1922 in which two Seminole women were raped; although there were no witnesses for the defense, the jury deliberated nearly three hours and freed the three white men accused of the crime.

In 1925 there occurred the first legal case involving Seminoles on both sides that lay within the jurisdiction of a local court. The leaders of two camps near Miami had a dispute that climaxed in an assault by one group upon the other. Several men of one camp were arrested and placed under a peace bond for a year by a justice of the peace.[36]

When the supply of furs and hides began to dwindle, some Seminoles looking about for ready cash found white people who wanted deer meat even if the hunting season had closed. Since they knew deer country well, they would kill a deer or two and take them to whites waiting in a camp or along a lonely road. In 1930 C. C. Woodward, Florida state game commissioner, commented that the Seminoles should confine their hunting activities to the reservations for their own use and not leave to sell game shot on or off the reservations. He pointed out that since the Seminoles had been made citizens in 1924, they should have no special privileges. Despite the objections of Woodward the Seminoles continued to hunt deer in most parts of south Florida, and, if they desired, to sell the meat to whites.

Social changes were also taking place in Seminole life. Formerly in accordance with tribal custom—marriages were arranged by couples agreeing to live together, and divorce was obtained by the man and woman separating. All such marriages were recognized by the state of Florida as common law marriages, and no divorce was needed, but in 1925 one Seminole couple obtained a marriage license and were married by a county official.[37] A bill introduced in the legislature that provided for the recording of Seminole marriages at the local county courthouse was not passed.

In 1920 Dr. O. S. Phillips, a special physician with the U.S. Indian Service, surveyed the Seminoles and found them to be enjoying better health than any tribe he had visited. The only diseases affecting them to any extent were sixteen cases of hookworm, twenty-two of influenza, sixteen of malaria, and three of bronchitis. He found no venereal disease. Many Seminoles had decay present in upper incisors. Dr. Phillips credited their excellent health to their outdoor life and their extensive physical exercise.

By 1924 the Seminoles had been making use in increasing numbers of the services offered by public health facilities and by private practices covered by federal dollars in Miami, Fort Myers, and other places. In July 1920 the wife of Ben Frank Tommie consented to have a white doctor in attendance at the birth of her first child. Still, due to the isolation of the camps, only twenty-four pregnant Seminole women saw white doctors in ten years. The rest went off into the sawgrass and hammocks, had the children, and came back to camp, often with permanent injuries inflicted by the childbirth.

According to Josie Billie, when a woman knew that it was time to have her baby, she retired to a tent erected some fifty feet from the camp.

> This tent has been prepared for the event. With her, the prospective mother takes another woman. Long ago, it was the custom to take a very old woman, but there are not many old left and they are unable to travel around the camp. This custom has been changed, so now the expectant mother takes one of her near relatives with her. Some times mother cries out with pain. "But not much," says Josie Billie. Miss Bedell, a missionary who has been working with the Seminoles for the past five years, said that she had been asked one time to attend a mother at childbirth. One dark stormy night several months ago two boys knocked at the mission door and spoke the girl's name, adding, "her baby, you come."[38]

The Seminole doctors began to make some changes in their procedures. No longer did they search the woods to secure leaves and herbs. At least one ordered prepared drugs from a wholesale drug company, and bottles containing prepared herbs, barks, and roots could be seen on the shelves of a doctor's chickee. Epsom salts and a green medicine for the relief of lumbago were popular, but rubbing alcohol was most often requested by patients.

One case in 1921 that helped build confidence in white physicians was that of Catathlee, a four-year-old orphan who suffered from a bad hernia. After much negotiation the boy was placed in Lee County Memorial Hospital at Fort Myers and underwent a successful operation with a prominent Seminole and his wife standing nearby. The procedure so impressed the Seminole that he placed his wife in the same hospital for kidney treatment and returned later for personal treatment. The federal expenditure for Seminole health care during fiscal year 1924 amounted to $1,360 for physicians, $346 for hospitals, $686.75 for medicine, and $302.85 for subsistence—a total of $2,695.20.[39]

In 1914 Henry Coppinger, who owned gardens along N.W. Seventh Street in Miami inhabited by some Seminoles, decided to charge a fee for tourists entering his Tropical Gardens and visiting their village. At first he did not pay the Seminoles, for they were able to sell dolls, toy canoes, and other artifacts to the Coppingers that the operators could offer for sale to tourists who visited the curio shop.[40] By 1918 the Seminoles were selling live baby alligators and stuffed small ones to tourists and shipping hides to northern factories. A few brave men were wrestling with the alligators, and a Seminole-style wedding was often presented, with the same actors playing the same roles time and again. In 1930 the pay at these villages averaged six dollars and food per week per family. Many of the several hundred Mikasuki village employees at Coppinger's, Musa Isle, St. Petersburg, and, later, Silver Springs became well-known personalities: Buffalo Tiger, Tony Tommie, Corey Osceola, Josie Billie, William McKinley Osceola, and Sam Huff. Some of them left Musa Isle or Coppinger's to establish small villages along the Tamiami Trail, where they sold curios and wrestled alligators. William McKinley Osceola was able to open an amusement camp on the Tamiami Trail, where he sold groceries and other merchandise and purchased and sold hides and furs; after keeping a close check on the hide and fur market prices, he was able to make a good profit.

One Seminole who had considerable business ingenuity was about to put together a rather large Seminole exhibition village at Musa Isle, which was described by an unidentified observer:

> Willie Willie, the well-known, educated young Seminole Indian is the proprietor and manager of an Indian village of his own on Musa Isle. He also has quite a display of alligators. The camp is called Oke-on-so-ho-ke-leia, which means, in Seminole, "Running Water City."
>
> The visitor is met by an Indian in native garb and conducted through the camp and shown and told all the interesting things of the camp and Indians. There is an Indian that enters a pen of vicious alligators and with bare hands captures one, subdues it, puts it asleep, and by opening its mouth gives the visitor an opportunity to see the terrible teeth, set in jaws that are faster and more powerful than the biggest steel trap. It takes experience and daring to accomplish such a feat and is well worth going miles to see.
>
> Alligators of all sizes, from the newly-hatched, tiny baby ones to the large, vicious ones, are in different pens. The small ones can be purchased by visitors desiring to send one home or raise a unique pet.
>
> There is a high and low class in every race, and the Indian has his caste, just as we have. Low caste tramp Indians are not tolerated at Willie Willie's camp. A visit to Oke-on-so-ho-ke-leia will show the difference between a well-kept village of high-class Seminole and one kept by low-caste ones.
>
> Unlike the Indians of the north and west, the Seminole Indian does not receive any compensation or aid from the government, nor have they had an opportunity to acquire the wealth acquired by the western

Exhibition group of Seminole Indians from Musa Isle, c. 1920. By permission of National Anthropological Archives, Bureau of American Ethnology, Smithsonian Institution, Washington, D.C.

Indian from oil wells and other sources. The Seminole today is, as he has always been, free and untrammeled by civilization.

Quite a few of the Indians speak English intelligibly and one can talk to them without any difficulty.

Another attraction is a real Indian princess, a descendant of Chief Osceola.

For a small silver coin, often used to make ornaments, one can get the Indians to pose for a picture. The coin is considered a gift, and these Indians are grateful for a gift from the whites, even though it may be accepted without comment or sign, for many of them do not know how to express in words their appreciation or thanks.

A jitney bus, taken at most any of the down-town corners, will take you to this camp by directing the driver to drive to Musa Isle Grove, Willie Willie's camp, and you will be well repaid for your visit.[41]

It was regrettable that Willie Willie lost the business to a white person.[42]

Seminole women and children employed at the villages lost their reluctance to talk to whites and engaged in conversation with white visitors. Seminole men watched to keep the women in check when they tried to sell articles to white men, but sometimes the glances were in vain, for some of the women valued the money more than they feared their husbands' displeasure. The children learned to badger the visitors for gifts of coins or candy.

The Industrial Station on the Hendry County reservation had reached such a deplorable state that some leading Seminoles held a meeting in January 1926 and recommended to the commissioner of Indian affairs that the Industrial Station be abandoned and that the funds saved be used for the care of sick and indigent Seminoles. If such a measure were taken, those not needed to care for the sick Seminoles could be employed by farmers and cattle ranchers; although the older Seminoles would not change by living and working among whites, the younger ones would adopt their way of life more readily.[43] Several weeks later the commissioner of Indian affairs and his staff endorsed the closing of the Industrial Station and the opening of Dania camp. Available evidence fails to reveal why Dania was selected as agency site instead of the Martin County reserve, which had better soil, was larger, and was closer to Seminoles who wanted training in modern ranching techniques.

On June 30, 1926, the Industrial Station was ordered closed and in its place a camp for sick and indigent Seminoles was planned on the reservation near Dania-Hollywood. Ten one-room frame cottages with no inside running water or electricity and a small administration building were to be erected. Plans were made to move the agency from Fort Myers as soon as the Dania reservation was ready.[44]

At the time no Seminoles lived on the reservation, and it took determined effort on the part of several persons to get some to relocate there. Agent Lucien Spencer asked Ivy Stranahan, longtime friend of the Seminoles, for help.[45] On a Monday morning she took Willie Jumper, Annie Tommie, and Frank Huff and his sister, Pocahontas, in her car to the reservation and explained how the federal government planned to assist the Seminoles.[46] When Stranahan said they would be paid $1.50 a day for clearing the wooded area, they began to clear away the palmettos so that cabins could be erected. Each day that week Stranahan returned with the Seminoles to work at clearing the land, and on Friday she wired the agent at Fort Myers that the Seminoles were willing to live on the reservation. The first families to move into the cottage complex included the Tommies, Osceolas, and Jumpers; the Jumper family had come from Miami, and the Osceola and Tommie families from hammocks near Fort Lauderdale.[47] Medicine woman Annie Tommie led her large family to the reservation, an action that helped persuade others to move, for she was well known as a doctor who treated both whites and Seminoles. The voluntary movement of these families to the reservation was an important landmark on the path of the Seminoles toward acceptance of the white way of life.

On September 18, 1926, a devastating hurricane struck southeastern Florida, killing many people, destroying many homes, and wrecking the cottages. Louis Capron, who helped carry supplies to the Seminoles from the American Legion in West Palm Beach, recalled how grateful they were to receive the clothes.[48] So far as can be ascertained no Seminoles lost their lives in the hurricane. Tony Tommie, the only white-educated Seminole at that time, served as liaison between the relief workers and the Seminoles and collected and distributed nearly $2,000 contributed by local civic groups.

The agency office was moved from Ft. Myers to Dania-Hollywood on July 1, 1927. The buildings constructed for the agency's new base of operation were the administration building, electric pumping plant, garage, school building, infirmary, laundry, and the ten two-room cottages. Squatters who had erected three buildings on the tract were evicted and their homes occupied by Seminoles. The agency was over a hundred miles from the bulk of the Seminole population, and it would be many years before the agent could properly supervise the Seminoles living in the Everglades, in Big Cypress, or on the land north of Lake Okeechobee. Still, during these days many Seminoles traveled from the Big Cypress Swamp to trade at Fort Lauderdale, which was near Dania–Hollywood, so the site served at least some of the scattered population.

Life in the ten double cottages at Dania–Hollywood seemed acceptable. Each three months the cottages were thoroughly cleaned and evidence indicated that the Seminoles were using the modern plumbing fixtures that had been installed, although a 1927 visit of a citizen's committee to the camp found "disorder and unsanitary conditions."[49] Many of the Seminoles built palmetto-thatched chickees near the cottages in which they preferred to cook, eat, and work.

One custom resisted the transition from chickee to cottage life. The Seminoles liked to keep clean by bathing in nearby lakes and streams, but none were available at Dania–Hollywood. As they were unable to accept the idea of using a tub or shower, some Seminoles waited until nightfall and then undressed and washed themselves with a garden hose. Spencer recommended that a swimming pool be built near the cottages for them to bathe in.

At first the cottages were intended for use by sick Seminoles, but when healthy Seminoles began to move into Dania–Hollywood, the whole concept of the cottages was changed. Betty Mae Tiger, who lived in one of the houses abandoned by the squatters, was not impressed by the ten-foot by eighteen-foot house, for the wood was rotten, the roof leaked, and rats lived in the crawlway. Finally the agent had the house torn down and a better one erected. Tiger was still not impressed, for the agent lived in a fine two-story frame house complete with offices, living quarters, and a fireplace, easily visible from the row of Seminole houses.[50] In 1930 Roy Nash reported that the traditional open-faced, thatched-roof chickee was much more clean and airy than the cottages or "dog kennels."[51]

The consumption of liquor became a most pressing problem during the late 1920s. Although the Seminoles did not manufacture or sell any whiskey on the reservation, it was easily obtained just beyond the reservation limits. That the Broward County sheriff and several deputies and policemen were currently under indictment for involvement in bootlegging operations was of no help to Spencer. Although Spencer was a special deputy, he hesitated to arrest most of the drunken Seminoles, for he was doing his best to induce them to move to the reservation. Finally he worked out a plan that kept the more obvious drinkers under some control. When they became boisterous, he arrested them and placed them in the Broward County jail for several days. When the judge found the Seminoles guilty as charged, he paroled them to the agent; if they were arrested again, they were sent to work sixty days on the county roads.[52]

According to Spencer the quality of liquor was such that "it drives the Indians crazy," and as a result two murders and a drowning took place. In May 1929 Carney Billie found a bootlegger's still, drank some of his loot, fell from his canoe, and drowned in the Miami Canal. On December 15, 1928, some drunken Seminoles walking along the Tamiami Trail had a fight during which Josie Billie stabbed Nuff-kee Roberts, who died from the wounds. Two months later Charlie Lee and Philip Billie obtained a gallon of liquor in LaBelle, and en route home Philip Billie killed Charlie Lee with a hunting knife. Although the local courts refused to hear cases in which Seminoles killed other Seminoles, on June 21, 1929, the Tribal Council tried Philip Billie and Josie Billie and acquitted them on the grounds that the murders were not premeditated.[53]

Since the first recorded incident in 1923 the number of venereal disease cases had remained within an annual rate of two or three, but in 1930 fourteen cases of gonorrhea were reported. As the total population of the Seminoles at this time included 314 adults, 214 children between five and nineteen, and 50 under five, a total of 578, the venereal disease rate reached epidemic proportions. According to two doctors who treated the cases, the two Seminole tourist camps in Miami—Musa Isle and Coppinger's Tropical Garden—were the major sources of infection.

Lucien Spencer had long realized that the Seminoles needed a school. The state of Florida had neglected them in its planning for the educational needs of its citizens, and only one school was situated near camp. The 152 Seminole children of school age were scattered over 5,000 square miles, making it nearly impossible to move enough into one area to establish a school for them.[54]

The move to initiate a school at the agency developed when the hurricane of September 1926 destroyed the camp. The assistant commissioner of Indian affairs, E. B. Merritt, decided to rebuild the camp and open a school. At a conference in Washington, D.C., December 16, 1926, officials from the Bureau of Indian Affairs made plans to erect a temporary building and to employ a full-blooded Seminole from Oklahoma, Lena King, to conduct the planned four-month school terms.[55] King had come from Oklahoma with her husband to help convert the Seminoles to the

Christian faith, but the visits of the Oklahomans had produced only ten converts between 1909 and 1923.

Just before the first day of class, an attempt was made to prevent the opening of the school. Tony Tommie and a few others visited the Seminole camp and claimed that all students would be vaccinated on opening day. As a result all but one family fled, and only three students appeared.[56] Spencer was able to repair the damage by selling his educational program to more parents, and enrollment climbed. Still he had trouble, for the leading student in the one-class school was a very intelligent six-year-old girl, and the teacher was forced to divide the school into three classes with three sessions so that there would be an equal division of talents.

Since the tribal leaders had successfully resisted education for so long, they regrouped and attempted to crush the opposition in another move. Willie Billie, one of the conservative leaders, appeared in February 1927 and somberly forbade anyone to attend classes. Spencer told him either to leave the camp by the next day or to face arrest. He left. Some widows told Spencer that they wanted their children in school but that they feared the reaction from the headmen. Accordingly Spencer decreed "no school, no food," and after no food for sixty days, the headmen ceased their opposition. The same opposition developed in the Indian Town camp, which was preparing to move to the Dania reservation. Once again Spencer refused to release food to the opponents of education, and within three weeks the Indian Town camp had moved to Dania and the children placed in school. Similar tactics were used to persuade the one family living in the Martin County reserve to move to Dania.

Once enrolled in the school, the Seminole children and their teacher still had a few problems. The one-room school building had no inside toilets and no living quarters for the teacher. At first the children were not well behaved; they loved to throw dirt through screens, leave class whenever they desired, and jump in and out through the windows instead of using the doors. Since kindness and patience were most important in dealing with the Seminole children, any infraction of the rules was not closely observed or noted. Generally speaking it was a member of the mother's family who administered punishment when it was needed, not the teacher. A close observer of Seminole life noted the following way in which the children were taught to obey:

> The Indian children are taught obedience from birth and as a rule are
> very well behaved, obeying all commands at once and without argu-

ment. However, in case they do need punishment, they are whipped with a switch. If this is not severe enough to bring a stubborn child under his parent's will, he is then scratched on the arm with a snake tooth. If the child still persists in "Raising hell," to quote Josie Billie, the scratching is continued until the blood comes. "Then he pretty quick stop raising hell," added Josie Billie. Sometimes many scars are seen.[57]

In addition to teaching in the one-room grade school, Lena King had classes in needlework and sewing for the women and night classes for the men who were employed during the day. When she resigned at the end of the term, one reason given was the lack of living quarters for the teacher on the reservation.

Mrs. John Marshall, wife of the agency farmer, took the teaching post. The daughter of Lucien Spencer, she had no experience and little training for the position of teacher, but she was available and willing— two important attributes. The school term was extended, lasting from November 5 to May 5, and instruction was begun in English instead of Muskogee. When they enrolled, all six children and two adult female students knew only their own language and according to the teacher took only one year to learn English. Accordingly, all work was given at the first-grade level. Night classes from six to seven o'clock were continued for the two adult men enrolled in the program.

The location of the agency school had certain drawbacks. Since Dania was distant from most of the Seminole settlements, parents either had to move to Dania or a boarding school needed to be established there. The Seminoles resisted both alternatives. In addition, the social environment at Dania was not acceptable to most of the Mikasuki and Muskogee leaders. Most of the social problems and venereal diseases had arisen at the Miami exhibition camps, and the Dania reservation residents were mostly those who were reported to be outcasts from the tribe. When observed by other Seminoles, the Dania-educated children were noted to be "obnoxious and bad mannered," and the other parents did not want their children to develop in such a way.[58]

In the spring of 1930 Lucien Spencer, while accompanying the federal census agent, died from the exertion of pulling his car from a waterlogged road on the Hendry County reservation. Spencer had helped establish the school at Dania-Hollywood, moved some Seminoles to the reservation, and fought the evils of liquor. The gains may not seem impressive, but they had been achieved over stubborn opposition engendered by the majority of Seminoles. Spencer had no clear-cut answer to the Seminoles' problem, but he offered a few practical solutions.[59] Perhaps his greatest failure was in supporting Brandon's Industrial Station plan, which had little chance of success when virtually all of the funds had been expended in erecting buildings and fences that saw little or no use. It may have been too late for Spencer to stop Brandon, who may have already authorized the construction of buildings and erection of the fence, but fences were not used by cattle ranchers in the area at that time.

One of the first events to take place after Spencer's death was the visit of social worker and writer Roy Nash, who was sent by Washington in 1930 to survey conditions among the Seminole Indians. Using oxen-drawn carts to visit the camps Nash found time to meet with two applicants for Spencer's position, Dr. John Gifford and Rev. Alexander Lynn. He discovered that Spencer had fired the caretaker of the Hendry County reservation because he had collected money from white hunters and allegedly cheated the Seminoles on sales of furs, pigs, and pumpkins. Nash hired sixty-two-year-old William Ivey Byrd as caretaker at the rate of twenty-five dollars a month to live at the reservation, repair the wire fence, and keep hunters off the land.

Nash's report, published in 1932, contained a most detailed account concerning the status of the Seminoles at that time and rates as one of the best ever written about the tribe. Nash hit hard at the educational progress of the Seminoles, with only 4 of nearly 600 persons able to speak acceptable English and the inability of the adults to obtain jobs that would enable them to advance above their present status on the lowest rung of the economic ladder. He provided a good survey of the various Seminole camps scattered throughout southern Florida.[60]

The economic situation was not good for the Seminoles in 1931. Most had no property rights to the land on which they resided. Thirty persons lived on the Dania-Hollywood Reservation, three or four families on the so-called Hendry County reservation, and the remaining 90 percent in thirty-five camps scattered throughout southern Florida. Since those not living on the federal land were squatters, they could be evicted from their homes and agricultural plots and their hogs shot. Nash recommended purchasing cattle to help the men, teaching the women to make saleable handicrafts, and buying better hogs to help both sexes.

Nash submitted the following conclusions to the commissioner of Indian affairs, Charles J. Rhoads: (1) Reservation land should be retained until real progress is made; (2) a public health nurse should be retained, and advances should be made in cattle development, handicraft work, and education; and (3) the Seminoles must be protected against bootleggers and those who sold their products. Perhaps the most cited of Nash's research figures was the estimate that from 50 to 75 percent of all money earned by the Seminoles was used to purchase hard liquor.[61]

By 1934 enrollment in the Dania school reached a record number of fifty students. An attempt was made to open a similar school in the Miami area, but when the assigned teacher became ill, the project was delayed. In 1936 the Dania school was closed because of poor attendance, and several of the students transferred to Cherokee Boarding School in North Carolina.

Laura Mae Osceola, one of the students who went to North Carolina, described her feelings at the time:

> My interest in Seminole people started when I was a little girl living on and off all three reservations. I use to think that if I grow up I want to help the people to improve their living and health conditions. I was one of the group who went away to boarding school in Cherokee, North Carolina because we couldn't attend public school here in Florida at that time. I wasn't sent away because I got in trouble or my mother wanted me to go away. I went because I wanted an education to be able to help myself and my people. At the young age I realized that the things we enjoyed at times like; swimming in the canal, walking through the woods and enjoying life of an Indian was not everything. I had smart kinfolks, who talked about the things to come because of white people coming to the pointed land (Florida).
>
> My uncles were people like Tony Tommie [who went to Carlisle Indian School in Pennsylvania], who was one of the first Seminole Indians in Florida who went away to school. Sam Tommie and Brownie Tommie, they were the ones who taught me to respect and help people. They were really talking to the boys in our family, but I took it all in by listening. Since I am a girl, I was suppose to be interested in what my grandmother taught me; how to be a good wife and mother, cooking, etc. When I hear my uncles talking, I use to think someday I'll do things for my people, and also take care of my clan members.[62]

11

Brighton and Big Cypress
Reservations

hen the Florida boom collapsed in 1926, Florida was the first state in the nation to feel the effects of the post–World War I recession: land values rapidly fell, large and small fortunes were lost, and many persons became unemployed. Since the white people could no longer find employment, they began to give the Seminoles competition in the search for food and available money, and by 1930 the Seminoles no longer played an important role in the hide trade. With the use of the automobile and construction of roads in southern Florida, the whites were able to penetrate most parts of the Big Cypress and remote sections adjacent to the Everglades. They controlled the hunting area for alligator, otter, and raccoon between LaBelle and the Devil's Garden, but the Seminoles held their own in the Big Cypress Swamp south of the Devil's Garden. Using electric battery lights, reflectors, and motor boats the whites held an excellent competitive edge over the Seminoles who, because of their conservative nature and lack of expensive equipment, continued to use the dugout canoe and torchlight. Besides taking control of the pelt trade, the whites began to compete in the search for cabbage palm hearts, coontie, and bullfrogs, whose legs had a considerable value.[1]

There had been some white intrusion in the lands west of Lake Okeechobee. The cattle ranchers from Fort Myers and the hunters and trappers operating from LaBelle exerted enough pressure to initiate a Seminole withdrawal from the Devil's Garden area into the Big Cypress Swamp. The extension of the Atlantic Coast Line Railroad, the construction of a hard surface road, the cultivation of extensive fields of sugar cane, and the erection of a refinery at Moore Haven forced the Seminoles to move from Fisheating Creek, their longtime residence.[2]

Of all the white pressures on the western part of the peninsula it was the construction of the Tamiami Trail, U.S. Highway 41, that changed Seminole life. After work on the Tamiami Trail came to a halt in 1918, a group known as the Trail Blazers decided to revive interest by traveling the forty-mile gap between the Dade and Lee county ends of the trail during the spring of 1923. Guided by two Seminole Indians the Blazers started the trip by car but could only reach the finish point by wading through the boggy terrain. After the trek had aroused interest in the project, construction on the highway was resumed and finally completed in April 1928.[3] According to the outstanding recorder of southern Florida's history, Charlton Tebeau, construction superintendents on the Tamiami Trail had found the Seminole Indians to be the most efficient and reliable workers they could employ, but with the opening of the road the Seminoles lost their front line of defense against the whites.[4] By using the trail and a feeder road from the Everglades to Immokalee, the white hunters and tourists were able to penetrate the heart of Seminole land.

The wave of white intruders disturbed in varying degrees the 520 Seminoles scattered in small groups from the northern end of Lake Okeechobee to Cape Sable on the Gulf of Mexico. With the opening of the Tamiami Trail and the falling of the water level, which made canoe travel difficult, the Seminole camps moved to cluster near the highway.[5] By 1940 the following camps were located within a mile or two of the trail from Miami to Ochopee: Jimmie Osceola, John White, Charley Tigertail, William McKinley, Frank Willie, Jimmie Tommie, John Motlow, Chestnut Billie, John Poole, Capt. Tony's wife, Corey Osceola, John Osceola, Josie Billie, and Ingraham Billie.[6] At first these camps were similar in nature to those located deep in the Everglades and Big Cypress, but soon some became miniature amusement camps similar to those at Miami. The Seminoles charged admission to their camps, sold Seminole-style products that had been made in the North, wrestled alligators, and allowed tourists to wander through their chickees. Some who had available funds opened small grocery stores.

Bill Osceola related why he had moved:

> I was born in the western part of Broward County in the glades not in the hospital. Along the Big Cypress swamp, the Seminoles lived and go all over in the glades hunting and fishing for their food and trading

First trustees of the Tribal Cattle Enterprise, 1939. By permission of National Anthropological Archives, Bureau of American Ethnology, Smithsonian Institution, Washington, D.C.

purposes. After the hunting trips, the Seminole would come back to the camps and make a garden and plant vegetables for their food supply. This is how the Seminole Indians of Florida lived. On one of these hunting trips, my parents settled in Broward County and that's where I was born. I grew up around the Big Cypress swamp and went hunting with my father until the state of Florida decided to drain the Everglades. With no water, the transportation was cut off for the Seminole Indians. Everybody started moving closer to nearby towns. My family moved to along the Tamiami Trail.[7]

After Spencer's death John Marshall, a farmer-laborer and son-in-law of Spencer, served until a permanent replacement, James L. Glenn, was appointed by Commissioner Rhoads. During the interval a contract was negotiated by which Seminole women picked oranges in nearby groves owned by whites and fifteen acres adjoining the Dania reservation were provided by the Florida legislature to support a Seminole gardening project.

Acting upon the recommendation of Roy Nash, federal authorities appointed Glenn from Collier County, aged thirty-nine and a Presbyterian, as financial clerk or special commissioner for the Seminole Indians. Before assuming his post Glenn was briefed in Washington by the heads of the health, education, land management, and living standards departments within the Bureau of Indian Affairs.[8] For his first full year in office, 1932–33, Glenn was allowed $11,899 for the administration of the several reservations within his jurisdiction, divided as follows: food for the aged, ill, and dependents, $1,800; employment of Seminole labor, $1,350; medical and health fund, $3,200; funerals, $150; and improvement of cottages, $500. Salaries for the four employees included financial clerk, $1,330; teacher, $1,356; caretaker for Hendry County reservation, $600; and B. L. Yates, general worker, $960.[9] One illustration of the terrible condition of the federal budget in 1932 can be seen in the bureau's refusal to purchase two new trucks to serve the scattered Seminoles to replace trucks that had seen ten years of hard use.[10]

Once Glenn understood the severe financial restrictions of his position, he began a program of reservation improvement and educational development. Finding the cottages to be small, hot, and crowded, he purchased lumber from a Pompano race track barn and enlarged them. Next he moved the cottages, school, and infirmary to sites that gave each cottage a large lawn, the school a more useful playground area, and the infirmary a better location and entrance. He extended the term of the day school from six to nine months and raised the position of the teacher who had replaced Mrs. Marshall to permanent civil service status. Teachers encouraged the fifteen students in the school to prepare the noon lunch, bathe twice a week, brush their teeth daily, and keep their hair free of lice. Adult educational opportunities introduced at this time included training in the use of machinery, and in fence building, canning, and clearing of land.

The new agent made a survey of the lands available for the Seminoles in Florida and found some conditions that needed correction. Altogether, 125,895 acres in federal and state land were available, but the tracts were so widely scattered as to be useless. Agent Jacob Brecht had acquired the 23,040-acre reservation in Hendry County for the Seminoles in 1894, but most of that land was in widely separated parcels, and the entire holdings could only support from 500 to 700 head of cattle. The 2,100 acres in Martin County was so poorly drained that the Seminoles refused to settle there, claiming "it was not good for their hogs."[11] A large tract embracing the state reservation of 99,200 acres in Monroe County seemed adequate until it was disclosed that much of the land was tide washed. Glenn attempted to exchange the state reservation land within the Everglades National Park for better land north of the Tamiami Trail, but Corey Osceola, William McKinley, and others opposed the transaction, claiming they would be killed if they signed the agreement. [12]

During the 1885–1930 period the Muskogee-speaking Seminoles withdrew from the Catfish Lake settlement (Lake Pierce) in Polk County across the Kissimmee prairie to the relatively unsettled central Florida area south of the headwaters of the St. Johns River. Some camps were situated in St. Lucie County and others near Indian Town but none could be found in the region between Indian Town and the Atlantic Ocean. In 1930 Roy Nash found three or four camps in the cabbage woods south of Brighton, some camps eight or ten miles northeast of Okeechobee City, several camps at Ten Mile Creek and the Blue Cypress, the camp of Billy Smith the medicine man six miles northeast of Fort Drum, several camps in western St. Lucie County, and one family living between Indian Town and Lake Okeechobee in Martin County.

Although the Muskogees maintained permanent camps, they moved about the countryside herding their hogs, gathering huckleberries to be sold in the towns, and during the spring working in the vegetable fields owned by the whites. Consequently, before the introduction of the automobile, they used horse- or oxen-drawn wagons to travel along the sandy trails and the nearby towns. When they needed utensils and goods, they sold alligator skins and huckleberries at Joe Bowers Trading Post at Indian Town and the Bowers Trading Post at Jupiter. They were not under white pressure to move, for they were living on land undesired by the whites at this time.

The Seminoles usually built their camps on a high place within a grove of pine trees or a cluster of palm trees in a hammock. Based on a general pattern the camps consisted of "a number of palm-thatched open-sided houses built around the outer zone of a clearing, with a cook house in the center." [13] Each family in the camp had its own dwelling, which served as sleeping quarters, a storage place for clothes, food, bedding, and other items, and a site where the women could work on household tasks. Equipment in the house included a Singer sewing machine, mosquito nets, lard cans, and a portable phonograph and records. [14]

At this time the federal government provided the Seminoles with infrequent visits by the agent from Dania with the services of a contract physician at Okeechobee. In 1932–33 Dr. C. L. Davis made 163 contacts with the Muskogees in treating a variety of ailments ranging from headaches to venereal disease.

By 1933 the national economic crisis impacted the Seminoles. The extension of roads into southern Florida allowed white hunters to penetrate almost all of the area. Their inroads, plus the canal development and drainage operations, greatly reduced the supply of wildlife. The Seminoles needed land reserved for their own use that would provide hunting grounds, grazing areas for stock, and sufficient fertile soil to produce good crops.

A fresh interpretation of federal-Seminole relations resulted from John Collier's 1933 appointment as commissioner of Indian affairs. Under Collier's prodding Congress passed the Indian Reorganization Act of 1934, which provided for the expansion of reservations, developmental aid for economic ventures, and encouragement of the American Indian way of life, including religion and arts and crafts. In line with the new philosophy, in January 1934 the assistant to the commissioner of Indian affairs, A. C. Monahan, made a detailed examination of the Seminole land requirements and proposed consolidating the landholdings and acquiring new tracts. Plans were formulated to secure a resettlement area near Miles City in Collier County by obtaining options on four sections of land, and options were also taken on four sections near Brighton.

In 1935, on the occasion of the one hundredth anniversary of the beginning of the Second Seminole War, the secretary of the interior, Harold Ickes, and the commissioner of Indian affairs, John Collier, and their staffs visited two Seminole reservations—West Palm Beach and Johnny Buster's camp in Collier County. An insight into the superficial briefing accorded the federal officials and his poor knowledge of the Seminoles was apparent in a book by Ickes in which he stated the principal reason he went to Florida was to talk to some old medicine men at the annual Sun Dance. Ickes found the Seminoles the wildest American Indians he had ever seen—also self-respecting and independent.

In honor of the visiting federal officials at West Palm Beach the Seminoles removed their shoes before coming into the room where the session was held. The following petition was submitted to Collier and Ickes:

We, a group of the Seminole Indians of Florida, assembled in conference on the one hundredth anniversary of the Seminole War, beg you to hear us:

Seminole Sun Dance, West Palm Beach. Courtesy of the Florida State Archives, Tallahassee.

The Seminole Indians have not been at war with the United States for one hundred years. The Seminole Indians live in peace and happiness in the Everglades, and have pleasant relations with the United States government. The Seminole Indians want a better understanding with the United States government and want to hear no more about war.

We have learned from our forefathers of the losses of our people in the Seminole War, and during recent years have witnessed the coming of the white man into the last remnant of our homeland.

We have seen them drain our lakes and waterways, cultivate our fields, harvest our forests, kill our game, and take possession of our hunting grounds and homes. We have found that it now grows more and more difficult to provide food and clothing for our wives and children.

We request and petition you to use your influence with the Congress and the President of the United States to obtain for us the following lands and benefits:

I. All of the lands in the State of Florida as marked on the map attached, hereto, including:
   (a) Lands in Collier, Hendry, Broward, and Dade counties known as Big Cypress.
   (b) Lands in Glades County known as Indian Prairie.

   (c) Lands in Martin and St. Lucie counties known as the Cow
      Creek country and the Blue Field section.

   (d) Lands in Indian River and Okeechobee counties known as the
      Ft. Drum swamp.

  II. For the loss of our other lands and our property an annuity of $15
     per capita per month.

  III. The full time nursing services of Indian nurses.[15]

The Seminoles included chief spokesmen Sam Tommie, Willie Jumper, Billie Stewart, Josie Billie, Jimmie Gopher, and Charley Billie, along with Amos Marks and Willie King, missionary–interpreters from Oklahoma. Some of them had more to say to Ickes and Collier. Jimmie Gopher said, "I want land. My cattle have vanished."[16] Charlie Cypress, the last of the old–time canoe makers, expressed the same views: he was happy, but since he had no hunting grounds, he wanted some land. Willie King, the missionary from Oklahoma, played the greatest role in circulating the petition among the Muskogees. After these conversations the Florida National Guard unit held a ceremony in which the "end" of the Second Seminole War was proclaimed.[17] Although most seemed pleased with the meeting, the board of directors of the Seminole Indian Association disagreed, calling it a "fake and a burlesque." Those Seminoles who took part in the meeting with Ickes and Collier were not given authority to act on behalf of either of the two Seminole groups.

Apart from the requests in the petition some Seminoles indicated that they wanted a voice in the affairs of the tribe as provided in the Indian Reorganization Act. They were given a chance to decide upon the matter in an election held on March 30, 1935, and the measure was approved 21 to 0. At first the Seminoles from Miami who had cast the twenty-one votes held out for self-government, but within a short time they adopted the attitude held by the majority of the tribe that they knew nothing about elections and issues and desired only to return to their camps, plant corn, and not bother anybody.

Glenn, the government's financial clerk and special commissioner, was informed by a letter from Washington on May 10, 1935, to begin negotiations for the purchase of the tracts of land requested by the Seminoles. Since the regional director of the Resettlement Administration, Dr. W. A. Hartman, had control of the necessary funds to make the purchase, all recommended tracts had to be approved by the Resettlement Administration. Glenn conferred with Hartman ten days later and discovered that, of the several tracts proposed by his office and the Seminoles, only four

Atlantic Ocean

Gulf of Mexico

Tampa Orient Road
□ Reservation

Brighton Reservation
□

N

Immokalee Farms □

State
□ Reservation
□ ⬚
Dania-Hollywood
Reservation

Big Cypress Reservation

Miccosukee Reservation □

Present-Day Seminole Reservations

sections of land in Indian Prairie were acceptable to Hartman. Such reasoning did not please Glenn, who believed Fort Drum Swamp was "potentially fitted for handling all phases of the social and economic life of these Indians." [18] Nevertheless, he had to go along with Hartman's ideas, for the resettlement administrator believed that the other tracts recommended by Glenn either were not suited for the Seminoles or were "real estate promoter's schemes to make more money." [19] Next Glenn tried to persuade the federal administrators to purchase land along the northwest shore of Lake Okeechobee for a game preserve or cattle range for the Seminoles and received some support from state of Florida officials, but the commissioner of Indian affairs would not approve the proposal.

The 2,500-acre tract of land known as Indian Prairie, northwest of Lake Okeechobee, was acquired for the Seminoles and became known as Brighton Reservation. (James B. Bright had developed Brighton in 1924 as a "boom time" project, and a hotel was erected in the town. As soon as the hotel was completed, a museum featuring Seminole items was opened, and a band of Seminoles who lived nearby came to the hotel to perform dances for the tourists. All of this came to an end when the boom collapsed in 1926.) Under the terms of the Appropriation Act of 1935 $25,000 was set aside for the purchase of additional land, and a comprehensive study of Seminole land needs was planned.[20] By 1938 the Brighton Reservation included 27,081 acres purchased by Resettlement Administration funds, 6,278 acres acquired with Indian Reorganization Agency funds, and 1,920 acres obtained by exchange with the state of Florida.[21] It would take many years for the land acquired by the Resettlement Administration to be transferred to the Bureau of Indian Affairs.

Other land transactions that benefited the Seminoles included the exchange of small tracts in Broward and Martin counties, not including Dania, for the Glades County tract. The state reservation land of 99,200 acres, little used by the Seminoles, was exchanged for another 104,000–acre tract adjoining the Big Cypress Reservation. By making exchanges with the state of Florida the federal officials were also able to consolidate the scattered tracts in Hendry County.[22]

The newly acquired reservation for the Muskogees seemed ideal, for it contained a number of palm hammocks ranging from one to twenty acres in area.[23] Those Seminoles living in St. Lucie and Martin counties had used these fertile hammocks for agricultural sites each spring to plant corn, pumpkins, and potatoes. In addition, junglelike undergrowth in the uncleared hammocks served as a haven for wild hogs, raccoons, quail, turkeys, and deer that they could hunt. Since there was an abundance of high ground in the hammocks, family groups would be able to establish campsites in separated areas as had been their custom. When the reservation was acquired, ten Seminole families lived on the tract. Plans were made to invite thirty more families to settle there, and by 1937 130 men, women, and children were living on the reservation.[24] Contrary to the practice adopted at Dania-Hollywood Reservation, no attempt was made to force the Seminoles to live in white-style houses. The Seminoles built chickees near the sixteen hammocks selected as their living areas and planted citrus trees, cabbage, carrots, beans, and tomatoes in the fields, which averaged five acres. Chickens, pigs, and cattle had been distributed to each family.

Within a short time the Muskogees learned about several negative features of the newly acquired reservation. When development of lands about the reservation took place, the white owners had built dikes, flood-water ditches, and canals, which caused an excessive amount of water to flow into the reserve; as a result much flood-control work was needed.

Also, the reservation land was not an intact area, for the Lykes brothers owned 480 acres within its bounds, and during the boom of the 1920s, at least forty persons acquired title to 11,640 acres within the reservation.[25]

On May 25, 1938, at a meeting of eighty Muskogee Seminoles and their leaders with William Zimmerman, assistant commissioner of Indian affairs, Richard Osceola expressed their need for a school, hospital, community building, and better cattle and horses. "My people think we need school for children. They can learn lots of things like white people. I would like to go to this school myself. Other men would like to go, too. Old people some day die. Young people need to learn to read and write so can do it when get big."[26]

Accordingly, federal authorities hired a husband-and-wife team, Mr. and Mrs. William D. Boehmer, to be responsible for educational work and community development. The school, offering English and the other usual studies, including poultry husbandry, garden making, and home-making, opened January 9, 1939. This school was more successful than the one at Dania, for there was great use of visual aids, and the pupils could leave the classroom to read books or perform manual labor whenever they desired. Mrs. Boehmer, whose official title was school housekeeper, assisted the Seminole women in various ways and advised the crafts organization. A bus made the rounds of the camps on the reservation to bring students to class in the morning and to return them home in the afternoon.

For the women the making of handicrafts would be a profitable venture. Until now, although some market for Seminole beadwork existed, the bulk of products sold in tourist stores and exhibition Seminole camps had been made in factories in Detroit and Jersey City, and Seminole children played with Seminole dolls purchased in Miami stores. In order to provide some livelihood for the women on Brighton Reservation besides work in the fields, Mrs. Boehmer wrote to the Indian Arts and Crafts Board in Washington, D.C., asking for advice. Alice Marriott from the Department of the Interior gave practical advice to the group, established standards, and wrote a constitution and bylaws. The women and young girls made dolls, costumes, beadwork, small canoes, and basketry according to standards established by the Seminole Crafts Guild of Glades County. Each article that passed inspection received a tag issued by the Seminole Indian Agency and was sold to tourists who visited Brighton School. Articles not meeting standards were exchanged for gasoline and groceries with neighboring stores and service stations.[27] At

Seminole cowboys at Brighton (1930s). Courtesy of the Florida State Archives, Tallahassee.

first articles were accepted for sale on a consignment basis, but after the guild had accumulated a revolving fund, it was able to pay cash to the women as they finished their products. By 1940 the Cohen brothers in Jacksonville were selling Seminole products distributed by the Seminole Crafts Guild.

The Seminoles acquired a livestock program in a somewhat unusual manner. Before the Seminole Wars the Seminoles possessed large herds of cattle, and as recently as 1925 Ada Tiger owned at least forty head before the end of the open range forced her out of business. Dr. Philip Weltner, regional director of the Resettlement Administration, decided to save the lives of some cattle and help the Seminoles; he transferred 547 head from the southwestern dust bowl to the Brighton Reservation and planned to ship 1,500 more. Most of the initial shipment died on arrival through lack of proper grazing lands and the long drive from the railroad to the reservation, but the survivors provided a nucleus for a growing herd.

Fred Montesdeoca, the agricultural agent for Okeechobee County, did most to put the Muskogees on the road to self-sufficiency.[28] He encouraged them to take an interest in the proper care, management, and treatment of cattle and hogs and in proper range control and improvement. Montesdeoca found a few people who were trained to work as range hands but had to teach the rest and in addition to obtain fertilizer, improve the grass, and place the cattle in suitable ranges. Cattle-raising techniques such as weaning yearlings, rotating pastures, and using good bulls were also part of the educational process, as well as helping the Seminoles overcome the consequences of poor native grass, no drainage, high water, and winter drought.[29]

With the growth of the cattle program it became necessary to at least give the appearance of including the Seminoles in the management phase of the operation. Administrators of the Bureau of Indian Affairs wrote a trust agreement in which nominations to the three trustee positions had to be approved by the Seminole agent and the commissioner of Indian affairs. To prepare the Muskogees for their first election on August 1, 1939, Fred Montesdeoca, with Willie King as interpreter, explained the need for elected trustees. The women gave scattered votes to virtually everybody, and Willie Gopher, a man who owned a horse but knew nothing about cattle, was elected, as were John Josh and Charlie Micco.[30] The requirements for the elected trustees at this time seemed to be a knowledge of English and skill in furthering good white-Seminole relations. Actually, the election meant very little, for Montesdeoca gave the orders.

Under the terms of an agreement that made the cattle-raising project self-sufficient, the Seminoles promised to repay the U.S. government in eighteen years for past expenditures. In 1940 receipts from the sale of bull calves and steers amounted to nearly $5,000, a sum sufficient to cover operating expenses and to provide for the purchase of forty-six head of yearling Hereford heifers from the Apaches at San Carlos, Arizona.[31] By 1953 the Seminoles had paid back the government $95,900 for cattle appraised in 1936 at $79,550; the Seminoles realized an average net profit of $19,000 a year.[32] Still, the average annual income per Seminole was only $700.

At Brighton almost every family owned some hogs, and the keep was very reasonable. Forage was based upon wild nuts and cabbage palm berries. When requested, the Glades County agricultural agent came to the reservation and for a small fee vaccinated the hogs against cholera, and close cooperation was maintained with the Everglades Experiment Station at Belle Glade and the Florida State Extension Service. This sideline of

Seminole Day School at Big Cypress, 1940. By permission of National Anthropological Archives, Bureau of American Ethnology, Smithsonian Institution, Washington, D.C.

hog raising became so profitable that in a two-month period in 1940, $1,000 worth of hogs were sold to a packer from Tampa.

In 1940 the Muskogees consisted of 175 persons living in twenty camps in the Brighton Reservation and at scattered sites west of Fort Pierce or Vero Beach. The only times all of the camps assembled were the Green Corn Dance in the summer and the Hunting Dance in the fall. As the men became engaged in ranch activities, more women worked as vegetable pickers in nearby farms or picked huckleberries, to sell in nearby towns. Food included sofkee, fry bread, boiled meat, boiled vegetables, coffee, boiled turtle, and fresh citrus.

At this time Brighton Reservation presented the following view to a white visitor:

> The administration building includes the Indian day school, the office, and the living quarters of the resident principal. There is a playground for the Seminole children, and a group of *chickees,* as Brighton Seminoles call their log and palmetto houses, standing a little apart from the other

buildings for the use of transient Indians. The administration building also houses a modern laundry with accompanying drying yard in the rear and the Seminole women take full advantage of this feature. The clothes lines are almost always hanging full of garments as colorful as Joseph's coat and probably much cleaner.

When Seminole women do their laundry they want every garment of their wardrobe washed. There must be no dirty ones left over. To this end, when all the clothing is laundered except that which they are wearing, they change into some of the freshly washed garments, even though they are wet, and then wash the soiled things they have just taken off.

Another modern innovation here, enjoyed by men, women and children alike, is the group of shower baths.

The advantage of living and working at the reservation is apparent when the money earned there can be traded at once for chewing gum, cakes, candy, syrup, and sugar, not to mention baker's bread, beef, coffee, and canned fruits. They soon discard the primitive mortar and pestle with which they formerly ground their meal and made coonti flour, and buy "store" flour. Their grits and meal can be ground at the reservation grist mill from the corn they themselves raise.

The Seminole at Brighton still like their "water-doughbread" however, a sort of pancake made by dropping thick flour-and-water batter by the spoonful into hot grease where it fries brown and crisp. This is considered the proper accompaniment for beef, venison, or fish.

Their ideas of home building and cooking have not changed. They still live in structures consisting, as they always have, of hand-hewn platforms supported by posts and sheltered from the elements by roofs thatched with palm leaves, thickly woven, reaching only a few feet from the ground and supported and weighted by more posts expertly held together. The cooking *chickee* is generally in the center of the camp with the sleeping *chickee* surrounding it. This floorless structure has the usual palm-thatched roof and here, or in the open a few feet distant, a fire is built in the ancient way, with logs placed like spokes of a wheel, the fire glowing at the hub where the pots of bubbling stew or *sofkee* are hung. The outer ends of the logs make convenient seats on which to squat while cooking, particularly if the weather is bad. In this case the cook has plenty of company for rain or a fall in temperature always brings a colony of dogs, pigs, and chickens to these outer spaces between the logs, where they drowse comfortably in the warmth from the central fire.

When a Seminole family takes permanent residence at Brighton Reservation, a camp site is prepared for it. The men of the CCC Camp clear an acre of ground and build as many *chickees* as necessary for the needs of the new family. This is done regardless of how many vacant *chickees* may be available, for the Seminole is particular and will rarely make a discarded camp his permanent home. The new resident is given a small garden plot near-by and a 5-acre farm site, usually farther back in the hammock. The 5-acre tract usually contains a patch of sugarcane. When mature, the cane may be ground and the syrup made at the community mill provided by the Government. The Seminole takes full advantage of this privilege.[33]

Through white contacts the Seminoles developed needs for certain material products of civilization. Nearly all of the men wished to own an automobile, and the young people listened to records and owned portable phonographs. Shopping trips were made to Okeechobee and Fort Pierce to buy dress goods for the women and Stetson hats and riding boots for the young men, and soon every camp possessed a sewing machine, iron pots, pans, and tools. A nurse made regular trips to the reservation, and when needed, a physician was called to render service without charge to the Seminole patient.[34]

Meanwhile the Mikasukis living to the south of Lake Okeechobee viewed with apprehension the planned opening of the Everglades National Park and further white intrusion and invited governor of Florida David Scholtz to meet with them. They chose a spot on a high pine island seventeen miles from the Everglades near the Tamiami Trail for the meeting place and spent ten days clearing the land and erecting a Seminole chickee for the "big white man from Tallahassee." Since D. Graham Copeland and the Baron Collier Company had provided money for the purchase of much food, 350 Seminoles were attracted to the feast and meeting with Scholtz. Meeting in a pine grove near a drainage canal on February 22, 1936, the governor, chief justice of the Florida Supreme Court, several members of the Florida cabinet, Josie Billie, Doctor Tiger, and Corey Osceola did not settle many matters. At the conclusion of the so-called pow wow and Sun Dance Scholtz nevertheless relayed a message from the Seminoles to the white world: the Seminoles wanted to be left alone. "They are afraid they will again be moved from the villages they occupy deep in the Everglades, they say they fear the white man will keep moving them until they are in the water . . . they did not ask for relief or aid of any kind, just to be left alone."[35]

It took some time for activities to be renewed at the Hendry County–Big Cypress Reservation. The agent had leased the land to C. W. Bartleson of Fort Myers for grazing purposes in exchange for keeping the fences and buildings in repair and hunters from using the tracts. Yet Bartleson brought no cattle to the reservation, and improvements fell into disrepair until William I. Byrd was appointed caretaker in 1931. Since the previous caretaker had allowed hunting on the reservation for a fee payable to him, Byrd had a difficult time keeping out hunters until he demonstrated that he was a tough man. Finally the real estate transaction in 1935–36 with the state of Florida consolidated the smaller tracts comprising the reservation into one large tract.

In response to a petition signed by ten Big Cypress Seminoles in 1941, 150 head of Florida cattle were acquired for the Big Cypress Reservation. Although only the lowest type of water-tolerant cattle were able to exist on the poorly drained pasture available at that time, the Seminoles eventually developed a herd of three-quarters Brahman stock.

By 1944 the Seminoles at Big Cypress Reservation wanted their own separate cattle trustees. At a March 18, 1944, meeting at Big Cypress, Josie Billie, accepted as spokesman for the Big Cypress group by the whites, said through interpreter Stanley Smith, "The Brighton Indians signed some type of paper, what was it?"[36] As a result the agent and the Seminoles drew up an agreement that provided for a livestock association at Big Cypress, approved by the commissioner of Indian affairs on August 8, 1945. The cost of acquiring a herd was assessed as a loan against each person who acquired cattle, with the long-term debt to be paid off as the cattle were sold. Since the government was spending over $200,000 a year for improvement of the pasture land, it raised grazing fees as costs mounted. As there was a limited amount of pasture land and each owner needed to be assured of a reasonable profit, the associates kept the size of a herd in 1965 to 200 head of cattle per owner.[37]

In 1935–36 Gene Stirling was assigned by the Applied Anthropology Unit of the Office of Indian Affairs to make a study of the Seminole Indians. Excerpts from his report, made available in 1936, follow:

> The location of the school at Dania has been the biggest stumbling block to getting the Seminoles to send their children to school. There are two primary reasons for this, geographical and social. The Agency at Dania is far removed from most of the Seminole settlements so that the children would either have to be put in a boarding school or the parents would have to move there. The Indians do not want either of these alternatives. They neither want to give up their children, or live at Dania

which is far removed from their sources of livelihood. Their other objection to sending their children to school at Dania is based upon the social environment that exists there. . . .

The Miami exhibition camps are the great sore spots in the Seminole picture. The camps especially desire families with children. The Indians are given their food and a few dollars a week per family. They have nothing to do except to be looked at by the tourists. Most of the cash they receive goes for liquor so that most of the nights are spent drinking. It is from these camps that most of the moral problems and venereal disease cases arise. They certainly offer a very unhealthy environment for the children to be brought up in. Two or three years of this loafing life with big city attractions makes the adults loath to take up a normal economic life again. The Seminoles are still too primitive to be in constant contact with a resort city like Miami without it doing them immeasurable harm. Part of the reason they go in these camps is on account of the increasing difficulty for them to make a living elsewhere. The camp owners use all manners of persuasion and threats to keep the Indians in the camps and prevent them from returning home. It is often necessary for them to sneak out of the camps in the middle of the night if they wish to leave.[38]

12

The New Deal, World War II, and the Advance of Christianity

 lthough the opening of Brighton Reservation and the realignment of Big Cypress critically affected Seminole life in southern Florida between 1931 and 1945, the Seminoles also felt at this time the effects of national and state economic and political activity—the depression, the New Deal in the form of the Civilian Conservation Corps, selective service, and a cattle tick epidemic that pitted Seminole against white cattle ranchers and legislators. Partly as a result of greater trust toward both Oklahoma Seminoles and whites, however, many Florida Seminoles adopted new religious beliefs during these years, and health problems that had arisen through increased contact with whites saw great improvement.

The Seminoles, although poor, had retained a limited amount of self-sufficiency, and the depression's unemployment and reduced budgets did not cause much added suffering among them. As they were classified within the limited income group, however, surplus army goods including uniforms, blankets, and heavy shoes were distributed among them during the Hoover administration (1929–33), and the Red Cross sent overalls, blankets, and sweaters—articles of little help in a subtropical land.

More useful and substantial help came during the Roosevelt administration, when an industrial program for the Seminoles was approved on November 23, 1933, under the provisions of the Civil Works Administration (CWA) Act. Projects undertaken during the CWA period included cutting palmettos from the land near the Dania-Hollywood campsite that was to serve as a base for visiting Seminoles, building a campsite at Miles City, laying sidewalks, constructing toilets, a kitchen, and bathrooms at the school, erecting a small hospital with two bedrooms, toilet, and bath, completing driveways, and setting up a quilt-sewing and clothes repair class for the women. In addition to the work performed by the Seminoles at the Dania agency, skilled white labor helped improve the school and hospital facilities. Altogether forty whites and Seminoles were employed in the CWA programs, which continued until February 1934.[1]

On January 22, 1934, federal authorities announced the creation of an Emergency Conservation Corps or Civilian Conservation Corps–Indian Division (CCC-ID) project with a budget of $3,000 for the Seminoles in Florida. Such projects were to be for the improvement of the reservations. Seminole men of any age could enroll in them, and their work camps could be of any size or form that the superintendent of the agency felt suitable. Since the Dania agency site resembled a jungle, choked by dead pine trees killed during the 1926 hurricane and a thick palmetto growth, work began there. Initially the Seminoles used hoes and axes to clear a small part of 140 acres, but later, trained by Glenn, they drove tractors and road graders purchased at bargain prices to clear out hard pockets of growth. According to the agent most of them worked well on the project, and when one became a slacker, he was reported by the others to the supervisor.[2] When word spread to the other camps that the work was available, many families traveled from the Tamiami Trail and Brighton to Dania-Hollywood and settled in tents and chickees on the newly cleared campground.[3] From March 31, 1933, to March 31, 1936, $30,058.08 was spent on Emergency Conservation Work projects at the Seminole reservations. Since Works Progress Administration and National Youth Administration programs were not established among the Seminoles, CCC-ID was virtually the only portion of the New Deal that was offered to them.

By 1936 the CCC projects had been extended to the newly opened reservation at Brighton and the much older Big Cypress Reservation in Hendry County. Working with a limited budget Superintendent Francis J. Scott employed thirty Seminoles grading truck trails on both reservations, fencing the Brighton Reservation, doing general cleanup, digging wells, posting the Big Cypress and Brighton reservations with No Trespass signs, and improving the public campground at Dania. Some problems on the CCC projects arose when most of the funds allotted had to be spent on equipment, materials, and supplies, leaving little for labor costs. Scott believed that work must be provided at subsistence wages for those attracted to the reservation and that the government could not expect the Seminoles to stay on the reservation if they could not earn a living there.[4]

As there was no experienced Seminole who could supervise the work, B. L. Yates, a resident of the area who spoke the language and had the confidence of the Seminoles, was hired as mechanic-supervisor. Of the 279 males included on the tribal rolls of 1934, ninety-two worked for the CCC.

The main purpose to which the CCC funds were put was revamping the three reservations into presentable and suitable places where the Seminoles would choose to live instead of moving to the exhibition villages. That administrators at Washington liked what was taking place became apparent when the budget rose from $8,486.75 in 1937 to $25,970 in 1938 and to $38,000 in 1939. The monthly publication of the Bureau of Indian Affairs and CCC-ID, *Indians at Work*, featured the Seminole cattle program in its March 1940 issue, and the front cover of the October 1939 issue showed some Seminoles (improbably attired in Seminole jackets) walking to work carrying hoes and shovels.

When the budget was reduced to $30,000 in 1940, Superintendent Scott protested to J. P. Kinney, general productions supervisor, but was told that budgets had been increased to pay for surveying Brighton and Big Cypress reservations and that, because the work had been completed, the budget should be reduced. The reduction meant that each enrollee in 1940–41 received a maximum of eleven days of work a month. Over the life of the program $4,530.73 was spent on buildings and plant and $164,516.52 on land and improvements.[5] Enrollees in CCC-ID received $30 a month plus food and lodging or commutation. White employees in 1938 received the following pay: W. Stanley Hanson, mechanic, $135 a month; B. L. Yates, general worker, $135 a month; and Frances Frost, clerk typist, $1,260 a year.

In 1939 and 1940 the *Miami Herald* featured celebrations held by the Seminoles at Dania-Hollywood in honor of the anniversaries of the establishment of CCC-ID. In 1939 a reporter wrote that in six years, CCC-ID had provided funds for 46 miles of fence, 21 miles of walks, 15 miles of truck trails, 12 miles of road, 1,293 acres of improved range, and the seeding of 663 acres.[6] An even more elaborate celebration took place a year later on April 11, 1940, when a softball game held the attention of spectators who refreshed themselves with ice cream, cake, and orangeade. The cause for celebration was the work done in one year by CCC-ID, which included building living quarters for two employees, drilling wells, erecting windmills, maintaining roads, constructing a ninety-foot bridge across Harney Pond Canal, installing seven miles of telephone line, constructing a sugar mill, and erecting sixteen miles of hog wire fence.[7] In February 1940 John Collier, commissioner of Indian affairs, and the CCC-ID director Daniel Murphy conferred in Florida with CCC-ID officials and Seminoles. On the trip from Dania-Hollywood to Brighton the administrator's car was pushed over soggy dirt roads by a truck, and when both vehicles became enmired, ten Seminoles shoved and used logs and jacks to rescue them.

Digging wells, fencing land, and repairing truck trails continued in 1941 under Dwight R. Gardin, former shop instructor, who took Scott's place. Superintendent Gardin protested the 1941 $4,094 decrease in funds and suggested to Washington that the Seminoles had been attracted to the reservation by the possibility of CCC-ID jobs and would develop home ties by raising hogs and chickens and planting a subsistence garden.[8] If the funds were reduced, the Seminoles would probably move back to the tourist camps of Miami or to the Tamiami Trail. It was important that funds be expended at the Big Cypress Reservation, where there was a serious attempt to introduce the livestock industry. When Washington would not respond to his appeals, Gardin ignored the budget and spent twice as much as the $31,000 allotted.[9] Ray Hall wrote Gardin that it was the worst case of financial mismanagement he had ever seen. Gardin was soon replaced by William B. Hill.

After the United States entered World War II, Congress decided to terminate the CCC program on July 2, 1942. In anticipation of the termination of the project, Daniel Murphy advised Hill in April 1942 to "close out as soon as possible, except forest protection, CCC-ID." If the army or navy needed CCC-ID property, it was to be transferred; if not, the Bureau of Indian Affairs could keep it. Of the CCC-ID property in Seminole land, $2,903.51 worth was transferred to the navy, and $1,134.59 in goods went to the Bureau of Indian Affairs.[10] The major value of the CCC-ID for the Seminoles was that it trained them in the fundamentals of beef production—range improvement, water control, fencing, and digging wells.[11]

Another problem that came to a head during these years was the clash between Big Cypress Reservation interests and those of cattle ranchers and hunters. Acting under the provisions of a law passed by Congress in 1906, the Department of Agriculture moved to eradicate the tropical cattle tick, *Boophilus annulatus,* variety *Australis,* which was infecting the cattle of the south and southwest, causing them to either decline in value for meat or hide purposes or die. One way to combat the effects of this disease was to establish quarantine areas in the states affected and to dip the cattle in a solution that killed the ticks. After $50 million had been spent on the program and fifteen states had been made relatively tick-free, only Florida and a small portion of Texas remained outside of this dip and quarantine program.[12]

In 1923 the Florida legislature began to cooperate with the Department of Agriculture by introducing the techniques that had worked so well elsewhere, but ticks kept coming back to infect cattle that had been previously dipped.[13] When ticks appeared on dipped cattle grazing near the swamps and parks in central and southern Florida, members of the Florida Livestock and Sanitary Board, believing that ticks from wild deer were infecting the cattle, ordered in 1937 the killing of all the deer in Highlands, Glades, and Osceola counties by professional hunters paid eighty dollars a month. When various groups protested this slaughter, the killing was temporarily stopped by an injunction but resumed after a favorable decision by the Florida Supreme Court. It has been estimated that as many as 7,000 to 8,000 deer were killed in this program, which virtually liquidated the deer population in southern Florida.

One sanctuary for the hard-pressed deer was the Big Cypress Reservation, and state officials tried to open it to the hunters. In December 1939 when representatives of the Florida Livestock and Sanitary Board met with Superintendent F. J. Scott at Dania, Scott pointed out that the Seminoles needed the deer for food and other uses; he refused to allow the hunters to enter the reservation. Nevertheless, hunters employed in the program had permission to cross Big Cypress Reservation into Collier County. During the hunting season in 1939 and 1940 private citizens obtained the same privilege when they paid a fee, and they were provided with the services of a Seminole to guide them across.[14] In March 1940, however, the Seminoles found that the hunters were killing deer on federal property in violation of the Ickes order, and all passage of non-Seminoles was prohibited. The principal reason the Seminoles wanted the traffic stopped was actually that they were losing too many hogs to the whites.[15]

With the approach of the 1941–42 hunting season, Floridians began to protest the action by the Seminoles. One group, headed by L. C. Betzner, wrote to Senator Claude Pepper in November 1941, "We want to hunt fifteen miles south of reservation in Hendry County. The only road to it crosses the reservation. We are willing to pay a fee."[16]

Commissioner of Indian Affairs Collier, under pressure from other agencies, conferred with Florida officials and with the Seminoles at Big Cypress. Taking the side of the Seminoles Collier proposed that a high fence be built around the reservation to keep the deer away from the cattle.[17] His stand angered cattle ranchers as well as state and other federal officials, and Florida senator Claude Pepper and representatives J. Hardin Peterson and Lex Green took an opposing position when they testified on bills to support eradication of the ticks on the reservations. The determined opposition of Representative Will Rogers, Jr., a Cherokee from Oklahoma, nevertheless allowed Secretary of the Interior Ickes to stall for time by insisting on proof of tick infestation before the Seminole deer could be killed by the hunters.[18] In late 1941, however, a fee was established permitting the deer hunters to cross the reservation.[19] In 1942, with gasoline rationing, the whole problem became academic; few automobiles made long trips in southern Florida during the 1942–45 period.

Two inspections of cattle by the Seminole agent on the Big Cypress Reservation in 1943 disclosed no cattle ticks and only seven wood ticks on about 600 head of cattle. An independent survey conducted by a National Audubon Society researcher, Roy Komarck, found no ticks carried by the fifty deer examined, and in a sample test conducted by Secretary of Agriculture Claude Wickard and Ickes, forty-two deer were killed but no ticks were found. When President Franklin Roosevelt supported Ickes, Wickard released the Big Cypress Reservation from federal quarantine restrictions, and the deer on the Big Cypress Reservation were safe for a time.[20]

On October 16, 1940, all eligible male residents of the United States between the ages of twenty-one and thirty-six registered for the first peacetime selective service in the history of the country. According to the 1940 census of the Seminoles, only 65 were eligible. At that time the Seminole population numbered 604 persons, with a little more than half on the reservations: 20 at Dania, 200 at Brighton, and 100 at Big Cypress. The remainder were scattered throughout the Everglades and Big Cypress Swamp. (Employed in helping the Seminoles were fifteen workers— three in administration, four in education, four in construction, three in health, and one in extension.)[21] At Brighton Reservation the extension agent, Fred Montesdeoca, and the school teacher, William Boehmer, served as a registration board and waited in the school building on October 16 for men to sign up.[22] During the day none appeared, although two women showed up and blew tobacco smoke on the building to protect any men that might register. Finally, under protection of darkness, two men came into the building and registered.[23] The registration process involved the filling in of sixty-one questions contained within an eight-page document and answering such questions required the knowledge of English.

The situation was at first equally discouraging at the Big Cypress registration center. When Josie Billie, medicine man from Big Cypress, visited the camps with W. Stanley Hanson, Conservation Corps employee, they found that many inhabitants had fled into the swamps when they learned about selective service registration. A few men returned to the camps when Josie Billie was able to contact them and explained their flight.

> Hanson learned of the misunderstanding between them and the agent of the Government who had demanded that they sign a "white ticket." To them this request meant disaster, and they refused. After listening to the experiences to which their misunderstanding had led some of them, Hanson wondered at their confidence in him and hastened to allay their fears. He reminded them that they had been hungry, their farms not having yielded for many moons, game and fish being scarce. During their time of need they had been cared for by the government. Some of them had been working on the W.P.A. and C.C.C. and should realize that their government would be just and fair.
>
> One young Indian stated that he would not go hungry, he could get a job and eat. He applied at a sawmill where he frequently worked. He was turned away. Until he brought his "white ticket" the boss man would not employ him. Hanson explained to the small group, the meaning of the "white ticket," and asked the Medicine Man to carry the message to the Indians hiding in the swamp of the Everglades. Asking for time for a consultation and with a promise to return soon with their decision, Hanson was left to await his return.
>
> In the small hours before dawn, the men followed by the squaws, the children and the faithful dogs, travelled slowly and silently back to their respective camps to take up their daily routine.[24]

Of the sixty-five Seminoles eligible for the registration, Josie Billie and Hanson were able to sign up twenty-nine.[25] First to volunteer for military service was Howard Tiger, who served in the U.S. Marine Corps at Guam and Iwo Jima. Others were Moses Jumper and Jack Osceola.

At first Gardin, the superintendent of the Seminole agency, showed little concern over the situation, for there seemed to be no doubt about the willingness of the Seminoles to fight for their country. In 1898 a group had shown their desire to fight against the Spanish, but the governor of Florida had rejected a bid to form a company of Seminoles.[26] Gardin pointed out that no Seminole had been drafted in World War I and that probably no Seminoles would be called for service in World War II, but he said that he urged the Seminoles to register during the remainder of the week. On October 29, 1940, he reported his lack of success to the commissioner of Indian affairs, John Collier. In response Collier requested Gardin to make a list of the names of those "recalcitrant" leaders who advised against registration and send the tabulation to the state selective service director who should "initiate necessary action based on law and facts." Accordingly Gardin reported to H. P. Baya, state director of selective service, the names of William McKinley Osceola, Corey Osceola, John Osceola, and Josie Billie, all living in villages along the Tamiami Trail. Gardin expressed the opinion that should the four be taken into custody, they would soon advise their people to register.[27] This recommendation would seem to indicate a breakdown in communications between Gardin and Hanson, for according to Hanson, Josie Billie, at least, had been very helpful in the first registration.[28] Hanson, a longtime friend of the Seminoles, fluent in Mikasuki, and one of two whites considered members of the Tribal Council, decided to make a thorough investigation concerning the attitude of the Seminoles toward selective service. In villages along the Tamiami Trail he found little or no desire on the Seminoles' part to register.

When the federal government had not gotten tough with those who failed to register in October 1940, would-be registrants for subsequent rolls decided to follow the lead of the recalcitrants. According to Josie Billie and Corey Osceola the Seminoles did not want to register but, if needed, would take their guns and fight for as long a period as desired by the whites. Hanson believed that some whites living near the Tamiami Trail had informed the Seminoles that they would not have to register for the draft because they were not citizens of the United States. Two Seminoles from Brighton who had gone to Miami to volunteer for army service had been rejected due to educational requirements. They had asked the recruiter, "Do you want us to write to the enemy or fight them?"

Officials in Washington and Hollywood initially wanted to adopt a tough stand toward the Seminoles and force almost complete registration, but that stand soon softened. Hanson was the first to conclude that forced registration would destroy the cordial relations between whites and Seminoles. Next the commissioner of Indian affairs sent out directions for a third registration, on February 16, 1941, for men who had reached their twentieth birthday by December 31, 1941, and had not passed their forty-fifth birthday by February 16, 1942.[29] It seemed better for someone not connected with the Seminole service to do the registering, but if no one were available, Hanson would do the job. In the third registration Hanson traveled 2,136 miles while locating and registering Seminoles from Silver Springs to Miami.

State selective service officials and Hanson realized the value of the Seminoles who were willing to assist the government in the war effort. Since coastal Florida was peppered with military and naval aviation training schools, the Seminoles could help with rescue work at any crash in the Everglades. Should enemy troops land by boat or parachute near or in the Everglades, the Seminoles would serve as guides in locating the invaders.[30] In June 1941 Hanson reported that the Seminoles were willing to serve on patrol and guide duty, and Secretary of the Interior Ickes and the secretary of war, Henry L. Stimson, referred the matter to the State Defense Council of Florida. So far as can be determined, no use was made of the Seminoles in those capacities.

By June 1, 1942, 67 of the 108 eligible Seminoles, 62 percent, had registered; opposition to registration was strongest among those not living on reservations. Hanson believed that, because a draft card was needed to secure employment, the holdouts would gradually register as they had in 1940.

"Captain Ralph W. Cooper of the Florida selective service was directed to make a thorough investigation of the matter and report to the state director. On February 25 and 26, 1942, he visited Dania-Hollywood, Brighton, Everglades, Fort Myers, and camps along the Tamiami Trail in a hurried trip and concluded that the Seminoles had little knowledge of English and were somewhat unsanitary. It would not be worthwhile to use force against the unregistered men for such action would produce poor results and arouse more distrust. By April 1942 the attorney general of the United States had decided that it was a state of Florida selective service matter. Florida selective service officials accepted Cooper's conclusion that, should all of the Seminoles be forced to register, the number accepted into service would not be worth the distrust aroused.[31]

The Seminoles played their role in the war effort as they saw fit.[32] Among them they purchased $40,000 worth of war bonds and savings stamps. Nineteen-year-old Betty Mae Tiger purchased the first war bond before joining three other Seminoles at school at Cherokee, North Car-

Ingraham Billie and his family in front of his store and camp along the Tamiami Trail, 1938. By permission of National Anthropological Archives, Bureau of American Ethnology, Smithsonian Institution, Washington, D.C.

olina. When sugar and other types of rationing took place, the Seminoles stood in line to accept their ration cards.

World War II produced some remarkable changes among the Seminoles. The wartime rationing of gasoline set back the tourist traffic in handicrafts and fees for hunting guides, agency services were curtailed, and the school established in 1940 at Big Cypress closed. On the positive side, when white workers in ranches, farms, and businesses went into the armed forces or moved to better-paying war jobs, employers were eager to hire the Seminoles. The work done for the Civilian Conservation Corps between 1935 and 1942 in fencing, operating heavy equipment, drilling wells, and constructing windmills had made the Seminoles highly employable. Even for those who had not been trained by the CCC or who preferred other work, the war years provided better means of economic sustenance. Extended family groups working together picked and planted crops for nearby farmers, and the Big Cypress Trail Seminoles developed their frog leg industry.[33] A few even went to Miami and parked cars at the parking lots and storage garages.

The Florida Seminoles were being increasingly assimilated not only economically into the white world but also spiritually into Christianity; 1945 saw the acceptance of the Christian faith by a record number of converts. Seminoles from Oklahoma—Willie King beginning in 1925 and Stanley Smith in 1943—worked hard to convert the Florida Seminoles, but results at first were poor. Rev. Eunah Tiger, who assisted Smith, said that according to Florida Seminole folklore Oklahoma Seminoles speaking English would come to Florida to take them back to Oklahoma. Florida Seminoles thus would not attend church even when food was offered.[34] Finally, when a delegation of twenty-seven Seminoles and nine Creeks came from Oklahoma to dedicate the unpainted frame building with wood shavings on the floor that had been built by the Seminoles, the First Seminole Baptist Church of Dania opened for services. The dedication was held on June 7, 1936, followed by a barbecue dinner in the yard of the church.

Stanley Smith began preaching at First Seminole Baptist with eleven members in the congregation, all women; Joe Bowers, the first male member, was baptized January 2, 1944.[35] Attendance at church climbed when it found that no one was seized and sent west. When Josie Billie, a leading medicine man, was converted to the Baptist faith in January 1945, others joined the church in record numbers: of 600 Indians in Florida, 102 had joined the church in Dania, 70 at Big Cypress, and 10 at Brighton.[36] Much progress was made in this area in 1946 when Junior Buster, Josie Billie, Barfield Johns, Billy Osceola, and Sam Tommie enrolled in the Florida Bible Institute at Lakeland, which offered courses on a three-year high school level to prospective religous leaders and adults desiring additional education.

By 1970 the Seminoles were in charge of seven churches. Of the two at Dania-Hollywood, the First Seminole Indian Baptist Church was founded in 1936 by Willie King and the Mekusokey Independent Baptist Church was founded in 1949. There are two churches at Big Cypress—the Independent Big Cypress Mission founded in 1966 and the Big Cypress First Baptist Church founded in 1948 as a mission. Both the Southern Baptist Mission and an independent Baptist group established churches at Brighton in 1951. In 1952 the Southern Baptists erected a building, but the independent group built a large chickee, which served as their church until

First Baptist Church, c. 1940. By permission of National Anthropological Archives, Bureau of American Ethnology, Smithsonian Institution, Washington, D.C.

they raised a building in 1958. The Southern Baptists called their church the First Indian Baptist Church of Brighton, and the independent Baptists, the Seminole Bible Baptist Church. When Baptist preachers began visiting persons along the Tamiami Trail, they erected a church building there in 1967 as well as a mission.

One observer noted that many of the Trail Seminoles had moved to the Big Cypress Reservation and become Christians out of a desire to improve their status. Since such positions as preacher or member of a church council were open to any who had ambition, men previously barred from high posts due to membership in the wrong clan began to join the church in order to gain prestigious posts.[37] The rise of Christianity among the Seminoles meant the emergence of a new type of leadership and the loss of power by the medicine men and council members.

Although the first contacts the missionaries from Oklahoma made were with the Creek-speaking and east coast Mikasuki-speaking Seminoles, the greatest number of conversions to Christianity occurred among the Mikasuki speakers at Big Cypress. So complete was the success of Christianity there that Big Cypress Seminoles within a short time no longer celebrated the Green Corn Dance, although the dance continued at Brighton and on the Tamiami Trail.

There was little real competition between the Green Corn Dance participants and members of the church. The Green Corn Dance was open to all Seminoles who wanted to take part, and they knew their role well in the ceremony. The dance made no attempt to change the ways of a participant but offered him an annual cleansing and renewal. Criticism of the Green Corn Dance by the Christians did not center upon the fact that it was a non–Christian religious event but that it was a period of "drinking and carousing." Such opposition was difficult to sell to young people during the 1970–80 period.

Deaconess Harriet Bedell, teacher for the Episcopal church who had worked among the American Indians in Oklahoma and Alaska, visited Miami and deemed a Seminole tourist exhibition village "disgraceful." When she heard the story of the abandoned Episcopal mission at Glade Cross, she decided to open a new mission at Everglades City in a small rented cottage. (The Episcopal church had tried valiantly to establish Seminole missions in four locations between 1893 and 1913, but their efforts had resulted in almost complete failure.) In the summer of 1933 Bedell began work with $25 a month from the South Florida Church Service League and the use of an old car. She found the Seminoles to be at first unresponsive and suspicious, and it took her three years to gain their confidence. Her travels took her from Everglades to Fort Myers, Miami, and Immokalee and to villages deep in the Big Cypress and Everglades. When the building of an airbase forced her to move from Everglades City, she leased another site and erected an assembly building along the Tamiami Trail. Slowly winning the confidence of the Seminoles, Deaconess Bedell taught them to improve their craft work and acted as agent for selling their handiwork to tourists. The Deaconess did not seek to change the Seminole style of religion abruptly, and she conducted some services in conjunction with the native religious leader.[38] She stayed with the Seminoles as long as her age and health permitted and then retired during the 1950s to a rest home in central Florida.[39]

The health of the Seminoles had been greatly affected by the increase in white contacts during the period from 1920 to 1945. In 1920 they were reportedly the healthiest American Indians in the United States, but after ten years of acculturation the story was less favorable. Since the Seminoles went barefoot and did not use proper latrines, few were free from hookworm. The lack of milk and fresh vegetables in their diet and the soft nature of the bulk of their food meant that virtually all suffered from pyorrhea.[40] The passing of the large wooden sofkee spoon from one person to another when eating stew seemed to be a major source of infection. They neither boiled clothing nor washed pots and dishes in hot water.[41] Malaria had been unknown among them, but when sawmills were opened in the Everglades in 1934, black employees were brought in from Georgia and within a short time malaria had spread by mosquito bite from the blacks to the Seminoles, with fifty cases in 1937–38. Atabrine and prompt medical treatment by white doctors eliminated the disease.

Better health measures and adequate food had increased the Seminole population from 208 in 1880 to 605 in 1940, 290.38 percent. In 1940 the children had a better chance to survive, for doctors and dentists working under federal contracts examined and treated the Seminoles. Contact with the whites had changed the medicine men's mode of treatment. They ordered prepared drugs from a wholesale drug company, and medicines such as Epsom salts, rubbing alcohol, and other popular drugstore items could be seen on the shelves of their chickees.[42] Josie Billie, a medicine man, referred cases to white doctors that his medications could not cure. Free medical services available included those of Dr. Pender of Everglades City, Dr. Rentz of Miami, a doctor at Fort Myers, and a visiting nurse, Miss Conrad, who managed to go to the camps and reservations. Unfortunately, visits to the doctor for more extensive treatment involved long trips to the settlements, and few physicians cared to make home calls at a chickee, but hospitalization was provided under federal contracts with the hospitals in Fort Pierce, Sebring, Miami, and Fort Lauderdale. In order to improve the diet, at least for the young Seminoles, children attending the Brighton Day School were given a hot lunch that included milk and green vegetables.

The World War II era in many ways proved a period of marking time for the Florida Seminoles; they neither lost nor gained much economic, social, or political ground, and old ways changed slowly. The end of the war, however, would galvanize many of the Seminoles no less than it did so many other Americans.

13

The Reservation Indians

ith the exception of the Second Seminole War, the post–World War II period produced perhaps the most startling changes ever felt by the Seminole community. Political, social, and economic developments included the consideration of Seminole claims before the Indian Claims Commission; the hearings for the possible termination of federal control and supervision; the growing popularity of automobiles, air boats, and frame or concrete dwellings; the marked advance of a successful livestock enterprise; the writing of a Seminole tribal constitution and election of officers; the separation of the Miccosukees and traditional Seminoles; the phasing out of one reservation school and the greater use of county educational facilities; a large number of conversions to the Christian faith; and the development of smoke shops and bingo.

In August 1946 Congress passed the Indian Claims Commission Act to provide a means to adjudicate claims arising from the acquisition of American Indian lands and to reduce or withdraw federal services to American Indians. Under the act, if frauds or mistakes had been committed, a tribe could receive according full and just compensation; the government was willing, as President Harry Truman had stated, to correct any mistakes that had been made. Yet the decision-making process moved at a snail's pace, with 588 claims filed, 108 dismissed, and only 50 awards, amounting to $94,915,000, made by January 1964.[1] The Claims Commission Act proved to be a bonanza for lawyers, a good research tool for the scholars who provided material for the attorneys, and of some benefit to those tribes that stipulated that part of the funds go for improvements such as roads and schools. The act also caused a split within the ranks of the Seminoles.

In order to understand how the Seminoles reacted to the provisions of the Indian Claims Commission Act, it is necessary to review the slow but steady progress of the tribe toward self-government. They had shown little inclination to form a tribal organization during the 1930s, content to remain as they had been since 1821 under the direct control of the agent and officials in Washington but resisting federal efforts to change their way of life. Then on August 8, 1945, the commissioner of Indian affairs, William A. Brophy, approved a new trust agreement for the management of the cattle industry on the two large Florida reservations. The pact provided for the establishment of two groups, the Brighton Agricultural and Livestock Enterprise and the Big Cypress Agricultural and Livestock Enterprise, with either group eligible to select three trustees, with the selection subject to approval by the agency superintendent and the commissioner of Indian affairs.[2]

An important feature of the new trust agreement was the provision for the selection of tribal trustees. Each of the two groups would select one trustee and the superintendent would appoint a third. The three selections would represent the entire tribe. In theory it was the first time a group was formed that would represent all of the Seminoles, but actually the trustees had little power. With the substitution of an appointive or elective power structure for the traditional one, those who had converted to the Christian faith moved into the top posts. Of the four elected to the Big Cypress positions, one was a former medicine man, two were active Christians, and one was to soon convert.[3]

Although the two livestock organizations and the tribal governmental unit seemed weak in political clout, they became the apparatus for a major move by the tribe. As early as October 1948 several younger and more acculturated Seminoles met with John O. Jackson, a Jacksonville attorney, and later with the superintendent, Kenneth A. Marmon, concerning the prosecution of tribal claims against the U.S. government. By October 15, 1949, a contract was signed with attorneys Jackson and Roger J. Waybright of Jacksonville to represent the Seminoles in the $50 million claim case to be tried before the Indian Claims Commission. Those who signed on behalf of the tribe were Brighton Agricultural and Livestock Enterprise trustees Frank Shore, Jack Smith, and John Henry Gopher; Big Cypress Agricultural and Livestock Enterprise trustees Morgan Smith, Junior Cypress, and Jimmy Cypress; Hollywood Reservation committee members Sam Tommie and Bill Osceola; and Seminole Tribe trustees Josie Billie, John Cypress, and Little Charlie Micco.[4] It should be noted that those who filed the claims were either cattle program directors, Baptists, or both. Nonreservation Seminoles representing 30 percent of the tribe were quick to claim that they were not represented in this grouping and that the superintendent had been the prime mover in the lawsuit and retention of attorneys.[5]

The claims, involving the request for payment for 39,132,000 acres plus interest, included these salient documents upon which the Seminoles based their case:

Justification for Claim
1. Camp Moultrie Treaty obtained by fraud and later breached, 30,000,000 acres, valued at $37,500,000.
2. Payne's Landing Treaty made ineffective by dilatory tactics of U.S., 4,032,940 acres, valued at $5,040,995.
3. The U.S. refused to pay just compensation for lands of Macomb Treaty, 5,000,000 acres, valued at $6,250,000.
4. Secretary of Interior requested State of Florida to take land without consent of Indians, 99,200 acres, valued at $992,000. Making a total of 39,132,140 acres, valued at $49,782,995.[6]

Matters became somewhat confused when the Seminoles from Oklahoma filed a petition in 1951 with the Indian Claims Commission asserting that the Florida Seminoles were actually "outlaws" and that all awards should be paid to the Oklahoma Seminoles. Two years later the commission ruled that the two groups should cooperate in a joint suit concerning claims one, two, and three, with division of award if given, and that claim four should be considered separately for the Florida Seminoles.[7]

The lawsuit would take several unanticipated turns during the next two decades. One group of nonreservation Seminoles challenged the suit as soon as it was filed. Because the group preferred an award of land rather than money, it finally broke away from the reservation Seminoles and called itself the Everglades Miccosukee Tribe of Seminole Indians. On April 27, 1976, the Indian Claims Commission entered a final judgment and award of $16 million. Guy Osceola, however, filed a suit on March 26, 1976, on behalf of a group known as the Traditional Seminoles living near Naples. Stating that the actions of the Claims Commission were in violation of the Constitution of the United States because they deprived the Traditional Seminoles of their rights and property without due process of law, the suit stopped the award process dead, and as late as 1992 none of the Seminoles had received any claims money.[8] Actually, the Seminole case received no slower treatment than the cases of other tribes, for twice the Claims Commission was granted five-year extensions to complete its case load; finally, in September 1978 when 133 of the cases were still undecided, they were transferred to the Court of Claims.

Other dealings with the federal government that arose during the 1950s concerned an attempt to remove the Seminoles from the list of tribes controlled by the Bureau of Indian Affairs and to end federal responsibility for them. Employees of the Bureau of Indian Affairs convinced Congress that Native Americans could supervise their own affairs without federal restraints, leading the Eighty-third Congress on August 1, 1953, to adopt House Concurrent Resolution 8, which expressed the opinion that the federal government should terminate its special services to the American Indians. Within a short time Congress passed a measure that gave the states power to extend their civil and criminal laws into the reservations.[9] By 1954 six tribes or groups lost their federal services, and events indicated that the Seminoles would be next.

On October 8 and 9, 1953, House Concurrent Resolution 8 and a proposed draft of a bill concerning the Seminoles were discussed at the agency headquarters at Dania-Hollywood, where an estimated crowd of 350 representing all three reservations and the Tamiami Trail groups took part in the two-day meetings. A tribal committee organized to examine the matter submitted to the Muskogee, Oklahoma, area director a report that took a firm stand against termination and expressed a desire to retain federal services for at least twenty-five years.[10] Their reasons included low income, land not sufficiently improved, public health picture slowly changing, poor roads, only two homes with running water and four with electricity, and much reservation land still not drained.

On March 1 and 2, 1954, joint hearings of the Senate and House subcommittees on the proposed termination project were held. Representatives of the reservation and Trail Indians presented the Seminole side of the picture along with representatives from Friends of the Seminoles, the Association of American Indian Affairs, and the Florida Federation of Women's Clubs.[11]

Sam Tommie, who lived on the Dania-Hollywood Reservation, testified before the committee regarding his reasons for the Seminole position against termination:

> I am from the Dania Reservation, representative of a group of 203 that represent the Dania Reservation. Dania Reservation voted in the Octo-

ber meeting and asked for protection; for Federal Government for 25 years they ask protection.

I came here to ask what this group in the reservation decides, to ask the protection. Why? They look into it in the reservation group and talk to the men in the school. They didn't have enough education to do themselves the work with the white people, but now they said, "We have schoolchildren. We are just going to wait until the schoolchildren get education to talk to the white people, our State our country officials. They can carry it on for themselves." . . .

Some people say, "Well, Seminoles have good education down in Florida." Yes, they have been studying books, but they can't do the business. Seminole Indians, they finish high school. Where I come from only 2 boys and 3 girls finished high school, but they never did attend college, and business school, business college. That is why the reservation group say, "Let's wait for these schoolchildren. They might be educated in the future."

REPRESENTATIVE BERRY (presiding). Sam, how many of your people can talk English?

MR. TOMMIE. Well, about my age—I am 53; I was born in 1901—well, I might say in the Dania group we have 203, and we might say about 40 or 45.

REPRESENTATIVE BERRY. In the younger group of about 20 years of age there are quite a few who can talk English; are there not?

MR. TOMMIE. Yes, they can talk.

REPRESENTATIVE BERRY. Maybe about half of them?

MR. TOMMIE. Yes, not quite half of them.[12]

Kenneth Marmon, superintendent of the Seminole Indian Agency, Dr. William Sturtevant, an anthropologist, and other white friends of the Seminoles were most effective in disclosing how far the Seminoles still had to go to compete with the white culture and how they could not successfully manage the cattle and land programs on their own for many years. Although a representative from Florida's governor, Charley Johns, spoke in favor of the termination of federal services, as a result of the firm stand taken at the hearings by their friends, the Seminoles were able to avoid the fate of the Menuminees of Wisconsin who were terminated in 1958; within a short time that tribe was reduced from one with considerable assets to one overwhelmed by "desperate poverty and ill health."[13] It was fortunate that the members of Congress changed their minds concerning the Seminoles, for the tribe, like the majority of American Indians, needed more time to manage their economic affairs before federal services were terminated.

In 1934 Congress passed the Wheeler-Howard Act or Indian Reorganization Act as part of the so-called Indian New Deal package devised by the commissioner of Indian affairs, John Collier. Title I of the act reaffirmed the right of each tribe living on a reservation to establish a system of self-government. When 25 percent of the adult population of any reservation requested home rule, a charter could be written that was subject to ratification by an approval vote of three-fifths of the adults.[14] Once approval had been given, the tribe would receive a charter of incorporation from the federal government and be able to establish enterprises and borrow money.

A plan to organize the Seminole Tribe under the terms of the Indian Reorganization Act begun in 1935 had been rejected by the tribe. Another proposal presented ten years later would have included four districts—Hollywood, Brighton, Big Cypress, and Tamiami Trail—with two or three representatives from each district being elected. Those living on the reservations were interested in such a plan, but since no interest was displayed by the Tamiami Trail group, the plan was dropped.[15] After discussions were held with Seminole leaders by the Muskogee, Oklahoma, area officer who had administrative control over the Florida agency, drafts of a Seminole constitution were prepared as early as January 1952, but they were not adequate. The main obstacle at this time was whether or not to have two constitutions—one for the entire tribe or separate ones for the off-reservation and the reservation groups.[16]

Administrators from the Area Office of Indian Affairs in Muskogee showed a revived interest in a constitution when they mailed ten copies of a proposed constitution and bylaws to Hollywood in October 1952. In January 1953 a constitutional committee met at the superintendent's office in Dania-Hollywood and reviewed half of the proposed constitution. When the committee had finished the work it was planned to discuss the proposed constitution at the various camps and reservations, but since the bulk of it had been written at Muskogee, the tribe did not support it or a subsequent revision.[17] When the Seminoles in Florida had prepared their own version of a constitution, it was rejected by Washington because of objections made by off-reservation Seminoles living along the Tamiami Trail.[18]

Once the Indian Reorganization Act had been passed by Congress, the Seminoles saw no reason to become incorporated, but by 1954 there were some compelling reasons to reconsider the decision. Both Bureau of Indian Affairs officials and a few tribal leaders were aware that the tribe had no control over reservation land or funds and wanted a change. Although the tribe seemingly possessed $116,000 engendered by oil and gas leases, it could not use those funds to improve the Dania-Hollywood Reservation and construct a community house because federal administrators, observing that the Seminoles had no legal organization, would not release the funds.[19] The state of Florida was also holding Seminole monies in trust.

In December 1954 Commissioner of Indian Affairs Glenn L. Emmons came to Florida to investigate political divisions among the Seminoles and met with six different groups at six different locations. As a result of his five days of discussion Emmons learned how difficult it was to establish a few points upon which all groups agreed. Emmons found the reservation people to be oriented away from the old ways of life and eager to adjust to new trends.

On December 20, 1955, a delegation of reservation Seminoles accompanied by their agency superintendent, Kenneth Marmon, appeared before Florida's Board of Commissioners of State Institutions, the custodian of the Seminole oil revenues accumulated from the lease of state reservation land. The delegation requested that the oil funds be released to the Seminoles, for money was needed for the older tribe members who could not provide for themselves, for clothing for sick children, and to install septic tanks and deeper wells to improve sanitary conditions. Former governor Millard Caldwell, the attorney for the nonreservation Seminoles, noted that he did not object to the proposal but did want the Seminoles to present a statement outlining what they were going to do with the money. Governor Leroy Collins suggested that the Seminoles should simply use the money to their best advantage. Fred C. Elliott, secretary engineer of the Internal Improvement Fund trustees, and one additional person to be selected from the attorney general's office, were appointed to contact the nonreservation group and get their opinion on the matter.[21] It would soon become apparent to the state officials that the nonreservation tribe members wanted land, not money.[22]

Some time was taken to determine the feelings of the various groups and to formulate a Seminole policy for the state of Florida. In a meeting of the Board of Commissioners of State Institutions on October 16, 1956, business committees from the three federal reservations proposed that $32,414 held in the oil and gas fund be expended for 1,420 acres of land. In response Fred Elliott proposed that a branch office be established and an advisory committee set up to formulate policy for the office.[23] On October 30 a committee composed of Ray Green, comp-

Governor and Mrs. LeRoy Collins visit with Seminole leaders at the Governor's Mansion (1956).

troller and chair, Richard Erwin, attorney general, and J. Edwin Larsen, treasurer, hired Colonel Max Denton as commissioner of Florida Seminole affairs at a salary of $400 a month. The group proposed that Denton assume his position on November 1, 1956, operate from Elliott's office or another site, and make a study of all laws pertaining to the Seminoles in Florida.[24] In this rather awkward set-up, Denton, with no prior experience in Seminole relations and with no Seminole advisers, headed the state of Florida's second venture into Seminole affairs.[25] The state's past record in this arena—establishing in 1917 a reservation on which no Seminoles would live—was unpromising.

Denton's appointment alarmed both the federal Indian officials and several organizations supporting the Seminoles. On the surface the move seemed rash, for funds to support the office might be taken from the oil and gas fund. Kenneth Marmon, superintendent of the Seminole agency at Dania-Hollywood, wrote to Collins inquiring into the status of the office and its source of funding.[26] In reply Collins noted that the $5,196 operating funds needed to open the office were borrowed from the oil and gas lease fund and would be repaid from general revenue, effective June 30, 1957.[27]

By April 1957 Denton had gathered some facts concerning the Seminoles of Florida and was ready for a conference in Washington with Commissioner Emmons, W. Barton Greenwood (the deputy commissioner), and eight other high bureau officials. In preparation for the meeting Emmons had met with the Board of Commissioners of State Institutions, trustees of the Internal Improvement Fund, and Denton in Tallahassee on March 20, 1957.[28] Issues agreed on in Washington by the state and federal officials included the following:

1. It was agreed that the Seminole Indians of Florida should be organized under a constitution and charters as soon as possible.
2. The current law and order status for state, civil and criminal jurisdictions was most satisfactory.
3. Director Denton should bring up the matter of more land for the Indians before the Board of Commissioners of State Institutions.
4. Tribal monies held in trust by Federal and State governments could not be given to the Indians until some type of governing body was organized by the Indians.[29]

Meanwhile Denton met with representatives of some of the off-reservation Seminoles at Everglades and with the Mikasukis at Jimmie Tiger's camp on the Tamiami Trail.[30]

On June 30, 1958, the Tribal Council of the Seminoles voted to request Governor Collins and the Board of Trustees of the Internal Improvement Fund for a distribution on a per capita basis among the 1,025 Indians of the $76,637.90 held in trust.[31] The request was not approved in total, but a rather miniscule sum of $18,000 was released for division among tribe. On October 26, 1958, more than 500 Seminoles gathered at Dania-Hollywood for the distribution of $25 apiece. Ninety-six-year-old Billy Bowlegs (of South Florida) decided to use the $25 to buy lumber for a new house, Frank Billie used the $75 available to his family for a car, and John Henry Gopher, his wife, and nine children placed their $275 in a bank.[32] Seminoles living off the reservation did not show up to receive their share of the funds. Judging from his creation of the rather weak Florida Office of Indian Affairs, the rejection of the purchase of the 1,420 acres of land, the distribution of $25 per Indian and the lack of a positive Seminole policy, the purportedly liberal Leroy Collins did not do much for the Seminoles of Florida.

In fact at this point the Seminoles were well on their way to taking care of themselves. In 1957, Rex Quinn, program officer of the Bureau of Indian Affairs and a Sioux, had come from Washington to help them prepare a suitable constitution.[33] Quinn and Superintendent Kenneth Marmon went over each paragraph of Quinn's draft with a committee selected by the Seminoles, debating each point and changing some concepts.[34] Marmon's and Quinn's goal was to draw up a constitution that would meet the guidelines regarding tribal government in *Indian Affairs Manual* 83-I, which would be issued on October 1, 1957.[35] On March 5, 1957, the committee met with the tribal attorney, Roger J. Waybright, for three hours discussing such points as governmental control over membership status, budget requests, and rules for election. The attorney explained that until members of the tribe proved that they were capable of managing themselves, some controls were needed.[36] Members of the constitutional committee included Bill Osceola, chair; Jackie Willie, Hollywood; Mike Osceola, Miami; John Henry Gopher, Brighton; Jimmie Osceola, Big Cypress; and Frank Billie, Big Cypress. The completed document, which included a constitution and charter, was ratified July 11, 1957, by Assistant Secretary of the Interior Roger Ernst and submitted to the tribe on August 21, 1957; it ratified the charter 223 for, 5 against. In a separate vote held on the same day, the constitution and bylaws of the tribe were approved by a vote of 241 for, 5 against. Since the vote had included 55 percent of the 448 eligible voters, the charter and constitution were considered to be legal and binding.

Bill Osceola, recalling some of these events, noted both the poverty of the Seminoles and the determination of some persons to have the tribe organized:

> We Seminoles found out about some money that was held by the State of Florida from the oil leases and tried to get it but the State said that we could not have it until we form an organization of some kind. A group of people were chosen to go to Tallahassee to ask for that money and they got a negative answer. On their way home, they were running out of money so they were splitting sandwiches to eat. That's how poor the Seminoles were trying to start some kind of organization for their people.
>
> When the delegates came back and had a meeting with the people, they decided to go ask the cattlemen in Brighton about raising some money in order to get help in organizing the tribe. Cattlemen told me, if I build a rodeo area in Dania, they would bring in the cattle to run the

The Constitutional Committee, 1957. By permission of National Anthropological Archives, Bureau of American Ethnology, Smithsonian Institution, Washington, D.C.

show and make money. I went to Broward County people for some lumber for the arena and they were happy to donate the lumber. The arena was built and we had the shows and made money for the expenses to take trips to Oklahoma and to Washington, D.C., asking for help in organizing our people into a tribe. When the funds were raised the Seminoles got together and selected a delegation from each reservation to travel to Oklahoma and to Washington, D.C. to negotiate with the Federal Government to help us organize our tribe. I was working with the people here in Dania reservation and Bill Osceola was working with the people in Brighton and Frank Billie had Big Cypress people. The people select Laura Mae Osceola to help us with the paper work. She was very young, but she was a good worker and helped us a great deal working toward the Tribal organization. Some people were against our work and saying leave the things as it is, but we kept working on it until the government sent one man down to work with us.

One day this man came and said "My name is Rex Quinn, I come to help you to write and set up the Constitution & By-Laws and Corporate Charter, I am an Indian." He was an Indian from far north.

This was the opportunity we were waiting for, a teacher to help us with the writing and setting up the Constitution & By-Laws and Corporate Charter. We met with Mr. Quinn and with our people and let them know who he was and why he was there for. He said he needed a committee to work with. The people select a committee and I was one of the committees to work with Mr. Quinn. He instruct us how to go about writing and setting up a Constitution & By-Laws and Corporate Charter. He told us which the other Indian tribes use and which is good and which is not so good. Some Tribes have only the Tribal Council. He recommend to us that it would be good to have Corporate Charter, which meant we would have two governing bodies. He kept teaching us until everyone understood the program and went to the people on the reservations and explained to them what was happening. We even went to Tamiami Trail, but the people there were not interested in organizing. Just the reservation people were interested in organizing the tribe. Three people were against the organization in voting and accepting. The tribal organization was finished and the election of the Officers was on.

We were elected, but everything seemed dark to us because we have never tried to operate a Tribe before. When we come against something we don't know, we would go to B.I.A. and ask for their assistance. As the Credit Office set up, people were getting loans for their homes or to purchase cattle to start a business.[37]

The constitution and bylaws provided for a Tribal Council of five members and for a chair, vice-chair, secretary, and treasurer. The constitution stipulated a council of five persons—an elected chair at large, one elected representative from each of the three reservations, and the president of the board of directors of the newly organized Seminole Tribe of Florida, Inc. The first chair of the council was Bill Osceola. Enactment of the constitution gave the tribe and its council limited control over the three reservations and power to enact regulations to safeguard the health, safety, and progress of the tribe.[38] Under resolutions adopted by the council, state and county civil and criminal authorities were given jurisdiction within the reservations, to be summoned only when a serious crime was committed or a white person was involved.

Organized at the same time as the constitutional tribal council was the Seminole Tribe of Florida, Inc., which was the business arm of the tribe. Each Seminole became a shareholder in the corporation, and Frank Billie was the first president of its board of directors. Formation of the corporation gave the tribe the legal right to administer the funds held in escrow by the U.S. government, but the authority of the five members of the board of directors was limited by control by the superintendent, the commissioner of Indian affairs, and the secretary of the interior. The board had little to do at first, for few funds were available for the creation and operation of enterprises.

Although the traditional leaders believed in a consensus or low-key approach, white-oriented leaders who arose at this time would tell the others what to do and took the place of the traditional leaders. Almost all of these new leaders had been trained in the methods and style of the Christian church and had a working knowledge of English and of give-and-take procedures common in church groups. Consequently, two of the most prominent ministers were elected as leading officers of the tribal organization for the next eight years.[39] At first the chair and council members were extremely conservative, but over the years they became more liberal. The philosophy of the present chair might be labeled proactive.

In 1963 the Seminole Tribe revised the constitution and bylaws. Reflecting Baptist influence, a supreme being was mentioned in the preamble of the revision. Official membership in the tribe for those born after 1963 was limited to those whose parents were at least one-quarter Seminole and were members of the tribe. For more speedy consideration of measures the Tribal Council was reduced from eight to five members; the term for members of the council was reduced from four years to two. The chair's term of office remained eight years, but it was made more difficult to secure the chair's recall; the chair was permitted to vote on all issues instead of only on tie votes. Finally, a bill of rights for all members of the tribe was added.

Over the postwar years the Seminoles continued to grow more independent both politically and economically. With the effects of drainage, approach of subdivisions, and use of the land and mineral resources, the swampy lowlands that had appeared so desolate to white eyes gradually began to improve in value. The Seminoles would never become as wealthy as the Osages, but the capital from all resources was growing. From the sale to the Florida Turnpike Authority of a right-of-way and other easements $200,241 was on deposit in the Treasury of the United States. The Seminole Tribe Rehabilitation Fund, which represented earnings from the Seminole Tribal Cattle Program from 1937 to 1953 and totaled $103,705.98, was on deposit with the regional disbursing officer of the U.S. Treasury Department at Kansas City. When the tribe was incorporated, these frozen funds became available for use by the Seminole Tribe of Florida, Inc.

With the tribe organized it was possible to initiate new programs and projects. A Corporate Revolving Credit Program was established to provide long-term emergency loans to individuals and for the construction of homes. Plans were made to move the Seminoles from farmhouses and chickees on the Dania-Hollywood Reservation into concrete block homes with city water and sanitary facilities. Under the program new houses were constructed and chickees modernized with the addition of septic tanks and running water at the Brighton and Big Cypress reservations. Another project was a land improvement lease with a vegetable company at Brighton Reservation, which called for the development of 320 acres.[40]

In the decade following the organization of the Seminole Tribe, several programs to improve the economic status of the Seminoles were initiated with varying success. In March 1960 the Seminole Arts and Crafts Center opened its doors to sell Seminole arts and crafts to the general public. During the same month the Seminole Okalee Indian Village Enterprise was created and became available to all as a display of early Seminole life and history. In December 1963 the two became the Seminole Indian Village and Crafts Enterprise. Other projects included Seminole Corporate and Tribal Building Enterprise (office facilities) in November 1959, Seminole Indian Land Development Enterprise (cattle production) in 1960, Seminole Indian Recreation Enterprise (overnight camping) and Seminole Indian Housing Rental Enterprise (low-cost housing) in November 1962, Revolving Credit Program (low-interest loans), Seminole Indian Estates (modern homes for Seminoles at Hollywood), housing developments at Big Cypress and Brighton, and adult education projects.[41] It was difficult to lure the Seminoles from their dependence upon federal programs and to attract private industry to the reservations because remote reservations such as Brighton and Big Cypress did not have adequate roads and utility services and because of the high cost of training workers ill prepared for industrial labor.

According to Bill Osceola, incorporation of the Seminole Tribe was a success.

> Twenty years ago there were no improved pastures on the reservations, the roads were muddy and the water everywhere and the vehicles

could not get around. Today it is all different. We the leaders have tried to help improve the conditions where the tribal members could benefit from it. A Big Cypress cattleman used to work a whole week trying to get his cattle together, but today it takes about thirty minutes to get the cattle in the pen. We have received many good things since we first organized.[42]

By 1960 the cattle enterprises were fairly successful. In a trust agreement approved on August 8, 1945, the Seminole Indians were to repay the Bureau of Indian Affairs "in kind" over the next ten years for the cattle received during the 1930s. Funds from the project paid for all improvements and operating costs, and the U.S. government was paid in full for the cattle. By 1953 tribal ownership was discarded in favor of private herds, and in March 1953, 2,150 purebred Hereford breeding animals were sold to forty-three families, leaving 1,300 animals to be sold in fall 1953.

So that a common herd could be operated on the reservation, the families that acquired cattle formed the Brighton Cattlemen's Association in April 1953. Its three directors were John Henry Gopher, Tobie Johns, and Andrew Bowers.[43] The pastureland at Brighton had been limed and fertilized and mostly cleared of palmettos, cabbage palms, and weeds, and it was hoped that such practices could improve the ratio of one cow per ten acres to one cow per three acres. Of the 35,795.03 acres at Brighton, 29,605.03 were used for grazing; 6,190 acres separated from the rest by a drainage canal could not be used and had been leased to whites. After September 1, 1953, a bridge was erected across the canal so that the tribe could use all of the land for grazing purposes.

In the first few years of the cattle venture duties were divided, with the association managing the livestock enterprise and Seminole Tribe, Inc., handling the finances. Although educational meetings were held to teach good breeding practices and proper range management, proper practices could not be enforced. Finally, in 1966, Seminole Tribe of Florida, Inc., assumed management of the program on the two reservations, and some of the owners of larger herds had a chance to become moderately wealthy.

The livestock programs on the Big Cypress Reservation were almost as productive as the ventures at Brighton. The extension agent concentrated on the production of native Florida cattle crossed with Brahmans; the breeding was done at first by the tribe and then by individual owners. The agent also assisted the Seminoles in the care of hogs, which some owned. By 1956 thirty-three families on the Big Cypress Reservation owned 1,700 head of cattle. As was the case with the individual owner program at Brighton, each family had its own marks and brands and had signed a mortgage to the Seminole Tribe for the cattle, with repayment plus interest to be made within eight years.

Between 1960 and 1975 the cattle program made slow but steady progress. Some pastureland was improved by leasing land to truck farmers who drained and ditched it and planted pangola or Bahia Pensacola grasses before returning it to the Seminoles after two years.[44] In former years some Seminoles tried to operate with small marginal herds, but in 1966 the cattlemen's association established rules for size of herds and use of the pastures.[45]

In addition to the cattle program Big Cypress instituted an agricultural and range-improvement operation. A five-year lease with S and M Farms provided the tribe with four dollars for each acre of tomatoes, cucumbers, and watermelons put under cultivation. As part of the program many acres of land were cleared and planted in improved grasses. In addition to the clearing and fertilization of land and the profit to the tribe, between twenty-five and thirty Seminoles were employed by S and M Farms.

The state of Florida continued to involve itself in Seminole affairs, sometimes in an advisory mode, sometimes more intrusively. When Farris Bryant became governor in 1961, he appointed William Kidd as state Indian commissioner, but the authority of the office was reduced. Kidd, a hydraulic engineer, showed some ability in assisting the Seminoles, but his title was downgraded to administrative assistant to Bryant in November 1961 and his department terminated.[46] In a further reduction Governor Bryant recommended in 1964 that Kidd be retained to work part-time on Seminole matters on the staff of the trustees of the Internal Improvement Fund.[47] When Kidd resigned on May 12, 1967, James W. Wilson, administrative assistant, became the governor's liaison officer for Indian affairs. Wilson continued in this position until Charles L. Knight was appointed on a part-time basis as Indian affairs consultant by Governor Claude Kirk in June 1968. State matters that were of concern to the Seminoles at this time included the need for a reduced toll for Seminoles using the newly constructed Alligator Alley and white protests regarding billboards placed on the state reservation along the same highway.[48]

During the 1960s Florida officials did their best to transfer title of the reservation land in Broward and Palm Beach counties to the U.S. government. In October 1965 Governor Hayden Burns, investigating the matter, found that if the reservation was transferred to the U.S. government, oil

Miccosukee tribal leaders present a jacket to the engineer for the Cabinet Trustees of the Internal Improvement Fund, on the steps of the State Capitol in Tallahassee, Florida. From left: Stanley Frank, Jimmie Tiger, John Poole, John Willie, William Kidd, Tommie Tiger, Calvin Sanders, Buffalo Tiger. Courtesy of the Florida State Archives, Tallahassee.

and mineral rights specified for the Seminoles would be a problem unless they were placed in trust.[49] Following a ruling by Attorney General Erwin, the Board of Commissioners of State Institutions withheld 50 percent of the revenue.[50] The groups were divided on what should be done with the state reservation: the Seminoles wanted to develop it; the off-reservation Miccosukees wanted to lease their share to oil and mineral interests. In 1971 the Seminoles received jurisdiction over one part of the state reservation and the Miccosukees over the remainder, both areas remained under the trusteeship of the Board of Trustees of the Internal Improvement Fund.[51]

Under terms of an executive order signed April 10, 1974, Governor Reubin Askew established the Florida Governor's Council on Indian Affairs, a private nonprofit organization. On the board were fifteen persons appointed by the governor; its cochairs were the chairs of the Seminole and Miccosukee tribes. The board's main task was to help the state carry out its responsibilities to the Seminoles and to other American Indians living in Florida. By 1982 $82,000 was allotted to the board from the state of Florida general revenue funds to take care of the needs of the office plus $350,000 derived from federal funds under the CETA program to provide for nonreservation American Indians living in Florida.

Progress in education since World War II has been uneven. During the 1954 trip of Commissioner Glenn L. Emmons to Florida, translation of his remarks was necessary at all six meetings, and few responses came from the adult audience in English; many responders spoke either Muskogee or Mikasuki. Yet strides in education were being made among young people not present at the meeting. The Brighton School grew so quickly that under the federal policy the school closed at the end of the 1953–54 year, and pupils were placed in nearby public schools. By 1956 the following Seminole enrollment in the nation's public schools was tabulated: Okeechobee, seventy; Stirling Grade School, fifty-three; McArthur Junior High School at West Hollywood, thirteen; Sequoyah Vocational School in Oklahoma, fourteen; Chilocco Agricultural School in Oklahoma, two; and Haskell Institution in Lawrence, Kansas, three.[52] In 1957 Joe Dan Osceola, the first Seminole to graduate from a public high school, graduated from Okeechobee High School.

The Big Cypress Day School was closed during World War II but opened with grades one to four in April 1951 under the direction of Houston L. Olson as teacher and Ilia Olson as housekeeping aide. Olson was interviewed in August by a *Tampa Tribune* reporter.

> "We expected enrollment to be 15, we prepared for 24, the actual enrollment was 31," he recalled. Average attendance was 23½ children per day. "Don't ask how that one-half kid got in—he was there, anyway," Olson laughed.
>
> Apparently the Indians like school. Olson reported that children arrived as early as 7 a.m., although the school did not open until 9 o'clock. The school building is a converted barn, but is very neat and clean.
>
> There was little or no equipment available when Olson took over. He arranged to borrow 23 desks from Hendry County schools, as well as other necessary equipment, and set up shop.
>
> When he opened the school, two-thirds of the enrollment was in the first grade. Half of these were in the first grade age category, the other half ranged in ages up to 14. His first grade pupils, Olson explained,

could not speak English. The other third of his class had some education, either at Dania Reservation, near Fort Lauderdale, or at public schools.

Olson's school runs through the sixth grade. Teaching the children is not an easy job, Olson said. One of his problems is the fact that Indian families migrate to wherever they find jobs, and the children's work must be geared so they can hold their own in any public school which they may be forced to attend if their parents leave the reservation.

Most of the Indians at Big Cypress are employed doing road work or as cowhands on the government cattle project sponsored for the Indians.

Olson made remarkable progress with the children during the nine weeks of school held here so far. At first he used older children with some schooling as interpreters.

"The children were very shy at first," Olson said. "They hid their faces or cupped their mouths with their hands when they talked."[53]

Students who had advanced to the fifth and sixth grades were sent to the Clewiston schools, and when they were promoted, they went to junior and senior high schools either in Clewiston or in Immokalee. (The pupils taking the ninety-mile rides to the two cities were probably setting records for busing.) Children living far from Clewiston or Immokalee were sent to the Cherokee Boarding School in North Carolina, but when boarding facilities were eliminated there in 1954 other nearby schools had to serve. In 1966 a modern educational facility and adjacent health clinic known as Ahfachkee (Happy) Day School was opened at Big Cypress, but the school experienced a high teacher turnover and students made slow progress. Special programs and intensive tutoring were added to remedy the situation.[54] More Seminole youths took advantage of the available educational facilities, and by 1988 as many as thirty were attending colleges and universities. Some graduated from college; one received his doctorate in education, and another with a law degree from Stetson University became a tribal attorney.

Even with the effort to raise educational levels at Brighton and Big Cypress, which included adult classes and transportation to and from schools, among high-school-age students the dropout rate was 30 percent. Educational progress was especially slow at the Big Cypress Reservation; only two persons had finished high school by 1987, and less than half of the tribe's under-eighteen population attended school. According to one Seminole, "Education is not right unless [the children] are ready and going after it."[55] By the time the young Seminoles become teenagers, some don't want to go to school; their parents do not urge them, and serious alcohol and drug problems and unemployment are the result.

After World War II some Seminoles moved from the chickee to the frame or concrete-block house, adopted white attire, and contracted the same diseases that affected the whites. Within the houses could be found refrigerators, washing machines, radios, electric sewing machines, and kerosene stoves. Moving to concrete-block houses brought on claustrophobia for some and a loss of community spirit; a few moved back to the chickees. The most popular foods were rice, grits, bacon, tomatoes, fried bread, and wild game. The consumption of large amounts of soft drinks and greasy food made obesity a problem with both sexes and all ages.[56] Virtually all of the Seminole families owned a car, and those who needed transportation through the swamps were using airboats and motorboats. Principal health problems by 1968 included sugar diabetes, deafness, pneumonia and other respiratory diseases, head lice (pediculosis), hookworms, and digestive ailments.[57]

The increasing availability of clinics, resident doctors, and contracts with neighboring hospitals have helped the Seminoles solve many of their major health problems and increase their population. Virtually all of the children are born in hospitals. Women come regularly to the clinics for birth control pills and routine immunization shots for their children and for others who need them. Since they had a life expectancy of forty-four years as contrasted to seventy years for whites, gains in this area have been important, for infant mortality, tuberculosis, and alcoholism rates were highest among all American Indians.

During the early 1970s 1,700 Florida Seminoles earned a living in various ways. Some worked in the vegetable fields and cattle ranches near the reservations, and a few made craft items such as Seminole shirts and dresses, miniature canoes, and dolls to be sold to tourists. Some worked at the Bureau of Indian Affairs office in Hollywood, at the reservations, and in various tribal enterprises. Programs of the Office of Economic Opportunity have provided such jobs as teaching aides in Head Start schools and social worker aides in the Community Action Program and the Neighborhood Youth Program. Some persons were able to work at the electronic components plant opened at Hollywood by the Industrial Development Program of the Bureau of Indian Affairs and others in flood control projects. Nevertheless, as late as 1973, some 60 percent of the families had incomes of less than $3,000 a year. In 1981 unemployment was about 40 percent at Big Cypress and Brighton and 25 percent at Hollywood. Of those employed, 75 percent worked for the tribe or in some federal or state program for the Seminoles.[58]

There was another side to reservation life that tribal officials were doing their best to erase. Studies made of reservation life noted the disorganization of the family, parental loss of control, indifference, disrespect for elders, and lower self-esteem of older children. In contrast the Miccosukees kept most of their families intact and were closer to mainstream conceptualizations of child-rearing.[59]

In 1971 Howard Tommie from Brighton, who had worked in the Neighborhood Youth Corps as a young man, became tribal chair. Guided by Richard Nixon's American Indian self-determination policy, Tommie began to deal with Seminoles who were not part of the older influential leadership and introduced free enterprise programs. In 1975 a group of Indians from the Colville Reservation in the state of Washington told Tommie about tax-free cigarette stores known as "smoke houses" that could be established on the reservation and become very profitable to the tribe. Marcellus Osceola and another Seminole received permission to open the first small cigarette sales store, or smoke shop, on the Dania-Hollywood reservation.

That the first cigarette shop should be opened on the reservation in southeastern Florida was appropriate, for it lay in the midst of a rapidly growing area and was a short drive from large population centers, including Fort Lauderdale and Boca Raton. When the small shop opened with cigarettes purchased from a firm in Alabama, long lines of cars formed along U.S. 441 to purchase cigarettes for $5.50 a carton, free of the $2.10 Florida tax. The loss in taxes to the state was $2,456,769 between April 1977 and February 1978. The Seminole reservation was not the only place where untaxed cigarettes could be obtained in Florida, however. Dozens of military installations and veterans' hospitals made the untaxed packs available, and the general public could order their cigarettes by mail from North Carolina. The Carolina Sales Company and the Tarheel Sales Company, two of the largest North Carolina mail-order houses, according to one estimate handled 40 percent of the $20 million in orders from Florida.

When Florida's Division of Alcoholic Beverages and Tobacco did not collect taxes from the Seminole smoke shop, the Broward County sheriff, Edward J. Stack, and Vending Unlimited–Ace Saxon, a cigarette vending company, petitioned the county court to force the collection. Why state officials did not act is difficult to ascertain, but they may have been afraid to tangle with federal reservation law, or Florida law may not have been adequate to enforce such collections. If Florida tried to seize the un-stamped cigarettes being moved from Alabama to Hollywood, it needed probable cause, proof that the cigarettes were not going to be sold only to Seminoles. Unless the cigarettes were in plain view, the truck carrying them could not be searched without a warrant.

The case eventually was transferred from Broward County courts to Leon County, where the Seminoles in March 1978 won a victory. When the decision was appealed, Judge Charles Miner, Jr., on May 25, 1978, supported the earlier decision—that under Florida law, cigarette taxes could not be collected on reservation land. His basis for the decision was a reading of the law to the effect that the tax was due from the wholesalers and not from the retail dealer. The burden of collecting the tax rested fully upon the wholesale dealer, and in the Seminoles' case, that dealer was in Alabama where Florida had no power to enforce its laws.[60]

Heartened by this success, Seminole leaders placed smoke shops on other reservations. They used the proceeds to employ other Seminoles and to improve the financial status of the impoverished tribe. When the shop established by Marcellus Osceola became inadequate to meet the demand, the tribe purchased it and built a new drive-in facility with funds provided by the sale of 51 percent of the project to Seminoles and 49 percent to whites. Two whites, George Simon and Eugene Weisman, raised the needed $2.5 million. Sometime later the tribe acquired full title to the building.[61] Now the Seminoles were ready to move ahead into bingo operations and, they hoped, to casinos.

Because the Bureau of Indian Affairs would not advance money for bingo halls and banks would not lend money because they could not foreclose on buildings on federal property, as in the case of the cigarette stores the Seminoles needed outside backing. In 1977 representatives of the Seminole Tribe contacted Eugene Weisman and George Simon, who agreed to find the necessary backers and open a bingo hall.[62] Profits would be split 45 percent to the backers, 55 percent to the tribe. A hall large enough to hold 1,500 persons, complete with valet parking, guards, closed-circuit television, a large tote board, and climate control was erected on the Hollywood Reservation at Stirling Road and U.S. 441 and opened for business in December 1979. Price of admission to the hall was $15, but one could also purchase chances to win from $10,000 to $110,000, and players paid an average of $20 in total fees.

Seminole bingo became very popular. Busloads of players arrived from places as far north as Jacksonville and as far west as St. Petersburg. After this success at Hollywood a smaller bingo hall was opened on the Brighton Reservation in November 1980. Such projects proved exceedingly profitable and, as could be predicted, were challenged in court by the state of Florida. Robert Butterworth, sheriff of Broward County, brought suit against the Seminoles, alleging that the bingo hall hours violated regulations established by the state of Florida restricting bingo hall hours and jackpots. When the case was heard in federal district court and the Fifth Circuit Court of Appeals, the Seminoles received a favorable decision.

When Seminole bones and artifacts were unearthed in the excavation of a site for the Fort Brooke Parking Garage in downtown Tampa, the city agreed that they could be placed in a museum that the Seminoles proposed to erect on an 8.5-acre reservation that the tribe had purchased for $85,000 at 5221 North Orient Road in Tampa.[63] The federal government then agreed to take the land in trust, and the Seminole tribe erected not only a museum and cultural center but a smoke shop and large bingo hall on the small reservation. This business venture at Orient Road prospered as well as had the one on the Hollywood Reservation.

Profits from the Seminole ventures other than tobacco and bingo were divided one-third to the tribal members involved, one-third to investors, and one-third to the tribe. Funds allotted to the tribe have been funneled into such projects as the Seminole Police Force, gymnasiums at Brighton and Big Cypress, a senior citizens' center, and the Cultural Heritage Project.[64] Bingo halls have reduced the unemployment rate among the Seminoles by 50 percent by employing tribe members in the halls and in projects bankrolled by bingo profits. Critics of the tobacco and bingo enterprises point out that these activities take advantage of smokers and of gambling weaknesses and are not in conformity with the traditional Seminole approach to life.

Much of the recent success of Seminole business operations has been due to the efforts of the flamboyant James Billie, who was forty-seven years old in 1992 and who has been tribal chair for the past eight years. Since taking office this controversial Vietnam veteran has raised the annual income of the tribe from $500,000 to $10 million and has instituted a revenue-sharing program in which each member of the tribe receives $1,200 a year.[65]

Under Billie's guidance the tribe in December 1984 opened an $11 million hotel and restaurant complex, Sheraton East, at the Orient Road site, paid for with a $1.9 million federal Urban Development Action grant and $6.5 million in borrowed funds and tribal reserves. Other ventures include citrus cultivation and real estate partnerships.[66] The big tests of James Billie's chairmanship will come when these business ventures give a full and complete accounting, when the number of young Seminoles who become high school, college, and technical school graduates are counted, and when the range of work opportunities available for the adult Seminole is broadened considerably.[67]

14
The Miccosukee and Trail Indians

ome Seminoles preferred to live outside the reservations in eight to ten villages located on private or state land along the Tamiami Trail or along the border of and in the Everglades National Park. Although acculturation was making rapid strides on all three reservations, these nonreservation Seminoles, known as the Trail Seminoles, resisted the advances of rapid acculturation by having the shaman and older men instruct the young people in plant life, animal lore, and tribal history. The Green Corn Dance—the central religious, social, and political focus of tribal life—was still an important event among some reservation Seminoles and those living along the Tamiami Trail. The shaman, or keeper of the medicine bundle, and the several member General Council that met at the Green Corn Dance provided the mechanism for making tribal decisions.[1] To the non-Christian Seminoles the "life of the tribe" would be gone forever without the medicine bundles and the Green Corn Dance, the forces that held the tribe together. The medicine man, or shaman, preserved the medicine bundle, which contained everything needed for the well-being of the Seminoles. It had the power to do great good but, if misused, could cause much harm. The carefully guarded bundle, wrapped in a deerskin, hair side out, contained pieces of horn, feathers, stones, and other items in buckskin bags. The medicine in the medicine bundle was described as war medicine so strong that if a woman approached too closely, it would knock her down. Before the end of the Seminole Wars, the tribe had only one medicine bundle, but with the scattering of the bands and removal of most of the tribe to the West, the original bundle in the charge of two persons was divided between those going west and those remaining in Florida. At one time there may have been as many as nine separate medicine bundles, but in 1900 after two had been destroyed in a fire there were only four.

In 1934 James L. Glenn, the financial clerk, reported that there were three Tribal Councils among the various bands of the Seminole Tribe consisting of one shaman and two or three council members each. Council members were chosen for life but could be impeached; after removal or death, a successor was named at the next Green Corn Dance. The Muskogee speakers living north of Lake Okeechobee had Billy Smith as shaman and two assistants, Smith's son Sam Jones and Billie Stewart.[2] The Mikasuki speakers had two bands, those at or near Miami and those at the Big Cypress Swamp. The names of the Miami council were unavailable to Glenn, but members of the Big Cypress council were Cuffney Tiger, the medicine man, plus Whitney Cypress, Charlie Cypress, and Billie Motlow.

By 1940 there was a different alignment and a new crop of councilmen. Listed as medicine men of the Muskogees were Sam Jones and Oscar Micco Jones and council members Na Ha Tiger, Tom Smith, and Charlie Micco. No longer was the Miami group represented, but the Mikasukis still had two bands—Big Cypress medicine men Coffney Tiger, John Osceola, and Josie Billie with council members Sam Willie, Corey Osceola, and William McKinley Osceola. The other division of Mikasukis, known as the Miles City group, consisted of medicine men Frank Charlie and Jimmie Billy and councilmen Charlie Cypress, Whitney Cypress, and John Cypress.[3]

When Josie Billie, the principal shaman since 1937 of the Trail Seminoles, became a practicing Baptist, he turned over possession of the medicine bundle to his brother Ingraham Billie, who thus became custodian of the medicine bundle and religious leader of the Trail group.[4] Assisting Ingraham Billie were other members of the council—Jimmie Billy, Frank Charlie, and Sam Jones.[5] Since he was the best-educated Seminole in the off-reservation group and could write, Buffalo Tiger served as interpreter and secretary for the council.

With some of the people tied to the old way of doing things and others swayed by the white culture, it was impossible for the Seminoles to present a united front on the issues that would face the tribe during the middle part of the twentieth century. Signs of this fragmentation became apparent as early as March 1935, when a small group of Seminoles presented a petition for a peace treaty and a request for some land in a meeting with Secretary of the Interior Ickes and Commissioner of Indian

Affairs Collier at West Palm Beach. Several weeks later Corey Osceola, William McKinley Osceola, Josie Billie, and others wrote the following message to the commissioner:

> We, the Chiefs, Leaders, Medicine Men, being the duly constituted authority to speak for and on behalf of the true Seminole Indians who live in the Big Cypress Country in Western Dade, Northern Monroe, Eastern Collier, Southern Lee and Hendry Counties, in the Southern portion of the State of Florida, desiring to voice the protest of our people and after consultation with the members of our tribe, desire to call attention of the Indian Commissioner to the fact that the Seminoles are not at peace and have never signed any Peace Treaty with the Government of the United States of America.
>
> The interest of the Seminole Indians in their residence in the Big Cypress Country in their hunting grounds is that of hundreds of years standing, and our homes are established thereat, and we are informed that the Indian Agent situated at Dania on the West Coast of Florida, miles distant from our habitation has, or will, present to the Honorable Indian Commissioner and to the Government's Council—Committee on Indian Affairs, a petition purporting to express the will of the Seminole Tribe of Florida, and we, the undersigned, being the hereditary and select head-men and councilors of the Seminole Tribe, respectfully protest against H.R. 7902 and S. 2755, being Legislation concerning Indian affairs, and expressly request the Honorable Committee on Indian affairs to exclude the Seminole Indians of the Big Cypress Country of South Florida from the operation and affects of said bill.[6]

The Seminoles displayed other signs of disunity at this time, but the act that caused the whites to recognize that the tribe had split apart was the filing in 1950 of a claim for $50 million by the reservation tribespeople. As soon as the lawsuit was filed, Corey Osceola and another Seminole council member submitted a statement to Sheriff L. J. Thorp of Collier County, which he transcribed and sent to U.S. Senator Spessard Holland of Florida:

> The Seminole Indians of Collier County do not desire and will not participate in the proposed suit; and wish to make this fact known to the powers that be. Cory [sic] Osceola tells me there are around 220 Indians of the Seminole Tribe living in Collier County; that they are well satisfied and wish to be let alone. These Indians are very superstitious

and seem to believe there is some underhanded motive for this suit. . . .
They feel that if a suit is brought in their name the Government (as they
do not realize the people of the U.S.A. are the Government) will take
some action as to removing them to some other territory.[7]

Other problems faced the non-reservation Seminoles. Some livestock
owners had begun fencing their land, interfering with hunting operations.
More serious was the dynamiting in the Everglades that was scaring game
and killing large numbers of fish and the operations of two oil derricks
engaged in drilling operations set up within a hundred yards of Jimmie
Tiger's village on the trail. The fabric of nonreservation Seminole independence and self-sufficiency was being threatened.

Dismayed by the stand taken by the reservation people, Ingraham
Billie and his tribal council group retained the services of Miami attorney
Morton Silver who had been recommended by young Buffalo Tiger,
whom Silver had represented when he secured a divorce from his white
wife.[8] After conferring with the council Silver consented to represent the
Trail Seminoles in 1952. Since the reservation group had already secured
the name Seminole, the council group took the name of Mikasuki, a
dialect that most of them spoke; they spelled it Miccosukee. By October 1,
1953, Silver sent a statement signed by Ingraham Billie, head medicine
man, in which the General Council disclaimed any part of the claims
lawsuit to the attorney general of the United States.[9]

Stronger action came in October 1955, when Silver protested the
activities of the agent at Dania-Hollywood and requested an investigation
by the secretary of the interior.[10] In reply the assistant secretary of the
interior, Orme Lewis, provided information concerning a future meeting
of a congressional committee that would deal with termination of federal
control over the Florida Seminoles. The relationship of the General Council to the tribe, Lewis noted, was not clear. Officials in Washington seemed
to feel that the claims of the General Council to represent a sizable
proportion of the Seminole population were false or at least had been
inflated by Silver.[11]

An opportunity for the nonreservation Seminoles to present their
views to both Congress and President Eisenhower came at the Washington hearings that Lewis had mentioned. A petition written on buckskin
decorated with egret feathers signed by a committee of ten council Seminoles was delivered to the White House and received by an aide to the
president.[12] In the petition the Seminoles pointed out that the suit filed

before the Indian Claims Commission had been instituted without the council's consent and that they wanted land, not money.[13] While the Buckskin Declaration was being presented, Silver and Buffalo Tiger were testifying before the congressional committee concerned with possible termination of the special status of the Seminoles.[14] Silver claimed that he had spent ten to twenty hours a week for the past year and a half working with the Miccosukees and that this Trail group had not received any federal aid at all. Buffalo Tiger spoke against termination in response to a question from Senator George Smathers of Florida:

> *Senator Smathers.* Buffalo, in other words, you say it is a matter of education and association with the white men, when you people get to know them better and associate with them more and have more confidence in them—you think that would be the time to take this bill up?
> *Mr. Tiger.* I guess you are right on that, because I am pretty sure that it is not time for Indians to take a thing like you have here. Myself I know something about the white man's way, but I couldn't understand a lot of things. I know a lot of people in the Glades that could not talk English, so it would be a bad thing for them. Just give them time, and the whole thing might change. Indian people might like the white people better, and they might do more for themselves if you just let things be, and that would be better for Indians and better for you, and there will be no hard feelings.[15]

In June 1954 the nonreservation Seminoles, exasperated by so little action on the part of Washington, dispatched a strong letter to President Eisenhower. Ingraham Billie, who signed the letter, stated that the "Miccosukee Seminoles" constituted an independent and unconquered nation, technically still at war with the United States. Eisenhower dispatched Commissioner Emmons to Florida in the fall of 1954 to investigate the status of affairs there. At first it seemed that only one meeting would be needed, but because the groups were so widely separated, it was necessary to schedule additional sessions. From December 16 to December 20, 1954, Emmons held six meetings with different Seminole groups, including the Ingraham Billie group at the Jimmie Tiger camp in the Everglades and sessions at the three reservations. An information officer, Morrill M. Tozier, noted that "from these many conversations there gradually emerged, for the first time, a reasonably coherent and comprehensive picture of the present situation among the Seminoles of Florida—a picture in many ways almost fantastically different from the badly distorted image which the Commissioner and the writer of this report took down to Florida with them."[16]

To Emmons and Tozier the Trail Seminoles presented an interesting contrast to the reservation tribe. The gathering at Jimmie Tiger's village was the largest of the six sessions held in Florida. After this meeting, and one held in Silver's office, Emmons emphasized a salient point: "The Miccosukee General Council may not represent a majority of the Florida Indians, (but) it certainly speaks for or comprises of [sic] a very substantial minority . . . that should not be overlooked."[17] In addition the white observers concluded that the General Council was neither a "red power" activist group recently organized nor one arranged by Silver, but an organization that had existed for many years and the only forum available to present problems that concerned all Seminoles.

Not all nonreservation Seminoles united behind the General Council. A village headed by Mike Osceola that was white-oriented had not joined. The Corey Osceola group, led by two brothers, Corey and John Osceola (Mike Osceola's uncles), which included fifteen to twenty adults, did not join with the General Council either, preferring to stay in the background most of the time. According to the reservation Seminoles there were approximately 150 nonreservation tribespeople, but Silver claimed that there were as many as 600.

Commissioner Emmons could not do much about the conflict between reservation and nonreservation Seminoles, for the issue became a matter for judicial settlement. During 1954 and 1955 Silver tried to have the 1950 claim filed by the Seminole Tribe with the Indian Claims Commission dismissed on the grounds that the Miccosukee Seminole Nation had never authorized such a suit.[18] The Indian Claims Commission on April 7, 1955, denied the General Council Indians a hearing by ruling that the ones who had filed the claims in 1950 represented all of the Seminoles living in Florida. On December 5, 1956, the Indian Claims Court dismissed Silver's appeal.[19]

Even at this, however, no real bitterness existed between the reservation and nonreservation groups. Buffalo Tiger, transplanting for Jimmie Billy, made this clear in 1955.

> Jimmie Billy say for his people, all we ask is for land, and if people live on reservation want the money, they can go ahead and take the money; we are not going to fight against them. And we don't want those people fight against us. All we want is hunting land and for our homes and our

rights and to be Indians, and he likes the life to be Indian. That is what he wants, and that is what most of them want down here.

So he says, if they want the money, they can go ahead and take the money and live on reservation. If they want that, we are not going to bother them, and as long as they don't bother us on this side, but he says you must recognize those people and us down here are two separate setups.[20]

By 1955, the Trail Indians were making specific demands for certain tracts of land. At first they claimed the entire southwestern section of Florida, minus several large communities, but on October 31, 1955, at a meeting in Washington with federal officials, Buffalo Tiger and attorneys Morton Silver and George Miller demanded a smaller area, 1.5 million acres that would include Florida Conservation Area Three, land in the Florida State Indian Reservation, and strips south and west about twelve to fifteen miles wide. They were not seeking title but exclusive and perpetual use of the land for hunting, fishing, grazing, and agricultural purposes. By March 1956 they were asking for exclusive hunting and fishing rights in the western part of Conservation Area Three, owned by the state; joint hunting and fishing rights in the remaining portion of Conservation Area Three, to be shared with non-Indians during hunting and fishing seasons; the right to catch frogs in a specified portion of the Everglades National Park; and authority to cut cypress for the building of chickees and canoes from the area west and south of the Big Cypress Reservation.[21] Since this land was controlled by the state of Florida, the Miccosukee land claim shifted from federal to state jurisdiction. The state of Florida had prepared for this situation by installing Max Denton in a newly created post, commissioner of Florida Seminole affairs.

On May 1, 1957, a meeting with the Miccosukees at Jimmie Tiger's camp on the Tamiami Trail was attended by from fifty to seventy-five Seminoles, who requested that Conservation Area Three of the Central and Southern Florida Flood Control District be assigned to the tribe and paid for from their claim pending against the U.S. government. In addition they agreed to prepare a constitution and bylaws to be approved by their people and thus establish a governing body. Denton endorsed the proposal.[22]

On July 30, 1957, the Everglades Miccosukee General Council (as it was now known) presented its constitution to the Board of Commissioners of State Institutions for approval. At the meeting Buffalo Tiger explained that of the 355 Seminoles living off the reservation, 201 had signed the constitution. Miccosukee attorneys Millard Caldwell and Dr. John Miller made detailed explanations of certain phases of the constitution, and the cabinet was assured that it was an agreement similar to municipal charters. Governor Leroy Collins explained that the two divisions could not be unified at this time and that approval of the constitution would not "detract from or deny recognition of the reservation group and their constitution." [23] The motion to recognize the Miccosukee Council as the Miccosukee governing body was unanimously adopted. [24]

As soon as the Miccosukee constitution had been approved, it seemed that assignment to the group of Conservation Area Three or 200,000 acres of land would come next. In a meeting at Miami Shores attended by eighty-six white sportsmen and several Miccosukees and their attorney Morton Silver on July 27, 1957, the Miccosukee Seminoles were questioned on their possible use of the land and refusal to allow hunting and fishing rights to others. Silver was alleged to have remarked: "Give us the land and after we have it we will sit down and negotiate your hunting and fishing privileges." The white audience laughed. Silver did say that the group wanted exclusive use of 100,000 acres but would permit whites to hunt and fish on the remainder. Rallying around the facts that 5,012 licenses had been sold for hunting and fishing in the Everglades but that only 400 Seminoles were involved in the issue, the sportsmen voted to hire an attorney and send a committee to talk to the governor to protest the allocation of land to the group. [25]

More facts were disclosed in a letter from B. F. Hyde, Jr., Executive Director of the Central and Southern Florida Flood Control District and custodian of Area Three. According to Hyde, 19,320 acres were owned by private interests, 1,960 acres in fee simple by his group, 15,360 by the State Board of Education, and the remainder controlled by trustees of the Internal Improvement Fund. Hyde did not object to hunting and fishing rights for the Seminoles, public hunting seasons, or exclusive frog gigging by the Seminoles but stressed that his organization had authority to flood the area. In addition, if cattle raising and agricultural activities were fostered in the area, extensive changes would be required, including construction of canals, dikes, and pumping stations. [26] By December 16, 1957, Denton and Van H. Ferguson, director of the Internal Improvement Fund trustees, submitted a proposal to Collins recommending the assignment of 138,430 acres in Area Three to the Seminole Indians of Florida for the protection of "their native religion, customs, tradition and economy in their native habitat."[27] At this point it seemed that the Seminoles would be given some exclusive rights within the involved land.

The plan submitted by Denton and Ferguson to Collins and the cabinet was sent to Attorney General Richard Erwin for review. Erwin found no legal authority by which the trustees of the Internal Improvement Fund could place state land in trust for the Seminoles or designate land for the exclusive use of a particular class. To remedy the situation Erwin suggested that a public hearing be held so that proper authority might be determined and, if some doubt concerning proper approval of the Denton-Ferguson plan still existed, the Florida legislature should grant such authority.[28] Erwin issued a strong statement on May 22, 1958, in which he said that if the state conceded that the Seminoles had a right to the land, "Florida would admit that the monetary debt owed to the Indians was for much more than the acreage actually being sought."[29]

One important factor in Erwin's decision was the agreement signed between attorney Morton Silver and the Everglades Miccosukee group on March 30, 1958 by which Silver was due a reasonable fee from the awards of money or land that the council would receive from the federal or state governments. As a result Silver would have a lien on these benefits, and such a lien could not be recognized by the state of Florida.[30] Consequently, after receiving the advice of Erwin, the state of Florida applied brakes to the efforts to give land to the Seminoles. As with the efforts to create a state reservation, the majority of white citizens never showed great enthusiasm for giving land to the Seminoles, and the Silver money issue provided an easy out to Collins and the cabinet.

In 1956 a split had taken place among the off-reservation Indians. Those headed by Ingraham Billie had hired Morton Silver in 1952, and in 1955 he was joined by George Miller and Millard Caldwell. By 1956 Ingraham Billie and the so-called traditionalists had broken with the lawyers, claiming that all the lawyers wanted was money, leaving Buffalo Tiger and some others to be represented by Silver. According to the Miccosukee Seminoles, who wrote Governor Collins, "the reason is that [Silver] refused to do what he wanted to do. He wants to do what he likes instead of what we want. Mr. Silver wants to get a title of land to which we do not believe in."[31] In reply Fred Elliott explained that Silver had no official connection with the trustees of the Internal Improvement Fund and that the board's dealings would be directly with the tribe or with a representative selected by them and certified by the board.

For their next moves Silver and the General Council tried two distinctly different modes of attack along the state front. First, Silver wrote a letter to the General Council, which in turn was forwarded to Governor Collins, stating that he had no intention of placing a lien on their land for payment of fees or of making the state of Florida responsible for such fees.[32] In their supporting letter the Miccosukee Seminoles noted that Collins had not met with them but had made a public announcement concerning the lawyers' fees, thus interfering with the land transaction.[33]

In a second move to put pressure on the federal authorities, the off-reservation group sought the assistance of other countries and international organizations. On November 20, 1958, several delegates visited the embassies of England, France, and Spain, presenting copies of treaties signed with these nations.[34] A conference was held at a village along the Tamiami Trail, attended by thirty-six tribal leaders from throughout the United States, in which the group voted to form a nation and to petition for membership in the United Nations.[35] It was decided to send a buckskin message to Fidel Castro, and within a short time several Miccosukees visited Cuba. These efforts directed at international assistance seemed to have been misdirected and hurt the efforts for suitable negotiation.

On November 7, 1958, Governor Collins appointed a committee composed of Chair Grady Crawford, William Baggs, John Pennekamp, Louis Capron, and Harold Vann to study the problems of the Seminoles of Florida. The group held meetings on December 4, 12, and 13, 1958, and on January 23, 1959, with various federal, state, and private individuals but with no Seminoles. In a report submitted February 16, 1959, to Governor Collins the committee found that the only "Indian tribe" as defined by the U.S. government was the Seminole Tribe of Florida, composed of Seminoles residing on federal reservations in Florida. Since all dealings with the tribes had been on the federal level, no tribe had a legitimate claim against a state. Finally, the committee noted that, since the Everglades Miccosukee Tribe of Seminole Indians had a pending claim against the state, "it would be impracticable or impossible for the state to make any grants, gifts or leases of land to the Indians."[36] Furthermore, the Everglades Miccosukee Tribe did not intend to live on the land sought from the state but intended to lease or use the land for profitable transactions.

Acting on the recommendation of the Crawford Committee the cabinet rejected the bid of the Miccosukee Seminoles for the 200,000 acres but agreed to acquire from private owners the land needed to place all of the eighteen or twenty campsites under state control. In addition the cabinet voted to release the $75,000 held in trust for all Seminoles for use by individual tribe members. Max Denton was instructed to work out a plan for the acquisition of the campsites, to help disperse the money from the trust fund, and finally to "encourage the Miccosukees to accept white schools, medical care and modern life." [37]

At this point the Miccosukee General Council could do little to protest the action of the cabinet, for the council had expended every weapon in its arsenal, but white friends were able to reverse the tide of battle. President Evelyn Harvey and the Miccosukee Seminole Indian Association circulated a petition supporting the land claim, which was to be sent to the Florida legislature, the cabinet, Collins, and Congress. An opening meeting was held in May at the Hialeah City Hall at which three members of the governor's committee were questioned by tribe members, their attorney, and white friends. A salient point stressed that the tribe had not yet seen the full committee report and had not been consulted in its preparation. [38] As a result of the mounting pressure the Florida legislature in June voted to set aside 143,400 acres of Everglades land for use by the Miccosukee Seminoles. [39]

Although there had been little or no formal communication between the reservation or "official" Seminole Tribe and those living away from the reservations, Commissioner of Indian Affairs Emmons was able to arrange a meeting in Miami at which most of the Florida groups were represented. On November 15, 1959, members of the board of directors of the Seminole Tribe of Florida and the Miccosukee Tribal Council met at the Everglades Hotel. The only group not represented was that from the area near Naples known as the Traditional Indians. [40] With a firm desire displayed by all to settle a serious problem, it was resolved that the reservation Seminoles would assert full control on the federal reservations, leaving the Miccosukees in control of all activities on the 143,620 acres. Such control of the area by the Miccosukee Council was at variance with a proposal submitted by Max Denton and Van Ferguson, the director of the Internal Improvement Fund trustees, who wanted the Tribal Council of the Seminole Tribe to have jurisdiction over the state land. [41]

Evidence that Governor Collins was not swayed by the action of the legislature was disclosed at a hearing of Seminole Indian problems by the Board of Commissioners of State Institutions held on November 17, 1959, in Tallahassee. Present at the meeting were leaders of the two tribal groups, Bureau of Indian Affairs officials, and white friends of the tribes, including Robert Mitchell, Bertram Scott, and Evelyn Harvey. First, Emmons pointed out that the Bureau of Indian Affairs would offer technical assistance but that the U.S. government at this time did not want to create any more federal reservations. Collins replied that he did not think anything could be settled in the meeting, for all types of legal questions could arise with property and the state was limited in action. Miccosukee Howard Osceola explained that the tribes had no claim against Florida but that both Seminole groups had agreed that the state land would be managed by the Miccosukees. Collins questioned the Seminole groups as to possible use of the land and brought out the fact that little research on land had been done by the Seminoles. He concluded that "in the first place we haven't any legal authority to convey this land or set it up in any irrevocable trust. . . . We do not have the authority to control the use of it and we can grant certain license and use and privileges."[42] Refusing to abide by the decision of the Miami meeting, Collins referred the matter back to the citizens' committee for further study. By April 5, 1960, the Board of Commissioners of State Institutions voted to make available to all the Seminole groups 143,620 acres in Flood Control Area Three for use in their traditional way. Yet, because some of the necessary paperwork was not completed, the attorney general ruled that action by the commissioners not binding.[43] As late as 1978 the tribes had limited use of a small portion of the land, but it was mostly used by the state as a water storage area.

During 1961 another internal dispute shook the Miccosukees. Evidence of a split between Buffalo Tiger and Silver were disclosed in a letter written by Tiger to former State Indian Commissioner Denton and incoming Commissioner Kidd on January 25, 1961. He claimed that Silver and the General Council no longer had an attorney–client relationship and desired a letter from the state officials stating that such action dismissing him was legal. Since Buffalo Tiger and his friends held control of the Miccosukee Council, the state found no objection, and Homer Kimbrell, an attorney recommended by Kidd, took Silver's place as attorney for the Miccosukees.[44]

In the 1960s American Indian involvement in their own programs was stressed by federal administrators, and many objectives previously believed unobtainable were realized on national and state levels by the various tribes in the United States. With the active cooperation of the Bureau of Indian Affairs, the clan leaders of the Miccosukees and Rex Quinn, from Washington, met at Jimmie Tiger's camp in the fall of 1961 and drafted a constitution. Voting in December 1961 at the old Micco-sukee headquarters on the Tamiami Trail, a number of the off-reservation Seminoles approved the document. On January 11, 1962, the constitution and bylaws of the Trail Indians were certified by the secretary of the interior, and the Miccosukee Tribe of Indians of Florida was officially recognized as an independent entity, distinct from the main body of the Seminoles.[45] The Miccosukee General Council, which included the chair, assistant chair, secretary, treasurer, and lawmaker, was recognized as the governing body of the Florida Miccosukees, responsible for membership, tribal government, law and order, education, and fiscal disbursement.[46]

With the tribe officially recognized by the federal government, certain benefits became available. R. C. Miller was appointed superintendent for the Miccosukee agency with offices at Homestead, Florida, to assist the Miccosukees in their relations with the federal government. Buffalo Tiger began to make plans for a restaurant, gasoline station, and bait-and-tackle shop to be constructed on land set aside for the Miccosukees by the state of Florida and financed by the Economic Development Program.[47] The National Park Service gave its approval to the lease of a small portion of the Everglades National Park for use by the Miccosukees, and the Dade County School Board made a portable schoolhouse available. Land along U.S. Highway 41, the Tamiami Trail, on the edge of the Everglades National Park provided for the Miccosukees was five hundred feet wide and five and one-half miles long. With the land and building available a school was opened on December 19, 1962, with instructional material provided by the Bureau of Indian Affairs, one teacher, and nineteen students. Some time later the staff grew to one principal teacher, two classroom teachers, one reading teacher, and four bilingual aides. An adult education program was put in operation and plans were made for an extensive summer program. A mobile lunch wagon already in operation became profitable, but there was a delay in establishing the restaurant, cattle program, and overnight campground. For the younger children there was a Head Start center. The bilingual program stressed the use of books printed in Mikasuki, and pertinent books in English were ordered for the school library.[48]

By 1965 the Bureau of Indian Affairs had erected a concrete block, stone, and wood building containing two classrooms, kitchen, serving area, and office. Besides facilities for tribal offices, there were also an auditorium–gymnasium, clinic, and housing and business headquarters. In addition to the educational and cultural center developed on the leased land along Highway 41, twenty-three wooden frame buildings were built to serve as family-type residences. Approximately one mile away from this center, a restaurant, grocery store, and service station became available in December 1964.

In 1970 the Miccosukees became one of the few tribes in the country to enter into a contract with the Bureau of Indian Affairs.[49] The agreement established a tribal nonprofit corporation to which funds were transferred from the bureau. The Miccosukees thus were able to control expenditures of funds and pay employees and, in fact, run all their own programs; they no longer needed the services of an agent. The Miccosukee Tribe of Indians of Florida and the Seminoles worked out an agreement with the state for administration of the 104,000-acre Florida State Reservation— 76,000 acres would be administered by the Miccosukee Tribe and 28,000 acres by the Seminoles.[50] Since much of this land was under water, it had little immediate value, but income derived from leases of productive land was diverted to the respective tribes.

In 1974 the Governor's Council on Criminal Justice, studying the problems of increasing crime on the reservations, concluded that the best means of providing proper law enforcement was to establish special improvement districts. Under the legislation enacted as a result the Miccosukees and Seminoles were able to plan and run their own law enforcement, public housing, health care, and other social services; they also became eligible for LEAA and other federal grants.[51] A new firehouse-police station was constructed, a senior high school program with thirty-two students was started with funds granted by an Upward Bound project in September 1976, and the Miccosukee Public Safety Department was set up in December 1976.

It is still difficult to determine the extent of the success achieved by the Miccosukee Indians since 1975. Certainly they gained a victory in being accorded the right to manage their own reservation, plan their own business ventures, and teach Seminole culture and history and the Mikasuki dialect in their schools.[52] The Cuban area of Miami, Little Havana, is expanding westward, and the question has been raised as to whether the Miccosukee children should not be learning Spanish rather than Mikasuki so that they will be able to obtain jobs in the rapidly changing southeastern Florida environment. Furthermore, the major source of income for the Miccosukees has been the limited proceeds of the tourist-oriented concerns—souvenir shops, exhibits, alligator wrestling, village exhibitions, and air boat rides. In 1986 these proceeds paid each of the 368 tribe members only $200. Although the tribe operated such enterprises as a restaurant and service station, it has no assets such as mineral rights; opportunities do exist for bingo games or smoke shops. Their lack of education and of work skills allow the Miccosukees limited chances to rise above the poverty level. They need all of the funding available to provide suitable vocational education for the young people.

Despite gains by the Miccosukee Tribe, some Mikasuki-speaking Seminoles living near Naples have refused to join either the recognized Miccosukee or Seminole leaders. Jimmy Wilson, Bobby Henry, O. B. White Osceola, Douglas Osceola, Bobby Clay, and others living in twelve villages near Naples were members of this group, the Traditional Seminoles, which would not cooperate in the land claims suit.[53] So far as can be ascertained, these Seminoles have few if any confirmed rights to land, education, or other benefits.

According to Guy Osceola, all of the Seminoles were once Traditional Seminoles, but one group broke away and formed the Seminole Tribe. Later another group seceded and formed the Miccosukees. The members of the tribe that have remained are the Traditional—they never broke away. Jimmy Wilson explains the views of the Traditional Seminoles:

> I live in a village 38 miles S.E. of Naples, Florida. I am spokesman for my village of 12 people. I hold no land deed by the whiteman's standard. I hold only my Indian title and right of occupancy to this land. My family and I live where we choose, as we always have. There are some Indian people who have turned their backs on their own people, their traditions, and way of life. These people speak for a small handful of people only. Our tradition is, by not being present at meetings, means a vote of no. There were many more Indian people not at the January meeting than there were people there who voted. I do not live on a reservation, and I was not informed of this meeting. If I had been, I and my people would not have voted for selling of our land. Our God gave us this land for us to live on, hunt, fish, and live in peace. Every year the whiteman tries to take more and more of our Indian land from us. He does not try to know and respect our ways of life. He tries to make us one of his. We are different from the whiteman, with different beliefs and customs by which we live. The selling of our land is against the way of life and custom for any true traditional Seminole Indian. We have always been in this land. We have always been able to hunt, fish, to cut wood for our homes, and live where we wished. We do not wish to give up our rightful claim to our land.[54]

Epilogue

Many changes have taken place for the Seminole Indians since 1858, when less than 300 remained on the peninsula only because the federal government could spare neither money nor men to remove them to Indian Territory. Today more than 1,500 Seminoles and Miccosukees live in Florida, including those living away from the three larger federal reservations. For many it is indeed a changing life, with more comfortable housing, food purchased at the supermarket, color television sets, the latest fashions in clothing, and late model cars.

Maintaining such a life-style, however, means that the Seminole can no longer go out into the Everglades and kill enough deer or alligators to exchange skins and hides for all of his and his family's food and clothing needs. Even the money flow engendered by work within the several reservations seems inadequate to satisfy the needs of most of the tribe's members. Some have done well by owning larger herds of cattle or by operating one or more of the smoke shops or bingo halls, but their number is small.

The others may have to choose between remaining on the reservation in a more spartan Seminole environment or leaving the reservation for a better chance at the luxuries enjoyed by some white Americans. To some older Seminoles, remaining on the reservation guarantees them the good life; it will be the young Seminoles whose choices decide the future of the tribe. If they have no desire to learn or use their language or if they think that life outside the reservation is better, changes will rapidly take place in Seminole land. Yet of all the tribes in the United States, the Seminoles of Florida have been the most reluctant to adjust themselves to the white world, and they still have reservations to which they can retreat from it. The Seminole Indians of Oklahoma are not as fortunate.

Appendix A.
Census of Seminole Indians
Made by Lucien Spencer
in July 1913
(by English name)

1. Abraham	1894	M
2. Amy Parker	—	F
3. Billy Bowlegs	1862	M
4. Billy Bowlegs Squaw	—	F
5. Billy Bowlegs Child	—	—
6. Billy Bowlegs Child	—	—
7. Billy Bowlegs Child	—	—
8. Billy Stewart	1875	M
9. Billy Stewart Squaw	—	F
10. Child	—	—
11. Big Charlie	—	M
12. Ben Parker	—	M
13. Billy Tom Head Man	—	M
14. Billy Stewart's Mother	—	F
15. Billy Buster	—	M
16. Billy Ham	1870	M
17. Squaw	—	F
18. Billy Tucker	—	M

19. Billy Smith Head Man	1850	M
20. Billy Smith Squaw	—	F
21. Daughter	—	F
22. Daughter	—	F
23. Daughter	—	F
24. Daughter	—	F
25. Daughter	—	F
26. Billy Smith's Daughter	—	F
27. Billy Doctor	—	M
28. Big Face	1898	M
29. Billy Connie	1893	M
30. Billy Charlie	1876	M
31. Squaw	—	F
32. Child	—	—
33. Billy Charley, Jr.	1892	M
34. Billy Doctor Johnny	1892	M
35. Billy	—	M
36. Blind Tom	1835	M
37. Billy Buck	1850	M
38. Squaw	—	F
39–42. Child	—	—
43. Billy Conepatchie [*sic*]	1860	M
44. Squaw	—	F
45–50. Child	—	—
51. Billy Concepatchie's Child [*sic*]	—	—
52. Billy Concepatchie's Child [*sic*]	—	—
53. Billy Josie	—	—
54. Hetutchatsee Billy Fewell	1846	M
55. Squaw	—	F
56–63. Child	—	—
64. Billy Harney	—	M
65. Billy Jim	1886	M
66. Squaw	—	F
67–69. Child	—	—

70. Billy Motlee	1853	M
71. Squaw	—	F
72. Billy Osceola	1892	M
73. Billy Roberts Osceola	1875	M
74. Squaw	—	F
75–77. Child	—	—
78. Ben Franklin	1886	M
79. Billy McKinley [sic]	1895	M
80. Brown Tiger	1886	M
81. Billy Buster	1860	M
82. Squaw	—	F
83–89. Child	—	—
90. Billy Buskenuggee	—	M
91. Billy Buckhorn	1858	M
92. Squaw	—	F
93–94. Child	—	—
95. Billy Jim (2)	1896	M
96. Squaw	—	F
97. Coffee Gopher	—	M
98. Squaw	—	F
99–102. Child	—	—
103. Charlie Snow	—	M
104. Charlie Micco	—	M
105. Charlie Buster	1875	M
106. Squaw	—	F
107–9. Child	—	—
110. Charlie Cypress	—	M
111. Squaw	—	F
112–14. Child	—	—
115. Charley Dixie Hall Negro	1878	M
116. Squaw	—	F
117. Son ¼ Negro	—	M
118. Son ¼ Negro	—	M
119. Daughter	—	F

120. Mother Negress	—	F
121. Charley Doctor	1890	M
122. Squaw	—	F
123–25. Child	—	—
126. E-faw-le-harjo Charley Osceola	1843	M
127. Charley Fewell	1863	M
128. Squaw	—	F
129–31. Child	—	—
132. Charley Jumper, Sr.	1855	M
133. Squaw	—	—
134–37. Child	—	—
138. Charley Jumper, Jr. (Little)	1880	M
139. Squaw	—	F
140–43. Child	—	—
144. Cooter Jumper	1888	M
145. Squaw	—	F
146–48. Child	—	—
149. Charley Peacock	—	M
150. Charley Tiger	1885	M
151. Coffee Tiger	1889	M
152. Coffney Tiger	—	M
153. Squaw	—	F
154. Cypress Tiger	1883	M
155. Charley Tigertail	1870	M
156. Mother	—	F
157. Sister	—	F
158. Charley Tommie (1)	1870	M
159. Squaw	—	F
160–61. Child	—	—
162. Charlie Willie	1865	M
163. Squaw	—	F
164–65. Child	—	—
166. Charley Carey	1899	M
167. Charley Ingraham	1892	M

168. Charley Tommie (2)	1880	M
169. Coffney Tiger	1881	M
170. Squaw	—	F
171. Charley Billie	—	M
172. Squaw	—	F
173–74. Child	—	—
175. Dan Parker	—	M
176. Duncan	—	—
177. Ch-ta-go-la-gee Dennis	—	M
178. Squaw	—	F
179. Son	—	M
180. Son	—	M
181. Daughter	—	F
182. DeSoto Tiger's Squaw	—	F
183. DeSoto Tiger's Son	—	M
184. Dick Smith	—	M
185. Squaw	—	F
186. Child	—	—
187. Doctor Johnnie Head Man	—	M
188. Squaw	—	F
189–91. Child	—	—
192. Doctor John Billy	—	M
193. Doctor Charley	1880	M
194. Squaw	—	F
195. Son	—	M
196. Doctor Jim's Boy	1894	M
197. Dave Poole Tigertail	1885	M
198. Squaw	—	F
199. Child	—	—
200. Doctor Tiger	1860	M
201. Dave Poole Tiger	—	M
202. Doctor Tommy	1880	M
203. Squaw	—	F
204–6. Child	—	—

207. Dan Parker's Mother	—	F
208. Dan Parker's Sister	—	F
209. Dan Parker's Sister	—	F
210. Elli Morgan	—	F
211. Etta Tiger	—	F
212. Frank Cypress	1892	M
213. Futch Cypress	1870	M
214. Squaw	—	F
215–16. Child	—	—
217. Funke Negress	—	F
218. Frank Doctor	—	M
219. Frank Tiger	1892	M
220. Squaw	—	F
221–23. Child	—	—
224. Frank Stranahan	1896 or 1898	M
225. Frank Tommy	1890	M
226. Fi-lan-a-hee	—	—
227. Frank Willie	1882	M
228. Squaw	—	F
229–30. Child	—	—
231. Girtman Billy	1890	M
232. Grover Billy	1896	M
233. Ginger Snaps	—	M
234. George Hendry Jim	1893	M
235. George Osceola	1890	M
236. Squaw	—	F
237. Child	—	—
238. George Hendry Osceola	1884	M
239. Squaw	—	F
240–41. Child	—	—
242. Grover Doctor	—	M
243. Harry Parker	—	M
244. Squaw	—	F
245. Daughter	—	F

246. Daughter	—	F
247. Hautlee	—	M
248. Hillard	—	M
249. Harry Doctor	1893	M
250. Henry Homespun	1890	M
251. John Osceola	—	M
252. Squaw	—	F
253–56. Child	—	—
257. Joe Bowers	—	M
258. Squaw	—	F
259–60. Child	—	—
261. Grandmother	—	F
262. John Billy (1)	—	M
263–67. Child	—	—
268. John Billy (2)	—	M
269. Squaw	—	F
270. Child	—	—
271. Joseph Billy (2)	1887	M
272. Squaw	—	F
273–74. Child	—	—
275. Henry Clay (1)	1870	M
276. Squaw	—	F
277–78. Child	—	—
279. Henry Clay (2)	—	M
280. Henry Parker	—	M
281. Ingraham Billy	—	M
282. Ingraham Tiger	—	M
283. Johnny Jumper	—	M
284. Squaw	—	F
285. Son Josh	—	M
286. Daughter	—	F
287. John Pierce	—	M
288. Lucy Bowles (Squaw)	—	F
289. Jimmy Gopher	1892	M

290. Squaw	—	F
291–97. Child	—	—
298. Jim Tuskenuggee	—	M
299. Joseph Billy (1)	1890	M
300. Jack Buster	1880	M
301. Son	—	M
302. Jackson Charley	—	M
303. Jimmy Henry	1893	M
304. Jim (Widow Doctor Jim)	—	M
305–8. Child	—	—
309. Joseph Jimmy	1885	M
310. Squaw	—	F
311–14. Child	—	—
315. Jack Osceola	1894	M
316. Jim Osceola	1855	M
317. Squaw	—	F
318–20. Child	—	—
321. Jim Jay Osceola	—	M
322. Johnny Willie	1870	M
323. Jimmy Willie	1890	M
324. Jack Tommy	1892	M
325. Johnny Osceola	—	M
326. Squaw	—	F
327–29. Child	—	—
330. John Miami Tiger	1878	M
331. Squaw	—	F
332–36. Child	—	—
337. Jim Tiger	—	M
338. Squaw	—	F
339–42. Child	—	—
343. Jack Tigertail	—	M
344. Squaw	—	F
345–48. Child	—	—
349. Jim Truitt	1888	M

350. John Osceola	1882	M
351. Squaw	—	F
352–53. Child	—	—
354. Jonie Tommy	1885	M
355. John Willy	1885	M
356. Squaw	—	F
357–61. Child	—	—
362. Jimmie Tiger	1883	M
363. Jose Billy	1895	M
364. John Willie	1893	M
365. Jose Jim	1893	M
366. Lewis Tucker	—	M
367. Little Billy	1888	M
368. Squaw	—	F
369–72. Child	—	—
373. Little John Billy	—	M
374. Little John	—	M
375. Lake Wilson	—	—
376. Squaw	—	F
377–85. Child	—	—
386. Little Billy Conipatci [*sic*]	—	M
387. Squaw	—	F
388–95. Child	—	—
396. Little Doctor	1892	M
397. Squaw	—	F
398. Child	—	—
399. Little Charley	—	M
400. Little Jim	—	M
401. Squaw	—	F
402–5. Child	—	—
406. Little Tiger	—	M
407–13. Child	—	—
414. Little Jimmy	—	M
415. Morthatigee	—	F

416. Macuffeeha	—	F
417. Mooschee	—	F
418. Miami Billy	1835	M
419. Miami Charley	1845	M
420. Miami Jim	1840	M
421. Mammy Jumper	1830	F
422. Naha	—	F
423. Nancy Tiger	—	F
424. Old Polly Parker	—	F
425. Miami Jimmy	1836	M
426. Squaw	—	F
427–32. Child	—	—
433. Nahah Tiger	—	F
434. Squaw	—	F
435. Mother	—	F
436–37. Child	—	—
438. Oscar Hall	—	M
439. Old Pinty	—	F
440. Old Tommy	1840	M
441. Old Charley	1840	M
442. Squaw	—	F
443. Old Jumper	—	—
444. Perty	—	—
445. Phillip Billy	1883	M
446. Squaw	—	F
447. Child	—	—
448. Rupe Cypress	—	—
449. Rithie [Ruthie] Parker	—	F
450. Robert Osceola's White Squaw	—	F
451. Child	—	—
452. Samson Snow	—	—
453. Sam Jones	—	M
454. Skin Tiger	—	—
455. Sam Willie	1886	M

Appendix A.

456. Squaw	—	F
457–58. Child	—	—
459. Sam Hough	1886	M
460. Sam Billy	—	M
461. Sho-y-o-chee Widow	—	F
462. Child	—	—
463. Tehim-cha	—	F
464. Bi-san-gee	—	F
465. Stem-l-h-eel	—	F
466. Sada Tiger	—	M
467. Squaw	—	F
468. Child	—	—
469. Smallpox Tommie	1890	M
470. Tallahassee Chipio [Chipco] (Head Man)	—	M
471. Squaw	—	F
472–73. Child	—	—
474. Tallahassee (boy)	—	M
475. TunVee Tiger	—	F
476. Tom Smith	—	M
477. Tom Billy's Squaw	—	F
478–80. Child	—	—
481. Tom Devil's Garden	1840	M
482. Tommy Doctor	—	M
483. Squaw	—	F
484–86. Child	—	—
487. Tommy Lootee	1870	M
488. Squaw	—	F
489–91. Child	—	—
492. Tom Smallpox	1888	M
493. Turkey Tiger	1894	M
494. Tiger Tiger	1874	M
495. Tom Tiger	1860	M
496. Tom	—	M

497. Tobasco Charley	—	M
498. Tony Tommy	1893	—
499. Tommy Doctor Billy	—	M
500. Tommy Osceola	—	M
501. Squaw	—	F
502–9. Child	—	—
510. Wildcat Tiger	—	—
511. Willie John	—	M
512. Squaw	—	F
513. Son Little Gopher	—	M
514. Daughter Nellie	—	F
515. Daughter Arna	—	F
516. Matottnee	—	F
517. Morilee	—	F
518. Marrylee	—	F
519. Willie Billie	1875	M
520. Squaw	—	F
521. Wilson Cypress	—	M
522. Squaw	—	F
523. Child	—	—
524. Wiltke Jim	—	M
525. Whitney Cypress	1865	M
526. Squaw	—	F
527–29. Child	—	—
530. Walter Tiger	1883	M
531. Squaw	—	F
532–33. Child	—	—
534. Willie Tiger	1870	M
535. Squaw	—	F
536–40. Child	—	—
541. Willie Jumper	—	M
542. Willie Willie (1)	—	M
543. Willie Willie (2)	—	M
544. Squaw	—	F

545–49. Child	—	—
550. Whip Jim	—	M
551. Young Tony	1880	M
552. Squaw	—	F
553–54. Child	—	—
555. Young Tommy	—	M
556. Squaw	—	F
557. Child	—	—
558–67. Unnamed widows & orphans	—	—

Appendix B.
Superintendents and
Agents for the
Federal Seminole Agency

November 1888–July 1889	Lilly Pierpoint (honorary position)
May 1892–January 1, 1899	Jacob E. Brecht
March 1, 1913–July 1, 1916	Lucien Spencer
July 1, 1916–March 19, 1917	W.S. Coleman
March 19, 1917–August 1917	Lucien Spencer
August 1917–November 1919	Frank Brandon
November 1919–April 1930	Lucien Spencer
April 1930–April 1931	John Marshall (acting agent)
April 1931–May 1936	James L. Glenn
September 1936–May 1940	Francis Scott
June 1940–June 1941	Dwight Gardin
July 1941–April 1942	William B. Hill
April 1942–September 1942	Chester Faris
September 1942–May 31, 1958	Kenneth A. Marmon
December 20, 1957–April 1, 1963	Virgil N. Harrington
April 29, 1963–May 21, 1965	Doyce L. Waldrip
May 23, 1965–July 14, 1967	Reginald W. Quinn
November 5, 1967–May 31, 1971	Eugene W. Barrett
June 13, 1971–1975	Duane C. Moxon

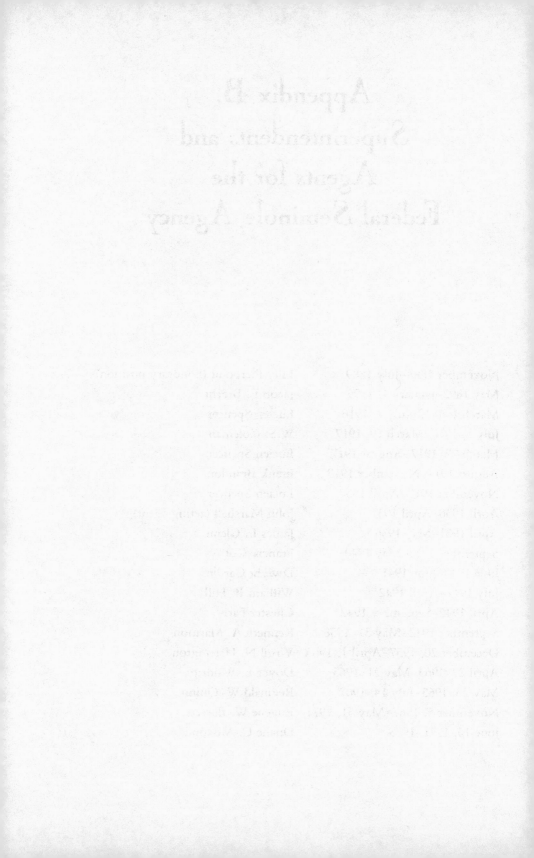

Appendix C.
State of Florida Indian Affairs
Consultants, Chairs, or
Commissioners

November 1, 1956–January 1961	Max Denton
January 1961–May 12, 1967	William Kidd
May 12, 1967–June 1968	James M. Wilson
June 1968–1974	Charles L. Knight
1974 to present	Governor's Council on Indian Affairs

Appendix D.
Boards of Directors and
Tribal Councils

BOARDS OF DIRECTORS

1957–1959

Frank Billie, president (resigned 8/16/58)	4-year term
Bill Osceola, vice-president	4-year term
John Henry Gopher (resigned 3/15/58)	4-year term
Dorothy Osceola (now Tommie)	4-year term
John Cypress	2-year term
Willie Frank	2-year term
Joe Johns	2-year term
Charlotte Osceola	2-year term
Andrew J. Bowers (replaced Gopher)	4-year term

1959–1961

Bill Osceola, president	(holdover)
Frank Billie, vice-president	(holdover)
Dorothy Osceola (Tommie) (resigned 8/60)	(holdover)
Andrew J. Bowers	(holdover)
Willie Frank	4-year term
Charlotte Osceola	4-year term
Toby Johns	4-year term
Betty Mae Jumper	4-year term
Dick Bowers (replaced Dorothy Osceola)	

1961–1963

Howard Tiger, president	4-year term
Jimmie Cypress, vice-president	4-year term
John Henry Gopher	4-year term
Bill Osceola	4-year term
Charlotte Osceola	(holdover)
Toby Johns	(holdover)
Willie Frank	(holdover)
Betty Mae Jumper	(holdover)

Constitution amended on March 14, 1963, requiring a change in elections, dates, procedures, etc.

1963–1965

Bill Osceola, president	4-year term
Billy Osceola, vice-president	4-year term
Joe Bowers (forfeited term 10/64)	2-year term
Willie Frank	2-year term
Fred Smith (inducted into army)	2-year term
Robert Osceola (elected 10/21/63 to replace Fred Smith)	
Mary Bowers (elected 11/30/64 to replace Joe Bowers)	

1965–1967

Bill Osceola, president	(holdover)
Billy Osceola, vice-president (resigned 11/66)	(holdover)
Willie Frank	2-year term
Mary Bowers	2-year term
Alice Snow	2-year term

1967–1969

Joe Dan Osceola, president	4-year term
Betty Mae Jumper, vice-president	4-year term
Joe Osceola, Sr.	2-year term
Willie Frank	2-year term
Henry Gopher (resigned 7/68)	2-year term
Tom Bowers (replaced Henry Gopher)	

Appendix D.

1969–1971

Joe Dan Osceola, president (resigned 1/71)	(holdover)
Betty Mae Jumper, vice-president	(holdover)
Willie Frank	2-year term
Howard Micco	2-year term
Joe Osceola, Sr.	2-year term

1971–1973

Fred Smith, president	4-year term
Howard Tommie, vice-president	4-year term
Willie Frank	2-year term
Tom Bowers	2-year term
JoAnn Micco (resigned 12/71)	2-year term
Mike Tiger (replaced JoAnn Micco)	

1973–1975

Fred Smith, president	(holdover)
Howard Tommie, vice-president	(holdover)
Willie Frank	2-year term
Archie Johns	2-year term
Steven D. Bowers	2-year term

1975–1977

Bill Osceola, president	4-year term
Howard Tommie, vice-president	4-year term
Willie Frank	2-year term
Archie Johns (held over to July reelection)	2-year term
Mike Tiger	2-year term

1977–1979

Bill Osceola, president	(holdover)
Howard Tommie, vice-president	(holdover)
Willie Frank	2-year term
Richard Smith	2-year term
Fred Smith (from July 1977)	2-year term

TRIBAL COUNCILS

1957–1959

Bill Osceola, chair	2-year term
Betty Mae Jumper, vice-chair	2-year term
Frank Billie	2-year term
Howard Tiger (installed 4/58)	2-year term
Charlotte Osceola	4-year term
Mike Osceola	4-year term
John Cypress (resigned 6/59)	4-year term
John Josh (resigned 6/59)	4-year term
Willie Frank (replaced John Cypress)	
Toby Johns (replaced John Josh)	

1959–1961

Willie Osceola, chair	4-year term
Howard Tiger, vice-chair	4-year term
Frank Billie	4-year term
Frank Huff	4-year term
Mike Osceola	(holdover)
Charlotte Osceola (resigned 6/60)	(holdover)
Toby Johns	(holdover)
Willie Frank	(holdover)
Jack Motlow (replaced Charlotte Osceola)	

1961–1963

Billy Osceola, chair	(holdover)
Mike Osceola, vice-chair	4-year term
Howard Tiger	(holdover)
Frank Billie	(holdover)
Frank Huff	(holdover)
Bill Osceola	4-year term
Toby Johns	4-year term
Jimmie Cypress	4-year term

Appendix D.

Constitution was amended March 14, 1963, requiring a change in elections, dates, procedures, etc.

1963

Billy Osceola, chair	4-year term
Bill Osceola, vice-chair	4-year term
Frank Billie	2-year term
Toby Johns	2-year term
Dan Osceola	2-year term

1965–1967

Billy Osceola, chair (resigned 11/66)	(holdover)
Bill Osceola, vice-chair	(holdover)
Frank Billie	2-year term
Jack Micco	2-year term
Dan Osceola	2-year term

1967–1969

Betty Mae Jumper, chair	4-year term
Joe Dan Osceola, vice-chair	4-year term
Bobby Frank (through 7/68)	2-year term
Rosie Buck	2-year term
Dan Osceola	2-year term
Don Osceola (replaced Bobby Frank)	

1969–1971

Betty Mae Jumper, chair	(holdover)
Joe Dan Osceola, vice-chair (resigned 1/71)	(holdover)
Frank Billie	2-year term
Richard Smith	2-year term
Bill Osceola	2-year term

1971–1973

Howard E. Tommie, chair	4-year term
Fred Smith, vice-chair	4-year term
Morgan Smith	2-year term

Richard Smith	2-year term
Cecil Johns	2-year term

1973–1975

Howard E. Tommie, chair	(holdover)
Fred Smith, vice-chair	(holdover)
Jimmie Cypress	2-year term
Joe Johns	2-year term
Marcellus Osceola	2-year term

1975–1977

Howard E. Tommie, chair	4-year term
Bill Osceola, vice-chair	4-year term
Paul Buster	2-year term
Stanlo Johns	2-year term
James Billie	2-year term

1977–1979

Howard E. Tommie, chair	(holdover)
Bill Osceola, vice-chair	(holdover)
Jimmie Cypress	2-year term
Rosie Buck	2-year term
Cecil Johns	2-year term

Source: 20th Anniversary of Tribal Organization, 1957–1977, Seminole Tribe of Florida (Privately printed, August 20, 1977), mimeo.

NOTES

The following abbreviations are used frequently in the notes:

ANR	Annual Narrative Report, BIA
ASP, FA	*American State Papers, Foreign Affairs*
ASP, IA	*American State Papers, Indian Affairs*
ASP, MA	*American State Papers, Military Affairs*
BIA	Letters received, Commissioner of Indian Affairs, Bureau of Indian Affairs, Record Group 75, National Archives
FRC	Bureau of Indian Affairs Records, Record Group 75, Federal Records Center, East Point, Georgia
OIA	Seminole Agency, Office of Indian Affairs, National Archives
SE	Seminole Emigration, Office of Indian Affairs, National Archives
T.P.	*The Territorial Papers of the United States,* Territory of Florida
WD	Department of Florida Records, War Department, National Archives
WPA Papers	Works Progress Administration Papers, Florida Historical Society, University of South Florida, Tampa

Chapter 1. The Seminoles Come to Florida

1. For the story of the 1704 Apalachee raid see Mark F. Boyd, Hale G. Smith, and John W. Griffin, eds., *Here They Once Stood;* Charles W. Arnade, "The English Invasion of Spanish Florida, 1700–1706."
2. James W. Covington, "The Apalachee Indians Move West," 221–25; John R. Swanton, "Early History of the Creek Indians and Their Neighbors," 123–28.
3. John J. TePaske, *The Governorship of Spanish Florida, 1700–1763,* 197. Verner W. Crane, *The Southern Frontier, 1670–1732,* 81; Lewis H. Larson, Jr., "Cultural Relationships between the Northern St. Johns Area and the Georgia Coast," 16–19.

4. Thomas Nairne to the Earl of Sunderland, July 10, 1709, Public Record Office, Colonial Office 5/382, No. 11 (hereafter PRO, CO).

5. See Henry F. Dobyns, *Their Number Became Thinned: Native American Population Dynamics in Eastern North America,* for examination of the effects of diseases upon the Florida Indians.

6. John M. Goggin and William C. Sturtevant, "The Calusa: A Stratified Non-agricultural Society with Notes on Sibling Marriage," in *Explorations in Cultural Anthropology: Essays in Honor of George Peter Murdock,* ed. Ward H. Goodenough (New York: McGraw-Hill, 1964), 187.

7. Jerald T. Milanich and Charles H. Fairbanks, *Florida Archaeology,* 236; William C. Sturtevant, "The Last of the South Florida Aborigines," 141–62.

8. *Key West Gazette,* January 11, 1832. Some survivors reportedly fled to Cuba in seventeen canoes.

9. TePaske, *Governorship of Spanish Florida,* 23; William C. Sturtevant, "Chakaika and the 'Spanish Indians': Documentary Sources Compared with Seminole Tradition," 37–38.

10. Bernard Romans, *A Concise Natural History of East and West Florida,* 291.

11. TePaske, *Governorship of Spanish Florida,* 224.

12. Robert L. Gold, "The East Florida Indians under Spanish and English Control, 1763–1765," 108; Gold, *Borderland Empires in Transition: The Triple Nation Transfer of Florida.*

13. Harold E. Driver, *Indians of North America,* 347. The Creek Confederation has been described as a collection of several score tribes usually called towns and somewhat similar to the collection of Greek city-states. According to John W. Caughey, *McGillivray of the Creeks,* 6–7, "the Creeks were notoriously undisciplined."

14. Robert S. Cotterill, *The Southern Indians: The Story of the Civilized Tribes before Removal,* 9. Still the most complete work concerning the early history of the Creeks is Swanton's "Early History." Harry A. Kersey, Jr., *The Florida Seminoles and the New Deal, 1933–1942,* 115. Other accounts of Creek history and life include: J. Leitch Wright, Jr., *Creeks and Seminoles: The Destruction and Regeneration of the Muscogulge People;* Charles M. Hudson, *The Southeastern Indians.*

15. Driver, *Indians of North America,* 345, 400–401.

16. Cotterill, *Southern Indians,* 12; Swanton, "Early History," 416.

17. Louis LeClerc Milford, *Memoirs, or a Quick Glance at My Various Travels and My Sojourn in the Creek Nation,* 94–95.

18. Milford, *Memoirs,* 106–7; Swanton, "Early History," 407–8. These two accounts differ slightly in interpretation of facts.

19. Milford, *Memoirs,* 108.

20. Swanton, "Early History," 409; Milford, *Memoirs,* 98.

21. Swanton, "Early History," 123–27.

22. Ibid., 110.

23. Ibid., 277–86.

24. Louis Capron, *The Medicine Bundles of the Florida Seminoles and the Green Corn Dance*, 180.

25. Ibid., 188–90.

26. Swanton, "Early History," 700.

27. Ibid., 358–59.

28. Ibid., 360–61.

29. Ibid., 363–65.

30. Ibid., 368–70.

31. Mark Boyd, "Asi-yahol or Osceola," 250–52.

32. James W. Covington, "Comments Upon Agent Spencer's 1913 Census of the Seminoles," *Florida Anthropologist* 39 (September 1986), 222–23.

33. Boyd, Smith, and Griffin, *Here They Once Stood*, 14; John R. Swanton, *The Indian Tribes of North America*, 128–29. In 1719, when a band of Creeks raided several American Indian villages near St. Augustine, they found at least sixteen Lower Creeks residing with the Yamassees there. Colonial Office 5/1265, No. 1441. According to Barcia, the son of a ruling Coweta chief visited St. Augustine in 1710. See *Barcia's Chronological History of the Continent of Florida*, ed. and trans. Anthony Kerrigan, 354.

34. Crane, *Southern Frontier*, 35–36; Herbert E. Bolton and Mary Ross, *The Debatable Land*, 48–50.

35. Crane, *Southern Frontier*, 162–86; TePaske, *Governorship of Spanish Florida*, 197–200.

36. Mark F. Boyd, ed. and trans., "Diego Peña's Expedition to Apalachee and Apalachicola in 1716"; Mark F. Boyd, ed., "Documents Describing the Second and Third Expeditions of Lieutenant Diego Peña to Apalachee and Apalachicola in 1717 and 1718."

37. Boyd, "Documents Describing Peña," 134; TePaske, *Governorship of Spanish Florida*, 203.

38. TePaske, *Governorship of Spanish Florida*, 205. Chiscalachisle, brother of Brims and a war chief, established an armed town at the juncture of the Flint and Chattahoochee rivers. See Kenneth W. Porter, "The Founder of the 'Seminole Nation'; Secoffee or Cowkeeper," 366–67.

39. TePaske, *Governorship of Spanish Florida*, 206; Boyd, "Documents Describing Peña," 109.

40. Don Juan Isidoro de Leon to Governor Manuel de Montiano, May 21, 1745, Lucy L. Wenhold, ed. and trans., "The Trials of Captain Isidoro de Leon," 249.

41. De Leon to de Montiano, June 26, 1747, ibid., 262.

42. Carol I. Mason, "Eighteenth Century Culture Change among the Lower

Creeks," 65–79; Charles H. Fairbanks, "Some Problems of the Origin of Creek Pottery," 53.

43. Francis Harper, ed., *The Travels of William Bartram*, 247. According to Porter, "Founder of the 'Seminole Nation'," 381, Bartram really meant the Lower Creeks and not the Upper Creeks when he stated that the Oconee first moved to the Creek lands and then southward. So far as can be determined, the exact site of Cuscowilla has not been located by historians or anthropologists. Thus, in connection with this most famous Seminole town, there are two mysteries—where it stood and the exact date of its establishment. Interview by the author with John Goggin, Gainesville, Florida, October 1962.

44. Harper, *Travels of William Bartram*, 240.

45. John M. Goggin, "Source Materials for the Study of the Florida Seminole Indians," 1.

46. Ibid.; Wright, *Creeks and Seminoles*, 117.

47. William C. Sturtevant, "Creek into Seminole," 105.

48. Cowkeeper, accompanied by forty-five warriors, came to Florida with James Oglethorpe in 1740, when the English attempted to seize the Castillo de San Marcos. *The Saint Augustine Expedition of 1740, A Report to the South Carolina General Assembly* (Columbia: South Carolina Archives Department, 1954), 55.

49. Coontie (Zamia integrifolia) or arrowroot was abundant in southern Florida. The large tubers needed to be ground into smaller sections, the poison contained within washed away, and the result put into shallow trays and dried in the sun. See "Seminole Bread—the Conti," *Journal of the New York Botanical Garden* 22 (July 1921), 121–31.

50. Milanich and Fairbanks, *Florida Archaeology*, 254–56. Martin F. Dickinson and Lucy B. Wayne, "The Seminole Indian Dispersed Settlement Pattern: An Example from Marion County, Florida," *Indians, Colonists and Slaves: Essays in Memory of Charles H. Fairbanks*, Florida Journal of Anthropology Special Publication No. 4 (1985), 222–23. For an account concerning Spanish loan words see William C. Sturtevant, "Spanish-Indian Relations in Southeastern North America," 50–53.

51. Little is known concerning the date when Talahasochte was founded. John T. Sprague, *The Origin, Progress, and Conclusion of the Florida War*, 19, states that the second band to come to Florida was the one led by Micco Hadjo that settled at Tallahassee.

52. Harper, *Travels of William Bartram*, 143.

53. James W. Covington, ed., *The British Meet the Seminoles*, 3.

54. Charles H. Fairbanks, *Ethnohistorical Report on the Florida Indians*, 120.

55. Harper, *Travels of William Bartram*, 88, 308.

56. Interview with Captain Daniel Burch, *Pensacola Gazette*, October 8, 1824.

57. Harper, *Travels of William Bartram*, 185–86. Myer M. Cohen claimed that the Ocklawaha band was composed of Yamassee descendants. Myer M. Cohen,

Notices of East Florida and the Campaigns, 33. See also facsimile edition with introduction by O. Z. Tyler, Jr. (Gainesville: University of Florida Press, 1964). Other bands of Yamassees probably migrated to the Upper Creeks and Mobile.

58. Gold, *Borderland in Transition,* 153–61.

59. John R. Alden, *John Stuart and the Southern Colonial Frontier, A Study of Indian Relations, War, Trade, and Land Problems in the Southern Wilderness,* 198–201.

60. Covington, *British Meet the Seminoles,* 23–25.

61. Ibid., 28; the book *Like Beads on a String: A Culture History of the Seminole Indians in North Peninsular Florida,* by Brent R. Weisman, gives an excellent account of the early history of the Seminoles. When the British learned that older leaders did not want to surrender any land, they considered postponing the conference; younger Seminoles who wanted rum and presents insisted that the conferences be held on schedule and that some land be given to the English. Gold, "East Florida Indians," 116.

62. For accounts of the 1765 and 1767 conferences, see Covington, *British Meet the Seminoles,* 18–37, 42–56; John Bartram, "Diary of a Journey through the Carolinas, Georgia and Florida"; Alden, *John Stuart,* 201–40; Charles L. Mowat, *East Florida as a British Province, 1763–1784, passim;* James W. Covington, "British Gifts to the Indians: 1765–1766," 71–75.

63. Fairbanks, *Ethnohistorical Report,* 157–59.

64. William S. Coker and Thomas D. Watson, *Indian Traders of the Southeastern Spanish Borderlands: Panton, Leslie and Company and John Forbes and Company, 1783–1847,* 33.

65. Ibid.

66. Ibid., 50–51.

67. Ibid., 14.

68. Ibid., 63.

69. Caughey, *McGillivray,* 25–26, 74–75. See also Helen Hornbeck Tanner, *Zéspedes in East Florida, 1784–1790,* 57–58; Jack D. L. Holmes, "Spanish Treaties with West Florida Indians, 1784–1802," 140–42.

70. Lyle N. McAlister, "Pensacola during the Second Spanish Period," 301.

71. Talk of Vicente Manuel de Zéspedes in Joseph B. Lockey, ed. and trans., *East Florida, 1783–1785,* 428–29.

72. Reply to talk of Vicente Manuel de Zéspedes, December 8, 1784, ibid., 429–30.

73. B. Lincoln, Cyrus Griffin, and D. Humphreys to Secretary of War, November 20, 1789, *ASP, IA,* 1:78–79.

74. Richard K. Murdoch, "Indian Presents: To Give or Not to Give, Governor White's Quandry," *F.H.Q.* 35 (April 1957), 337.

75. Jack D. L. Holmes, "The Southern Boundary Commission, the Chattahoochee River and the Florida Seminoles, 1799," 301.

76. Holmes, "Southern Boundary," 329–30.
77. Andrew Ellicott, *The Journal of Andrew Ellicott,* 221.
78. Coker and Watson, *Indian Traders,* 189.
79. Wright, J. Leitch, Jr., *William Augustus Bowles, Director-General of the Creek Nation,* 58–60.
80. Caughey, *McGillivray,* 298–300; Wright, *Bowles,* 59–60.
81. Wright, *Bowles,* 67–72.
82. Cotterill, *Southern Indians,* 100–103.
83. Coker and Watson, *Indian Traders,* 232.
84. Milford, *Memoirs,* 62–63.
85. Coker and Watson, *Indian Traders,* 237–38.
86. John Forbes, "Journal, May, 1803."
87. Wright, *Bowles,* 162–64; Coker and Watson, *Indian Traders,* 241–42.
88. Coker and Watson, *Indian Traders,* 239.
89. Ibid., 241–42.
90. John C. Upchurch, "Aspects of the Development and Exploration of the Forbes Purchase," 119.
91. Coker and Watson, *Indian Traders,* 269–70.
92. Charles H. Fairbanks, "Excavations at Horseshoe Bend, Alabama," 51–52; Mason, "Eighteenth Century Culture Change," 65–80.
93. *Narrative of a Voyage to the Spanish Main in the Ship "Two Friends,"* 164. Part of this account has been reprinted in John W. Griffin, ed., "Some Comments on the Seminole in 1818," *Florida Anthropologist* 10 (November 1957), 41–49.
94. William H. Simmons, *Notices of East Florida with an Account of the Seminole Nation of Indians by a Recent Traveller in the Province,* 25.
95. James G. Forbes, *Sketches, Historical and Topographical of the Floridas: More Particularly of East Florida,* 103, 105. See also facsimile edition with introduction by James W. Covington (Gainesville: University of Florida Press, 1964).
96. Jack D. L. Holmes, "Two Spanish Expeditions to Southwest Florida, 1783–1793," 102. The 1757 map of Tampa Bay, drawn by Francisco Maria Celi, shows one Seminole village along the southern shore. Charles W. Arnade, "Three Early Spanish Tampa Bay Maps," 88.
97. Holmes, "Two Spanish Expeditions," 105–6. In 1814, 1819, and 1820, Seminole leaders from Tampa Bay were reported to have visited Havana. Sturtevant, "Chakaika and the 'Spanish Indians,'" 38–39.
98. James W. Covington, "Trade Relations between Southwestern Florida and Cuba, 1600–1840."
99. James W. Covington, ed., "A Petition from Some Latin-American Fishermen, 1838," *Tequesta* 14 (1954), 62.
100. Thelma Peters, ed., "William Adee Whitehead's Reminiscences of Key West," 38.

Notes

101. John Lee Williams, *The Territory of Florida*, 26. See also facsimile edition with introduction by Herbert J. Doherty, Jr. (Gainesville: University of Florida Press, 1962).

Chapter 2. Early Conflicts with White Americans

1. *Dictionary of American Biography*, s.v. "Mathews, George."
2. Kenneth W. Porter, "Negroes and the East Florida Annexation Plot, 1811–1813."
3. T. Frederick Davis, ed., "United States Troops in Spanish East Florida, 1812–1813 (Letters of Lt. Col. T. A. Smith)," 3–23.
4. Rembert W. Patrick, *Florida Fiasco: Rampant Rebels on the Georgia-Florida Border, 1810–1815*, 180, 185.
5. Ibid., 185.
6. Ibid.
7. Ibid., 207.
8. Simmons, *Notices of East Florida*, 76–77.
9. Augusta *Chronicle*, October 20, 1815. News of Payne's death and migration of his village reached Georgia by January 1813. Hawkins to Secretary of War, January 18, 1813, *ASP, IA* 1:838.
10. Patrick, *Florida Fiasco*, 229–30.
11. Ibid., 233.
12. Lieutenant Colonel Thomas Smith to General Thomas Flournoy, February 24, 1813, Davis, "United States Troops," 271–74. As late as 1822 William Simmons saw the ruins of Bowlegs's house, traced the paths used by the Seminoles, and observed the cowpens, which were marked by trees growing along the lines. Simmons, *Notices of East Florida*, 51.
13. Fairbanks, *Ethnohistorical Report*, 214–15.
14. Frank Lawrence Owsley, Jr., *The Struggle for the Gulf Borderlands: The Creek War and the Battle of New Orleans;* Big Warrior to Hawkins, August 4, 1813, *ASP, IA* 1:851; H. S. Halbert and T. H. Ball, *The Creek War of 1813 and 1814;* R. David Edmunds, *Tecumseh and the Quest for Indian Leadership*, 148–50; Theron A. Nuñez, "Creek Nativism and the Creek War of 1813–14."
15. See James W. Holland, *Andrew Jackson and the Creek War: Victory at Horseshoe.*
16. See *ASP, IA* 1:837; Charles J. Kappler, comp. and ed., *Indian Affairs, Laws and Treaties* 2:108–9.
17. John Sugden, "The Southern Indians in the War of 1812—The Closing Phase," 291.
18. Earl Bathurst to Charles Cameron, March 30, 1814, Admiral Alexander Cochrane Papers (hereafter cited as CP).
19. Coker and Watson, *Indian Traders*, 279–80; Sugden, "Southern Indians," 280.

20. J. Leitch Wright, Jr., *Britain and the American Frontier, 1783–1815* (Athens: University of Georgia Press, 1975), 162–65. News that the English had landed at Deer Island reached Hawkins in central Alabama by mid-June 1814. Hawkins to Big Warrior, Little Prince, and other Creek chiefs, June 16, 1814, *ASP, IA* 1:845.

21. Captain Hugh Pigot to Lieutenant George Woodbine, May 10, 1814, CP. In January 1813 the Spanish commander at St. Marks and Seminoles living near the juncture of the Flint and Chattahoochee rivers were certain that British troops would arrive "some place in the South and West." Hawkins to Secretary of War, January 18, 1813, *ASP, IA* 2:839.

22. Hawkins to Secretary of War, June 14 and 15, 1814, *ASP, IA* 1:859.

23. Coker and Watson, *Indian Traders*, 281.

24. Woodbine to Pigot, May 31, 1814, CP.

25. Hawkins to Secretary of War, August 16, 1814, *ASP, IA* 1:860.

26. Ibid.

27. Frank L. Owsley, Jr., "British and Indian Activities in Spanish West Florida during the War of 1812," 118.

28. Edward Nicolls to Cochrane, December 3, 1814, CP; General Orders town of Mobile, September 17, 1814, Inspector General A. P. Hayne, *ASP, IA* 1:861.

29. William Rawlins to Cochrane, January 16, 1815, CP.

30. Sugden, "Southern Indians," 312; this earthen fortification was sited two miles below the juncture of the Flint and Chattahoochee rivers near present-day Chattahoochee.

31. Treaty of March 10, 1815, signed by thirty American Indian leaders including prominent Seminoles enclosed in letter of Nicolls to Benjamin Hawkins, June 12, 1815, Public Record Office, Foreign Office (hereafter Foreign Office) 5/139.

32. Nicolls to B. Hawkins, April 28, 1815, *ASP, FA* 4:548.

33. B. Hawkins to Nicolls, May 24, 1815, ibid., 549.

34. Sugden, "Southern Indians," 308.

35. Arbuthnot to Nicolls, August 26, 1817, Public Record Office, Foreign Office 5/139 (hereafter PRO, FO).

36. James W. Silver, *Edmund Pendleton Gaines, Frontier General*, 54.

37. Ibid., 57.

38. Major Thomas Freeman to General Edmund P. Gaines, May 22, 1816, National Archives, Roll 414, Letters received by Secretary of War, Registered Series 1801–1860, December 1815–December 1816, D–L, G–37 (9).

39. General Andrew Jackson to Gaines, March 12, 1816; Gaines to Secretary of War, April 6, 1816, ibid.

40. Gaines to Secretary of War, April 30, 1816, ibid.

41. Humble Representation of the Chiefs of the Creek Nation to His Excellency Governor Cameron (no date), in *Narrative of a Voyage to the Spanish Main*, 219.

42. Arbuthnot to Nicolls, August 26, 1817, *Narrative of a Voyage,* 225–26.

43. Ochlockonee Sound, located ten or twelve miles to the west of St. Marks, may have had better facilities, for it had been selected by Bowles as a port.

44. Bowlegs to Coppinger (no date), *The Trials of A. Arbuthnot and R. C. Ambrister Charged with Inciting the Seminole Indians to War,* 34–35.

45. W. A. Croffut, ed., *Fifty Years in Camp and Field: Diary of Major-General Ethan Allen Hitchcock, USA,* 152; T. Frederick Davis, "Milly Francis and Duncan McKrimmon, an Authentic Florida Pocahontas," 251–58.

46. Arbuthnot's Journal, *ASP, FA* 4:609.

47. Ibid.

48. Ibid., 610.

49. Ibid.

50. Gaines to the Seminole Chiefs (no date), *Narrative of a Voyage,* 221.

51. Ibid., 221–22.

52. Gaines to Jackson, November 21, 1817, *ASP, MA* 1:686.

53. Ibid.

54. Gaines to Secretary of War, November 26, 1817, ibid.

55. David B. Mitchell to Governor Graham, December 14, 1817, ibid., 688.

56. Gaines to Secretary of War, December 2, 1817, ibid., 687.

57. Mark Boyd, "Events at Prospect Bluff, on the Apalachicola River, 1808–1818," 88; *National Intelligencer,* February 24, 1818.

58. John S. Bassett, ed., *Correspondence of Andrew Jackson* 2:341.

59. Ibid., 347.

60. Edwin C. McReynolds, *The Seminoles,* 83.

61. Jackson's orders to Captain Isaac McKeever, *ASP, FA* 4:573.

62. Jackson to John C. Calhoun, March 25, 1818, *ASP, FA* 4:573. The body of Kinache was identified by Hambly but one author believed that Kinache, surviving the battle, fled to Nassau in 1819 and returned to Florida at Plantation Key the same year. Wright, *Creeks and Seminoles* (Lincoln, Nebr.: University of Nebraska Press, 214).

63. Jackson to John C. Calhoun, May 5, 1818, *ASP, FA* 4:601.

64. Alexander Arbuthnot to John Arbuthnot, ibid., 581.

65. James Parton, *Life of Andrew Jackson* 1:456–57.

66. Kenneth W. Porter, "The Negro Abraham," 1–8.

67. Ibid.

68. Jackson to J. C. Calhoun, April 20, 1818, *ASP, MA* 1:700–701.

69. Ibid. Alan Craig and Christopher S. Peeples, "Captain Young's Sketch Map," 176–79; Mark Boyd, ed., "Hugh Young, A Topographical Memoir on East and West Florida."

70. Charlton W. Tebeau, *A History of Florida,* 112–13.

71. Statement of John Arbuthnot, August 6, 1818, PRO, CO 23/67; transcript in Joseph B. Lockey Collection.

72. Deposition of John Fenix, July 22, 1818; transcript from PRO, ibid.

73. For trial record see *Trials Arbuthnot and Ambrister* and also *ASP, MA* 1:721–34.

74. Parton, *Life of Jackson* 1:270–80; *Niles Weekly Register,* June 6, 1818.

75. Fairbanks, *Ethnohistorical Report*, 229–30.

76. Boyd, "Osceola," 255–57.

77. Simmons, *Notices of East Florida*, 59.

78. See John M. Goggin, "The Seminole Negroes of Andros Island, Bahamas," 200–206, and Kenneth W. Porter, "Notes on Seminole Negroes in the Bahamas," 56–60.

79. Weisman, *Like Beads on a String*, 80.

80. Ibid.; Sturtevant, "Creek into Seminole," 106.

Chapter 3. Prelude to War, 1821–1833

1. Secretary of War to Jean A. Penieres, March 31, 1821, *The Territorial Papers of the United States,* edited by Clarence E. Carter, 22:26–27. Hereafter cited as *T.P.*

2. Secretary of War to Governor DuVal, June 11, 1822, *T.P.,* 452–55.

3. Fairbanks, *Ethnohistorical Report,* 229–30.

4. Mark F. Boyd, "Horatio S. Dexter and Events Leading to the Treaty of Moultrie Creek with the Seminoles." See lists of towns as contained in Boyd, "Hugh Young," and Swanton, "Early History," 406–7.

5. DuVal to Secretary of War, September 22, 1822, *T.P.* 22:533–34.

6. Proclamation of Governor DuVal, July 29, 1822, *T.P.* 22:504.

7. Thomas Wright to Acting Governor Walton, December 7, 1822, *T.P.* 22: 576–77; see also Walton to Secretary of War, January 9, 1823, *T.P.* 22:597.

8. Arrell M. Gibson, *The American Indian: Prehistory to the Present,* 299.

9. Secretary of War to James Gadsden and Bernardo Suqui, April 7, 1823, *T.P.* 22:659–61.

10. James Gadsden to Secretary of War, June 11, 1823, *T.P.* 22:694–96.

11. John K. Mahon, *History of the Second Seminole War, 1835–1842,* 43.

12. Ibid., 364.

13. Indian Commissioners to Secretary of War, September 26, 1823, *T.P.* 22: 747–51.

14. See James W. Covington, "Federal Relations with the Apalachicola Indians: 1823–1838."

15. Dr. Andrew Welch claimed that the following articles in the treaty were disregarded by the federal government: article 2, the boundary line was not

checked by the Seminoles; article 3, part of the $5,000 annual annuity was paid in the form of high-priced whiskey and gun powder; article 6, the agent represented the government, not the Seminoles; and of the thirty-two Seminoles present, only six signed the treaty, and the commissioners filled in the remaining names. Andrew Welch, *A Narrative of the Early Days and Remembrances of Osceola Nikkandochee, Prince of Econchati, a Young Seminole Indian, Son of Econchati-Mico, King of the Red Hills in Florida,* 212–14.

16. See Donald L. Chamberlin, "Fort Brooke: Frontier Outpost, 1824–1842"; James W. Covington, "The Establishment of Fort Brooke," 273–78; and George A. McCall, *Letters from the Frontier,* 135–83.

17. *ASP, IA* 2:430.

18. Gad Humphreys to DuVal, April 7, 1824; DuVal to Calhoun, July 17, 1824, ibid., 617, 619.

19. DuVal to Calhoun, July 29, 1824, ibid., 621.

20. McCall, *Letters from the Frontier,* 152.

21. Ibid., 156.

22. Gadsden to Secretary of War, March 20, 1824, *T.P.* 22:905–7, and June 15, 1824, *T.P.* 22:968–70.

23. DuVal to Secretary of War, July 22, 1824, *ASP, IA* 2:620.

24. Receipts by Indian Chiefs for Payment of Improvements, November 12, 1824, *T.P.* 23:102–5.

25. DuVal to Humphreys, November 27, 1828, ibid., 115–16.

26. Kenneth W. Porter, "Thlonoto-sassa: A Note on an Obscure Seminole Village of the Early 1820s," 118.

27. Boyd, "Horatio S. Dexter," 91–92.

28. Brent Weisman, "On the Trail of Osceola's Seminoles in Florida."

29. Brent Weisman, "Cove of the Withlacoochee Archaeological Project," 7.

30. Cantonment Brooke had been established at Tampa in 1824 to keep a watch upon the Seminoles and to prevent them from communicating with traders from Cuba. George M. Brooke, Jr. "Early Days at Fort Brooke"; James W. Covington, "Life at Fort Brooke 1824–1836," *F.H.Q.* 36:319–30; Chamberlin, "Fort Brooke," 5–29.

31. Humphreys to Superintendent Thomas L. McKenney, September 20, 1825, *T.P.* 23:323–24.

32. George M. Brooke to Colonel George Gibson, December 20, 1825, *ASP, IA* 2:655.

33. Eloise R. Ott, "Fort King: A Brief History."

34. James Barbour to Gadsden, May 2, 1826, *T.P.* 23:527–28.

35. Talk by the delegation of Florida Indians, delivered by Tuckasee Mothla (John Hicks), May 17, 1826, *T.P.* 23:548–51.

36. Humphreys to Secretary of War, October 10, 1828; see also DuVal to Humphreys, September 22, 1828, both cited in Sprague, *Origin,* 60–62.

37. Sprague, *Origin*, 50–51; Daniel F. Littlefield, Jr., *Africans and Seminoles: From Removal to Emancipation*, 8–9.

38. The best account of the removal of the northern tribes can be found in Grant Foreman, *Last Trek of the Indians* (Norman: University of Oklahoma Press, 1946), and for the southern tribes, by the same author, *Indian Removal: The Emigration of the Five Civilized Tribes of Indians*.

39. See Walter L. Williams, ed., *Southeastern Indians since the Removal Era*.

40. John K. Mahon, "Two Seminole Treaties: Payne's Landing, 1832, and Fort Gibson, 1833," 8.

41. Kappler, *Indian Affairs*, 2:344–45.

42. Ibid., 344, 394.

43. Croffut, *Fifty Years*, 79–80.

44. Mahon, "Two Seminole Treaties," 20.

45. DuVal to McKenney, July 17, 1828, *T.P.* 24:42–43.

46. On May 30, 1829, the president of the United States set aside part of section nos. 14–15, township 3, range 7N and W, for an agency adjoining the Apalachicola reserves. Ibid., 222.

47. McKenney to DuVal, April 13, 1830, *T.P.* 24:392–93.

48. Acting Governor James D. Westcott, Jr., to Abraham Bellamy, February 2, 1832, ibid., 668–70.

49. Gadsden to Secretary of War, August 30, 1832, *T.P.* 24:727.

50. DuVal to Acting Secretary of War John Robb, October 11, 1832, ibid., 740.

51. Wiley Thompson to Elbert Herring, August 6, 1834, National Archives, Office of Indian Affairs, Apalachicola Reserve and Emigration, 1826–34 (hereafter cited as A.R.E.).

52. Gadsden to Secretary of War Lewis Cass, April 16, 1833, *T.P.* 24:752–54.

53. Memorandum of Convention between Blount, Davy, and Westcott, October 28, 1833, A.R.E. Westcott took DuVal's place during the spring, summer, and most of fall 1833 while DuVal was in Kentucky.

54. Johnson took John Vacca, the son of Mulatto King, to Washington, and he returned to Florida by stagecoach. John's brother and another boy died of cholera in Kentucky, but the others including Billy, son of Blount, survived. After the five returned to Florida, another educational group including three from the original band was organized and sent to the Kentucky school in January 1834.

55. David M. Sheffield to DuVal, February 23, 1833, *ASP, IA* 2:456.

56. Herring to Thompson, December 23, 1834, *T.P.* 25:83. In November 1834 it appeared that Econchatimico and Mulatto King might go to Texas. Blount's wife was a daughter of Mulatto King, and Econchatimico would go wherever Mulatto King desired. Blount's death, however, ended any chance of removal to Texas. See Herring to Thompson, December 2, 1834, ibid., 71.

57. John Walker to Thompson, July 28, 1835, *ASP, MA* 2:463.

58. Sheffield to Secretary of War Lewis Cass, February 9, 1836, *T.P.* 25:567–68.
59. Econchatimico to Congress of the United States, April 2, 1836, ibid., 462.
60. Resolution by Citizens of Gadsden County, May 14, 1836, ibid., 284–85.
61. Gibson to Archibald Smith, Jr., June 14, 1836, ibid., 312.
62. Walker to Lieutenant Joseph W. Harris, May 21, 1838, ibid., 506–7.
63. Daniel Boyd to Indian Commissioner Crawford, January 26, 1839, Florida Superintendency, A.R.E.
64. Boyd's survey report is found in ibid., *T.P.* 25:619–20. A good summary of the Apalachicolas' final days in Florida is McReynolds, *The Seminoles*, 214–15.

Chapter 4. The Second Seminole War, Phase I, 1835–1838

1. For a summary of the difficulties endured during the war see Mahon, *Second Seminole War*, 324–27; Wright, *Creeks and Seminoles*, 252–80, and Sturtevant, "Creek into Seminole," 108–10.
2. Kenneth W. Porter, "Negroes and the Seminole War, 1835–1842," 430–31; Williams, *Territory of Florida*, 237.
3. Senate, *Abstract of Council*, 24th Cong., 1st sess., 1835, S. Doc. 152, 20–21; T. Frederick Davis, "The Seminole Council, October 23–25, 1834."
4. The best accounts of Osceola's life are contained in the complete issue of *F.H.Q.* 33 (January–April 1955); Brent Weisman, "Cove of the Withlacoochee," 5.
5. Davis, "Seminole Council," 340–41.
6. Ibid., 349.
7. Senate, *Minutes of Council of December 27, 1834*, 24th Cong., 1st sess., 1835, S. Doc. 152, 29–32. In the April 24, 1835, meeting eight leaders gave their approval to the treaty; when Micanopy, Jumper, Alligator, Sam Jones, and Black Dirt refused to sign, Thompson crossed their names from the list of Chiefs. Sprague, *Origin*, 84–85.
8. Woodburne Potter, *The War in Florida, Being an Exposition of Its Causes, and an Accurate History of the Campaigns of Generals Clinch, Gaines, and Scott*, 88–91.
9. House, *Supplemental Report on Causes of Hostilities*, 24 Cong., 1st sess., 1836, H. Doc. 271, 197.
10. For various proposals concerning the planned removal see *American State Papers, Military Affairs* 6:520–35.
11. Mahon, *Second Seminole War*, 99, has an excellent account of the events that preceded the actual hostilities.
12. Ibid., 114–34.
13. Charley Emathla, who had a cornfield and herd of cattle near the agency, had earlier migrated south from the Chattahoochee River. Wright, *Creeks and Seminoles*, 250–51.

14. Potter, *War in Florida*, 93–94.

15. James H. Howard, *Oklahoma Seminoles, Medicines, Magic, and Religion*, 231. Throughout the various battles Seminole leaders could be heard lecturing their warriors.

16. Howard, *Oklahoma Seminoles*, 231.

17. Jacob Mickler Report, August 28, 1857, M143, Box 28, National Archives, Department of Florida Records, War Department (hereafter WD).

18. Richard K. Call to President Andrew Jackson, December 22, 1835, *T.P.*, 25:217.

19. Potter, *War in Florida*, 100–101.

20. A very readable and well-researched account of the battle is Frank Laumer, *Massacre* (Gainesville: University of Florida Press, 1968); also see W. S. Steele, "Last Command: The Dade Massacre," 35–47.

21. Sprague, *Origin*, 90; see also Captain Ethan Allen Hitchcock to General Edmund Gaines, February 22, 1836, *ASP, MA* 7:425.

22. Laumer, *Massacre*, 150–52. Colonel Duncan L. Clinch to AAG, December 29, 1835, *T.P.* 25:218.

23. George C. Bittle, "The Florida Militia's Role in the Battle of Withlacoochee," 304; Herbert J. Doherty, Jr., *Richard Keith Call: Southern Unionist*, 96–97.

24. Weisman, *Like Beads on a String*, 92–94; Weisman, "Cove of the Withlacoochee," 20–21.

25. Frank Laumer, "Encounter by the River," *F.H.Q.* 46 (April 1968), 338.

26. Cohen, *Notices of East Florida*, 126; to James Gadsden, the white people of Florida were like a "ship tossed on an angry ocean without helm, the mariner asleep and crew divided." Gadsden to the President, January 14, 1836, *T.P.* 25:224–26.

27. Mahon, *Second Seminole War*, 324; Henry Prince Diary, P. K. Yonge Library of Florida History, University of Florida, Gainesville (hereafter Prince Diary).

28. Williams, *Territory of Florida*, 272–75.

29. Charles W. Elliott, *Winfield Scott, the Soldier and the Man*, 299–300; John K. Mahon, ed., "The Journal of A. B. Meek and the Second Seminole War, 1836," 302–18.

30. Silver, *Gaines*, 178; Potter, *War in Florida*, 156; Elliott, *Winfield Scott*, 301.

31. Croffut, *Fifty Years*, 93–95; *Army and Navy Chronicle*, August 11, 1836; Prince Diary.

32. Joshua Giddings, *The Exiles of Florida*, 122–23.

33. Tom Knotts, "History of the Blockhouse on the Withlacoochee," 245–54.

34. Samuel G. Drake, *Aboriginal Races of North America*, 431–32.

35. Williams, *Territory of Florida*, 252.

36. Ibid., 247.

37. Cass to Governor Richard K. Call, June 20, 1836, *T.P.* 25:314–15.

38. Doherty, *Call,* 104–5; Call to Acting Secretary of War, December 2, 1836, *T.P.* 25:445–46.

39. Boyd, "Osceola," 292.

40. Charles H. Coe, *Red Patriots: The Story of the Seminoles,* 74–77.

41. Croffut, *Fifty Years,* 110–11.

42. Bones of many Seminoles were found when the city of Tampa was erecting the Fort Brooke Garage. The bones were buried on a Seminole reservation near Tampa created for the purpose, and artifacts found with the bones are on display in a museum on the facility. Weisman, *Like Beads on a String,* 85–91.

43. Mahon, *Second Seminole War,* 210–11.

44. Samuel Forry to J. W. Phelps, October 31, 1837, Samuel Forry, "Letters of Samuel Forry, Surgeon, U.S. Army, 1837–38," 7:94 (hereafter Forry Letters).

45. Forry to Phelps, October 19, 1837, ibid., 88.

46. Forry Letters, 94.

47. Jacob Rhett Motte, *Journey into Wilderness: An Army Surgeon's Account of Life in Camp and Field during the Creek and Seminole Wars, 1836–1838,* 119–20.

48. Boyd, "Osceola," 295.

49. "The White Flag"; Motte, *Journey,* 138.

50. Forry Letters, 93.

51. Foreman, *Indian Removal,* 332.

52. Littlefield, *Africans and Seminoles,* 16.

53. Gary E. Moulton, "Cherokees and the Second Seminole War," 296–305; Motte, *Journey,* 149.

54. J. Floyd Monk, "Christmas Day in Florida," 30–31.

55. U.S. Congress, *Congressional Globe* 6:165–66; *Army and Navy Chronicle* 6:71; Sprague, *Origin,* 203–13.

56. Foreman, *Indian Removal,* 363. It was estimated that some 2,968 Seminoles were shipped out from 1836 to March 1841 and 934 from April 1841 to April 1842, a total of 3,902. In January 1847 Captain John C. Sprague estimated there were 120 warriors in the various bands. Captain John C. Casey compiled a list of the 126 Seminole men that was printed in the *Florida News,* August 27, 1853.

Chapter 5. The Second Seminole War, Phase 2, 1838–1842

1. Mahon, *Second Seminole War,* 249–51.

2. Ibid., 253.

3. Halleck Tustenuggee claimed to have lived along the Withlacoochee River all of his life and had resided in the Long Swamp, six miles from Fort King, for the past three years. Frank F. White, ed., "Macomb's Mission to the Seminoles, John T. Sprague's Journal Kept during April and May, 1839," 169.

4. Ibid., 178–86. According to Sandy, a black, who, under orders from Harney, contacted Sam Jones and was given assurances that Jones and all of his warriors wanted an end to the war and accepted the terms; ibid., 177.

5. George R. Adams, "Caloosahatchee Massacre: Its Significance in the Second Seminole War," 376.

6. James W. Covington, "Cuban Bloodhounds and the Seminoles."

7. Lieutenant C. R. Gates to Lieutenant Colonel Newman S. Clarke, July 3, 1841, copy of letter in Col. Newman S. Clarke folder, "Scouting the Withlacoochee Cove Area," Box 3, Keenan-Brown Collection, P. K. Yonge Library.

8. Hester Perrine Walker, "Massacre at Indian Key, August 7, 1840, and the Death of Dr. Henry Perrine"; Motte, *Journey*, 227–28.

9. Sturtevant, "Chakaika and the 'Spanish Indians'."

10. Sprague, *Origin*, 248–49.

11. Mahon, *Second Seminole War*, 298.

12. Ibid., 270.

13. Sprague, *Origin*, 272.

14. Ibid., 274.

15. Ibid., 281.

16. Ibid., 287.

17. Ibid., 288.

18. Ibid., 300.

19. Ibid., 316.

20. McCall, *Letters from the Frontier*, 404–6; Sprague, *Origin*, 465–68.

21. Croffut, *Fifty Years*, 172.

22. Secretary of War John C. Spencer to General Winfield Scott, May 10, 1842, *T.P.* 26:471–72; James W. Covington, "The Agreement of 1842 and Its Effect upon Seminole History."

23. William J. Worth to A.A.G., July 24, 1842, *T.P.* 26:515–18.

24. Worth to A.A.G., August 12, 1842, ibid., 524–25; McCall, *Letters*, 411–12.

25. Cooper, A.A.G. General Order, 28, *T.P.* 26:519.

26. Sprague, *Origin*, 498–99.

27. Ibid., 499–500.

28. Sturtevant, "Creek into Seminole," 108.

Chapter 6. A Period of Crisis

1. *Statutes at Large of the United States* 4:420; see Roy M. Robbins, *Our Landed Heritage: The Public Domain, 1776–1936*, 49–50, and Benjamin H. Hibbard, *A History of the Public Land Policies* (New York: Macmillan, 1924), 152–53.

2. *Statutes at Large* 6:502. The area open to settlement was corrected on June 15, 1844. Ibid., 5:671; James W. Covington, "Armed Occupation Act of 1842."

3. A complete list of settlers can be found in U.S. Congress, Senate, *Report of the Commissioner of the Land Office on the Armed Occupation Act* and in James W. Covington, *Story of Southwestern Florida* 1:422–51.

4. Although the order of President James Polk is not listed in James D. Richardson, *A Compilation of the Messages and Papers of the Presidents, 1789–1897,* it is mentioned in Secretary of the Interior Orlando Brown to Commissioner, General Land Office, J. Butterfield, July 25, 1849, U.S. Congress, Senate, *Relative to the Hostilities Committed by the Seminole Indians in Florida during the Past Year . . . ,* 114–15. Butterfield to Brown, August 4, 1849, ibid.

5. J. Butterfield, Commissioner, General Land Office, to Thomas Ewing, Secretary of the Interior, May 16, 1850, *Relative to the Hostilities,* 160.

6. George Ballentine, *Autobiography of an English Soldier in the United States Army,* 105.

7. Thomas P. Kennedy to Captain John T. Sprague, October 2, 1845, John C. Casey Papers, Gilcrease Museum.

8. Joah Griffin to Kennedy, September 27, 1845, Casey Papers.

9. Michael G. Schene, "Not a Shot Fired: Fort Chokonikla and the 'Indian War' of 1849–1850," 21.

10. Governor William D. Moseley to James Polk, December 29, 1848, Seminole Agency, 1846–55, National Archives, Office of Indian Affairs (hereafter OIA). *Acts and Resolutions of the Second General Assembly* (Tallahassee: State of Florida, 1846), 56, 57; *Acts and Resolutions of the Fourth General Assembly* (Tallahassee: State of Florida, 1849), 71.

11. Captain John C. Casey to A.A.G., U.S. Congress, Senate, *Operations in Florida,* July 23, 1849, 116 (hereafter cited as *Operations in Florida*).

12. John T. Sprague to Major General R. Jones, January 11, 1847, S26 Seminole Agency, OIA, printed as Covington, ed., "The Florida Seminoles in 1847." On Holata Micco, see Carolyn T. Foreman, "Billy Bowlegs," and Kenneth W. Porter, "Billy Bowlegs (Holata Micco) in the Seminole Wars." Goggin, in "Source Materials," writes, "Of course, the Muskogee and Mikasuki dialects were related but not mutually intelligible"; because it was the practice for the married Seminole male to live at the camp of his in-laws, some mixing of the Mikasuki and Muskogee groups occurred. The Yuchi had joined the Seminoles during the eighteenth and nineteenth centuries; one of their towns was at Spring Garden, in present-day Volusia County; see Swanton, *Indian Tribes of North America,* 119. It is difficult to believe that Choctaws were living in southern Florida at this time, but other persons had so indicated; for a Florida Choctaw's account of this tribe, see Horace Ridaught, *Hell's Branch Office.*

13. Casey to Jones, June 18, 1849, *Relative to the Hostilities,* 23–24.

14. Orlando Brown to Spencer, July 25, 1849, ibid., 113–14. See Commissioner of Indian Affairs W. Medill to Spencer, June 7, 1849, ibid., 108–9; Spencer to Thomas Ewing, Secretary of the Interior, June 25, 1849, ibid., 111–12.

15. Spencer to Ewing, June 29, 1849, ibid., 109. Spencer to Orlando Brown, October 1, 1849, ibid., 138–39; Ewing to Brown, September 19, 1849, ibid., 139.

16. Schene, "Not a Shot Fired," 21.

17. Disposition of William and Nancy McCullough, August 11, 1849, *Relative to the Hostilities,* 161–63.

18. Casey Diary, Casey Papers.

19. Casey to A.A.G., September 6, 1849, *Operations in Florida, 121.*

20. Ibid. Subsequent reports state that five were involved in the attacks. Item from *Florida Republican,* July 21, 1849, in unidentified clipping, "Collection of Clippings from Contemporary Newspapers, 1836–1865," Jacksonville, Florida, Public Library. J. H. Bronson, B. A. Putnam, and Joseph Hernandez to George W. Crawford, Secretary of War, July 31, 1849, *Relative to the Hostilities,* 30–31.

21. Casey Diary, Casey Papers.

22. The site of the store located just north of present-day Wauchula became known as Chokkonickla or Burnt House.

23. Disposition of William and Nancy McCullough. Casey to A.A.G. July 29, 1849, *Relative to the Hostilities,* 38–39.

24. Smith to A.A.G., July 17, 1849, ibid., 25.

25. Governor Moseley to Captain William Fisher, July 30, 1849, ibid., 52–53.

26. William W. Morris to A.A.G., August 13, 1849, ibid., 119–20. It has been suggested that one of the raids had been prompted by dishonest dealing on the part of William Barker, who had been a trader. Andrew Canova, *Life and Adventures in South Florida,* 53.

27. Casey to A.A.G., August 20, 1849, *Relative to the Hostilities,* 116–17; Coe, *Red Patriots,* 196–97. Since this version was taken from Casey's diary it seems more correct.

28. Twiggs to Crawford, September 23, 1849, *Operations in Florida,* 49–52.

29. Quoted in New York *Journal of Commerce,* October 8, 1849.

30. Twiggs to A.A.G., October 19, 1849, *Operations in Florida,* 133–34.

31. Agent Marcellus DuVal claimed that Sam Jones protected the life of the fifth murderer, that others had taken part in the killings, and that the three were delivered as a sacrifice to save others. DuVal to Governor Thomas Brown, November 19, 1849, *Relative to the Hostilities,* 140–41; according to the diary of Casey, the three were guilty, but Chipco and several others had taken part in the Peace River attack. Casey Papers.

32. Unidentified clipping, "Collection of Clippings."

33. Ibid.

34. Coe, *Red Patriots,* 193.

35. Ibid., 193–94.

36. Twiggs to A.A.G., October 3, 1849, *Operations in Florida,* 126–28.

37. DuVal to Brown, November 5, 1849, *Relative to the Hostilities,* 143–44.

38. Casey to Crawford, March 1, 1850, *Operations in Florida,* 54.

39. Casey to David E. Twiggs, April 15, 1850, *Relative to the Hostilities,* 96.

40. St. Augustine *Ancient City,* June 10, 1852.

41. Secretary of War to Captain John Casey, October 7, 1850, Casey Papers.

42. Jesse Sumner to Casey, November 20, 1850, ibid.

43. Secretary of War to Casey, October 7, 1850, ibid.

44. Casey Diary, January 10, 1851, ibid.

45. Notes of Council, April 13, 1851, Casey Diary, ibid.

46. Notes, May 13, 1851, ibid.

47. Casey Diary, ibid.

48. Ibid.

49. Ibid. See Helen Byrd, "Genealogical Sketch of the Whidden Family," Hillsborough County Historical Commission, Tampa, Florida; statement of Justice of the Peace Simon Turman, August 24, 1852, U.S. Congress, Senate, *On the Case of L. Blake, June 19,* 27.

50. Casey to Commissioner of Indian Affairs, February 9, 1851, National Archives, Office of Indian Affairs, C571, Seminole Emigration (hereafter SE).

51. Alexander Stuart to Commissioner of Indian Affairs Luke Lea, April 19, 1851, S81, SE.

52. Luther Blake to Lea, May 15, 1851, B915, SE.

53. Casey Diary, Casey Papers.

54. Agreement of September 20, 1852, A800, SE.

55. *Gleason's Pictorial Magazine,* May 1, 1852.

56. Clipping, Casey Diary, Casey Papers.

57. Casey to Blake, October 11, 1852, B127, SE. For an account of Casey's activities, see Fred C. Wallace, "The Story of Captain John C. Casey."

58. Blake to Comptroller, September 24, 1853, B274, SE.

59. Aaron Jernigan to Brown, February 9, 1852. *Case of L. Blake,* 57; the law approved January 20, 1851, provided for the raising of a regiment of mounted volunteers and the extension of Florida laws into the reserve.

60. Benjamin Hopkins to Brown, March 25, 1852, ibid., 68; Arthur Thompson, "A Massachusetts Traveller on the Florida Frontier," 134–36.

61. Message of Millard Fillmore, January 18, 1853, Richardson, *Messages and Papers of the Presidents* 4:2720–21.

62. Jacksonville *News,* January 10, 1853; Tallahassee *Floridian and Journal,* March 5, 26, 1853.

63. John T. Sprague to Secretary of Interior Jacob Thompson, June 25, 1857, T400, OIA.

64. Jefferson Davis to Stephen Mallory and August Maxwell, August 5, 1854, Tallahassee *Floridian and Democrat,* September 9, 1854. As early as December

1851 after George Cabell had talked to the commissioner of Indian affairs and secretary of the interior a bill was prepared that provided for the surveying of all land in Florida. Cabell to Brown, December 1851, Letters Book of Governor Thomas Brown, Florida State Archives, Tallahassee.

65. See Memoirs of Reconnaissance with maps during the Florida campaign, April 13, 1854, to December 1855, compiled by Major Francis Page, WD; John M. Schofield, *Forty-six Years in the Army;* selection from B. J. Lossing, *Memoirs of Lt. Col. John Greble,* printed in *Tampa Tribune,* May 4, 1958.

Chapter 7. The Final War, 1855–1858

1. Tampa *Herald,* December 15, 1855.

2. John Parrish, *Battling the Seminoles,* 215.

3. Ray B. Seley, Jr., "Lieutenant Hartsuff and the Banana Plants," 10.

4. Gary R. Mormino, ed., "The Firing of Guns and Crackers Continued till Light," 59.

5. Seley, "Hartsuff," 13–14.

6. Each company was required to have seventy-four privates, two musicians, four corporals, four sergeants, one second lieutenant, one first lieutenant, and one captain. Captain A. Gibson to Adjutant General, April 12, 1856. Letters received, Orders and Ordnance returns, 1856, War Department, RG75, National Archives. Contemporary records indicated that it was very difficult to recruit foot soldiers; Governor James Broome to Jefferson Davis, December 31, 1855, Florida *House Journal,* 1856, 35–36; Broome to John Monroe, February 4, *House Journal,* 1856, 40–41.

7. The headquarters of the four state mounted companies were: Kendrick, Fort Broome (Hernando County frontier); Durrance, Fort Fraser (area east of Peace River); Lesley, site unselected (Lower Peace and Manatee river areas), and Jernigan, Fort Gatlin (one half of the company operating east of St. Johns River and other half cooperating with Johnson's company). See message of Governor Broome, November 24, 1856, *House Journal,* 1856, 12; Broome to General Jesse Carter, February 4, 1856, *House Journal,* 1856, 25–26.

8. Carter to Captain William Kendrick, February 27, 1856, *House Journal,* 67. Captain John Casey and James McKay estimated that in 1854 the Seminoles had 185 men, 200 women, 90 children under the age of fifteen, and 40 old warriors. From 1854 to 1857 some 20 youngsters may have become of age to join the fighting force. Tampa *Florida Peninsular,* August 24, 1857.

9. Tampa *Florida Peninsular,* March 8, 1856; Ernest L. Robinson, *History of Hillsborough County,* 38.

10. Albert DeVane, conversation with author, December 6, 1962.

11. Tampa *Florida Peninsular,* February 2, 1856.

12. Alexander S. Webb, "Campaigning in Florida in 1855," 410–12.

13. Mormino, "Firing," 66.

14. Canova, *Life*, 60–62; Lillie B. McDuffee, *Lures of the Manatee: A True Story of South Florida and Its Glamorous Past*, 91–92.

15. Tampa *Florida Peninsular*, April 5, 1856; for accounts of the attack on the Braden plantation see Carter to Broome, April 12, 1856, *House Journal*, 1856, appendix 85–86, and Tampa *Florida Peninsular*, April 12, 1856. Also see John Monroe to A.A.G. Samuel Cooper, April 16, 1856, M265, Box 27, WD.

16. J. A. Hendley, *History of Pasco County, Florida*, 4, 16; Tallahassee *Floridian and Journal*, May 31, 1856; Samuel Churchill, Inspector General, to Monroe, May 15, 1856, C3, Box 27, WD.

17. Gibson to Lieutenant Thomas Vincent, April 18, 1856, G3, Box 27, WD.

18. Tampa *Florida Peninsular*, May 24, 1856; *Tampa Tribune*, December 4, 1965; Hubbard L. Hart to James Campbell, Postmaster General, July 19, 1856, *House Journal*, 1856, 29–31; Monroe to Hart, July 6, 1856, *House Journal*, 1856, 31; Postmaster to Campbell, July 6, 1856, *House Journal*, 1856, 31–32.

19. Canova, *Life*, 55–56.

20. *Fort Meade Leader*, cited in *Tampa Tribune*, October 26, 1958; *House Journal*, 1856, 13.

21. Francis M. Durrance to Carter, June 16, 1856, *House Journal*, 1856, 21; Albert DeVane, article in "Pioneer Florida," *Tampa Tribune*, June 19, 1960.

22. Morris to Captain Francis N. Page, July 26, 1856, M120, Box 30, WD.

23. Robert Bradley to Davis, March 22, 1856, B23, Box 26, WD.

24. Davis to Broome, June 11, 1856, Indian Office Letter Book 39, page 142, Office of Indian Records, National Archives.

25. Carter to Durrance, April 23, 1856, *House Journal*, 1856, 96.

26. William S. Harney to A.A.G., November 25, 1856, Box 27, WD. For details of the Harney disaster at the Caloosahatchee River and subsequent revenge see Adams, "Caloosahatchee Massacre," 368–80, and Sturtevant, "Chakaika and the 'Spanish Indians,'" 36–73.

27. Captain Alfred Pleasonton, General Orders No. 2, January 5, 1857, Box 28, WD.

28. Memorandum of Plan of Operations, March 6, 1857, signed by A.A.G. Cooper, A28, Box 28, WD.

29. George E. Buker, "Francis's Metallic Life Boats and the Third Seminole War," 150.

30. Bertha R. Comstock, "History of the Capron Trail," Works Progress Administration Papers, Florida Historical Society, University of South Florida (hereafter WPA Papers).

31. Article in 1886 copy of *Philadelphia Times*, quoted in Karl Grismer, *The Story of Fort Myers*, 72.

32. Jacob Mickler Report, August 28, 1857, M143, Box 28, WD.

33. Canova, *Life*, 14–15.

34. Oliver O. Howard, *Autobiography* 1:76.

35. David Ramsey, ed., "Abner Doubleday and the Third Seminole War," 323–24.

36. John A. Bethell, *Bethell's History of Point Pinellas*, 81.

37. Tampa *Florida Peninsular*, October 3, 1857.

38. Ramsey, "Abner Doubleday," 327.

39. Canova, *Life*, 69–70.

40. S. Rogers to A.A.G., January 9, 1858, Box 32, WD.

41. Kappler, *Indian Affairs*, 2:756–63.

42. Elias Rector to Captain John Pope, February 22, 1858, R9, Box 32, WD.

43. Rector to Commissioner of Indian Affairs Charles Mix, March 16, 1858, R514, 1858, OIA.

44. McReynolds, *The Seminoles*, 287.

Chapter 8. Early Contacts and Establishment of a Reservation

1. Robert A. Taylor, "Unforgettable Threat: South Florida Seminoles in the Civil War," paper read at the May 1989 meeting of the Florida Historical Society, Gainesville.

2. Ibid.

3. State of Florida Constitution 1868, Section 7, 8; *Florida Statutes Annotated* 26:465; in December 1862 the Confederate legislature of Florida passed a law providing for the hiring of an Indian agent at $1,500 a year and for the posting of a reservation south of Lake Okeechobee. *Acts and Resolutions Adopted at the 12th Annual Assembly of Florida* (Tallahassee: State of Florida, 1862), 39. In 1864 George Lewis and a Mr. Griffin were reported to be Confederate Indian agents who traded cloth, tobacco, lead, and rifle caps for hogs. Rodney E. Dillon, Jr., "The Little Affair: The Southwest Florida Campaign, 1863–1864," 325.

4. Charles W. Pierce, *Pioneer Life in Southeast Florida*, 39.

5. "Life Among the Indians," Federal Writer's Project, Works Progress Administration Papers, P. K. Yonge Library; for other accounts of Seminole life at this time see J. W. Ewan, "The Seminole Christmas" and "A Seminole Reminiscence," 39–46.

6. See articles by Albert DeVane in "Pioneer Florida," *Tampa Tribune*, July 15, April 2, 1950. Chipco died in 1884, but his nephew, Tallahassee, had assumed his position as leader by 1877.

7. *Lake Wales Highlander*, September 25, 1925. An excellent account of Seminole life in the Everglades during the 1880s can be found in John F. Reiger, ed., "Sailing in South Florida Waters in the Early 1880s."

8. W. Stanley Hanson and Carl Liddle, "Indians and Indian Life," WPA Papers.

9. Fort Myers *Press*, March 31, 1889. A Seminole encampment at this time

usually consisted of a man, his wife, unmarried children, and married daughters and their husbands and children. Married men went to live with their wives' families, usually occupying a chickee erected fairly near that of the senior couple. For other details of Seminole life along the Kissimmee and Caloosahatchee rivers during this period, see Pat Dodson, ed., *Journey through the Everglades: The Log of the Minnehaha,* 31, 51, 52.

10. The purpose of the hunting dance was to insure good hunting and to protect the hunters from snakebite. Louis Capron, "Notes on the Hunting Dance of the Cow Creek Seminole," 67–78.

11. Charles B. Cory, *Hunting and Fishing in Florida* (Boston: Estes and Lauriat, 1896), 29.

12. A scholarly and detailed account of the Green Corn Dance is Capron, *Medicine Bundles;* Mrs. Frank Stranahan stated that she refused to attend the Green Corn Dances for some had turned into drunken brawls. Dwight Gardin to Carita Corse, January 14, 1937, WPA Papers.

13. Albert DeVane, "A Brief Biographical Sketch of Josie Billy—Cocha-No-Gof-Dee of Big Cypress Reservation," Seminole Papers, Florida Historical Society, University of South Florida, Tampa.

14. Interview with Phillip Youmans, WPA Papers.

15. Interview with Hanson and Liddle.

16. Capron, *Medicine Bundles,* 197–98.

17. Robert F. Greenlee, "Ceremonial Practices of the Modern Seminoles," WPA Papers; other sources include Robert F. Greenlee, "Medicine and Curing Practices of the Modern Florida Seminoles," 317–27; William C. Sturtevant, "The Medicine Bundles and Busks of the Florida Seminoles," 31–70.

18. Mr. D. B. McKay, the pioneer historian, mayor, and newspaper editor, recalled the visits of Tallahassee to Tampa.

19. Fort Myers *Press,* November 14, 1889.

20. Marjory Stoneman Douglas, *The Everglades: River of Grass,* 278. Bess Burdine recalled that her father stocked bolts of vivid calico for the Seminoles and that they approached in single file to shop at Burdine's on Flagler Street. Dorothy D. Davidson, "Pioneer Pictures," 6; Alan Craig and David McJunkin, "Stranahan's: Last of the Seminole Trading Posts," 49.

21. Dora Doster Utz, "Life on the Loxahatchee," 46–47.

22. The best account of Seminole clothing in transition is the article by Hilda J. Davis, "The History of Seminole Clothing and Its Multi-colored Designs."

23. E. Adamson Hoebel and Karen Daniels Peterson, commentary, *A Cheyenne Sketchbook by Cohoe,* 7.

24. L. D. Darrell to Commissioner Hiram Price, September 16, 1882, 16908–82, Letters Received, Commissioner of Indian Affairs, Bureau of Indian Affairs, Record Group 75, National Archives (hereafter BIA).

25. Secretary of Interior Teller to Commissioner of Indian Affairs, September 16, 1882, 16908–82, BIA.

26. Henry Caruthers to Commissioner of Indian Affairs, October 24, 1882, 6764–82, BIA.

27. Caruthers to Commissioner of Indian Affairs, March 10, 1883, 5011–83, BIA.

28. Commissioner E. J. Brooks to First Lieutenant Richard H. Pratt, June 9, 1879, in William C. Sturtevant, presenter and annotator, "R. H. Pratt's Report on the Seminole in 1879," 3–4.

29. Ibid., 13.

30. Ibid., 14. Slaves were kept by Old Tigertail, who lived near Cutler. Ewan, "Seminole Reminiscence," 46.

31. Clay MacCauley, *The Seminole Indians of Florida,* 447–78.

32. Alfred Jackson Hanna and Kathryn Abbey Hanna, *Lake Okeechobee: Wellspring of the Everglades,* 332; *Statutes at Large* 23:95.

33. Sturtevant, "Creek into Seminole," 111.

34. Patsy West, "Seminole Indian Settlement at Pine Island, Broward County, Florida: An Overview," *Florida Anthropologist* 42 (March 1989), 48; William C. Sturtevant, "A Seminole Personal Document," 57–58.

35. Cyrus Beede to Commissioner of Indian Affairs, April 6, 1885, 7652–85, BIA.

36. An excellent account of the trade between the storekeepers and the Seminoles is Harry A. Kersey, Jr., *Pelts, Plumes, and Hides: White Traders among the Seminole Indians, 1870–1930.*

37. Lorenzo Creel, Special Agent, to Commissioner of Indian Affairs, March 20, 1911, 24816–1911, BIA.

38. Dora Doster Utz, "West Palm Beach," 62.

39. Thelma Peters, "The First County Road from Lantana to Lemon City," 4; Bertha Comstock, "James D. Girtman, Pioneer and Indian Trader," WPA Papers.

40. U.S. Indian Inspector Charles F. Nesler to Secretary of the Interior Ethan A. Hitchcock, February 23, 1904, with File 126–1909, BIA.

41. New York *Sun* of July 1886, cited in Tampa *Times,* January 20, 1934.

42. Lilly Pierpont to Mrs. Grover Cleveland, January 1, 1887, 1858–87, BIA.

43. E. M. Wilson to Commissioner of Indian Affairs, November 3, 1887, 30447–87, BIA.

44. *Annual Report of Women's National Indian Association,* 15. Although the Women's National Indian Association had auxiliaries scattered throughout the eastern United States, the Winter Park, Florida, Kentucky, and Philadelphia auxiliaries made special contributions to the Seminole mission.

45. Mrs. Quinton to Commissioner of Indian Affairs, March 21, 1892, 10792–92, BIA.

46. Jacob E. Brecht, "Report," *Sixty-Second Annual Report of the Commissioner of Indian Affairs to Secretary of Interior* (Washington, D.C.: GPO, 1893), 356.

47. Charlton W. Tebeau, *Florida's Last Frontier: The History of Collier County,* 197.

48. Fort Myers *Press,* January 17, 1896.

49. Brecht, "Report," 369.

50. *Lake Worth Historian* clipping, n.d., Kirk Munroe Papers, Parcel 22, Library of Congress, Washington, D.C.

51. Brecht, "Report," 66.

52. *Acts and Resolutions Adopted by Legislature of Florida at Its Third Regular Session under Constitution, AD 1885* (Tallahassee: State of Florida, 1891), 216.

53. Report of James A. Ingraham, Chairman, to Governor W. O. Bloxham as copied in letter of Special Agent Lorenzo Creel to Commissioner of Indian Affairs, March 29, 1911, 27957–1911, BIA.

54. Harry A. Kersey, Jr., "Private Societies and the Maintenance of Seminole Tribal Integrity, 1899–1957," 305.

55. Charles F. Nesler, U.S. Indian Inspector, to Ethan A. Hitchcock, Secretary of the Interior, February 23, 1904. With File 176F2–1909, BIA.

56. *Acts and Resolutions Adopted by the Legislature of Florida at Its Seventh Regular Session under Constitution AD 1885* (Tallahassee: State of Florida, 1899), 148.

57. Minnie Moore-Wilson, *The Seminoles of Florida,* 148. For further details concerning the incident see Harry A. Kersey, Jr., "The Case of Tom Tiger's Horse: An Early Foray into Indian Rights," 306–18.

58. Sections of this chapter have been taken from James W. Covington, "Federal and State Relations with the Florida Seminoles, 1875–1901."

Chapter 9. Missionary Efforts and New Federal Reservations

1. In October 1892 the Missionary Jurisdiction of Southern Florida had been established by the General Convention of the Protestant Episcopal Church meeting at Baltimore, and Bishop Gray was appointed the first bishop of the new diocese. He was fifty-nine years old when appointed and had served all of his time as priest in the Diocese of Tennessee. For details of the mission see Harry A. Kersey, Jr., and Donald E. Pullease, "Bishop William Crane Gray's Mission to the Seminole Indians in Florida, 1893–1914," 257–73.

2. Bishop Henry Benjamin Whipple (1822–1901) of the Protestant Episcopal Church was a leading reformer of U.S. Indian policy. Active among the Sioux and Chippewa, he was called by them "Straight Tongue." *Dictionary of American Biography,* s.v. Whipple, Henry Benjamin.

3. Bishop Gray to Albert Smiley, Proprietor of Lake Mohonk Hotel, October 9, 1908, 74485–08, BIA. The Lake Mohonk Conference, started in 1883 by Albert Smiley, was "an unofficial coordinating agency for the reformers." Federal officials, members of Congress, and reformers attended the four-day sessions held at Lake Mohonk, New York, and recommended policies that were usually followed by the Bureau of Indian Affairs. William Hagan, *American Indians,* 124.

4. Tebeau, *Florida's Last Frontier,* 72; as late as 1936 land at Immokalee was owned by the church, and several Seminoles were buried in the cemetery there.

5. Harriet Randolph Parkhill, *The Mission to the Seminoles in the Everglades of Florida,* 10.

6. Tebeau, *Florida's Last Frontier,* 72. William H. Brown, a former British sailor, established a store at Immokalee and then moved to Boat Landing in 1896, where he purchased a trading post that had been erected by Wilson, reportedly a Baptist minister who tried to convert the Seminoles. Rev. George W. Gatewood, a Methodist minister at Everglade, had been able to lure a few Seminoles into attending his services but none were converted.

7. The Cashbook of Brecht, Industrial Teacher and Special Disbursing Agent for the Seminole Indians, is in File 1378, Florida 1892–1899, BIA. It contains receipts for July 28, 1892–July 25, 1899, when orders were given to sell all property to the highest bidder. The sum of $185 was realized.

8. Davis, "Seminole Clothing," 975.

9. Parkhill, *Mission,* 12.

10. Gray to Smiley, October 9, 1908, 74485–1908, BIA.

11. Ibid. For details of friction between the Seminoles and whites over the theft of Tom Tiger's bones, Harry A. Kersey, Jr., "The Seminole 'Uprising' of 1907," 49–58.

12. Tebeau, *Florida's Last Frontier,* 73; at present Boat Landing is in the middle of the Big Cypress Reservation.

13. Letter of Rev. Irenaeus Trout to Commissioner of Indian Affairs, March 6, 1909, 17682–1909, BIA. Attached to the note was a census of the Seminole Indians. Also see James W. Covington, "The Seminole Indians in 1908," 99–104.

14. *Tampa Tribune,* December 5, 1909.

15. Special Agent Lorenzo Creel to Commissioner of Indian Affairs, March 20, 1911, 24816–1911, BIA.

16. William J. Godden to Gray, June 11, 1910, 51288–1910, BIA.

17. Extract from Lorenzo Creel's "Report of March 29, 1911, on Conditions Among the Seminole Indians of Florida" attached to letter of Walter L. Fisher, Secretary of the Interior, to President William Taft, June 15, 1911, 20817–1911, BIA.

18. Creel to Commissioner of Indian Affairs, December 15, 1910, 99716–1910, BIA.

19. Hitchcock to Commissioner of Indian Affairs, February 27, 1904, 14019–1904, BIA.

20. Commissioner of Indian Affairs Robert G. Valentine to Gray, May 25, 1910, 51288–1910, BIA.

21. Charles F. Hauke to Gray, July 20, 1910, ibid.

22. Gray to Commissioner of Indian Affairs, July 29, 1910, 62518–1910, BIA. The *Tampa Tribune* (December 5, 1909) reported that Frank Brown had given the land to the church, but he had sold it to the U.S. government.

23. Creel to Commissioner of Indian Affairs, January 27, March 20, 1911, 24816–1911, BIA.

24. Commissioner of Indian Affairs to Secretary of the Interior, March 5, 1914, 101916–1915, BIA. In September 1913 Bishop Gray had requested the use of sections 29 and 32 for an experimental farm and sections 29–32 for grazing rights. Lucien A. Spencer to Commissioner of Indian Affairs, September 15, 1913, 111683–1913, BIA.

25. Note from Secretary of Interior, March 9, 1914, 101916–1915, BIA.

26. Upon retirement Gray went back to Tennessee but continued to visit Florida until his death in 1919.

27. Fort Myers *Press,* March 23, 1914.

28. Ibid., October 2, 1914. In early September 1914, when Godden gave a talk to a group in Fort Myers, he claimed that the Seminoles were in a critical situation due to the disruption of fur markets by World War I and the near extinction of fur-bearing animals. Ibid., September 22, 1914.

29. A picture of the missionary party appears opposite page 177 in McReynolds, *The Seminoles;* John F. Brown to Hauke, Second Assistant Commissioner of Indian Affairs, March 24, 1911, 26789–1911, BIA. John F. Brown, Jr., was the son of a white doctor who had married the daughter of John Jumper when he accompanied the removal party to the West.

30. Hauke to Brown, March 17, 1911, 26789–1911, BIA.

31. Creel to Commissioner of Indian Affairs, March 20, 1911, 24816–1911, BIA. All of these early efforts by the Oklahoma group to convert the Florida Seminoles failed, for in 1931 there were no Seminoles attending church, no buildings, and no missionaries. See Sturtevant, "Seminole Personal Document," 75 n. 24.

32. James O. Buswell III, "Florida Seminole Religious Ritual: Resistance and Change," 257.

33. Ibid., 259.

34. Creek to Commissioner of Indian Affairs, March 29, 1911, 27957–1911, BIA. Andrew J. Duncan, brother-in-law of President William McKinley, visited the Florida Seminoles and made a report concerning them in 1898. He recommended that 300,000 acres be purchased for them by the government and set aside as a reservation, and that certain lands frequented by the Seminoles be withdrawn from inclusion in the Swamp and Overflowed Land Act provision. Coe, *Red Patriots,* 256; the only one of Duncan's recommendations that was carried out was the acquisition of the twelve 40-acre tracts near Dania.

35. Hauke to E. E. Watson, Deputy Clerk of Lee County, Florida, February 18, 1911, 27957–1911, BIA. The same situation occurred in Dade County in 1913. See L. Spencer to Commissioner of Indian Affairs, September 18, 1913, 113468–1913, BIA.

36. *New York Herald* clipping, n.d., Munroe Papers.

37. Kirk Munroe to Ingraham, July 20, 1907, 25954–1911, BIA.

38. Interior Departmental Order of November 27, 1907, cited in Hauke to Commissioner of the General Land Office, April 6, 1911, BIA (no file number).
39. Creel to Commissioner of Indian Affairs, March 9, 1911, 24175–1911, BIA.
40. Inspector Frank Churchill to Secretary of Interior, April 29, 1909, 33652–1911, BIA. In February 1911 Nathan P. Bryan was selected by the Florida legislature to serve as U.S. senator.
41. *Statutes at Large* 38:1632. This land included NW/4 NE/4 Sec 1 T 518R 418.
42. Ibid., 274.
43. The land in Broward, Collier, and Martin counties was reserved for the Seminoles in Executive Order 1379 signed by William H. Taft on June 28, 1911. *Presidential Executive Orders*, 122. In addition to the land reserved at Dania by President Taft, 2,200 acres in Martin County and 960 acres in Collier County were reserved by the same order. Annual Narrative Report, 1914, Special Commissioner Lucien Spencer to Commissioner of Indian Affairs (hereafter ANR). Parts of this chapter were taken from James W. Covington, "The Florida Seminoles: 1900–1914," and "Seminole Indians in 1908."
44. Creel to Commissioner of Indian Affairs, March 29, 1911, 27957–1911, BIA.
45. *House Journal*, 1913, 2427; *Senate Journal*, 1913, 2233.
46. *House Journal*, 1913, 2578–80; some time later a citizen purchased 60,000 acres of this desired tract for $4.20 an acre.

Chapter 10. Lucien A. Spencer and His Work, 1913–1931

1. U.S. Congress, Senate, *A Survey of the Seminole Indians of Florida*, 65 (hereafter *Survey*).
2. Kersey and Pullease, "Bishop Gray's Mission," 257–73.
3. ANR, 1913.
4. L. Spencer to Commissioner of Indian Affairs, September 18, 1915, 1915–1916, BIA.
5. In October 1913 Spencer conferred with the superintendent of public instruction so that Tony Tommie could attend school. In November 1913 the headmen of Tommie's clan gave their consent for his school attendance. Special Report of L. Spencer to Commissioner of Indian Affairs, 2678–1914, BIA (no date).
6. ANR, 1915.
7. ANR, 1918. Likewise, the Annie School experiment did not last long.
8. William C. Sturtevant, "Notes on Modern Seminole Traditions of Osceola," 209.
9. Lucien Spencer, Indian Census Rolls, Indians of Florida, Seminoles of Florida, 1913–40, M595, Rolls 486–87, submitted by Superintendent in Charge of Agency Records, BIA.

10. Spencer to Commissioner of Indian Affairs, September 18, 1915, 1915–1916, BIA.

11. ANR, 1915, Fort Myers *Press,* September 22, 1914.

12. ANR, 1913.

13. For information concerning the Indian Rights Association see Francis P. Prucha, *American Indian Policy in Crisis: Christian Reformers and the Indian, 1865–1900,* 138–43; Jack T. Ericson, ed., *A Guide to Microfilm Edition, Indian Rights Association Papers, 1864–1973.*

14. Kenneth R. Philip, *John Collier's Crusade for Indian Reform, 1920–1954,* 127. See commentary by Robert F. Berkhofer, Jr., in Jane F. Smith and Robert Kvasnicka, eds., *Indian-White Relations: A Persistent Paradox,* 83–85, and Benay Blend, "The Indian Rights Association, the Allotment Policy, and the Five Civilized Tribes, 1923–1936," 68–69.

15. Matthew Sniffen to Herbert Welsh, February 1, 1916, Roll 30, Indian Rights Association Papers, Historical Society of Pennsylvania, Philadelphia. The microfilm copy is the only one available to the researcher at the Pennsylvania Historical Society (hereafter IRA Papers).

16. Matthew K. Sniffen, "Florida's Obligation to the Seminole Indians: A Plea for Justice," 1–8.

17. Minnie Moore-Willson to Joseph Elkington, March 15, 1916, Roll 30, IRA Papers.

18. Kersey, "Private Societies," 307–8; Moore-Willson to Ivy Stranahan, January 7, 1917, Roll 32, IRA Papers.

19. May Mann Jennings to Moore-Willson, May 12, 1915, Minnie Moore-Willson Collection, Otto G. Richter Library, University of Miami, Coral Gables, Florida. In her letter to Moore-Willson, Jennings stated it was her belief that obtaining much worthless land would prevent the legislature from giving the Seminoles anything more desirable in future years. It was better to decide what was wanted and to keep asking for it until it was obtained. Looking back, Jennings was correct; Moore-Willson, not understanding the situation, would obtain the worthless land.

20. Testimony of May Mann Jennings, "Condition of the Florida Seminoles," *Hearings before the Committee on Investigation of the Indian Service,* House of Representatives, 65th Cong., 1st sess., March 12–14, 1917, 100.

21. Ibid., 12–14, 95–96. Sears wanted more land and money for the Seminoles. In March 1917, when the House of Representatives Committee met at St. Augustine, it was felt that most of the members desired a small reservation for the Seminoles in Florida.

22. For an account of the patronage of Sidney Catts, see Wayne Flynt, *Cracker Messiah: Governor Sidney J. Catts of Florida,* 108, 111; Tampa *Times,* March 10, 1917; David R. Colburn and Richard K. Scher, *Florida's Gubernatorial Politics in the Twentieth Century,* 136–37.

23. Moore-Willson to Sniffen, January 15, 1917, IRA Papers.

24. Sidney Catts to Sniffen, February 5, 1917, IRA Papers.

25. Ibid., February 13, 1917; Catts to Welsh, February 12, 1917, ibid.

26. Jacksonville *Times Union,* May 10, 1917; *Laws of Florida, 1917,* 1:131–32.

27. *Survey,* 57–59.

28. *Tampa Tribune,* July 21, 1982. In August 1950 the Board of Commissioners of State Institutions had allowed the Central and Southern Florida Flood Central District to use 16,000 acres of state reservation land for water storage. The Seminoles were not consulted. Such use made the land useless for all other purposes.

29. *Survey,* 67–68; ANR, 1918.

30. J. F. Jaudon and George W. Storter, "Seminole Indian Life," WPA Papers.

31. Isabelle Sanderson, "The Hendry County Reservation," WPA Papers.

32. Ibid.

33. ANR, 1922.

34. ANR, 1919.

35. ANR, 1922; *Survey,* 56.

36. ANR, 1925.

37. Ibid.

38. Gladys Buck, "Indian Questionnaire," WPA Papers.

39. ANR, 1925.

40. Dorothy Downs, "Coppinger's Tropical Gardens: The First Commercial Indian Village in Florida," 227. One of the first exhibition villages had been operated by Bert Lasher on the North Fork of the New River in Fort Lauderdale. Many of the people who worked at Coppingers had learned how to endure the stares and curiosity of tourists at the Fort Lauderdale attraction. Patsy West, "Seminoles in Broward County: The Pine Island Legacy," *New River News* 23 (Fall, 1985), 4–11.

41. Patsy West, "The Miami Indian Tourist Attraction: A History and Analysis of a Transitional Mikasuki Seminole Environment," 200.

42. Ibid.

43. ANR, 1926. In 1936 the Hendry County Reservation was renamed Big Cypress Reservation, and 2,380 acres was added to its area; an additional 18,356 acres added later enlarged the reservation to 42,697 acres.

44. Much of this section was taken from James W. Covington, "Dania Reservation: 1911–1927."

45. Ibid.

46. August Burghard, *Mrs. Frank Stranahan: Pioneer,* 18.

47. *Survey,* 70.

48. Louis Capron, Interview, June 28, 1971, Duke American Indian Oral History Project, P. K. Yonge Library of Florida History, Gainesville.

49. ANR, 1929.

50. James Lafayette Glenn, *My Work among the Seminoles,* 13–14.
51. *Survey,* 35
52. ANR, 1929.
53. Ibid.
54. For a general view of the Seminole educational situation see Harry A. Kersey, Jr., "Educating the Seminole Indians of Florida, 1879–1969."
55. ANR, 1927.
56. Ibid. Ivy Stranahan helped prepare the way for the introduction of the school by teaching classes of six to twelve young Seminoles. Using pictorial Sunday school lesson cards issued by the Presbyterian church, she taught the elements of English to students who sat on logs in the woods or on the running board of her car. See Burghard, *Mrs. Frank Stranahan.*
57. Buck, "Indian Questionnaire."
58. U.S. Department of the Interior, "Report on the Seminole Indians of Florida."
59. Signs of the Seminoles' determined opposition to Spencer can be found in the annual census returns for the period 1920–30; some Seminoles refused to give their names to Spencer. See Spencer, Indian Census Rolls.
60. *Survey,* 20–22.
61. Ibid., 74–86.
62. *20th Anniversary of Tribal Organization, 1957–1977, Seminole Tribe of Florida.*

Chapter 11. Brighton and Big Cypress Reservations

1. ANR, 1934.
2. *Survey,* 20.
3. Tebeau, *Florida's Last Frontier,* 23.
4. Charlton W. Tebeau, *Man in the Everglades,* 55.
5. Hanna and Hanna, *Lake Okeechobee,* 293.
6. *Seminole Indians in Florida,* State Department of Agriculture (Tallahassee: State of Florida, 1940), map.
7. *20th Anniversary,* Bill Osceola, n.p.
8. James L. Glenn, Interview, October 22, 25, 1976, Fort Lauderdale Historical Society, Fort Lauderdale, Florida.
9. James L. Glenn, "Saga of Florida Indians," section 3, ibid.
10. Ibid.
11. ANR, 1933.
12. Ibid.
13. Alexander Spoehr, "Camp, Clan, and Kin among the Cow Creek Seminoles of Florida," 12.
14. Ibid.

15. ANR, 1935.

16. *Palm Beach Post,* March 21, 1935; *Miami Herald,* March 20, 1935.

17. Although the narrative report for 1935 places the meeting in a hotel room, Ickes recalls that it took place on a wooden platform under a blazing sun in an arena surrounded on three sides by bleachers and on the fourth, by open water. Harold Ickes, *The Secret Diary of Harold L. Ickes,* 324.

18. ANR, 1935.

19. J. W. Stewart, Director of Lands, to Lawrence E. Lindley, Washington Representative, Indian Rights Association, May 7, 1936, Central Files 1907–37, 17027–34–310, BIA.

20. Ibid.

21. J. E. Scott, Superintendent, Seminole Indian Agency, to Commissioner of Indian Affairs, February 19, 1938, 10581–1938, BIA. George H. Dacy, Assistant Economist, Bureau of Indian Affairs, Report on the Seminole Indians of Florida for the National Resources Planning Board, Dania, Florida, 1941 (hereafter Dacy Report). Land at Brighton was at first under the Department of Agriculture, but in 1938 by Executive Order 7868 it was transferred to the secretary of the interior. Full title to the land was not granted to the Seminoles until much later. Commissioner Emmons to Legislative Counsel, Office of the Solicitor, March 19, 1956, BIA.

22. William Zimmerman, Jr., Assistant Commissioner, to J. Peterson, July 31, 1935, 59942–1935, BIA; Congress approved of the exchange on June 14, 1935.

23. Preliminary Report, "Federal Indian Reorganizational Land Program, Seminole Indians in South Florida," Central Files 1907–37, 17027–34–310, Seminole Part 2, BIA. A description of Billie Stewart's and Billie Buster's camps near Brighton in 1932 can be found in Frances Densmore, *Seminole Music,* 11–12.

24. ANR, 1935.

25. Dacy Report.

26. *Florida Times Union,* May 26, 1938.

27. Dacy Report.

28. Fred Montesdeoca, a native of Keenansville, Florida, had a degree in animal husbandry from the University of Florida, owned a ranch at Lorida, and had developed an interest in the Seminoles during his days as a university student. In 1955 he was given the unofficial title of "assistant county agent for Indian Affairs." He stayed on his job until 1969, when he retired to work on his ranch. He died on December 11, 1974. *Tampa Tribune,* December 15, 1974.

29. Merwyn S. Garbarino, *Big Cypress: A Changing Seminole Community,* 106.

30. Ibid., 118.

31. Dacy Report.

32. U.S. Congress, Subcommittee of the Committees on Interior and Insular Affairs, *Joint Hearings on Termination of Federal Supervision over Certain Tribes of Indians,* 1105 (hereafter *Termination*).

33. Works Progress Administration, Federal Writers Program, *Seminole Indians in Florida,* 13–18.
34. Ethel Cutter Freeman, "Cultural Stability and Change among the Seminoles of Florida," 251.
35. Jacksonville *Times Union*, February 23, 1936. As a result of this meeting, the state of Florida began to issue free automobile tags to the Seminoles.
36. Superintendent Kenneth Marmon to Commissioner of Indian Affairs John Collier, March 18, 1944, Stock Raising Record 930, Record Group 75, Records of the Bureau of Indian Affairs, Federal Records Center, East Point, Georgia (hereafter FRC).
37. Portions of this chapter were published in James W. Covington, "Brighton Indian Reservation, Florida, 1935–1938."
38. U.S. Department of the Interior, "The Seminole Indians of Florida."

Chapter 12. The New Deal, World War II, and the Advance of Christianity

1. ANR, 1934.
2. Ibid.
3. Ibid.
4. Agent Francis J. Scott to Commissioner of Indian Affairs, July 24, 1939, 40290–39, BIA.
5. "Final Report of Indian Emergency Conservation Work and Civilian Conservation Corps," Indian Division, table 6, BIA.
6. *Miami Herald,* April 27, 1939.
7. Ibid., April 11, 1940. In 1942 when the number of families at Dania-Hollywood had declined to six, the agency was transferred back to the federal building at Fort Myers.
8. Agent Dwight Gardin to Murphy, October 4, 1940, 67133–40, BIA.
9. Murphy to Gardin, January 21, 1941, BIA (no file number).
10. "Final Report," table 7.
11. Much of the section concerning CCC-ID is taken from James W. Covington, "The Seminoles and Civilian Conservation Corps," *Florida Anthropologist* 34 (December 1981), 232–37.
12. See Kenneth R. Philip, "Turmoil at Big Cypress: Seminole Deer and the Florida Cattle Tick Controversy."
13. Testimony of Dr. T. H. Applewhite, Inspector in Charge of Tick Eradication, U.S. Bureau of Animal Industry, before U.S. Congress, House Committee on Indian Affairs, *Hearings on Eradicating Cattle Ticks on the Seminole Indian Reservation,* 1942, 42.
14. Superintendent Dwight R. Gardin to Collier, January 4, 1941, 83148–40, BIA.

15. W. Stanley Hanson to Gardin, January 24, 1941, 5676–41, BIA.

16. L. C. Betzner, et al. to Senator Claude Pepper, November 5, 1941, 66133–41, BIA; James Owens, Jr., County Assessor, Palm Beach County, to Collier, November 1, 1941, 66133–41 BIA.

17. Philip, "Turmoil," 43.

18. *Miami Herald,* May 3, 1943.

19. Collier to Representative Pat Cannon, November 19, 1941, 67462–41, BIA.

20. Report of Harold Peters, "Seminole Indian Project, September 16, 1942–December 10, 1942," BIA (no file number).

21. Brochure issued by the Seminole Indian Agency, Dania, Florida, July 1, 1941, Florida History Collection, P. K. Yonge Library of Florida History, Gainesville, Florida.

22. *New York Times,* October 17, 1940.

23. Personal communication with William Boehmer, February 12, 1979.

24. Claire W. Angell, "The Seminoles and the White Paper," WPA Papers.

25. Captain Ralph Cooper to Henry P. Baya, Director of Selective Service, State of Florida, February 27, 1942, Selective Service Record [SSR] 820, FRC.

26. Coe, *Red Patriots,* 242.

27. Dwight Gardin to Baya, November 7, 1940, 77334–40, SSR 820, FRC.

28. W. Stanley Hanson to Superintendent William Hill, March 10, 1942, SSR 820, FRC.

29. Commissioner of Indian Affairs H. Harlan Greenwood, Circular to All Superintendents, January 16, 1942, Circular 3368H, SSR 820, FRC.

30. William Zimmerman, Assistant Commissioner of Indian Affairs, to Mrs. Ethel Cutler Freeman, October 22, 1942, 46058–42, BIA.

31. It was established that in 1942 there were 637 Seminoles: two-thirds were Mikasuki and the rest Muskogee. Females outnumbered males 329 to 308. The 172 families had a yearly average income of less than $500, but only 5 received relief payments, $3.85 per month per person.

    Most of the material in this chapter concerning selective service was taken from James W. Covington, "The Seminoles and Selective Service in World War II."

32. Superintendent Kenneth Marmon to Commissioner of Indian Affairs, October 9, 1943, War Savings Bonds 220.1, FRC.

33. Freeman, "Cultural Stability," 251. When women began to work in the fields during the war, they abandoned the mass of neck beads and adopted an eyeshade hairdo. Ethel Cutter Freeman, "Fashions among Modern Seminoles," *Scenic Highlands of Florida* (Miami, 1952), n.p., and "Our Unique Indians: The Seminoles of Florida," 15.

34. *Miami Herald,* June 7, 1936.

35. Ibid., June 19, 1949.

36. Buswell, "Florida Seminole Religious Ritual," 282.

37. Freeman, "Cultural Stability," 251.

38. Account concerning Deaconess Bedell, WPA Papers.

39. Tebeau, *Florida's Last Frontier*, 74–82.

40. J. L. Glenn, ANR, 1934.

41. W. Stanley Hanson, "Seminole Wash Day," WPA Papers.

42. Greenlee, "Ceremonial Practices."

Chapter 13. The Reservation Indians

1. *Statutes at Large* 60:1049; William A. Brophy and Sophia A. Aberle, comps., *The Indian, America's Unfinished Business: Report of the Commissioner on the Rights, Liberties, and Responsibilities of the American Indian*, 29.

2. Superintendent Kenneth Marmon to W. O. Roberts, Area Director, March 30, 1951, Tribal Relations, FRC.

3. Buswell, "Florida Seminole Religious Ritual," 419–20.

4. Marmon to Roberts, March 30, 1951, FRC.

5. U.S. Congress, Senate Select Committee on Indian Affairs, *Hearings on Distribution of Seminole Judgement Funds*, 217 (hereafter *Distribution*).

6. Information on claims filed by Seminole Indians of Florida and Claims of Morton Silver in letters to the Secretary of the Interior and to the President of the United States—Claim for $49,732,975 plus 5% interest. CIA 182 #58, Box 286, 163050, BIA (n.d.). The land included within the Everglades National Park had been taken in 1944.

7. LeVerne Madigan, "The Most Independent People—A Field Report on Indians in Florida," 3.

8. Affidavit of Bobby Clay, March 29, 1976, *Distribution*, 451–53.

9. Angie Debo, *A History of the Indians of the United States*, 352–53.

10. No objection was held to termination of law and order and education services. Annual Report of Seminole Agency to the Muskogee Area Office for Fiscal Year Ending June 30, 1954, 1956–17462, BIA.

11. See *Termination*.

12. James S. Olson and Raymond Wilson, *Native Americans in the Twentieth Century*, 1984), 1118.

13. Ibid., 149–50.

14. *Statutes at Large* 48:984–88; see also Kenneth R. Philip, "John Collier and the Controversy over the Wheeler-Howard Bill," 171–200.

15. Marmon to D'Arcy McNickle, Chief, Branch of Tribal Relations, Bureau of Indian Affairs, March 22, 1951, Tribal Relations, FRC.

16. Secretary of the Interior Douglas McKay to Morton H. Silver, November 5, 1953, Division of Programs, PRS-1931, BIA.

17. Betty Jumper, Secretary, Committee of Seminole Indians, to Area Director, Muskogee Area Office, Oklahoma, October 16, 1953, BIA.

18. Madigan, "Independent People," 3.

19. Minutes of Board of Directors of Seminole Tribe, April 4, 1955, Tribal Matters 064, FRC.

20. Report on the Florida Seminoles, December 1954, by Morrill M. Tozier, Bureau of Indian Affairs Information Officer, Seminole of Florida File 163-050, Box 286, CIA 182, Federal Records Center, Suitland, Maryland (hereafter Tozier Report).

21. Minutes of Board of Commissioners of State Institutions, December 20, 1955, Florida State Archives (hereafter BCSI Minutes).

22. BCSI Minutes, March 20, 1956.

23. Report to the Board of Commissioners of State Institutions and to the Trustees of the Internal Improvement Fund, May 29, 1956. Governor Leroy Collins, Administrative Correspondence, Florida State Archives, Tallahassee. (hereafter Collins Correspondence).

24. Harry Smith to Max Denton, December 18, 1956, Collins Correspondence; another duty of the commissioner of Indian affairs was the issuing of license tags to the Seminoles.

25. October 16, 1956, BCSI Minutes.

26. October 30, 1956, Report of Director of Committee, BCSI Minutes. At the same time Denton was appointed, Bertram D. Scott, executive director of the Seminole Indian Association of Florida nominated Fred Montesdeoca for the position. Montesdeoca, who had nearly twenty years of experience in dealing with the Seminoles, would have probably been a better choice. Scott to Collins, October 30, 1956, Collins Correspondence.

27. Collins to Marmon, December 21, 1956, Collins Correspondence.

28. Report to the Board of Commissioners of State Institutions and trustees of the Internal Improvement Fund on the Seminole Indians, Denton to Collins, March 21, 1957, Collins Correspondence.

29. Denton to Board of Commissioners of State Institutions, April 8, 1957, Collins Correspondence.

30. Denton to Board of Commissioners of State Institutions, July 19, 1957, Collins Correspondence.

31. Resolution C–49-59, Tribal Council, Seminole Indians of Florida, Collins Correspondence.

32. *Miami Herald,* October 26, 1958.

33. James W. Covington, "Seminole Leadership: Changing Substance, 1858–1958," *Tequesta* 40 (1980), 35.

34. Robert T. King, "Clan Affiliation and Leadership among the Twentieth Century Florida Indians," 148.

35. *Indian Affairs Manual,* 83–1, Tribal Government, Bureau of Indian Affairs, Department of the Interior (Washington, D.C.: GPO, 1959).

36. Roger J. Waybright to Rex Quinn, April 15, 1957, Rex Quinn Papers, P. K. Yonge Library of Florida History, Gainesville, Florida.

37. *20th Anniversary*.

38. Constitution and Bylaws of the Seminole Tribe of Florida. Amendments were adopted in 1963 and subsequent years. Small reservations that were created later are represented in the council. Tampa Reservation is considered part of Brighton, and Immokalee, part of Big Cypress. Immokalee has a nonvoting member of the board.

39. Robert T. King, "The Florida Seminole Polity, 1858–1978," 170.

40. Minutes of Board of Directors, Seminole Tribal Council, May 18, 1959, BIA.

41. Seminole Tribe of Florida Community Action Program, Quinn Papers.

42. *Seminole Tribe of Florida*.

43. The Seminoles felt that control of the cattle program came from the Area Office at Muskogee, and that they had little say about it. "Trip to Seminole Agency," December 13–24, 1957, Rex Quinn to Commissioner of Indian Affairs, December 27, 1957, Quinn Papers.

44. King, "Seminole Polity," 119. During the 1970s the federal government acquired a tract of under ten acres at Immokalee to serve the Seminoles at that city, which might be deemed another federal reservation.

45. Charles Fairbanks, *The Florida Seminole People,* 42–43; some criticism of the cattle program at Big Cypress is given in Garbarino, *Big Cypress,* 122–24.

46. State Indian Commissioner William Kidd to Dr. G. M. Davis, November 2, 1961, Governor Farris Bryant, Administrative Correspondence, Florida State Archives, Tallahassee (hereafter Bryant Correspondence).

47. Governor Farris Bryant to Robert Parker, Director, Internal Improvement Fund, November 30, 1964, Bryant Correspondence.

48. Betty Mae Jumper to Governor Claude Kirk, September 18, 1968, and Resolution of Board of Directors, Naples Chamber of Commerce, September 11, 1968, Governor Claude Kirk, Jr., Administrative Correspondence, Florida State Archives, Tallahassee.

49. Governor Hayden Burns to Rex Quinn, Superintendent of Seminole Agency, and John Miller, Superintendent of Miccosukee Agency, October 7, 1965, Hayden Burns, Administrative Correspondence, Florida State Archives; *Laws of Florida, 1965,* 65–249.

50. Erwin to Board of Control of State Institutions, December 3, 1956; Kidd to Burns, July 7, 1965, Burns Correspondence.

51. *Laws of Florida, 1971,* 71–286.

52. Marmon to Mrs. Leon Freeman, November 6, 1956, BIA; Seminole children, mostly from Dania, attended the Cherokee Indian School in North Carolina from 1937 to 1954. Their expenses were underwritten by Friends of the Seminoles and Daughters of the American Revolution. In 1945 Agnes Parker and Betty Mae Tiger graduated from the Cherokee high school.

53. *Tampa Tribune,* August 5, 1951.

54. James C. Nicholas et al., *Recommendations Concerning Employment, Income and Educational Opportunities for the Seminole and Miccosukee Tribes in Florida,* 458.

55. *Tampa Tribune,* December 12, 1988.

56. Nicholas, *Recommendations,* 463; see Sandra Joos, "Obesity and Diabetes Mellitus among the Florida Seminole Indians," *Florida Scientist* 43 (Summer 1980), 148–52.

57. Community Development Officer to Superintendent, July 20, 1967, Quinn Papers.

58. *Tampa Tribune,* March 29, 1981.

59. Harriet P. Lefley, "Acculturation, Child-Rearing and Self-Esteem in Two North American Indian Tribes," *Ethnos* (Fall 1976), 397–98.

60. Decision of Judge Charles E. Miner, Case 77–1933, March 3, 1978. Office of the Clerk, Records of the Courts, Circuit Court of Leon County, Leon County Courthouse, Record Book 898, 475. In 1979 the legislature gave permission for the Seminoles to sell untaxed cigarettes on reservation land. *Laws of Florida, 1979,* 79–136, 79–317, 1679.

61. *Tampa Tribune,* March 29, 1981.

62. Ibid.

63. When the Seminoles acquired the land, they said that they would use it to bury American Indian bones uncovered when construction was undertaken for the Fort Brooke Parking Garage in downtown Tampa. However, within a short time the bones were buried and the site marked with a wooden marker, artifacts found with the bones were displayed in a smaller museum, and the smoke shop and bingo hall were constructed. This property is listed on the Hillsborough County tax rolls as U.S. government trust property, although another 308-acre adjacent tract is listed as property of the Seminole Tribe of Florida, and taxes amounting to $83,535 for three years have not been paid. Ibid., December 15, 1986.

64. Ibid., March 16, June 12, 1987; October 6, 1981.

65. *Florida Trend* 28 (January 1985), 111.

66. Margot Ammidown, "The Seminole Tribe, Inc.: Winning and Losing at the White Man's Game," 238–40; *Tampa Tribune,* June 9, 1982. Each Seminole received in 1982 a check for $300, with $1,000 projected for 1983 (*USA Today,* June 13, 1983).

67. An example of inadequate planning developed with the opening of the world's largest bingo hall at Big Cypress: employees were not paid, and winners were unable to collect their prizes. *Tampa Tribune,* April 2, 1988.

Chapter 14. The Miccosukee and Trail Indians

1. Capron, *Medicine Bundles,* 159–210, and Buswell, "Florida Seminole Religious Ritual," 67–69; Sturtevant, "Creek into Seminole," 115–17.

2. Glenn to Commissioner of Indian Affairs, August 15, 1934, Tribal Matters 064, FRC.

3. Gardin to Commissioner of Indian Affairs, July 31, 1941, Tribal Relations 063, FRC.

4. Ingraham Billie, son of Little Billie and Nancy Osceola, was born in 1890. His brother was Josie Billie, who became a medicine man, convert to Christianity, and assistant pastor of a Baptist church. Ingraham Billie and his wife, Effie Tiger Billie, had five children. He was a member of the Panther Clan. *"20th Anniversary,"* 626.

5. Kenneth Marmon, Superintendent Seminole Agency, to Paul Fickinger, Area Director, Muskogee, Oklahoma, May 2, 1955, Business Committee, Indian 067, FRC.

6. *Distribution,* 148.

7. Ibid.

8. Statement of Jimmie Tiger and thirteen others, September 28, 1950, ibid., 226, 227. Ingraham Billie was listed among the thirteen, but Buffalo Tiger was not. Morton H. Silver, born in 1926, graduated from the University of Florida Law School and was admitted to the Florida Bar in 1950.

9. Ingraham Billie to Silver, October 1, 1953, *Distribution,* 230, 231.

10. Tozier Report.

11. Ibid.

12. Miccosukee General Council to President Dwight D. Eisenhower, file 452B, Miccosukee Papers, National Anthropological Library, Smithsonian Institution (hereafter Miccosukee Papers).

13. In reply to the declaration, Gerald D. Morgan, administrative assistant to the president, drafted a brief note of receipt and promised "thorough consideration." Morgan to Ingraham Billie, March 4, 1954, Miccosukee Papers.

14. *Termination,* 1078–95. Reservation Seminoles who testified were selected by popular vote and their travel expenses paid; the Miccosukees took care of their own expenses.

15. Ibid., 1090.

16. Tozier Report, 3.

17. Ibid.

18. Special appearance and motion to quash filed by Silver and Alpert on September 17, 1954, before the Indian Claims Commission, *Distribution,* 43–47; Silver to Edgar E. Witt, April 7, 1955, ibid., 279–82.

19. Roger J. Waybright to Marmon, December 7, 1956, File 163–050, BIA.

20. Testimony of Jimmie Billy, April 6, 7, 1955, cited in "Seminole Land Rights in Florida," *American Indian Journal of the Institute for the Development of Indian Law* 4 (August 1978), 20.

21. Members of the Everglades Miccosukee General Council in July 1957, including: Buffalo Tiger (chair), Howard Osceola, Bill McKinley Osceola, Jr., Sam

Willie, Little Doctor, John Osceola, John Poole, Henry Sam, John Willie, Tommie Tiger, and Jimmie Tiger, BCSI Minutes, July 30, 1957.

22. Denton to Board of Commissioners of State Institutions, n.d., Collins Correspondence.

23. Denton to Board of Commissioners of State Institutions, July 19, 1957, ibid.

24. BCSI Minutes, July 30, 1957, ibid.

25. Minutes of Protest Meeting, July 27, 1957, signed by C. E. McLane, Director, Airboat Association of Florida, ibid.

26. Hyde to Van Ferguson, Director, Trustees, Internal Improvement Fund, November 14, 1957, ibid.

27. Denton and Ferguson to Collins, December 16, 1957, ibid.

28. Dan Livingstone to Collins, November 6, 1958, ibid.

29. Madigan, "Independent People," 5.

30. Annex K, Miccosukee Papers.

31. Ingraham Billie et al. to Collins, October 25, 1956, Collins Correspondence.

32. Silver to Executive Council, November 10, 1958, ibid.

33. Bill McKinley Osceola, Bobby Tiger, and Buffalo Tiger to Collins, November 12, 1958, ibid.

34. *New York Times,* April 2, 1959.

35. Edmund Wilson, *Apologies to the Iroquois* (New York: Farrar, Straus and Cudahy, 1960), 27.

36. Grady L. Crawford to Collins, February 16, 1959, Collins Correspondence.

37. *Tampa Tribune,* March 5, 1959; *Miami Herald,* March 5, 1959.

38. *Hialeah-Miami Springs Journal,* May 21, 1959.

39. *Laws of Florida, 1959,* 285.14, 285.15, 1492–494.

40. Minutes of Special Board of Directors Meeting, Everglades Hotel, Miami, Florida, November 15, 1959, B/A, SM.

41. Max Denton and Van Ferguson to Board of Commissioners of State Institutions, August 11, 1959, Collins Correspondence.

42. Typescript of tape of meeting, November 17, 1959, ibid.

43. *Tampa Tribune,* July 31, 1977. This ruling did not settle the matter, for the Miccosukees brought suit in federal court claiming that a federal flood control project flooded much land that they had claimed since 1839. The state of Florida agreed to a settlement that would give them $975,000 for land and 265,000 acres in the Everglades for hunting and fishing privileges, including a 76,800-acre federal reservation. *Tampa Tribune,* December 9, 1982. Congress approved the transaction by January 1983.

44. Buffalo Tiger, Miccosukee Tribe of Seminole Indians, 1833 N.W. 45th St., Miami, Florida, to Denton and Kidd, March 15, 1961, Bryant Correspondence.

45. An earlier constitution had been written, and the organization known as "The

Everglades Miccosukee Tribe of Seminole Indians" had been recognized by Commissioner Emmons on January 27, 1958, as "qualified to speak for and on behalf of those Indians who have affiliated with the organization by signing their names to the roll." Emmons to Executive Council, January 27, 1958, Annex G, Miccosukee Papers. Such recognition in fact meant very little.

46. Miccosukee Tribe, "The Miccosukee Tribe of Indians of Florida" (n.p., n.d.); in 1976 the Business and General Council of the Miccosukee Tribe of Indians of Florida included Buffalo Tiger (chair), Billie Cypress (assistant chair), Bobby Billie (secretary), and Henry Bert (lawmaker). Letterhead, Miccosukee Papers.

47. Buffalo Tiger to Commissioner of Indian Affairs, October 8, 1963, Bryant Correspondence (copy). In a meeting in Miami, June 11, 1963, Florida officials had set aside Areas 12A and 12B of Conservation Area Three in the Central and South Florida Flood District for use by the Seminoles. Miller to G. E. Dail, Director, Central and South Florida Flood Control District, September 17, 1963, Bryant Correspondence. Under Miccosukee control was a strip of land 5.5 miles long and 500 feet wide totaling 333.3 acres that had been leased for fifty years from the Bureau of Indian Affairs and the National Park Service. Three other tracts of land, 600 feet by 65 feet, had been given in perpetuity by the state of Florida. U.S. Department of Commerce, *Federal and State Indian Reservations and Indian Trust Areas,* 187, 188.

48. Nicholas et al., *Recommendations,* 469–70.

49. In January 1968 a motion to intervene in the Seminole claims case was filed on behalf of the Miccosukee Tribe by Buffalo Tiger and Sonny Billie. Their attorney was Arthur Lazarus, Jr., of Strasser, Spregelburg, Fried, Frank and Kampelman of Washington, D.C. In 1977 S. Bobo Dean of the same firm represented the Indians.

50. *Laws of Florida, 1971,* 71–286.

51. *Laws of Florida, 1974,* 74–175.

52. The Miccosukees also gained equality with the Seminoles in regard to scholarships. *Laws of Florida, 1971,* 286, 1451–52.

53. See affidavits of these Miccosukees in *Distribution,* 443–53.

54. *Distribution,* 443.

BIBLIOGRAPHY

Manuscript and Document Sources

Federal Records Center, East Point, Georgia
  Bureau of Indian Affairs Records. Record Group 75.

Florida Historical Society, University of South Florida, Tampa
  Seminole Papers.
  Works Progress Administration Papers.

Florida State Archives, Tallahassee
  Records of the Office of the Governor.
  Brown, Thomas, Administrative Correspondence, 1849–53, Letterbook, Record Group 101, Series 755.
  Burns, Hayden, Administrative Correspondence, 1965–67, Box 29, Record Group 102, Series 131.
  Collins, Leroy, Administrative Correspondence, 1955–58, Boxes 19 (First Term) and 87 (Second Term), Record Group 102, Series 776.
  Kirk, Claude, Administrative Correspondence, 1967–71, Box 54, Record Group 102, Series 927.
  Minutes of Meetings of the Board of Commissioners of State Institutions, 1956–1965, Series 431, Record Group 145.

Gilcrease Museum, Tulsa, Oklahoma
  Casey, John C., Papers.

Historical Society of Pennsylvania, Philadelphia
  Indian Rights Association Papers.

Leon County Courthouse, Tallahassee
  Records of the Courts. Summary of Case 77–1933, March 3, 1978, Decision of Judge Charles E. Miner.

Library of Congress, Washington, D.C.
  Munroe, Kirk, Papers.

National Anthropological Library, Smithsonian Institution, Washington, D.C.
  Miccosukee Papers.

National Archives and Records Service, Washington, D.C., and Suitland, Maryland
  Department of the Army Records. Record Group 94. Letters Received by the Adjutant General's Office, 1780s–1917.

Bureau of Indian Affairs Records. Record Group 75. Letters Received by the Office of Indian Affairs, 1824–1980.

Department of the Navy Records. Record Group 45. Letters Received by Secretary of the Navy from Captains, 1805–61.

National Library of Scotland, Edinburgh
Cochrane, Admiral Alexander, Papers (MS 2328, 2336).

P. K. Yonge Library of Florida History, Gainesville, Florida
Florida History Collection.
Florida Writers' Program Papers.
Greenslade Papers.
Keenan–Brown Collection.
Lockey, Joseph B., Collection.
Prince, Henry, Diary.
Quinn, Rex, Papers.
Works Progress Administration Papers.

Public Record Office, London
Colonial Office 5 (America and the West Indies).
Foreign Office 5 (United States).

Newspapers

Army and Navy Chronicle, 1835–42

Augusta *Chronicle,* 1815

Florida Republican, 1849

Florida Times Union, 1938

Fort Myers *Press,* 1885–14

Gleason's Pictorial Magazine, 1852

Hialeah-Miami Springs Journal, 1959

Jacksonville *News,* 1853

Jacksonville *Times Union,* 1917–36

Key West Gazette, 1832

Lake Wales Highlander, 1925

Miami Herald, 1939, 1940, 1959

New York *Journal of Commerce,* 1849

New York Times, 1940, 1959

Niles Weekly Register, 1818

Palm Beach Post, 1935

Pensacola Gazette, 1824

St. Augustine *Ancient City,* 1852

Tallahassee *Floridian and Journal,* 1853–54

Bibliography

Tampa *Florida Peninsular,* 1856
Tampa *Herald,* 1855
Tampa *Times,* 1917, 1934
Tampa Tribune, 1909–87
USA Today, 1983

Books and Articles

Adams, George R. "Caloosahatchee Massacre: Its Significance in the Second Seminole War." *Florida Historical Quarterly* 48 [hereafter cited as *F.H.Q.*] (April 1970): 368–80.

Alden, John R. *John Stuart and the Southern Colonial Frontier: A Study of Indian Relations, War, Trade, and Land Problems in the Southern Wilderness.* Ann Arbor: University of Michigan Press, 1941.

American State Papers: Documents, Legislative and Executive of the Congress of the United States: I and II: Indian Affairs. IV: Foreign Affairs. V: Military Affairs. 1890–1938.

Ammidown, Margot. "The Seminole Tribe, Inc.: Winning and Losing at the White Man's Game." *Florida Anthropologist* 34 (December 1981): 238–42.

Annual Report of Women's National Indian Association. Privately printed, 1981.

Arnade, Charles W. "The English Invasion of Spanish Florida, 1700–1706." *F.H.Q.* 41 (July 1962): 29–37.

———. "Three Early Spanish Tampa Bay Maps." *Tequesta* 25 (1965): 83–96.

Ballentine, George. *Autobiography of an English Soldier in the United States Army.* New York: Stringer and Tounsend, 1853.

Bartram, John. "Diary of a Journey through the Carolinas, Georgia and Florida." *Transactions of the American Philosophical Society,* New Series, 33 (1942): part 1, 1–120.

Bemis, Samuel F. *John Quincy Adams and the Foundations of American Foreign Policy.* New York: Knopf, 1949.

Bethell, John A. *Bethell's History of Point Pinellas.* St. Petersburg, Fla.: Great Outdoors, 1962.

Bittle, George C. "The First Battle of the Second Seminole War." *F.H.Q.* 46 (July 1967): 39–45.

———. "The Florida Militia's Role in the Battle of Withlacoochee." *F.H.Q.* 44 (April 1966): 303–11.

Blakey, Arch Frederic. "Military Duty in Antebellum Florida: The Experiences of John Henry Winder." *F.H.Q.* 63 (October 1984): 152–71.

Blend, Benay. "The Indian Rights Association, the Allotment Policy, and the Five Civilized Tribes, 1923–1936." *American Indian Quarterly* 7 (Spring 1983): 67–80.

Bolton, Herbert E., and Mary Ross. *The Debatable Land.* Berkeley: University of California Press, 1925.

Boyd, Mark F. "Asi-yaholo or Osceola." *F.H.Q.* 33 (January-April 1955): 249–305.

———. "Events at Prospect Bluff on the Apalachicola River, 1808–1818." *F.H.Q.* 16 (October 1937): 55–96.

———. "Horatio S. Dexter and Events Leading to the Treaty of Moultrie Creek with the Seminoles." *Florida Anthropologist* 11 (September 1958): 65–95.

———. "Map of the Road from Pensacola to St. Augustine, 1778."*F.H.Q.* 17 (July 1938): 15–23.

———, ed. "Documents Describing the Second and Third Expeditions of Lieutenant Diego Peña to Apalachee and Apalachicola in 1717 and 1718." *F.H.Q.* 31 (October 1952): 109–39.

———. "Hugh Young, A Topographical Memoir on East and West Florida." *F.H.Q.* 13 (October 1934): 20–50.

——— and trans. "Diego Peña's Expedition to Apalachee and Apalachicola in 1716." *F.H.Q.* 28 (July 1949): 1–27.

Boyd, Mark F., Hale G. Smith, and John W. Griffin, eds. *Here They Once Stood.* Gainesville: University of Florida Press, 1951.

Brooke, George M., Jr. "Early Days at Fort Brooke." *Sunland Tribune* 1 (1974): 1–14.

Brophy, William A., and Sophia A. Aberle, comps. *The Indian, America's Unfinished Business: Report of the Commissioner on the Rights, Liberties, and Responsibilities of the American Indian.* Norman: University of Oklahoma Press, 1966.

Buker, George E. "Francis's Metallic Life Boats and the Third Seminole War." *F.H.Q.* 58 (October 1984): 139–51.

Burghard, August. *Mrs. Frank Stranahan: Pioneer.* Fort Lauderdale: Historical Society of Fort Lauderdale, 1968.

———, and Phillip Weidling. *Checkered Sunshine: History of Fort Lauderdale, 1793–1955* Gainesville: University of Florida Press, 1966.

Buswell, James O., III. "Florida Seminole Religious Ritual: Resistance and Change." Ph.D. diss., St. Louis University, 1972.

Canova, Andrew. *Life and Adventures in South Florida.* Tampa: Tribune, 1906.

Capron, Louis. *The Medicine Bundles of the Florida Seminoles and the Green Corn Dance.* Anthropological Papers 35, Bureau of American Ethnology Bulletin 151, Washington, D.C.: GPO, 1953.

———. "Notes on the Hunting Dance of the Cow Creek Seminole." *Florida Anthropologist* (December 1956), 67–78.

Caughey, John W. *McGillivray of the Creeks.* Norman: University of Oklahoma Press, 1959.

Chamberlin, Donald L. "Fort Brooke: Frontier Outpost, 1824–1842." *Tampa Bay History* 7 (Spring, Summer 1985): 5–29.

Coe, Charles H. *Red Patriots: The Story of the Seminoles,* Cincinnati: Editor, 1898.

Cohen, Myer M. *Notices of East Florida and the Campaigns.* New York: Burges and Honour, 1836.

Coker, William S., and Thomas D. Watson. *Indian Traders of the Southeastern Spanish Borderlands: Panton, Leslie and Company and John Forbes and Company, 1783–1847.* Pensacola: University of West Florida Press, 1986.

Bibliography

Colburn, David R., and Richard K. Scher. *Florida's Gubernatorial Politics in the Twentieth Century*. Tallahassee: Florida State University Press, 1980.

Constitution and Bylaws of the Seminole Tribe of Florida. Privately printed, 1963.

Cotterill, Robert S. *The Southern Indians: The Story of the Civilized Tribes before Removal*. Norman: University of Oklahoma Press, 1954.

Covington, James W. "The Agreement of 1842 and Its Effect upon Seminole History." *Florida Anthropologist* 31 (March 1978): 8–11.

———. "The Apalachee Indians Move West." *Florida Anthropologist* 17 (December 1964): 221–25.

———. "Armed Occupation Act of 1842." *F.H.Q.* 40 (July 1961): 41–52.

———. *The Billy Bowlegs War*. Chuluota, Fla.: Mickler, 1982.

———. "Brighton Indian Reservation, Florida, 1935–38." *Tequesta* 36 (1976): 54–65.

———. "British Gifts to the Indians: 1765–1766." *Florida Anthropologist* 13 (September 1960), 71–75.

———. "Cuban Bloodhounds and the Seminoles." *F.H.Q.* 33 (October 1954): 111–19.

———. "Dania Reservation: 1911–1927." *Florida Anthropologist* 29 (December 1976): 137–44.

———. "The Establishment of Fort Brooke." *F.H.Q.* 31 (April 1953), 273–78.

———. "Federal and State Relations with the Florida Seminoles, 1875–1901." *Tequesta* 32 (1972): 17–27.

———. "Federal Relations with the Apalachicola Indians: 1823–1839." *F.H.Q.* 42 (October 1963): 125–41.

———. "The Florida Seminoles: 1900–1914." *F.H.Q.* 56 (October 1974): 181–97.

———. "The Seminole Indians in 1908." *Florida Anthropologist* 26 (September 1973): 99–104.

———. "The Seminoles and Selective Service in World War II." *Florida Anthropologist* 32 (June 1979): 46–51.

———. *Story of Southwestern Florida*. 2 vols. New York: Lewis Historical, 1957.

———. "Trade Relations between Southwestern Florida and Cuba: 1610–1840." *F.H.Q.* 38 (October 1959): 114–28.

———. "Trail Indians of Florida." *F.H.Q.* 58 (July 1979): 37–57.

———, ed. *The British Meet the Seminoles*. Contributions of the Florida State Museum, Social Science No. 7. University of Florida Press: Gainesville, 1961.

———. "The Florida Seminoles in 1847." *Tequesta* 24 (1964): 49–57.

Craig, Alan, and Christopher S. Peeples. "Captain Young's Sketch Map." *F.H.Q.* 48 (October 1969): 176–79.

Craig, Alan, and David McJunkin. "Stranahan's: Last of the Seminole Trading Posts." *Florida Anthropologist* 24 (June 1971): 45–49.

Crane, Verner W. *The Southern Frontier, 1670–1732*. Ann Arbor: University of Michigan Press, 1956.

Croffut, W. A., ed. *Fifty Years in Camp and Field: Diary of Major-General Ethan Allen Hitchcock, USA*. New York: Putnam, 1909.

Davidson, Dorothy D. "Pioneer Pictures." *Update* 2 (October 1974): 4–6.

Davis, Hilda J. "The History of Seminole Clothing and Its Multi-colored Designs." *American Anthropologist* 52 (October 1955): 974–80.

Davis, T. Frederick. "Milly Francis and Duncan McKrimmon, an Authentic Florida Pocahontas." *F.H.Q.* 21 (January 1943): 251–58.

———. "The Seminole Council, October 23–25, 1834." *F.H.Q.* 7 (April 1929): 330–50.

———, ed. "United States Troops in Spanish East Florida, 1812–1813 (Letters of Lt. Col. T. A. Smith)." *F.H.Q.* 9 (July 1930): 3–23.

Debo, Angie. *A History of the Indians of the United States*. Norman: University of Oklahoma Press, 1970.

Densmore, Frances. *Seminole Music*. Bureau of American Ethnology Bulletin 161. Washington, D.C.: Smithsonian, 1956.

Dillon, Rodney E., Jr. "The Little Affair: The Southwest Florida Campaign, 1863–1864" *F.H.Q.* 62 (January 1984): 314–31.

Dobyns, Henry F. *Their Number Became Thinned: Native American Population Dynamics in Eastern North America*. Knoxville: University of Tennessee Press, 1983.

Dodson, Pat, ed. *Journey through the Everglades: The Log of the Minnehaha*. Tampa: Trend House, 1973.

Doherty, Herbert J., Jr. *Richard Keith Call: Southern Unionist*. Gainesville: University of Florida Press, 1961.

Douglas, Marjory Stoneman. *The Everglades: River of Grass*. New York: Rinehart, 1947.

Downs, Dorothy. "Coppinger's Tropical Gardens: The First Commercial Indian Village in Florida." *Florida Anthropologist* 34 (December 1981): 225–31.

Drake, Samuel G. *Aboriginal Races of North America*. New York: Hurst, 1880.

Driver, Howard E. *Indians of North America*. Chicago: University of Chicago Press, 1961.

Edmunds, R. David. *Tecumseh and the Quest for Indian Leadership*. Boston: Little, Brown, 1984.

Ellicott, Andrew. *The Journal of Andrew Ellicott*. Chicago: Quadrangle, 1962.

Elliott, Charles Winslow. *Winfield Scott, the Soldier and the Man*. New York: Arno, 1979.

Ericson, Jack T., ed. *A Guide to Microfilm Edition, Indian Rights Association Papers, 1864–1973*. Glen Rock, N.Y.: Microfilming Corporation of America, 1975.

Ewan, J. W. "The Seminole Christmas." *Tequesta* 40 (1980): 39–42.

———. "A Seminole Reminiscence." *Tequesta* 40 (1980): 43–46.

Fairbanks, Charles H. *Ethnohistorical Report on the Florida Indians*. 3 vols. New York: Garland, 1974.

———. "Excavations at Horseshoe Bend, Alabama." *Florida Anthropologist* 15 (June 1962): 41–56.

———. *The Florida Seminole People*. Phoenix: Indian Tribal Series, 1973.

———. "Some Problems of the Origin of Creek Pottery." *Florida Anthropologist* 11 (June 1959), 58–64.

Flynt, Wayne. *Cracker Messiah: Governor Sidney J. Catts of Florida*. Baton Rouge: University of Louisiana Press, 1977.

Bibliography

Forbes, James G. *Sketches, Historical and Topographical of the Floridas: More Particularly of East Florida.* New York: Van Winkle, 1821.

Forbes, John. "Journal, May, 1803." *F.H.Q.* (April 1931): 279–89.

Foreman, Carolyn T. "Billy Bowlegs." *Chronicles of Oklahoma* 33 (Winter 1955): 512–22.

Foreman, Grant, *Indian Removal: The Emigration of the Five Civilized Tribes of Indians.* Norman: University of Oklahoma Press, 1953.

Forry, Samuel. "Letters of Samuel Forry, Surgeon, U.S. Army, 1837–38." *F.H.Q.* 6 (January–April 1928): 133–48, 206–19; *F.H.Q.* 7 (July 1928): 88–105.

Freeman, Ethel Cutter. "Cultural Stability and Change among the Seminoles of Florida." In *Man and Cultures: Selected Papers of the Fifth International Congress of Anthropological and Ethnological Sciences, Philadelphia, September 1–9, 1956,* ed. Anthony F. C. Wallace, 249–54. Philadelphia: University of Pennsylvania Press, 1960.

———. "Our Unique Indians: The Seminoles of Florida." *American Indian* 2 (Winter 1944–45): 14–28.

Garbarino, Merwyn S. *Big Cypress: A Changing Seminole Community.* New York: Holt, Rinehart & Winston, 1972.

Gibson, Arrell M. *The American Indian: Prehistory to the Present.* Lexington, Mass.: Heath, 1980.

Giddings, Joshua. *The Exiles of Florida.* Columbus, Ohio: Follett, Foster, 1858.

Glenn, James Lafayette. *My Work among the Seminoles.* Edited by Harry A. Kersey, Jr. Gainesville: University of Florida Press, 1982.

Goggin, John M. "The Seminole Negroes of Andros Island, Bahamas." *F.H.Q.* 24 (January 1946): 201–6.

———. "Source Materials for the Study of the Florida Seminole Indians." Laboratory Notes No. 3, Anthropology Department, University of Florida, Gainesville, August 1959. Mimeo.

Gold, Robert. *Borderland Empires in Transition: The Triple Nation Transfer of Florida.* Carbondale: University of Southern Illinois Press, 1969.

———. "The East Florida Indians under Spanish and English Control, 1763–1765." *F.H.Q.* 44 (July 1965): 105–20.

Greenlee, Robert. "Medicine and Curing Practices of the Modern Florida Seminoles." *American Anthropologist* 40 (July, September 1944): 317–27.

Grismer, Karl. *The Story of Fort Myers.* St. Petersburg, Fla., 1949.

Hagan, William. *American Indians.* Chicago: University of Chicago Press, 1961.

Halbert, H. S., and T. H. Ball. *The Creek War of 1813 and 1814.* University: University of Alabama Press, 1969.

Hanna, Alfred Jackson, and Kathryn Abbey Hanna. *Lake Okeechobee: Wellspring of the Everglades.* Indianapolis: Bobbs-Merrill, 1948.

Harper, Francis, ed. *The Travels of William Bartram.* New Haven, Conn.: Yale University Press, 1958.

Hendley, J. A. *History of Pasco County, Florida.* Dade City, Fla., n.d.

Hoebel, E. Adamson, and Karen Daniels Peterson, commentary. *A Cheyenne Sketchbook by Cohoe.* Norman: University of Oklahoma Press, 1964.

Holland, James W. *Andrew Jackson and the Creek War: Victory at Horseshoe.* University: University of Alabama Press, 1969.

Holmes, Jack D. L. "The Southern Boundary Commission, the Chattahoochee River and the Florida Seminoles, 1799." *F.H.Q.* 44 (January–April 1966): 265–84.

———. "Spanish Treaties with West Florida Indians, 1784–1802." *F.H.Q.* 48 (October 1969): 140–54.

———. "Two Spanish Expeditions to Southwest Florida, 1783–1793." *Tequesta* 25 (1965): 97–107.

Howard, James H. *Oklahoma Seminoles, Medicines, Magic, and Religion.* Norman: University of Oklahoma Press, 1984.

Howard, Oliver O. *Autobiography.* 2 vols. New York: Baker and Taylor, 1908.

Hudson, Charles M. *The Southeastern Indians.* Knoxville: University of Tennessee Press, 1976.

Ickes, Harold. *The Secret Diary of Harold L. Ickes.* New York: Simon & Schuster, 1953.

Kappler, Charles J., comp. and ed. *Indian Affairs, Laws and Treaties.* 2d ed. 2 vols. Washington, D.C.: GPO, 1904.

Kerrigan, Anthony, ed. and trans. *Barcia's Chronological History of the Continent of Florida.* Gainesville: University of Florida Press, 1951.

Kersey, Harry A., Jr. "The Case of Tom Tiger's Horse: An Early Foray into Indian Rights." *F.H.Q.* 53 (January 1975): 306–18.

———. "Educating the Seminole Indians of Florida, 1879–1969." *F.H.Q.* 49 (July 1970): 16–35.

———. *Pelts, Plumes, and Hides: White Traders among the Seminole Indians, 1870–1930.* Gainesville: University Presses of Florida, 1975.

———. "Private Societies and the Maintenance of Seminole Tribal Integrity, 1899–1957." *F.H.Q.* 61 (January 1978): 297–316.

———. "The Seminole 'Uprising' of 1907." *Florida Anthropologist* 26 (June 1974): 49–58.

Kersey, Harry A. *The Florida Seminoles and the New Deal, 1933–1942.* Boca Raton: Florida Atlantic University Press, 1989.

Kersey, Harry A., Jr., and Pullease, Donald E. "Bishop William Crane Gray's Mission to the Seminole Indians in Florida, 1893–1914." *Historical Magazine of the Protestant Episcopal Church* 42 (September 1973): 257–73.

King, Robert T. "Clan Affiliation and Leadership among the Twentieth Century Florida Indians." *F.H.Q.* 55 (October 1976): 138–52.

———. "The Florida Seminole Polity, 1858–1978." Ph.D. diss., University of Florida, 1978.

Knotts, Tom. "History of the Blockhouse on the Withlacoochee." *F.H.Q.* 49 (January 1971): 245–55.

Lanning, John Tate. *Saint Augustine Expedition: A Report to the South Carolina General Assembly.* Columbia: South Carolina Archives Department, 1954.

Larson, Lewis H., Jr. "Cultural Relationships between the Northern St. Johns Area and the Georgia Coast." *Florida Anthropologist* 11 (February 1958): 16–19.

Bibliography

Littlefield, Daniel F., Jr. *Africans and Seminoles: From Removal to Emancipation.* Westport, Conn.: Greenwood, 1977.

Lockey, Joseph Byrne, ed. and trans. *East Florida, 1783–1785.* Berkeley: University of California Press, 1949.

McAlister, Lyle N. "Pensacola during the Second Spanish Period." *F.H.Q.* 37 (January 1959): 281–327.

McCall, George A. *Letters from the Frontier.* Philadelphia: Lippincott, 1868.

MacCauley, Clay. *The Seminole Indians of Florida.* Bureau of American Ethnology Fifth Annual Report 1883–1884. Washington, D.C.: GPO, 1887.

McDuffee, Lillie. *Lures of the Manatee: A True Story of South Florida and Its Glamorous Past.* 2d ed. Bradenton, Fla.: Privately printed, 1961.

McKay, D. B., ed. *Pioneer Florida.* 2 vols. Tampa: Southern, 1959.

McReynolds, Edwin C. *The Seminoles.* Norman: University of Oklahoma Press, 1957.

Madigan, LaVerne. "The Most Independent People—A Field Report on Indians in Florida." *Indian Affairs,* no. 31 (April 1959): 1–9.

Mahon, John K. "British Strategy & Southern Indians: War of 1812." *F.H.Q.* 44 (April 1966): 285–302.

———. *History of the Second Seminole War, 1835–1842.* Gainesville: University of Florida Press, 1967.

———. "The Treaty of Moultrie Creek." *F.H.Q.* 40 (April 1962): 350–72.

———. "Two Seminole Treaties: Payne's Landing, 1832, and Fort Gibson, 1833." *F.H.Q.* 41 (July 1962): 1–21.

Mason, Carol I. "Eighteenth Century Culture Change among the Lower Creeks." *Florida Anthropologist* 16 (September 1963): 65–82.

Milanich, Jerald T., and Charles H. Fairbanks. *Florida Archaeology.* New York: Academic, 1980.

Milford, Louis LeClerc. *Memoirs, or a Quick Glance at My Various Travels and My Sojourn in the Creek Nation.* Edited and translated by Ben C. McCary. Savannah, Ga.: Beehive, 1959.

Mitchem, Jeffrey, and Brent Weisman. "Changing Settlement Patterns and Pottery Types in the Withlacoochee Cove Region of Florida." *Florida Anthropologist* 40 (June 1987): 154–66.

Monk, J. Floyd. "Christmas Day in Florida." *Tequesta* 38 (1978): 5–38.

Moore-Willson, Minnie. *The Seminoles of Florida.* New York: Privately printed, 1910.

Mormino, Gary, ed. "The Firing of Guns and Crackers Continued till Light." *Tequesta* 45 (1985): 48–72.

Motte, Jacob R. *Journey into Wilderness: An Army Surgeon's Account of Life in Camp and Field during the Creek and Seminole Wars, 1836–1838.* Edited by James F. Sunderman. Gainesville: University of Florida Press, 1953.

Moulton, Gary E. "Cherokees and the Second Seminole War." *F.H.Q.* 53 (January 1975): 296–305.

Mowat, Charles L. *East Florida as a British Province, 1763–1784.* Berkeley: University of California Press, 1943.

Narrative of a Voyage to the Spanish Main in the Ship "Two Friends." London: Printed for John Miller, 1819. Facsimile. Gainesville: University of Florida Press, 1978.

Nicholas, James C., et al. *Recommendations Concerning Employment, Income and Educational Opportunities for the Seminole and Miccosukee Tribes in Florida.* Springfield, Va.: Department of the Interior, National Information Service, 1974.

Nuñez, Theron. "Creek Nativism and the Creek War of 1813–14." *Ethnohistory* 5 (Winter, Spring, Summer 1958): 1–47, 131–75, 202–301.

Olson, James, and Raymond Wilson. *Native Americans in the Twentieth Century.* Urbana: University of Illinois Press, 1984.

Ott, Eloise. "Fort King: A Brief History." *F.H.Q.* 46 (July 1967): 29–38.

Otto, John S. "Hillsborough County (1850): A Community in the South Florida Flatwoods." *F.H.Q.* 62 (October 1983): 180–93.

———. "Range Cattle in Southern Florida." *F.H.Q.* 65 (January 1987): 317–28.

Owsley, Frank L., Jr. "British and Indian Activities in Spanish West Florida during the War of 1812." *F.H.Q.* 41 (October 1967): 111–40.

———. *The Struggle for the Gulf Borderlands: The Creek War and the Battle of New Orleans.* Gainesville: University of Florida Press, 1981.

"Panton, Leslie, Papers: Letters of Edmund Doyle, 1815." *F.H.Q.* 17 (January 1939): 54–58.

Parkhill, Harriet R. *The Mission to the Seminoles in the Everglades of Florida.* Orlando: Privately printed, 1910.

Parrish, John O. *Battling the Seminoles.* Lakeland, Fla.: Southern Printing, 1930.

Parton, James. *Life of Andrew Jackson.* 3 vols. New York: Mason, 1860.

Patrick, Rembert W. *Florida Fiasco: Rampant Rebels on the Georgia-Florida Border, 1810–1815.* Athens: University of Georgia Press, 1954.

Peters, Thelma. "The First County Road from Latana to Lemon City." *Update* 1 (December 1973): 3–4.

———, ed. "William Adee Whitehead's Reminiscences of Key West." *Tequesta* 25 (1965): 3–42.

Peterson, Karen S. *Plains Indian Art from Fort Marion.* Norman: University of Oklahoma Press, 1971.

Philip, Kenneth R. "John Collier and the Controversy over the Wheeler-Howard Bill." In *Indian-White Relations: A Persistent Paradox,* edited by Jane F. Smith and Robert M. Krasnick. Washington, D.C.: Howard University Press, 1976.

———. *John Collier's Crusade for Indian Reform, 1920–1954.* Tucson: University of Arizona Press, 1977.

———. "Turmoil at Big Cypress: Seminole Deer and the Florida Cattle Tick Controversy." *F.H.Q.* 56 (July 1977): 29–44.

Pierce, Charles W. *Pioneer Life in Southeast Florida.* Edited by Donald W. Curl. Coral Gables, Fla.: University of Miami Press, 1970.

Porter, Kenneth W. "Billy Bowlegs (Holata Micco) in the Seminole Wars." Part 1. *F.H.Q.* 45 (January 1967): 219–42.

———. "The Founder of the 'Seminole Nation'; Secoffee or Cowkeeper." *F.H.Q.* 27 (April 1949): 362–84.

————. "The Negro Abraham." *F.H.Q.* 25 (July 1946): 1–43.

————. "Negroes and the East Florida Annexation Plot, 1811–1813" in *The American Negro: His History and Literature*, edited by Kenneth Porter. New York: Arno, 1971.

————. "Negroes and the Seminole War, 1835–1842." *Journal of Southern History* 30 (November 1964): 427–50.

————. "Notes on Seminole Negroes in the Bahamas." *F.H.Q.* 24 (July 1945): 56–60.

————. "Thlonoto-sassa: A Note on an Obscure Seminole Village in the Early 1820s." *Florida Anthropologist* 13 (December 1960): 113–19.

————, ed. "The Journal of A. B. Meek and the Second Seminole War, 1836." *F.H.Q.* 38 (April 1960): 302–18.

Potter, Woodburne. *The War in Florida, Being an Exposition of Its Causes and an Accurate History of the Campaigns of Generals Clinch, Gaines, and Scott.* Baltimore: Lewis & Coleman, 1836.

Presidential Executive Orders. Vol. 1. Compiled by WPA Historical Records Survey. Washington, D.C.: GPO, 1944.

Prucha, Francis P. *American Indian Policy in Crisis: Christian Reformers and the Indian, 1865–1900.* Norman: University of Oklahoma Press, 1976.

Ramsey, David, ed. "Abner Doubleday and the Third Seminole War." *F.H.Q.* 59 (January 1981): 314–34.

Reiger, John F., ed. "Sailing in South Florida Waters in the Early 1880s." *Tequesta* 26 (1971): 43–66.

Richardson, James D., ed. *A Compilation of the Messages and Papers of the Presidents, 1789–1897.* 10 vols. Washington, D.C.: GPO, 1896–99.

Ridaught, Horace. *Hell's Branch Office.* Citra, Fla.: Privately printed, 1957.

Robbins, Roy M. *Our Landed Heritage: The Public Domain, 1776–1936.* Lincoln: University of Nebraska Press, 1962.

Robinson, Ernest L. *History of Hillsborough County.* St. Augustine, Fla.: Record, 1928.

Romans, Bernard. *A Concise Natural History of East and West Florida.* New Orleans: Pelican, 1961.

Schene, Michael G. "Not a Shot Fired: Fort Chokonikla and the 'Indian War' of 1849–1850." *Tequesta* 37 (1977): 19–37.

Schofield, John M. *Forty-six Years in the Army.* New York: Century, 1897.

Seley, Ray B., Jr. "Lieutenant Hartsuff and the Banana Plants." *Tequesta* 23 (1963): 3–14.

Silver, James W. *Edmund Pendleton Gaines, Frontier General.* Baton Rouge: Louisiana State University Press, 1949.

Simmons, William H. *Notices of East Florida with an Account of the Seminole Nation of Indians by a Recent Traveller in the Province.* Charleston, S.C.: Privately printed by A. E. Miller, 1822.

Smith, Jane F., and Robert Kvasnicka, eds. *Indian-White Relations: A Persistent Paradox.* Washington, D.C.: GPO, 1976.

Sniffen, Matthew K. "Florida's Obligation to the Seminole Indians: A Plea for Justice." *Indian Rights Association,* 2d series, February 20, 1917, no. 111.

Spoehr, Alexander. "Camp, Clan, and Kin among the Cow Creek Seminoles of

Florida." *Anthropological Series* 33 (August 1941), no. 1, Field Museum of Natural History.

Sprague, John T. *The Origin, Progress, and Conclusion of the Florida War*. New York: Appleton, 1848.

Statutes at Large of the United States, 1821–1980. 90 vols. Washington, D.C.: GPO, 1821–1980.

Steele, W. S. "Last Command: The Dade Massacre." *Tequesta* 46 (1986): 35–47.

Sturtevant, William C. "Chakaika and the 'Spanish Indians': Documentary Sources Compared with Seminole Tradition." *Tequesta* 13 (1953): 35–73.

———. "Creek into Seminole." In *North American Indians in Historical Perspective*, edited by Eleanor B. Leacock and Nancy O. Lurie. New York: Random House, 1971.

———. "The Last of the South Florida Aborigines." In *Tacachale: Essays on the Indians of Florida and Southeastern Georgia during This Historic Period*, edited by Jerald T. Milanich and Samuel Proctor. Gainesville: University of Florida Press, 1978.

———. "The Medicine Bundles and Busks of the Florida Seminoles." *Florida Anthropologist* 7 (March 1954): 31–70.

———. "Notes on Modern Seminole Traditions of Osceola." *F.H.Q.* 33 (January–April 1955): 206–17.

———. "A Seminole Personal Document." *Tequesta* 16 (1956): 55–75.

———. "Spanish-Indian Relations in Southeastern North America." *Ethnohistory* 9 (Winter 1962): 41–94.

———, presenter and annotator. "R. H. Pratt's Report on the Seminole in 1879." *Florida Anthropologist* 9 (March 1956): 1–24.

Sugden, John. "The Southern Indians in the War of 1812—The Closing Phase." *F.H.Q.* 60 (January 1982): 273–312.

Swanton, John R. "Early History of the Creek Indians and Their Neighbors." Bureau of American Ethnology Bulletin 73. Washington, D.C.: GPO, 1922.

———. *The Indian Tribes of North America*. Bureau of American Ethnology Bulletin 145. Washington, D.C.: GPO, 1952.

Tanner, Helen Hornbeck. *Zéspedes in East Florida, 1784–1790*. Coral Gables, Fla.: University of Miami Press, 1963.

Tebeau, Charlton W. *Florida's Last Frontier: The History of Collier County*. Coral Gables, Fla.: University of Miami Press, 1957.

———. *A History of Florida*. Coral Gables, Fla.: University of Miami Press, 1971.

———. *Man in the Everglades*. Coral Gables, Fla.: University of Miami Press, 1969.

TePaske, John J. *The Governorship of Spanish Florida, 1700–1763*. Durham, N.C.: Duke University Press, 1964.

The Territorial Papers of the United States. Edited by Clarence E. Carter. Vols. 22–26: *Territory of Florida, 1821–1824*. Washington, D.C.: GPO, 1934–62.

Thompson, Arthur. "A Massachusetts Traveller on the Florida Frontier." *F.H.Q.* 38 (October 1959): 129–41.

The Trials of A. Arbuthnot and R. C. Ambrister Charged with Inciting the Seminole Indians to War from the Official Documents Which Were Laid by the President before Congress. London: James Ridgway, 1819.

Bibliography

20th Anniversary of Tribal Organization, 1957–1977, Seminole Tribe of Florida. Privately printed, August 20, 1977.

U.S. Congress. *Congressional Globe.* Debates and Proceedings, 1833–73. 109 vols. Washington, D.C.: GPO, 1833–73.

U.S. Congress. House. Committee on Indian Affairs. *Hearings on Eradicating Cattle Ticks on the Seminole Indian Reservation, Florida, November 5, 1941–February 25, 1942.* 77th Cong., 1st sess., 1942.

———. *Condition of the Florida Seminole.* 65th Cong., 1st sess., 1917. H. Doc.

———. *Supplemental Report on Causes of Hostilities.* 24th Cong., 1st sess., 1836. H. Doc. 271.

U.S. Congress. Senate. *Abstract of Council.* 24th Cong., 1st sess., 1835. S. Doc. 152.

———. *Florida Seminole Agency.* 67th Cong., 2d sess., 1921. S. Exec. Doc. 102.

———. *On the Case of L. Blake, June 19.* 33d Cong., 1st sess., 1853. S. Exec. Doc. 71.

———. *Operations in Florida.* 31st Cong., 1st sess., vol. 3, pt. 1, 1849. S. Exec. Doc. 1.

———. *Relative to the Hostilities Committed by the Seminole Indians in Florida during the Past Year, Their Removal, etc.* 31st Cong., 1st sess., 1849. S. Exec. Doc. 49.

———. *Report of the Commissioner of the Land Office on the Armed Occupation Act.* 30th Cong., 1st sess., 1848 S. Doc. 39.

———. *Report of Military Operations.* 31st Cong., 1st sess., 1849. S. Exec. Doc. 1.

———. Select Committee on Indian Affairs. *Hearings on Distribution of Seminole Judgement Funds, March 2, 1978.* 95th Cong., 2d sess. Washington, D.C.: GPO, 1978.

———. *A Survey of the Seminole Indians of Florida.* Report by Roy Nash. 71st Cong., 3d sess., 1931. S. Doc. 314.

U.S. Congress. Subcommittee of the Committees on Interior and Insular Affairs. *Joint Hearings on Termination of Federal Supervision over Certain Tribes of Indians.* Part 8, Seminole Indian, Florida. 83d Cong., 1st sess. Washington, D.C.: GPO, 1954.

U.S. Department of Commerce. *Federal and State Indian Reservations and Indian Trust Areas.* Washington D.C.: GPO, 1974.

U.S. Department of the Interior. Bureau of Indian Affairs. *Indian Affairs, Manual 83–1: Tribal Government.* Washington, D.C., 1959.

———. Narrative Reports of the Superintendents of the Florida Seminole Agency and Special Commissioners. Washington, D.C., 1893–1940.

———. "Report on the Seminole Indians of Florida." Report by Gene Stirling. Doc. 126567. Applied Anthropology Unit, Office of Indian Affairs. Washington, D.C., 1936. Mimeo.

Upchurch, John C. "Aspects of the Development and Exploration of the Forbes Purchase." *F.H.Q.* 48 (October 1969): 117–39.

Utz, Dora Dogter. "Life on the Loxahatchee." *Tequesta* 32 (1972): 38–57.

———. "West Palm Beach." *Tequesta* 33 (1973): 43–66.

Walker, Hester Perrine. "Massacre at Indian Key, August 7, 1840, and the Death of Dr. Henry Perrine." *F.H.Q.* 5 (July 1926): 18–42.

Wallace, Fred C. "The Story of Captain John C. Casey." *F.H.Q.* 42 (October 1962): 127–44.

Waylor, Theodore W. *The States and Their Indian Citizens.* Washington, D.C., 1972.

Webb, Alexander S. "Campaigning in Florida in 1855." *Journal of the Military Service Institutions.* November, December 1912: 399–429.

Weisman, Brent Richards. "Cove of the Withlacoochee Archaelogical Project." *Florida State Museum Miscellaneous Project Report Series,* no. 24, August 1985.

———. *Like Beads on a String: A Culture History of the Seminole Indians in North Peninsular Florida.* University: University of Alabama Press, 1989.

———. "On the Trail of Osceola's Seminoles in Florida." Paper distributed by the Order of Indian Wars, January 1988.

Welch, Andrew, *A Narrative of the Early Days and Remembrances of Osceola Nikkan-dochee, Prince of Econchati, a Young Seminole Indian, Son of Econchati-Mico, King of the Red Hills in Florida.* Edited and annotated by Frank Laumer. Gainesville: University of Florida Press, 1977.

Wenhold, Lucy L., ed. and trans. "The Trials of Captain Isidoro de Leon." *F.H.Q.* 35 (January 1957): 246–65.

West, Patsy. "The Miami Indian Tourist Attraction: A History and Analysis of a Transitional Mikasuki Seminole Environment." *Florida Anthropologist* 34 (December 1981): 200–20.

———. "Seminole Indian Settlements at Pine Island, Broward County, Florida: An Overview." *Florida Anthropologist* 42 (March 1989): 43–56.

White, Frank F., ed. "Macomb's Mission to the Seminoles, John T. Sprague's Journal Kept during April and May, 1839." *F.H.Q.* 35 (October 1956): 130–93.

"The White Flag." *F.H.Q.* (January–April 1955): 218–34.

Williams, John Lee. *The Territory of Florida.* New York: Goodrich, 1837.

Williams, Walter L., ed. *Southeastern Indians since the Removal Era.* Athens: University of Georgia Press, 1979.

Works Progress Administration, Federal Writers Program. *Seminole Indians in Florida.* Tallahassee, Fla.: Department of Agriculture, 1940.

Wright, J. Leitch, Jr. *Creeks and Seminoles: The Destruction and Regeneration of the Muscogulge People.* Lincoln: University of Nebraska Press, 1987.

———. *William Augustus Bowles, Director-General of the Creek Nation.* Athens: University of Georgia Press, 1967.

INDEX

Colville (Wash.) Reservation, 253
Comanche Indians, 154
Community Action Program, 252
Conepatchie, Billy. *See* Konipatci,
Billy
Confederacy: Seminoles under, 145–
46, 320n.3
Congress, U.S.: and Indian auton-
omy, 236–37; Seminole appeals to,
261, 267, 337n.14
Conrad (visiting nurse), 232
Constitution: written tribal, 233, 238,
241, 242–45, 335n.38; committee of,
243 (illus.); Miccosukee, 263–64,
269, 338n.45
Cook, Jim, 137–38
Cookman Institute, 155
Coontie, 13, 59, 88, 99, 148, 158, 201,
302n.49
Cooper, Ralph W., 227
Copeland, D. Graham, 216
Coppinger, Henry, 190–91, 196,
328n.40
Corn, 147, 148
Cow Creek, 156, 208
Coweta (Creek town), 6, 10, 35
Coweta Indians, 301n.33
Cowkeeper (Oconee chief), 12, 13, 18,
19, 25, 29, 302n.48; as Spanish
scourge, 14; vs. Yamassee/British,
17
Crawford, George W., 116
Crawford, Grady, 266
Creek Confederacy: nature of, 5,
300n.13; Seminoles in, 3, 12–13. *See
also* Creeks
Creeks: Apalachicolas vs., 70; and
banishment as punishment, 8; blacks
captured by, 94; Blount assaulted
by, 68; children of, 8, 9; and
divorce, 9; in Florida, 101, 113, 115
(*see also* Muskogees; Octiarche;
Tiger Tail); Indian Territory
promoted by, 141; language of (*see*
Muskogee [lang.]); McGillivray
and, 19; and menstruation, 8; and

murder, 8; nomenclature of, 9; in
Oklahoma, 73, 75, 141, 229; religion
of, 6; removal to Oklahoma of, 63,
64, 71, 109; Seminoles and, 32,
45–46; Seminoles as, 5–6; social
organization of, 6–9; Spaniards and,
20; U.S. vs. Alabama, 88; as U.S.
Army allies, 43, 89; warriors of, 9.
See also Creek Confederacy; Creek
War; Lower Creeks; Upper Creeks
Creek Seminole and Wichita Baptist
Association, 172
Creek War, 33, 100, 109; Florida exiles
from, 101; Lower Creeks as U.S.
allies during, 53; Seminole role in,
34–35
Creel, Lorenzo S., 169, 171, 173, 175
Crews, Edward, 122
Crime, 196; punishment of, 149–51; on
reservations, 270. *See also* Green
Corn Dance, criminal docket
relative to
Crops: of Creeks, 5; Seminole, 13, 58,
81, 98, 99, 100, 102, 104, 113, 114,
138, 140, 141, 147, 153, 155, 158, 169,
181, 203, 206, 210. *See also* Citrus
crops; Coontie; Corn; Sugar cane
Cuba: Florida Indians flee to, 4, 14;
Miccosukee delegation to, 266;
Seminole arms from, 53, 77, 83,
102, 309n.30; Seminole excursions
to, 13; slave revolt in, 98
Cubans: as Gulf Coast fishermen, 27;
as Indian employers, 4, 300n.8;
Seminoles and, 5, 27
Cultural Heritage Project, 255
Cunningham, William, 23
Curry family, 146
Cuscowilla (town), 12, 13, 15 (map),
22, 23, 302n.43; Payne in, 29. *See
also* Cowkeeper
CWA (Civil Works Administration),
219–20
Cypress (tree): importance to
Seminoles of, 263
Cypress, Billie, 339n.46

Index

Mandarin (settlement), 105
Mann, Cameron, 171
Marks, Amos, 208
Marmon, Kenneth A., 234, 237, 239, 240, 242
Marriage, 189; Creeks and, 7, 8–9; as tourist attraction, 191
Marriott, Alice, 211
Marrylee, 180
Marsh, Oren, 57
Marshall, John, 203
Marshall, Mrs. John, 198
Martin County: reservations in, 175, 326n.43
Matheos, Antonio, 9
Mathews, George, 28–29
Matottnee, 180
Measles, 4, 93, 167; U.S. troops ravaged by, 85, 88
Meat, 13. *See also* Cattle; Deer, Seminole dependence on; Hogs
Medicine bundles, 257–58
Medicine men. *See* Shamans
Mekusokey Independent Baptist Church, 229
Menéndez de Avilés, Pedro, 4
Menuminee Indians, 237
Merritt, E. B., 196
Miami: bootleg whiskey in, 159; Cuban section of, 270; Miccosukees of, 258; Seminole car parkers in, 229; Seminole depredations near, 131; Seminoles on display in, 190–91, 218, 222, 231, 328n.40; Seminole visits to, 177; as Spencer base, 177–78, 181; trading post at, 158
Miami River, 156, 157
Micanopy (chief), 33, 48, 55–56, 75, 90–91, 101; and black slaves, 62; capture of, 95; at Dade Massacre, 79; and Payne's Landing treaty, 64–65, 311n.7; peace overtures of, 90; in Second Seminole War, 84; at Silver Springs council, 73, 74; in Washington, 61
Micco, Charlie, 213, 258

Micco, Holata. *See* Bowlegs, Billy (of South Florida)
Micco, Little Charlie, 234
Miccos: Creek, 6
Miccosukee, Lake, 26, 43, 45, 47
Miccosukee (Bowles schooner), 24
Miccosukee Seminole Indian Association, 267
Miccosukee Tribe of Indians of Florida, 235, 269–71, 338–39n.45, 339nn.46,49
Mickler, Jacob E., 137–39
Mikasuki Indians, 55–56, 101, 107, 113, 115, 130, 137, 181, 249–50; and Bureau of Indian Affairs, 270, 339n.49; clans of, 149; councils of, 258, 263–64, 267–69, 337–38n.21; family strength of, 253; after First Seminole War, 47, 48; as independent nation, 261 (*see also* Miccosukee Tribe of Indians of Florida); Osceola supported by, 76; in Second Seminole War, 83, 90; separationist activities of, 233, 235, 258–71; as tourist attraction, 270. *See also* Big Cypress Seminole Indian Reservation; Billie, Ingraham; Everglades, Seminoles of; Jones, Sam; Neamathla; Philip; Tamiami Trail, Seminoles of
Mikasuki (lang.), 12, 26, 156, 315n.12; English and, 269
Mikasuki (town), 15 (map), 15–16, 19, 24, 25
Miles City, 219, 258
Miller, George, 263, 265
Miller, John (Bahamas businessman), 22–23
Miller, John (Miccosukee attorney), 264
Miller, R.C., 269
Milton, John (Florida governor), 145
Miner, Charles, Jr., 254
Mink, trade in, 154
Miro, Esteban, 20
Missionaries, 160. *See also* Baptists;